The
Women's
West

The Women's West

Edited and with Introductions by
Susan Armitage and Elizabeth Jameson

University of Oklahoma Press : Norman and London

The articles by Jameson, Van Kirk, Graulich, Murphy, Johnson, Harris, and Bush appeared in *Frontiers,* Vol. 7, No. 3 (1984); the Zavella article appeared in *Frontiers,* Vol. 8, No. 1 (1984). They are reproduced here in modified form with permission.

Library of Congress Cataloging-in-Publication Data

The Women's West.
   Includes bibliographies and index.
   1. Women—West (U.S.)—History.   2. Frontier and pioneer life—West (U.S.) —History.   3. Women—United   States—History—19th   Century.   I Armitage, Susan H. (Susan Hodge).   II. Jameson, Elizabeth.
HQ1418.W66   1987   305.4'0978   86–14672
ISBN 0–8061–2043–6 (cloth)
ISBN 0–8061–2067–3 (pbk.)

Dedication

For Our Mothers, Julia Merritt Hodge and Grace Klein Jameson

Contents

Illustrations

Acknowledgments

Scores of people, over several years, contributed to the success of the Women's West Conference of 1983, and we are grateful to them all. From the conference emerged this book, a permanent organization—the Coalition for Western Women's History—and many fast friendships and working partnerships. The conference presentations are the core of this volume, and we are especially grateful to the members of the Program Committee, and particularly to its co-chairs, Patricia Albers and Paula Petrik, who created shape out of many diverse submissions. We also thank Richard Hart and Marcia Jones, then of the Institute of the American West, conference co-sponsor; and Melissa Hield, who joined us on the Steering Committee. We are grateful to the organizations that helped fund the 1983 conference: the Association for the Humanities in Idaho, the Anheuser-Busch Company, and the state-based humanities programs of Alaska, Colorado, Montana, New Mexico, and Washington.

To all who have enhanced our westward journey and who helped make this book possible, again our thanks.

Pullman, Washington　　　　　　　　　　SUSAN ARMITAGE
El Rancho, Colorado　　　　　　　　　ELIZABETH JAMESON

The
Women's
West

Editors' Introduction

No other region of the United States has so shaped the image of our national identity as has the West. Ever since Frederick Jackson Turner articulated his famous "frontier thesis" in 1893,[1] historians have debated how and to what extent the frontier nourished American individualism and democracy. The contribution of the western frontier to our national mythology is less debatable. From Daniel Boone to John Wayne, our national folklore is replete with white male "rugged individuals" finding their selfhood in the freedom of an untamed land. This image, like most other stereotypes, is one-dimensional and historically inaccurate and incomplete. It leaves out most westerners, including the original inhabitants of the land, American Indians, and Hispanics; men who came West, not as loners, but with their kin; and women of all ethnic groups and social classes.

Recently western and women's historians have begun to address the omissions of the older western history, and the articles in this book represent pioneering efforts to reexamine the West through women's eyes. They are based on papers presented at the first Women's West Conference, in Sun Valley, Idaho, in August, 1983. The Women's West Conference was the first national meeting devoted to western women's history, and the work in this volume represents the most diverse and detailed examination yet undertaken of women's pasts in the West. As organizers and participants, we saw the conference as an important step in the development of a new area of historical inquiry. It brought together historians, both independent and institution-based, and provided us an opportunity to share and compare work with other researchers and with westerners whose lives are part of the history we seek to record. It was an exciting conference, full of the delight of discovery and the satisfaction of confirmation.

The articles in this book are important because of the ways in which they describe women's roles in western history and add the experiences of western women to national scholarship in women's history. Women have been virtually absent from traditional western history. This omission has severely distorted our understanding of the settlement and development of the American West. Sadly, ignorance of western women has been nearly as pervasive in the much newer field of American women's history. We start, then, with the obvious assertion that there *were* women "in them thar hills," that historians are now recording their experiences, and that western women's history offers important insights into our national past.

3

The absence of women from older western histories reflects in part a narrow concentration on the early Euro-American[2] frontier period, when, especially in mining areas and boom towns, women were scarce. More were present on agricultural frontiers, which were frequently settled by families. But whether one defines the frontier as a place characterized by a low ratio of people to inhabitable space or as the process by which a place is settled and cultural forms are established, the narrow focus on a brief historical epoch obscures the lives of the original inhabitants and of later settlers whose experience changed over time. There were, in fact, many frontiers, beginning with the arrivals of the first Europeans and Africans on the East Coast in the seventeenth century. In this volume, however, we focus not on the frontier but on the trans-Mississippi West, defined as the area west of the ninety-eighth meridian. That is, of course, a very large area. It was settled at different times by people of different ethnic heritages, and it includes a variety of geography, climate, and regional economies. That diversity is demonstrated by the careful studies of women's experiences in different times and places in this book. Central to the articles is the recognition that the diversity of western experiences requires us to understand the different circumstances of western women's lives before we can arrive at large generalizations about what the West has been for women.

Early scholarship on western women asked the same questions that researchers trained in western history or in women's history brought with them. From western history we inherited the question of whether or not the frontier was a liberating environment for women. From women's history we inherited scholarship based in prescriptive literature which told Victorian women what the dominant culture considered their appropriate roles, and we asked whether these roles and values were challenged in the West.[3] We think that many of the studies in this book demonstrate that a more complex set of questions is posed by the lives of western women and that the current state of scholarship calls for more such detailed histories of actual lives.

One purpose of many of the articles is to identify and then begin to correct some of the oversights and omissions in earlier histories of the West. It is not enough to put a few western heroines into our stories of a heroic and masculine nineteenth-century frontier. Many of the topics of the new women's history do not "fit" into older accounts. In fact, the more we learn about work and family roles, the more we become convinced that much male experience is also omitted from the older western history.

What does the new research on western women offer to the general field of American women's history? Many of the articles consider how idealized eastern sex roles were changed in the West. A number of authors look at the impact of role definitions on women who could not achieve them, and ask whether the contradiction between daily reality and idealized expectations produced new roles for western women and men. In this way western women's history contributes to all of women's history by providing studies of how ideal definitions of womanhood were accepted, rejected, or adapted by nineteenth-century women, in this instance western women. Other articles indicate the limits of beginning with the role prescriptions of the Victorian elite. They show that many different understandings of sex roles were held by many different westerners, and begin to explain how these changed over time.

Thus this volume has been shaped by our interest in western history *and* women's history. This dual focus has led us to break with the nineteenth-century frontier format and to raise new issues that apply to men as well as women. As we have confronted the inadequacy of older scholarship, we have, inevitably, examined the methodological tools and theoretical assumptions with which we began and have searched for new materials and new ways to achieve a more complete historical understanding of western women. How can we document the lives of millions of women who are not represented in historical archives? How can we include the experiences of women who lived in the region before written history? How can we include the important variables of ethnicity, class, regional economy, period of settlement, family status, and women's life cycles without losing the forest for the trees? We are beginning to see the need to forge new tools and new models. That is what these articles are *most* about: What analytical tools do we need, to ask and to unravel the important questions?

We believe that western women's history must be inclusive. It should offer a multicultural economic perspective that includes all races and classes, in addition to both sexes. It begins with the histories of American Indians and of Spanish conquest, not with Euro-American settlement in the nineteenth century. We will need to use the tools and insights of archaeologists and anthropologists to reconstruct part of the history of western women. In addition, it is important to pay more attention to economic class than do some of the older accounts. The recent interdisciplinary work in the fields of American Indian, Hispanic and Chicano, black, and Asian-American studies is crucial to the achievement of an accurate and inclusive history. Other new questions, insights, and techniques will emerge as we continue to explore.

We think that a new and more comprehensive framework is desirable. We have tried to provide one in the organization of this volume, which reflects our sense of the rethinking implied by the term the "Women's West." We begin with a section on images of western women because we believe that the first step, and probably the hardest, is to free ourselves from the all-pervasive masculinity of the popular image of the American West. Until that basic re-vision occurs, we cannot see women in their own right. Authors who write about western women without confronting this most basic reconceptualization fail, in our opinion, to meet the challenge posed by western women's history.

Then we move not to the nineteenth-century Euro-American pioneers but to the original inhabitants of the West and their interactions with the newcomers. This section challenges the customary "pioneer" framework of traditional western history. It is not as extensive as we would like, which reflects how recently we have recognized that a major new topic is emerging between traditional American Indian history and traditional frontier history.

Following that, two central sections consider persistence and innovation in gender roles, which is a central issue for women's history. Part Three, entitled, "Emotional Continuities," introduces methodologies developed by literary critics that women's historians have long considered vital for the analysis of private documents, though they may be less familiar to other historians. In Part Four the concerns and methods of the new women's history are applied to western women to explore how gender roles were defined in the West and how women acted to change their roles.

A final section, Part Five, moves into the twentieth century and into a range of topics (suffrage, ethnicity, patterns of women's work) that are connected with research undertaken by women's historians studying other regions but have not yet received detailed attention in the West. Within this organization four articles—those by Susan Armitage, Elizabeth Jameson, Rosalinda Méndez González, and Suzan Shown Harjo—provide general overviews of conceptualization and methodology. Many of the articles speak directly or implicitly to the need for a new history, and that need has informed the organization of the articles and our introductory comments.

The contributors to this volume add many new perspectives and layers of detail to our portrait of the American West, and they demonstrate that the detail and dailiness of western women's lives can be as compelling as mythic images remote from our own experience. We hope that, as it develops as a field, western women's history will change our image of the American West and contribute to a more inclusive women's history, therefore ultimately changing our interpretations of our national past. It is an exciting exploration. If the Women's West Conference and this volume are indications, western women's history will involve sharing insights, questioning older assumptions, and the pleasure of learning from one another.

Notes

1. Frederick Jackson Turner, "The Significance of the Frontier in American History," in *Annual Report of the American Historical Association for the Year 1893* (Washington, D.C.: U.S. Government Printing Office, 1894).

2. By "Euro-Americans" we mean all Americans of European ancestry except those of Spanish ancestry. We distinguish Chicanas and Hispanas from others of European heritage to differentiate their historical experiences from those of later European immigrants.

3. For an example of a recent work influenced by the questions of western history, see Sandra L. Myres, *Westering Women and the Frontier Experience, 1800–1915* (Albuquerque: University of New Mexico Press, 1982). For a work influenced by the assumptions of prescriptive literature and women's history, see Julie Roy Jeffrey, *Frontier Women: The Trans-Mississippi West, 1840–1880* (New York: Hill and Wang, 1979).

PART ONE

Myths

In all fields of women's history, a first step has been to analyze images of women in the existing literature. This has been a logical starting point because, as is generally acknowledged, until recently the usual subject of history has been great and famous men. "Ordinary" men, ethnic minorities, and women were incidental to the story.

The crucial step in women's history is to see women as actors, not as onlookers in history. No longer are women and women's concerns marginal; now they are central. Women's history looks different from its predecessors, simply because the perspective is different. Women occupy center stage. By breaking through the images that others have imposed, we can now discover what women thought and did for themselves.

Breaking free of stereotypes is never particularly easy, and it may be especially difficult in the field of western history. The drama of the West, the frontier myth, and the sense of adventure continue to enthrall us. The western legend evokes a sense of people challenged by the pioneering experience, made larger and better for it. We may not at first realize that all the people being challenged in this myth are men. The gender bias underlying the western story has led us to believe that the West was built by stalwart men and incidental, unimportant women. The men are so dominant that the women have been all but crowded off the stage.

Correcting this imbalance has been a starting point for much of western women's history, and the first step was to examine common stereotypes. There have been many different formulations, but a number of us feel a special debt to folklorist Beverly Stoeltje, whose article "A Helpmate for Man Indeed" outlined three images—refined lady, helpmate, and bad woman—and linked them with corresponding male figures.[1] The three chapters in Part One follow Stoeltje's lead. They attest both to the power of the stereotypes and to the importance of challenging them.

Most stereotypes have some basis in reality, but they tend to be one-dimensional distortions of that reality. If we are to understand what is accurate in older images of western women, analyzing the stereotypes is the essential first step. Once dissected and understood, the images no longer loom so large. Now we can take what is true and useful and discard the rest. We begin to see with our own eyes rather than those of others.

Note

1. Beverly Stoeltje, "A Helpmate for Man Indeed: The Image of the Frontier Woman," *Journal of American Folklore* 88, No. 347 (January–March, 1975). See also Sheryll Patterson-Black, "Women Homesteaders on the Great Plains Frontier," *Frontiers* 1, no. 2 (Spring, 1976) for an early challenge to the image of western women as "reluctant pioneers."

1

Through Women's Eyes: A New View of the West

SUSAN ARMITAGE

In the following article, Susan Armitage examines stereotypes to make a larger point. Criticizing the omissions of western history is important, she says, and criticizing its underlying assumptions is essential. The spirit *of much of traditional western history—male-dominated, racist, romantic— must be challenged. A sensitive understanding of female stereotypes reveals these assumptions and helps us understand what must be different in western women's history. If historians of women simply replace old male-dominated stereotypes with new ones, not much will change in our thinking about western history. Instead, Armitage dissects the older images to uncover biases that need to be corrected, and to find hints of the realities of women's lives that they may suggest. She demonstrates how focusing on women's experiences challenges the unspoken assumptions of the older western history. Armitage thus argues not only that western women's history is valuable in its own right; it also provides a starting point from which to rethink western history as a whole.*

There is a region of America that I have come to call Hisland. In a magnificent western landscape, under perpetually cloudless western skies, a cast of heroic characters engages in dramatic combat, sometimes with nature, sometimes with each other. Occupationally, these heroes are diverse: they are mountain men, cowboys, Indians, soldiers, farmers, miners, and desperadoes, but they share one distinguishing characteristic—they are all men. It seems that all rational demography has ended at the Mississippi River: all the land west of it is occupied only by men. This mythical land is America's most enduring contribution to folklore: the legendary Wild West.

When Charlotte Perkins Gilman wrote a utopian novel about an all-female world called Herland, she knew that she was writing a fantasy. The problem with Hisland is that many people believe it is history, and some of those people are historians.

Western American history is a diverse field, and it is manifestly unjust to characterize all or even the majority of western historians as Hislanders. Nevertheless, it is true that the general tenor of the field, as reflected in textbooks and courses offered, has a strong Hisland flavor.

Indian women pulling in a whale on the Pacific Coast. Ashael Curtis photograph.
Courtesy Washington State Historical Society, Tacoma.

Most histories of the American West are heroic tales: stories of adventure, exploration, and conflict. While these are fine stories, with narrative drive and drama, their coherence is achieved by a narrowing of focus. Most western historians write about the nineteenth-century period between the opening of the frontier and its official closing in the 1890s. They focus on the westward expansion of the Euro-American settlers, paying scant attention to the native peoples whose lands and cultures were invaded. They seldom write about the period before European settlement, and few have ventured to write about the twentieth-century West. Within the frontier time frame most western specialists write about a limited number of events—the fur trade, the gold rushes, the cattle drives, the Indian wars, the political struggles to establish territorial governments and policies. Historians tell and retell these events in great detail. Women are either absent or incidental to the story.

Of course, there are reasons for this historical approach. The most common reason is the continuing popular and scholarly interest in the frontier period. Without question, the heroic Hisland story has a firm hold on the public imagination. A second rationale for the Hisland approach is its coherence. Without this unifying approach, how could one organize all the variety and complexity of historical experience in the West? A third reason, surely, is simply that the Hisland story is tried and true. The narrow focus and male bias are examples of an older kind of historical writing that has not yet gone out of style in the West.

Clearly, western history is in need of some evaluation and renovation. Many in the field share this opinion and some have published their views.[1] Suggestions for change have come from many different perspectives: ethnic historians, social historians, labor historians, among others. This criticism comes at a good time for those of us engaged in western women's history. In our research we have found a new western woman; through her eyes we see a new view of the West. We do not wish to create a sweet little cameo version of western history that will slip right into the Hisland story. We want to change the way the story is written. We are eager to communicate our findings and to share in the rewriting of western history.

Women's history sources—diaries, letters, journals, memoirs, novels, poems, children's books, and oral histories—provide information from which to build a new view of the West. Many of these women's sources have been in the archives all along, but earlier historians apparently found them uninteresting and simply passed them over. Now, however, we realize what a treasure trove those sources are. Precisely because their perspective is different from what we are used to, women's accounts can help us to see the frontier experience in a new light.

In the past few years I have used a variety of images to explain what the women's perspective can mean. One good image is that of the stereopticon, found in so many Victorian parlors. The card with two nearly identical photos is uninteresting until placed in the viewer and focused: then a sharp three-dimensional picture emerges. Women's history, like the picture in the stereopticon, can contribute a missing dimension to our western history.

Certainly there are large areas where men and women of the same race, economic class, and general background will agree on interpretation. But because of differences in socialization and life experience, men and women do not see the world identically: these are the differences that produce the three-dimensional picture in the stereopticon. In the past, men have believed that they could speak for everyone. Now we know that we must ask what women have to say for themselves because Hisland history has not spoken accurately for western women.

In Hisland the few women who do appear are strictly stereotyped. There are three common images: the refined lady, the helpmate, and the bad woman. The lady, who may be a schoolteacher, a missionary, or merely a woman with some civilized tastes, is defined as being too genteel for the rough and ready West. She is either uncomfortable, unhappy, or is driven literally crazy by the frontier. Apparently the only way she can prove her gentility is to become a victim. On the other hand, the strong and uncomplaining helpmate adapts to the West, but in the process becomes a workworn superwoman, losing all her individuality. The bad woman has both glamour and power, but she loses them along with her life as she comes rapidly to her appropriate end—a bad one.[2]

Unless we can see women as they really were, we cannot understand their lives and feelings, or their perspective on the West. Nevertheless, as I can testify from years of struggle, it is remarkably hard to shake one's mind free of these stereotypes. I began by finding women who *did not* fit the mold. This is not hard to do. Perhaps the best example is that late-frontier figure, the single woman homesteader. She is no man's helpmate, and her education and culture do not hinder her from going it alone and enjoying it.[3] Then there is someone like Dame Shirley, who used her civilized skills and values to draw such a vivid picture of a California gold rush camp that Bret Harte couldn't resist stealing some of her plots for his much more famous stories.[4] As Mary Murphy shows later in this volume, easiest of all to disprove is the stereotype of the prostitute with the heart of gold.

On the other hand, realizing that every stereotype contains a grain of truth, one can usefully rethink the stereotypes from the woman's perspective, as I did with the image of the reluctant pioneer, a variant on the refined lady theme. I returned to one of my favorite sources, the diary of Amelia Buss, which she kept during her first year on a lonely homestead near Fort Collins, Colorado, in 1866–67.[5] She came West unwillingly, leaving friends and family behind. She filled her diary with details of daily housekeeping in a primitive cabin, and with complaints about hard work, isolation, and loneliness. Here is a typical complaint:

George went to the mountains yesterday morning to be gon all week . . . after he had gon gave vent to my feelings in a flood of tears. It may seem foolish to those that have neighbors and friends around them. I get a long very well through the day but the long evening and nights are *horrible*.

Amelia developed rituals to sustain herself in her new surroundings. On Sunday she held Bible readings with her young daughter, evoking warm memories of companionable Sabbaths in the East. She lived for letters from home. And she used her diary, which her sisters gave her as a parting gift, as a place to acknowledge her private fears.

Her diary ends with a retrospective entry, dated exactly one year after her arrival in Colorado. She has become resigned: "Now I have settled down with the belief that here I shall end my days and the sooner I make it home the better." She went on: "This little book may seem full of trifling troubles to you, but at the same time they were great to me, more than I knew how to bear . . . and now farewell little book you shall not carry more complaint to my friends at home."

At first glance Amelia Buss appears to be a perfect example of the western stereotype of the lonely, frail woman, too gentle for the harshness of the West. We pity her. But consider the reasons for her unhappiness. She has left behind her emotional supports, including a large and supportive kin network and her associates in close religious fellowship. Her husband is often away and his economic misfortunes add to her insecurity. She does monotonous work in primitive and isolated conditions. Her health is uncertain. In spite of her efforts to make the best of things, she is desperately lonely. Of course she is—why wouldn't she be? Once the distorting prism of the sentimental stereotype is removed, Amelia Buss is revealed as a realist. Her reasons for unhappiness were valid. She certainly hoped for a better future, but in the meantime she saw things as they were. The effect of the pitiful stereotyping has been to deny us her reality and that of other unhappy pioneers. Not all women were reluctant pioneers or permanently reluctant. In Amelia Buss's case, reluctance gave way to adaptation: "Now I have settled down with the belief that here I shall end my days and the sooner I make it home the better." We can move beyond pity to find a wider use for the diaries of reluctant pioneer women.

The traditional frontier history has been a success story; we do not know much about the "failures" or about the pressures and anxieties that everyone, male and female, encountered. Typically, it has been more permissible for women to confide their hopes and fears to their diaries than it has been for men. While being publicly supportive of their men's adventures, some women sought a private outlet for the very fears that men, focused optimistically on the future, might not be able to admit to themselves. For this reason, such women's sources are essential to serious efforts to describe the full complexity of the pioneer experience.

Let us look at another stereotype, woman as civilizer. In western legend, women were "gentle tamers." Their very presence on the frontier was enough to make rough and rowdy men think about polite behavior and the establishment of civilized institutions like schools, churches, and libraries. What is striking about this stereotype is the unbelievable passivity of the women. Women did not have to *do* anything; they simply had to be there, and men would build communities around them. The women I have found in my historical research were never that passive. They played an active role in building their communities. They selected community projects, lobbied for them, and raised money for them. But when the moment of formal organization came, the women stepped back. Men were elected as officials and were often given credit for the entire enterprise. The official story and the informal story are not the same. Because newspapers document the official facts, not the informal ones, historians who have relied solely on newspapers in research perpetuate the invisibility of women. It is still possible to read books and articles about community-building that never mention a woman! As Elizabeth Jameson shows so clearly in her article, oral histories have been a major source to document women's informal community activities, and to make us examine our assumptions. But think about it: who could seriously imagine a frontier populated by ineffectual, ornamental women?

We are talking about real women who led real lives, people we could meet and talk to and share concerns with, not condescendingly pity or look up to in childlike awe. Pity and awe are the signs of stereotyping and mythologizing, of what I call "golly gee whiz" history. The fact is that even the most heroic people lead ordinary lives 99 percent of the time— and that is what we are looking for to construct a realistic western history. Because some men in western history have achieved heroic stature, we may think that we need to create female figures in the same mold. I think that would be a mistake. Ordinary lives are the true story of the West, for men as well as for women.

Frequently the pity and awe come not from the stereotype but from ourselves. We are so shocked by the painful and narrow lives we find in our research that it is difficult to see those lives as they seemed to the women who lived them. For example, every year I have some students who are awed by the heroism of the brave women who came west on the Overland Trail. Nonsense. Those women did not see themselves as heroic. They were doing what had to be done. Whatever our final opinion of their lives, we must start with their own self-explanations. In this respect, I have always found Gerda Lerner's definition of women's history very useful: "The true history of women is the history of their ongoing functioning in [the] male-defined world, *on their own terms.*" [6] Understanding those terms is what makes the woman's perspective and what we have to be clear about.

Here is another example of the danger of stereotyping. In the Pacific Northwest, by far the best known female figure is Sacajawea, the American Indian woman who accompanied Lewis and Clark. We know almost nothing about the real Sacajawea—she is largely a myth created out of a pitifully few historical facts. In the past I have said, "Fine—now at least there is a token woman in company with Paul Bunyan, Mike Fink, Pecos Bill, and pals." But I was wrong. The Sacajawea myth is nothing more than Pocahontas in western dress—the same old white stereotype of the "princess" who mediates between white and American Indian by siding with the white man. That is no more useful an image of Indian women than is the other prevalent image of the squaw, used and later abandoned by the white explorer or fur trader. [7] Similarly insulting are the images of Hispanic and Asian women portrayed either as sex objects or toiling drudges. Our efforts to reject, revise, and re-examine stereotypes must be multicultural.

The principle is important: we want to look at the experience of women of all races, not just white women. When we do that, the starting point of western history changes. Conventional "firsts" such as "the first white woman over the Rockies" and "the first white child born in Oregon Territory" are seen for what they are: unconscious racism. Western history began long before that.

Anthropologists are now working to recover a true picture of the lives of American Indian women. Because traditional western histories have regarded Indians primarily as an obstacle to be removed, the emphasis inevitably has been on conflict between whites and Indians. It is true that Indians were killed or removed by force as white settlement advanced. But frequently this removal happened after considerable peaceful contact had occurred between whites and Indians. Many white women's diaries, letters, and memoirs tell of frequent encounters between whites and Indians. Usually the Indians asked for food. Because white women controlled and distributed the family food supply, they, not their husbands, were usually the central actors in these encounters. The female response was anxious, uneasy, placating, not violent. These peaceful "everyday encounters" provide another perspective from that of the violent military stories.[8] I suspect that such encounters were widespread on the frontier.

Of course, culture contact is two-sided. The American Indian side of the story is now being at least partly restored to our historical understanding. Here is one testimonial from Ironteeth, a Northern Cheyenne woman:

I used to cry every time anything reminded me of the killing of my husband and my son. But I now have become old enough to talk quietly of them. I used to hate all white people, especially their soldiers. But my heart has become changed to softer feelings. Some of the white people are good, maybe as good as Indians.[9]

These examples show how women's sources round out our historical understanding and, at least to some extent, modify the emphasis on violence.

A focus on the experience of all women lengthens the time frame of western history, and the time frame can expand forward, as well as backward. Consider the long history of Chicano culture in the Southwest and California; the migration of blacks to the West during and following World War II; and the twentieth-century immigration to the West Coast of Chinese and other Asian women. None of those experiences is a part of western history as we understand it today. Traditionally, western history has focused on the experience of white, predominantly American settlers and *their* pioneer period, roughly 1840 to 1880. But what of the later pioneers? I suggest another perspective, a history of waves of settlement (beginning of course with the first settlers, the American Indians), tied together by a focus on the family experience of adaptation. This would provide a new, unifying principle, one in which we could look at all of western history, not just a few brief years. Two articles in this collection—on women, work, and family by Patricia Zavella and Micaela di Leonardo—point the way to a twentieth-century consideration of these issues.

Frederick Jackson Turner understood that the frontier experience was a continuous process. He wrote of the way in which successive waves of settlers at first reverted to primitive customs, then gradually altered and finally "civilized" the wilderness. Turner also argued that the frontier was a liberating influence both personally and socially. The individual who moved west was liberated from the economic and psychological constraints of civilized society. Likewise, the free frontier society was a democratizing force which kept the entire American society fluid and open.

Maybe so, maybe not, and especially maybe not for women. Historians have been arguing about the validity of the frontier thesis for a long time. The frontier *process* strikes a responsive chord in almost all of us, perhaps especially in those of us who are not native westerners. When we moved west we felt like different people, and we want to know if the pioneers felt the same. But it has always seemed to me that it is not the drama and the heroism, but the very dailiness and ordinariness of the frontier story that we find so compelling. We want to know how people traveled to the West, what difficulties they encountered, how they coped, and how the story turned out in the end. And we want that history of real people to make sense in our lives as westerners today. Conventional heroic western history, whether about men or women, does not meet those needs.

Although Turner was right about the process, he was wrong about something else. By focusing on adaptation by individuals, rather than by families or groups, he perpetuated the biases of the frontier myth: adventure, individualism, and violence. In the frontier myth the historical facts of the frontier process become the stuff of heroic tale. The contours of the frontier myth are probably most familiar to us in literature: the encounter with wilderness, the excitement of danger and challenge, the violent act of confrontation and commitment, the final slow surrender of freedom to advancing civilization.[10] The myth in all its varied forms—literature, art, history, popular culture—is deeply compelling for it is *the* American myth, the story of how we learned to identify with the land, how we came to say "this land is our land." Or alternatively, how the West was won, conquered, overcome, pillaged. For unmistakably, the frontier myth is a violent myth, preoccupied with stereotypically male issues like courage, physical bravery, honor, and male friendship. It could hardly be otherwise, considering that until recently men have been not only our historians but our mythmakers as well.

Still today the frontier myth holds a powerful and evocative fascination for us. Films, novels, and histories tell and retell the familiar stories. Again and again the stereotyped figures act out adventurous, individualistic, and violent dramas. Clearly, many people find these stereotyped images appealing. But is it history?

Women's sources do not support the exclusive preoccupation with adventure, individualism, and violence. Recent studies of the Overland Trail have revealed that few women diarists saw their westward journey as an adventure. They were much more concerned with separation, loss, tedium, fatigue, and the daily effort of living.[11] Similarly, the mythic stress on individualism turns out to be overdone. For example, upon close examination that heroic individualist, the fur trapper, becomes, if not precisely a family man, certainly not the loner of legend. Sylvia Van Kirk's work on the Canadian fur trade has shown how dependent the trappers were on Indian society, which they joined through their marriages and relationships with Indian women.[12] Her work does what we all need to do—examine a stereotype (in this case, the trapper), hold it up to the light, shake it out, and lo and behold!—a new and much more complex historical reality emerges—one in which women matter.

Of all the qualities of the frontier myth, surely the most troublesome is the emphasis on violence. Protection of white women often was used as a reason for violence against Indians. I have already suggested that women's sources tell another, more peaceful version of white-Indian contact. There may be other kinds of violence, like the vigilantism in mining towns, where women's sources can provide new information as well. Still other kinds of violence, in particular violence against women, have not been considered and need to be. Melody Graulich's work asks important new questions about the effect of domestic violence on the lives of western women. She has identified the subject through her study of women's novels; we must try to trace it historically. It is important to reconsider the issue of violence precisely because it has been so celebrated. In literature and drama, and I suppose in reality as well, violence is often the expression of hidden fear and a means of resolution. In real life, however, the resolution is not so simple: violent acts have consequences for all concerned, victor as well as victim. We need to move beyond the simple celebration of the act of violence to a complex historical consideration of its effects.

Today there is no room for the real, actual western woman in Hisland. She does not fit in: like the genteel lady, she cannot adapt. But, unlike the stereotype, she is not to blame. The Hisland version of western history is to blame, and it must be changed to tell the real story of the settlement of the West, from the beginning to the present. Much more than the history of women is at issue. Women's history provides a new perspective for the rethinking and reconceptualization that lie ahead. As we discover the real lives of western women, we will destroy both the female stereotypes—the lady, the helpmate, and the bad woman—and the male myths of adventure, individualism, and violence. Once we have removed the old distortions, we can concentrate on the rewriting of western history. We can use all of our sources, female and male, to write a new history of the West, one that many of us have wanted for a long time.

Notes

1. Michael P. Malone, ed., *Historians and the American West* (Lincoln: University of Nebraska Press, 1983).

2. These stereotypes were first clearly delineated by Beverly Stoeltje in "A Helpmate for Man Indeed: The Image of the Frontier Woman," *Journal of American Folklore* 88, no. 347 (January–March, 1975): 25–41.

3. See Sheryll Patterson-Black, "Women Homesteaders on the Great Plains Frontier," *Frontiers*, 1, no. 2 (Spring, 1976): 67–88.

4. Louise A. K. S. Clappe, *The Shirley Letters* (Santa Barbara, Calif.: Peregrine Smith Inc., 1970).

5. A descendant donated the original diary to the Special Collections of Colorado State University Library, Fort Collins. A local historian, Evadene Swanson, was instrumental in arranging the donation. Earlier, typescript copies prepared by another family member had been given to the archives at Colorado State University and the University of Colorado at Boulder.

6. Gerda Lerner, "Placing Women in History: A 1975 Perspective," in Bernice Carroll, ed., *Liberating Women's History* (Urbana: University of Illinois Press, 1976), p. 359.

7. Patricia Albers and Beatrice Medicine, *The Hidden Half: Studies of Plains Indian Women* (Washington, D.C.: University Press of America, 1983) p. 3.

8. Susan Armitage, "Women's Literature and the American Frontier," in Lawrence Lee and Merrill Lewis, eds., *Women, Women Writers, and the West* (New York: Witson Publishing, 1979); and Glenda Riley, *Women and Indians on the Frontier* (Albuquerque: University of New Mexico Press, 1984).

9. "Ironteeth, A Northern Cheyenne Woman" in Thomas B. Marquis, *The Cheyennes of Montana* (Algonac, Mich.: Reference Publication, 1978).

10. Richard Slotkin, *Regeneration Through Violence* (Middletown, Conn.: Wesleyan University Press, 1973), thoroughly discusses the frontier myth in American literature, though not from a feminist perspective.

11. See especially John Faragher, *Women and Men on the Overland Trail* (New Haven, Conn.: Yale University Press, 1979); Lillian Schlissel, *Women's Diaries of the Westward Journey* (New York: Schocken Books, 1982).

12. Sylvia Van Kirk, *Many Tender Ties: Women in Fur Trade Society, 1670–1870* (Norman: University of Oklahoma Press, 1983), and her article in this book.

2.
_____

The Way We Weren't: Images of Women and Men in Cowboy Art

CORLANN GEE BUSH

In this article Corlann Gee Bush analyzes the images of women and men in cowboy art. If "seeing is believing," we need look no further for reasons why inaccurate and demeaning stereotypes of western women persist. Bush uses standard techniques of artistic criticism to explicate the conventions of this genre of western art. She reveals that an apparently realistic art form is actually devoted to preserving a never-never land of male fantasy. Bush helps us see the ways in which cowboy art perpetuates myths of heroic males who never really existed in the first place. Her feminist analysis exposes the politics of an extremely popular and widespread art form. The next time you see a piece of traditional cowboy art, analyze the message. You may not like what you really see.

The scene boils with action: Indians are attacking the wagon train. A courageous man stands on the platform of his covered wagon, shooting around a board hastily placed there for protection. Wounded, a warrior falls off his white stallion, while another brave surges past him, tomahawk raised. Yet another Indian draws back his bow. In the foreground a bearded white man astride one of the rearing horses of the team pulling the wagon fires point-blank at an Indian with upraised tomahawk. Yet another brave is shot from behind just as he prepares to strike a blow with his war club. From the rear of the wagon runs a band of rescuers: a white man, a young boy, and several others bent on saving the beleagured party. In the wagon a young man falls back, blood gushing from a wound over his heart. Cradling him in her arms, a young woman with long blonde hair attempts to staunch the blood. Behind her an older woman with dark hair turns away, shielding a baby. Fear on her face, she stares over her shoulder at the distant viewer, as if pleading for help.

The painting *Attack on an Emigrant Train,* by Charles Wimar, tells everything one needs to know about the history of the American West as seen through the eyes of cowboy artists: he fights; she cringes. The purpose of this article is not to retell such an already familiar story but to show how paintings helped mold—and continue to reinforce—the myth of the West as *his land.*[1] Cowboy art is today one of the most vital and popular of the junta of American mythmakers: paintings, motion pictures,

The Fight for the Waterhole, by Frederic Remington. Courtesy Museum of Fine Arts, Houston, Texas.

paperback novels, and traditional American history. The assumptions, images, narrative techniques, and values portrayed in these media are interdependent, relying on and cross-referencing each other to tell the same story.

For example, Frederic Remington's *The Fall of the Cowboy* depicts a scene that would be unintelligible to a viewer who knew nothing of the popular history of the West. In it two cowboys approach a fence at the end of a long, cold day. Snow covers the ground, and a blanket of dense, gray clouds threatens a blizzard. Although they must smell the barn barely visible in the distance, the horses' heads are down, their legs splayed from exhaustion. One bearded cowboy remains in the saddle; his partner has dismounted to open the wooden gate of a barbed-wire fence. The mood is somber, the colors dark; even the footsteps in the snow seem sad and pathetic.

But what is going on here? Why the sorrow? Why are these men not happy to be home at the end of a long day? The answer is, of course, that the fence is barbed wire, and "we all know" that barbed wire meant the end of the open range. Thus we are witnessing not merely the end of a cowboy's day but the end of his era. In this painting the technique itself, its title, our knowledge of American history, the western movies we have seen, the cowboy novels we have read—all contribute to make this not so much a work of art as an artifact of popular culture.

Western art, or "cowboy art," as its artists and patrons prefer to call it, is narrative and representational. It tells a story based on the frontier myth and set against a natural backdrop. Further, it uses realistic detail and specific artistic techniques to convey traditional values about the roles of men and women in the West. That the paintings tell false and stereotyped stories is, in fact, the point, for cowboy artists do not paint the real West. They paint, instead, the romantic West, the West of myth and legend, the West the way the culture wants it to have been. The function of cowboy art, therefore, has been to paint stories that freeze the frontier myth in the cultural subconscious.

Almost always these stories present men and women differently. Although there were a few exceptional heroines, such as Mountain Kate, who is shown fighting a bear on the cover of one of Beadle's dime novels, the images and stories about the frontier woman have almost always emphasized her gentility and passivity. Painting after painting features a woman in a wagon, babe in arms, being led across the plains. Metaphorically carrying American civilization westward as she literally cradles the next generation, the pioneer woman has little opportunity to act as an individual in her own right. Men, on the other hand, lead very exciting lives, for their encounters with the frontier free them from their domestic roles and liberate them from the constraints of society. Cowboy art for men is the tale of action and adventure, danger and violence. Paintings such as Charles M. Russell's *The Jerk Line,* Wimar's *Attack on an Emigrant Train,* and Remington's *Stampeded by Lightning* are so charged with energy that they almost jump from the canvas. Even paintings that do not depict action scenes have an intense, barely suppressed potential for explosion. Remington's *The Hold Up,* Russell's *When Shadows Hint Death,* and O. C. Seltzer's *Carrying the Mail* are famous representatives of such paintings, while Marv Ennes's *Men of the Madison* and Tom Lovell's *Long Time till New Grass* are more recent treatments of the same themes.

The classic painting of the western male experience is Remington's *The Fight for the Waterhole,* which contains all the elements of narrative and style that make cowboy art unique. In it five men and their six horses have taken shelter from Indian attack in an almost dry waterhole. The small puddle of water reflects a far-off mountain. The horses bunch together in the bottom of the depression; the men have taken up defensive positions around the rim. A dozen Indians on horses circle in the distance; the smoke from one rifle makes a faint white streak against the yellow sand. Two men in the foreground stare at the distant enemy; spent shells litter the sand beneath their rifles. The angle of the shadows indicates that if these men are not shot or captured they will die of thirst. Yet all show courage and determination in the face of almost certain death; they will fight to the last man.

Gray sand dominates the foreground and forms the waterhole; dusty yellows stretch to gray mountains, then blue-gray, cloudless sky. The cowboys are dressed in grays and browns except for the jaunty, carefully knotted red bandana on the mustachioed veteran closest to the viewer. The other cowboy in the foreground is young, yet he too aims his rifle with steely determination. The defender in the middle distance exudes confidence, his hand resting on his hip a moment before drawing his pistol. Here are the men who won the West.

Remington's painting is dramatic because it combines the prime themes of action, adventure, individualism, and violence into a tale of danger, heroism, courage, and male bonding. It is compelling because the vastness and austerity of the landscape form a backdrop appropriate to the drama. Here is the mythic, American, "male psychodrama" experienced on canvas.

For women, however, the myths and thus the paintings are markedly different. If *Fight for the Waterhole* is the quintessential masculine painting, then *The Madonna of the Prairie*, by W. H. D. Koerner, represents its feminine counterpart. In this work a beautiful young woman with clear eyes and rouged cheeks, seated on a covered wagon, stares past the viewer into the land beyond. The canvas of the wagon forms a halo around her head. She is tastefully dressed: the brooch, obviously an heirloom, sets off the white collar of her dress, itself is a rich red-brown. Her bright-crimson shawl has slipped off her shoulders and can be seen beside her on the seat and wrapped over her right arm. Its color accentuates her lips, complements her dress. She holds the heavy black reins in delicate hands. The painting conveys a sense of peaceful waiting, an atmosphere of equal parts serenity and anticipation.

Called a "madonna" in the painting's title, the woman is clearly not pregnant and is not shown with children, a rarity in the few western paintings that portray women.[2] This seeming contradiction is resolved by a closer reading of the painting: The woman expects to become pregnant, she expects to have her children on the prairie, she expects to settle the West. She is, symbolically, the expectant mother. It is her attitude and her femininity—not her specific individual condition—that fit her for her holy work.

In terms of technique this painting is almost the complete antithesis of *Fight for the Waterhole*. The female figure is centered in the picture and framed by the canvas; the five cowboys are arrayed across the picture and set against a vast, hostile landscape.[3] The framing of the female figure serves to protect her from danger, to erase her individualism, to elevate her to symbolic status. However, the five men are not only unframed; they actually break the frame of the waterhole, emphasizing not only their separateness but also their dominance over the landscape.

These paintings are typical of cowboy art in more than the use of impressionistic background. Color and detail are equally important. In presentations of men the palette is somber and monochromatic, using shades of brown, black, and gray to emphasize the barrenness of the landscape, their masculinity, and their seriousness of purpose. In presentations of women, the colors are rich, the tones warm; reds, greens, rusts, even golds give off an almost reverential glow. Such use of color serves to set

The Madonna of the Prairie, by W. H. D. Koerner. Courtesy Buffalo Bill Historical Center, Cody, Wyoming.

women apart from the scenes they are in, giving them a separate symbolic reality.

In addition, the use of detail varies dramatically when men and women are depicted. For women, the details of dress and clothing are richly colored and specific, while the items in their surroundings are merely suggestive. For example, the brooch and the buttons on the madonna's dress glint in the light; a wisp of hair begins to escape its pins; her luminous hands reveal trimmed nails. Yet the details of the wagon and its gear are only suggested; even the canvas of the wagon is painted with broad strokes, its frame barely visible. She holds the reins in such a way that they will be jerked out of her hands if the horses suddenly shy. The emphasis on personal detail to the exclusion of the impersonal says that this is Woman; she is universal, belonging to no particular place, part of no specific event. In contrast, the details of *Fight for the Waterhole* are extremely specific: the spent shell casings on the sand where they have been ejected from the rifle, the saddles and packs on the horses in the water hole, the loose strap of the canteen on the closest defender's back, the length and angle of the shadows. All such details of place and time serve to particularize the scene and make it real.

The painterly conventions differ for men and for women in one other aspect: eye contact. Men are almost always involved in the action, and their eyes focus on specific objects, in or out of the picture. Women, on the other hand, most frequently look out of the picture frame at the viewer or beyond, into the distance. John Berger calls this the "looking at being looked at" look and says:

One might simplify this by saying *men act* and *women appear*. Men look at women. Women watch themselves being looked at. This determines not only most relations between men and women but also the relation of women to themselves. The surveyor of woman in herself is male: the surveyed female. Thus she turns herself into an object—and most particularly an object of vision: a sight.[4]

The truth of these generalizations is frequently demonstrated by the absence of a particular convention in paintings of males. For example, Harvey Dunn's *The Homesteader's Wife* shows a woman alone in a vast landscape. She is unframed and seems almost naked, for there is no bonnet on her head or Conestoga wagon to shelter her. She leads an ox across a field of dried, yellow grass; the sun beats down on her; she stares at the ground ahead of her. Here is a woman beaten down by the elements. The homesteader's wife is the reluctant pioneer who is not, like a man, liberated by the forces of nature but is destroyed by them. Similarly, Seltzer's drawing *Pioneer Mother* shows a woman with a rifle, protecting her two children, who cling to her skirts. The look on her face is one of horror and desperation, a sharp contrast to the look of courageous determination on the face of the boy, in equally desperate straits, in Remington's *The Emigrants*.

Regardless of artist or era, cowboy art tells the same story of independent men and dependent women. In William Ranney's *The Pioneers* and John Clymer's *The Homesteaders* the differing conventions for men and women are evident in the same painting. Ranney presents a *tableau vivant:* a family of five, two oxen, one white horse, a covered wagon, and two dogs frozen for a moment in their journey across the endless prairie. The father, dressed in brown, walks at the head of the team of oxen, long rifle on his shoulder; he stares vigilantly ahead. The distant horizon and the gray cloudscape emphasize his strength and diligence.

Behind him in the wagon two children are being cared for by an older woman, dressed in lighter, richer brown. However, the focus of interest in the painting is the younger woman in the left center foreground. Riding sidesaddle on a white horse, she wears a green dress with matching sunbonnet, the green of the hat accented by a band of red. The whiteness of her fichu intensifies the green of her dress and echoes the creamy white of her horse. The colors of her saddle blanket pick up and complement the colors of her ensemble. This part of the scene—the woman-occupied space—is serene and reverential, in stark contrast to the sense of purposefulness of her husband's stride.

This woman and the three figures on the wagon look into the distance, but not one is staring in the same direction as the father. He is looking at something specific; they merely stare ahead into the unknown. The differences in the use of color are likewise remarkable. The woman on the horse is painted in rich, luminous colors that modulate as the viewer's eye sweeps across the group in the wagon, finally dulling to the dark, dignified tones of the father-leader. That the woman's dress is greener than the grass of the prairie is not accidental, for she represents the spring of new hope. Finally, in this painting Ranney uses the same framing conventions noted earlier: the man walking free under the skies; the wife and children sheltered from the wildness of the landscape by the canvas of the wagon, just as they are protected from danger by the man and his rifle.

In like manner, John Clymer's *The Homesteaders* shows another family group on the overland trail. Five people, three horses, a colt, two cows, a dog, a caged chicken, and a wagon crowd the scene. In the foreground, about to stride out of the picture frame, is a man in his early thirties. He carries a rifle, wears a startlingly white shirt with suspenders, brown pants with mud on the knees and high-top boots. He looks directly and piercingly at the viewers as if to determine if we are friend or foe. As the whiteness of his shirt and the firmness of his step indicate, there is nothing indeterminate about this man. His son, about ten, is dressed in an off-white shirt and is riding his father's horse. As children will, he has let his gaze wander from the task at hand, so his father leads the horse. Behind the boy, his mother drives the Conestoga wagon; a young girl seated beside her, plays with a doll. Both are dressed in blue sunbonnets and purple-toned dresses—the mother in lavender, the child in plum. They are framed by an open rib of the wagon; its closed canvas forms a glowing backdrop. From the back and sides of the wagon protrude the farm tools (a moldboard plow) and household goods (a rocking chair) that the family will use to make a new life. Behind the wagon an elderly, bearded man drives two cows forward.

Despite the overcrowding of the scene, the three males take up considerably more space than the two females. For example, the father steps resolutely forward into the wilderness, connected to, but not limited by, his family. The boy, as befits his youth, is partly framed by the wagon behind him—indicating that he will be, for a while longer, sheltered and protected by his father. The grandfather's shoulders break the horizon. The two women, on the other hand, are totally enclosed, not only by the wagon but also by their menfolk. They go where they are led; they remain where they are protected.

Again the details of the painting are meticulously rendered: the viewer can see the trigger on the rifle, the sight on its barrel, the intricacies of horse collar and bridle. The details of dress and posture are clear. Yet despite its fidelity to detail, this painting errs in significant ways. First, we are asked to believe that this man would carry a heavy rifle as he walked, especially when his horse with rifle scabbard is within arm's reach. Second, his knees are muddy, but his high-top boots are not. And his shirt . . . how does his wife get it so white without *Tide?* Finally, the animals are well fed, the people healthy; no one is dirty or disheveled. Even the man's suspender clips are polished and, of all things, level. Either this family has just begun its westward journey and the details that describe them are therefore true, or something other than a realistic representation of a family headed west is being portrayed. Since both the landscape and the vegetation belie the former conclusion, we are left to wonder why the artist would paint such a patently unreal scene with such *intricately* real detail. The answer, of course, is that the realism of the details seduces the viewer into believing that the *story* is equally true and real. This false verisimilitude, in turn, discourages the viewer from further examining the story by checking it against the lives of real people. The mind freezes.

Several other paintings seduce their viewers into believing in the truth of an obvious falsity. Charles M. Russell, who should have known better,[5] was frequently guilty of such incongruities, especially in his five Keeoma portraits. In them he presents the realistic objects of a native woman's life and then uses these to convince us of Keeoma's carnality and wantonness. Painted in either reclining or "hip-slung" poses, Keeoma is sexualized in a way that white women never are in western art. The message is clear: white women are too pure to be shown as specifically sexual creatures. In fact, although white women are frequently painted with children in their arms, they are never portrayed as pregnant. Native American women, on the other hand, are seen as more "natural," less civilized and civilizing than white women; they are painted with all the sensuality and spirit denied white women.

This inability of white male artists to accept the sexuality of white women and its artistic transference to Indian women is illustrated by the history of the Keeoma paintings themselves. Although legend has it that Russell had an unrequited love affair with a Blood "maiden" named Keeoma and that he painted his love for her in his portraits, the truth is that Russell's wife, Nancy, was the model for the paintings.[6] To pose, she dressed in buckskin and surrounded herself with artifacts. Russell painted the objects realistically; he painted her as an Indian. In this way he was able to paint his wife as the sensual woman he knew her to be while preserving her place within the moral code of white society. Nancy Russell was able to play the seductress without publicly revealing her own sexuality. This repressed sexuality was transposed onto an Indian woman who did not exist but who lived, nonetheless, deep in the subconscious of white American males.

When white women are painted or sculptured as sexual beings, the renditions almost always say more about the women's supposed relationship to a man than they say about the woman herself. For example, another of Russell's works shows four scenes from a cowboy's life. The first watercolor, titled *Just a Little Sunshine,* shows a cowboy sitting in the shadow cast by his horse, the only spot of shade in the yellow landscape. *Just a Little Rain* reveals the same cowboy wearing a slicker, rain cascading from a gray sky, his horse standing in a puddle, water sluicing from his hat. *Just a Little Pleasure* shows us the same cowhand, drunk, sitting on the edge of a bed. His hat, a glass, one boot, and some coins litter the floor. A handsome woman in a low-cut blue gown pulls off his other boot as he brandishes a five-dollar bill in her face. *Just a Little Pain* reveals our hero dosing himself against venereal disease. The paintings are bawdy and humorous in a typically western, understated way, yet the message about female sexuality is as clear as the comedy.

Seltzer, a friend and colleague of Russell, sketched two portraits of women that likewise focus on the implied presence (or absence) of men in their lives. One, the *Dance Hall Girl,* shows a hardened, cold-eyed prostitute sitting in a chair at a card table; the drink in one hand and the cigarette in the other testify to her life of depravity. *Pioneer Mother,* on the other hand, shows a woman attempting to load a muzzle-loading rifle that is almost as big as she is. With two children cowering around her skirts and panic written clearly on her face, the viewer feels compelled to ask, "Why has she been left alone?"

This sense that women must be protected by white men from the ravages of Indian men is also a favorite theme of cowboy artists. Paintings such as Wimar's *The Abduction of Boone's Daughter by the Indians* show defenseless white women enslaved or about to be captured by Indians. Such paintings functioned in complex ways. First, by assuming that white men would be incensed over this threat to the virtue of white women, they persuaded men to see themselves as the protectors of defenseless women. Second, by instilling fear of rape and capture in women, such paintings encouraged women to see themselves as defenseless and in need of protection. Since many of these paintings and drawings were used as illustrations in popular magazines, they served at the time to induce fear of Indians and the unknown and to limit women's mobility. Finally, these paintings reinforced the cultural view that Indian men were heathens and savages, a class of "others" who deserved killing because they threatened white women. Thus, by portraying white men as courageous defenders of virtue, by showing white women helpless at the hands of ravening savages, this subgenre of cowboy art reveals how inextricibly racism is connected to sexism in the American subconscious.

A few western paintings seem to defy the conventions of the rapacious savage/defenseless madonna subgenre by depicting Indian men and women as noble representatives from a different culture. The best of these are Remington's *Ridden Down,* which shows a dust-encrusted brave standing next to his exhausted horse and singing his death chant; and Henry Farny's *The Sorcerer,* which depicts a shaman, surrounded by his sacred medicine, dancing and drumming his invocation to the spirits. In addition, most works by George Catlin, particularly his portraits, present his native subjects as strong, intelligent, unsentimentalized individuals. In all of these, the details of dress and artifact are rendered with fidelity. Nonetheless, even these sympathetic works emphasize the exotic "otherness," not the common humanity, of the subject.

It is, in fact, the distance between the realism of the painted artifacts and the unreality of the depicted lives that helps account for the continuing popularity of cowboy art. People enjoy cowboy art because they believe it to be history; they want to hang the West on the wall above the couch. Contemporary patrons of cowboy art want to entertain, watch television, argue, and make love under paintings that console them, that recall simpler times, that seduce them into believing in the myths of Hisland history. Such artistic seduction is, of course, abetted by the absence of women's history; but, for the most part, the paintings accomplish the seduction themselves. Cowboy art "works" for its viewers because story and technique intertwine.

Analysis of these paintings, then, shows that for men the story is a heroic tale, an epic quest for freedom filled with action, adventure, individualism, and violence. This story is told, artistically, by the use of one or more of the following techniques:

1. The men in the paintings have direct eye contact with something or someone either within the painting itself or implied by it. This convention is used to demonstrate the individuality and integrity of the subject.

2. The palette is restricted and austere, employing black, brown, and gray tones to emphasize the seriousness of the story. These somber tones are occasionally relieved by a spot of vibrant color, usually red, to stress the individuality and courage of the subject.

3. Black and white contrasts reinforce the story as a battle between good and evil.

4. Vast, impressionistic landscapes form the backdrop for the epic action. This convention acts as a metaphor for the enormity of the American West at the same time that it masculinizes the western landscape.

5. Objects in the painting are rendered in realistic detail, thus seducing

the viewer into believing that the story is as realistically portrayed as the surroundings.

6. Subjects are portrayed holding guns and other weapons to underscore the elements of violence and danger in the story.

7. The subjects of paintings are shown in noncontiguous groups (i.e., arrayed across the canvas) in order to emphasize the loneliness and isolation of the frontier. No matter how many men are depicted in a scene, each is portrayed as separate and apart, a man alone in an epic, individual battle.

For women, the western story is not an epic but an allegory, a tale of passivity, dependence, gentility, and, frequently, victimization. As courage is for men, sexuality is the important characteristic of women portrayed in cowboy art. Yet, the emphasis is not on a woman's personal sexuality but on her generic, symbolic womanhood. Whether fallen or chaste, whether native or white, whether victim or madonna, the heroine of western paintings is a stranger in *his land,* an interloper into the epic. In order to relate the allegories of woman as gentle tamer or wild temptress, cowboy artists make use of the following techniques:

1. Women stare beyond the picture frame at the viewer, presumably male—in Berger's phrase, looking at being looked at. This convention makes women the objects of viewing, not the actors in a drama.

2. The palette is rich, warm, and earthy, using gold, green, and ochre tones to emphasize the femininity and "naturalness" of the subject.

3. Most female subjects are bathed in a warm, luminous, sometimes reverential glow to emphasize their state of blessedness. Sharp contrasts are used only to portray fallen women or women as victims.

4. Women are set against a close and limiting backdrop which holds them within the scene, confining them and limiting their action. This convention serves as a metaphor of protection and emphasizes women's docility and dependence.

5. The objects and artifacts of the surroundings are painted abstractly, thus narrowing the focus of the painting and removing the subject from the particularities of time or event. This convention emphasizes the symbolic, rather than the specific, context of women's lives.

6. Subjects of paintings are shown in close, contiguous groups, frequently holding children. This shows women's story to be allegorical and communal, rather than epic and individual.

7. Women are seldom shown using weapons or even tools. When a woman does hold a gun, it is frequently bigger than she is or she is frightened of it. Western women are supposed to be defenseless and dependent.

In western art, image and techniques reciprocate to tell remarkably different stories for men and women. By examining how cowboy artists use these conventions to "paint their narratives," we learn how art reinforces myth and freezes it in the popular mind. By understanding these conventions we can begin to change them, a task that some contemporary cowboy artists have already begun. Among these are well-known artists such as M. C. Poulsen, Jim Bama, Steven Saylor, and Jaune Quick-to-See Smith and lesser known artists such as Douglas Kent Hall and Shawn Williams.

Williams's *Joy Riding* shows a young woman riding a large white horse, brown hair streaming out behind her, her hand reaching for her hat as she exhilarates in the speed of her ride. This painting upsets the traditional narrative themes by depicting a woman who is anything but passive and dependent. Hall's *Mesquite Texas,* a silver print from a photograph, ignores tradition in another way; it shows only the boots and lower legs of a dozen cowboys standing together at a bar, a rodeo, or a roundup—it is difficult to tell which for there is no background or landscape. Every detail of their jeans, boots, and spurs is so exquisitely rendered that the sheer variety begins to blur into sameness while the similarities split into difference and individuality. This wonderful work of cowboy art turns several conventions on their heads: there is no action or danger, no eye contact, no separateness, no landscape, no narrative. Yet the detail and the use of black, gray, and white contrasts tell us volumes about these working cowboys and their lives.

Poulsen, Bama, and Saylor focus on character rather than narrative. Bama's *Lucylle Moon Hall* shows an elderly woman with graying hair, wrinkled hands, weathered face. She wears a well used cowboy hat, a red shirt, and fringed buckskin vest; a red silk scarf is knotted below her left ear. Her pose is contemplative; her face strong. Here is a woman of the West who fits none of the stereotypes. Most of Bama's other paintings employ the techniques used in this work: the lack of landscape or natural setting, broad-ranging palette, warm and luminous colors, use of detail to illuminate character rather than narrative. In fact, Bama's concentration on character and avoidance of narrative are conscious; he says: "I always felt out of place with anecdotal paintings of historical scenes, roundups, and brandings. My venture into the world of western art convinced me that I was being boxed in by subject matter.[7]

While Bama usually avoids setting in order to focus on character, Saylor uses details of setting and background to highlight it. His *Last of the Constables,* for example, shows an elderly lawman at his desk, a kerosene lamp lighting the objects from a vanishing life. *Landrums* shows two men in a small town cafe; one strums a chord on his guitar while the owner listens with a half bored, half quizzical expression. Two jukeboxes and a poster on the door remind the viewer of the world of country-western music that remains beyond the singer's reach. Saylor's paintings are more humorous and self-deprecating than those of most other cowboy artists, and he uses color more quixotically. *Beans and Whiskey,* for example, shows an old hand seated with his back to a stone wall, plate of beans in hand. He wears, of all things, a purple coat. Likewise, the wrangler in *Crossin' the Carson* wears a still-blue denim jacket and uses a bright red, fringed Navajo saddle blanket. Saylor's large work, *Bar Talk,* is both wry and hilarious, using unusual colors and exaggerated scale to show us contem-

Lucylle Moon Hall, by Jim Bama.

porary western characters who are at once silly and sad. We recognize ourselves in them immediately.

If Bama and Saylor have redefined the traditions of cowboy art, Poulsen and Smith have managed to defy them without denying them. While some of Poulsen's work, notably *Portrait of a Pioneer* and *And the Hearts of the Children Shall Turn to Their Fathers,* are heavily imitative of Bama's character portraits, *Wrangler in Yellow Slicker* and *Chuck Poulsen, Outfitter 1922–1977* are profoundly different. The latter shows a strong man caught at a moment of rest, the faded denim of the clothing testifying to his hard life. As usual the details are precise and clear. All seems traditional, yet something is wrong: Chuck Poulsen stares ahead with vacant eyes, looking at nothing in particular; the white pearl handle of his six gun is unscratched and oddly oversized; he wears large stones on the ring fingers of each hand and kneels in an uncomfortable pose halfway between squatting and sitting. He is still, yet somehow moving; neither in the painting nor out of it. Its details serve to locate him in no time or place. This is Poulsen's loving, yet ambiguous, eulogy to his father, an outfitter killed in a hunting accident.[8]

Wrangler in Yellow Slicker is, on the other hand, firmly located in space if not in time. A cowboy riding a mud-spattered horse slogs into a tent camp. There is snow on the ground, but mud clogs the path, spatters the tents, and obscures the horse's white stockings. The wrangler's slicker shines so brightly in a ray of late afternoon sun that it almost hurts the eyes. The tents, the lodgepole pine in the background, the jutting tent pole, all serve to confine the wrangler in this late-fall camp, to frame him solidly within the painting. Yet this painting tells no story, contains no moral, describes no action. It does not focus on character, nor is it located in time. This could be any wrangler, today or one hundred years ago.

If the thrust of the best, contemporary, untraditional cowboy art has been to strip paintings of their story, then Smith's work confounds even the iconoclasts, for her work is wholly story. But it is story without narrative. Smith's paintings are, fittingly, like Indian petroglyphs: we almost seem to understand their specific meaning; we try to translate but cannot. Her Kalispell and Wallowa Water Hole series combine small-scale line drawings of horses, tipis, warriors, shamans, fences, and travois with broad, pastel blocks and abstract geometric forms. As Mary Carroll Nelson describes Smith's recent work:

She has adapted both the figurative work of [native American] men and the abstract designs of women. . . . Demarcations of field have fused creating a vigorously active surface of colors layered one upon the other, with figurative elements in thickened strokes. . . . These [are] cryptic, scratchy notations that [can] be "read" as a collection of component parts in an anecdote, but each reader's version of the story would differ, depending on memory and understanding.[9]

Each reader's version differs, depending on memory and understanding. Gone are the assumptions of shared cultural history, the stereotypes reinforced by movies and pulp novels, the allusion to allegory, the prescriptions of epic that have characterized cowboy art. Myths about men and women in the West, once thought universal, have, at last, been made personal and idiosyncratic.

Thus, by stripping their work of narrative and stereotype, by concentrating on character or moment, by combining themes and mixing conventions, the best of the new cowboy artists—Hall, Bama, Poulsen, and Smith—require us to re-examine the meaning of the traditions perpetuated by their predecessors. As they unpaint the culture's western myths, they challenge us to learn the truth about the ways we really were in the West.

Notes

1. Susan Armitage, "Through Women's Eyes: A New View of the West," *The Women's West,* this book.
2. Paintings that portray single men or men in groups outnumber paintings of women ten to one.

3. What Matthew Baigell says of Remington's paintings is true of *Fight for the Water-hole* and descriptive of cowboy art in general: "Remington's frontier really has no location. He usually indicated landscape features with schematically rendered detail—some under-brush, a distant mountain. More precise definition of background details would have imposed reality upon the dream." (Matthew Baigell, *The Western Art of Frederic Remington* [New York: Ballantine Books, 1976], p. 24.)

4. John Berger, *Ways of Seeing* (London: British Broadcasting Corporation, 1973), p. 47.

5. Ironically, we owe to Russell some of the few paintings of strong, capable, native American women. His *In the Wake of the Buffalo Runners* and *Indian Women Moving Camp* are excellent paintings which violate all the conventions about how Indian women were to be painted. Nonetheless, he created few paintings of strong competent white women, despite the fact that his wife, Nancy Cooper Russell, was his business manager and agent.

6. Frederick G. Renner, *Charles M. Russell: Paintings, Drawings and Sculpture from the Amon G. Carter Collection* (Austin: University of Texas Press, 1972), p. 45.

7. Lorry McGehee, "Bama," *Art West,* 6, no. 1 (December, 1982): 41.

8. Dale Burk, *A Brush With the West* (Missoula, Mont.: Mountain Press Publishing Company, 1980), p. 69.

9. Mary Carroll Nelson, "Jaune Quick-To-See Smith," *Art West* 6, no. 4 (May–June, 1983): 70–74.

3.
_____

Illusion and Illumination: Visual Images of American Indian Women in the West

PATRICIA C. ALBERS AND WILLIAM R. JAMES

Historians of women are recovering the lives of those who have been over-looked in earlier histories often through the use of unconventional topics and research methods. The following article is a good example of the fruitfulness of such an approach. It explores a neglected topic, the stereo-typing of American Indian women, by analyzing changing images on post-cards, a popular medium which reached a wide audience beginning in the late nineteenth century. The results are illuminating. The authors' careful consideration of changing historical contexts allows us to see how subtly pervasive and destructive the values of the dominant culture can be.

The disruption of American Indian cultures by Euro-Americans is a basic theme in western history. When we consider that conflict, however, most of us think in military and political terms, of the battles and removals of the nineteenth century. However, we see in the example explored in this article how the real lives of American Indian women were progressively, though peacefully, denied. We come to realize that we need to see culture conflict as pervasive, ongoing, and basic to our understanding of western history.

During the past century, the most familiar image of the American Indian has been masculine.[1] As stereotypically portrayed, the Indian is a tipi-dwelling, buffalo-hunting, equestrian warrior replete with warbonnet and fringed buckskin clothes. Originally promoted and popularized in the Wild West Shows of the late nineteenth and early twentieth centuries, and later in Hollywood movies, this stereotyped symbol has become the only image that scores of urban Americans and Europeans recognize as Indian.[2]

When it comes to visual images of American Indian women, however, it is less easy to isolate one pictorial stereotype as pervasive as the war-bonneted "warrior." If a uniform caricature has existed, it has been the image of the Indian "princess" (Illustration 1). Although popular in recent years, this female figure has not always dominated the visual representa-tions of western Indian women, nor has it been prevalent in all areas of the West.

Visual portrayals of Indian women, while generally less prevalent than those of men, exhibit much greater variation in their content and themes.

ILLUSTRATION 1. This New Year's greeting card is the work of early-twentieth-century illustrator Ellen Clappsaddle. The card was published by the International Art Publishing Company of New York around 1908. Postcard in authors' collection.

Instead of a single homogenized image, there have been a range of pictorial motifs, variation in the settings and attire in which female subjects appear, and diversity in poses. Unifying visual themes can be isolated, of course; but in general, these tend to be greatly modified by the culturally specific backgrounds of the women who are pictured, and they tend to change with shifts in the meaning and uses of the media in which the pictures appear.

Tracing the history and range of pictures that represent Indian women in the West reveals a great deal about the bias and subjectivity inherent in the production and mass release of these images over time. It also offers a critical perspective for interpreting the role that the visual media play in creating popularized images of American Indian women.

One medium suited to this type of understanding is the picture postcard. Since the late nineteenth century thousands of pictures depicting Indian females have been printed on postcards. Their images have been featured on cards sold in artistic and collectible series, and on cards with greeting, comic, and advertising messages. Finally, they have been popular subjects on a wide range of pictorial views issued for local consumption and tourism. Since postcards have been widely available during the past century, they have been one of the primary sources from which the public has drawn its visual image of Indian women in the West.

TOWARD A CRITICAL INTERPRETATION OF VISUAL IMAGES

To photograph people is to violate them, by seeing them as they never see themselves, by having knowledge of them they can never have; it turns people into objects that can be symbolically possessed.[3]

Susan Sontag's words about photography provide an apt beginning for a critical interpretation of the visual images of Indian women that appear on postcards. Along with other popular media, the postcard has fostered and perpetuated a "way of seeing" Indian women that is estranged from their *lived* experience. Rather than seeing these women as "real" people, the postcard has turned them into caricatures from some romantic fantasy promoted in novels and film. When caricatures of Indian women appear on postcards reproduced from paintings and drawings (Illustration 1), the image is obviously the artist's interpretation. There is no presumption that the image is real. But in postcards produced from photographs, the subjective and mythical qualities of the picture are more elusive. Unlike paintings, photographs convey images that seem real. A photograph, after all, directly records a trace of an appearance that existed in some time and place. As such, it gives the illusion that it represents something that is "true" to life. When confronted with a photograph, we accept it as an objective representation because the camera does not "lie."[4]

But even though the camera is neutral, those who take and reproduce its photographs are not. What is recorded by a camera involves a complex dialectical relationship between the direct appearance of a sight and the

ILLUSTRATION 2. This modern chrome card depicts Navajo women in Arizona. Pictured, from left to right, are Emma Sharty, Louise Claw, Helen Boone, Dolly Turquoise, and Julia Turquoise. Distributed on a postcard in the late 1950s, this photograph is the work of Bob Bradshaw, a well-known southwestern photographer. Postcard in authors' collection.

photographer's interpretation of that appearance. In many postcard pictures of American Indian women, the "truth" of an image does not derive from the reality of the subject's own experience. While such images are often informed by the past or present cultures of their Indian subjects, they distort the appearance of these cultures in a way that conforms to the photographer's understanding of what constitutes "authenticity" in Indian life. The standards by which photographers judge the genuineness of their images are determined, more often than not, by popularly held symbols and stereotypes, rather than by conditions intrinsic to the everyday lives of the subjects pictured.[5]

The Navajo, for example, are the most widely photographed Indian group in the Southwest. Of the hundreds of pictures of Navajo that have been printed on postcards, over half show women weaving rugs, standing in front of hogans, or posed against natural attractions such as Canyon de Chelly or Monument Valley (Illustration 2). While many of these views approximate the lifestyles of a few Navajo women, they do not represent the experiences of the vast majority. But it is these images that continue to appear on postcards, not views of Navajo women as nurses, teachers, lawyers, secretaries, or assemblyline workers. By focusing attention only on the unique and exotic, postcards contribute to the public's misinformed vision of what life is like for most women in contemporary Navajo society.

The way in which a postcard picture is interpreted and the meanings it conveys cannot be understood apart from the context in which it originates and the uses to which it is put.[6] It is important, therefore, to distinguish between what John Berger[7] identifies as the "private" and "public" uses of photographs.

Photographs printed on postcards for private use represent, in Berger's words, "a memento from a life being lived."[8] These pictures are grounded directly in the experiences of those who are photographed and who see the images. Postcard pictures that Indian people have taken for their own use and that fill the pages of their family albums are of this order. The meaning of these images is personal and drawn from the lives and histories of those who are associated with the pictures.

Far different in their meaning are photographs, and the renditions of them, that are reproduced on postcards for public use. These pictures are detached completely from the historical contexts in which they were taken and from the experiences of those who participated in their production. The images convey depersonalized and ahistorical messages. Consequently, they are easily subjected to uses and interpretations that have nothing to do with the lives of the women who are pictured. Public postcard pictures of Indian women have been manipulated in the interest of public fantasies and stereotypes, and they confirm Sontag's observation that photographs violate their subjects when they are placed in contexts, and are ascribed meanings, over which the subject has no control or knowledge.

The historical process by which postcard images of Indian women in the West have become increasingly fetishized and alien to their own experiences can be further illustrated by examining substantive and stylistic changes in postcards which reproduce photographs that are related to actual historical contexts and those that are not (e.g., portraits).

PICTURES FROM A LIFE BEING LIVED

The most varied and historically accurate postcard pictures of Indian women in the West come from the early decades of the twentieth century, when the postcard was a popular medium for reproducing photographs of private and local interest. In the years before 1925, studio and itinerant photographers earned a livelihood from the sale of postcards depicting people, events, and places in western communities. Photographers who lived near, or traveled to, reservation communities took pictures of life as it was being lived by Indian people. Most of these views were issued in small numbers and printed on photographic stock. They were sold by the studio photographer or by local retailers, including druggists, stationery, and variety store owners. Pictures for which there was a larger demand were generally reproduced by national or regional postcard manufacturers using various lithographic processes.

What is striking about the postcard pictures of Indian women produced for local sale is their ordinariness. The pictures depict women in the places

ILLUSTRATION 3. This privately taken photograph was printed on postcard stock around 1910. It shows Dakota women in the Fort Totten Trading Post in North Dakota. Postcard in authors' collection.

where they customarily lived and traveled, in the clothing they commonly wore, and in poses that were unpretentious and candid. Many of the photographs taken of Dakota (Sioux) women from North and South Dakota were of this order (Illustration 3). In this type of postcard, the images were drawn directly from the day-to-day experience of the female subjects.

The pictures were also connected to the personal lives of those who viewed and mailed them, as is revealed in the messages written on the backs of locally issued postcards. When these refer to the postcard's picture, they suggest that the sender is either acquainted with the subjects personally or knows from direct experience something about the Indian people in the area. For example, the message on the back of one postcard from South Dakota reads:

This is Thomas Little Dog and his squaw seated by their campfire. The stuff hanging up at the corner of the tent which looks like clothes is meat they had up to dry. They had just eaten their breakfast when I got there.

Yours truly,
"Polly"

It is clear from this message and others like it that the subjects pictured on the postcards are not strangers; they were people with whom the viewer had some direct and concrete connection.

Although not without their own kinds of racial biases, the early locally produced cards of Indian women in the West revealed an authentic appearance. The dominant images of these private pictures were not severed from the life that Indian women lived and their neighbors witnessed.[9]

PICTURES FROM A LIFE AS SPECTACLE

In contrast to the postcard pictures which drew their interest from the lives of local people, Indian and white alike, tourist and collectible-type cards were directed at strangers who had little or no direct knowledge of the Indian women pictured. Consequently, many of these images took on appearances and interpretations that were largely divorced from the lived-in experiences of their female subjects.

In the years before 1925, tourist and collectible postcards existed alongside views produced primarily for local consumption. In an era when few people owned cameras and when photographs were not reproduced regularly in newspapers and magazines, the postcard was the predominant visual medium. It was the primary means by which Americans and Canadians gained their visual images of Indian people in near and distant places.[10]

In this early period, there was some overlap between the subjects and themes of postcards used in local, private contexts and those issued for outsiders—tourists and collectors in far-removed urban centers. More often than in postcards of Indian men, women appeared in identifiable native settings and were engaged in some kind of traditional activity. In much of the West, postcards picturing Indian people in their home surroundings and occupied in work were dominated by female subjects. And in some areas, such as the Southwest and the Great Basin, the bulk of early postcards pictured women, in contrast to the Plains region where views of men in portrait-type pictures prevailed.

The pre-1925 postcards that were sold primarily to national and regional-tourist audiences emphasized the exotic in Indian life rather than the ordinary. In general, what began to emerge in these pictures was a disparity between the everyday life of Indian women and the images that outsiders saw of their lives.

An important reason for the discrepancy was the not uncommon practice of reproducing photographs taken in the nineteenth century on postcards issued in 1915 and later, a practice especially common in the Southwest (Illustration 4). Obviously, profound changes had occurred in the lives of Indian women since the photographs were taken. But, instead of documenting this change, postcards continued to project a romantic and anachronistic view of Indian life, one which was totally out of step with the contemporary experiences of Indian women.

Some postcard pictures, to be sure, did convey something of the experiential reality of certain Indian women. But the reality that was pictured represented only a very narrow aspect of their lives. It was a reality conforming to the stereotyped ideas that tourists held, or to the staged settings in which tourists encountered these women. After 1915 postcards increasingly pictured women engaged in crafts aimed at local tourist and art mar-

ILLUSTRATION 4. The woman pictured on this postcard is probably a Yavapai (not Papago, as indicated by the caption) from the Fort McDowell Reservation, near Phoenix, Arizona. Reprinted from a photograph by George Wharton James, the picture appeared on many postcards published between 1905 and 1950. The card illustrated here was distributed by Lollesgard Specialty Company of Tucson around 1945 and published by the Curteich Company of Chicago. Postcard in authors' collection.

ILLUSTRATION 5. The women pictured here are probably Achomawi from the Susanville area of California. The photo was taken by Eastman's Studio. Postcard in authors' collection.

kets, or performing roles at tourist attractions, such as the Gallup Indian Ceremonials in New Mexico, Lake Tahoe in Nevada, and Pawnee Bill's 101 Ranch in Oklahoma.

In the years after 1925, when postcards were no longer a medium for reproducing pictures of local interest,[11] the only views of Indian women that remained were those appealing to tourist audiences. In areas of the West where culturally unique and exotic aspects of Indian life were no longer significant to local tourism or could no longer be photographed, postcard images of Indian women either vanished or conformed to popular stereotypes.

In California and the Great Basin, where postcard pictures of Indian women weaving baskets, milling acorns, and cooking in domestic surroundings were once common, they virtually disappeared in the years after 1930. Only in tourist places, such as Yosemite, Palm Springs, Death Valley, Disneyland, and Knott's Berry Farm, did postcard pictures of Indian women remain. In contrast to the older ones, the newer images tended to be staged, and usually depicted local Indian women in costumes based on stereotyped models rather than indigenous ones (Illustration 5).[12] The growing disparity between daily life and what appeared on postcards was also found in other regions of the West. Increasingly, postcard pictures recreated facsimiles of indigenous life, either for purposes of the photograph or for tourist audiences in places such as the Pendleton Round-up, in Oregon, and Indian City, in Anadarko, Oklahoma.

ILLUSTRATION 6. A studio portrait of Oklahoma Indian women mailed from Waynoka, Oklahoma. Postcard in authors' collection.

Only in the Southwest and the Arctic do we continue to see postcard pictures that originate in genuine, indigenous settings, in which at least some Indian women live. Southwestern settlements like Taos, Acoma, and Monument Valley are not only the homes of Indian people but they have become major tourist attractions as well. Therefore, one of the major reasons that indigenous views of Southwestern Indian women have remained so popular, at least until quite recently, is the vital role that these women and their communities play in regional tourism.

Generally speaking, postcards used in tourism presented profoundly different images of Indian women. What was witnessed at tourist attractions, and what appeared on postcards, was a partial and, in some cases, a false "reality." Conforming to popular stereotypes promoted in other media such as films and advertising, the images of Indian women in the West had little to do with much of their life experience.

PICTURES AS PORTRAITS

As postcards moved away from picturing the daily experiences of Indian women and emphasized images of these women as spectacles for national and tourist audiences, there was another important shift in imagery: an increasing tendency to isolate Indian women from identifiable surroundings. Portraiture, which had always been a popular mode of presenting female subjects, eventually dominated postcard pictures of Indian women in most regions of the West.

Among the many changes in female portraiture in postcards over time, the most striking has been a decline in diversity. This is evident not only in poses but also in the range of subjects. As with postcard pictures of Indian men,[13] there has been a general trend toward the creation of a standardized or homogenized public image of native women. In part, the increasing uniformity in postcard image making has been related to the more limited function of this medium in modern times.

In the years before 1925, when the postcard still functioned as a medium for reproducing private and local photographs, Indian women were often posed in popular portrait modes of the period (Illustration 6). Alone or with others, they faced the camera directly, as in the style immortalized in the 1930 Grant Wood painting, *American Gothic*. They were photographed against backdrops and with props identical to those used in photographing whites. Outdoor settings were undifferentiated (that is, they were not prominent or symbolically significant).[14] Finally, Indian women were pictured in their customary dress, whether indigenous or European in origin.

In photographs used for tourist and collectible postcards, Indian female subjects were posed differently. More often than not, women were photographed in profile and angular poses (Illustration 7). In contrast to the mundane look of frontal poses, the more contrived poses lent an aura of grandeur. The subjects became ennobling and transcendent figures whose images could be mythologized and severed from their true historical place.[15]

However, these caricatured portraits of Indian women never became dominant on tourist and collectible-type postcards. In contrast to postcards picturing Indian men, those depicting women were more likely to be contexturalized—that is, taken in surroundings, and with accouterments

ILLUSTRATION 7. A Laguna woman from New Mexico whose portrait was taken by Karl Moon in the late nineteenth century and reproduced on several postcards distributed by the Fred Harvey Company of Albuquerque from 1904 to 1945. Postcard in authors' collection.

ILLUSTRATION 8. This modern stock postcard of a Plateau Indian woman from Oregon or Washington was published by the Dexter Company of New York in the early 1960s. Postcard in authors' collection.

that clearly located the subject in a particular time and place. In addition, the identities of Indian women rarely spoke for themselves as pictures of Indian men did. Women were less likely to be photographed alone or outside an identifiable setting, and were more likely to be anonymous. It is rare to find postcard pictures that identified Indian women by their personal names. Instead they were given abstract labels, such as "squaw," "maiden," or "princess,"[16] or their identity was submerged in that of a man's: a husband, father, or brother.

Another interesting trend has been the decline in the overall number of postcards that picture Indian women. In most areas of the West, with the possible exception of the Southwest where pictures of Indian women continue to prevail, there has been a significant decrease in postcards with female subjects[17] and a general drop in the variety of women pictured on postcards. Again, before 1925, women of all age groups and many different ethnic groups were well represented on postcard pictures. In the years thereafter, however, fewer pictures show women of middle age or older. Youthful appearances dominate as was the trend in popular photography in general.

The visual image of Indian women as "maiden" or "princess" has increased in popularity over time.[18] Although portraits of younger Indian women have always been common, before 1925 they were usually posed in clothing indigenous to their own cultures. But after 1925, there was a decided trend towards portraying young Indian women in stereotypic "princess" costumes—namely, fringed buckskin dresses and beaded headband (Illustration 8). At the same time, Indian men were increasingly depicted in warbonnets, even in areas where these were not present indigenously, such as California and Florida.[19]

Since World War II, the "princess" figure has come to dominate popular portraits of Indian women in most areas of the West. It has also become the image most commonly seen on the stock cards issued by national postcard manufacturers. The Indian women pictured on these cards are totally anonymous; they are personally nameless, and there is no reference to their tribal identity or to their geographic origins. Sold in areas far from the homes of the subjects pictured, stock images are abstractions, devoid of any concrete historical role and meaning. For example, Illustration 8, which pictures an Indian woman from the Plateau region, was sold in resort areas in Wisconsin during the 1960s. What matters in stock images is not the accuracy of the picture and its context but its fidelity to the public's stereotyped caricatures.

Lacking contextualization, as provided by scenes of human activity and its associated lived-in environments, portraits are easily subjected to multiple and external meanings which have nothing to do with the experiences of those pictured. In the case of the "princess" image and other stereotyped portraits of Indian women, the public does not read the pictures in terms of meanings intrinsic to the subject's own experience and culture. Rather, the public interprets them in terms of pat stereotypes, which reinforce and play to popular notions of Indian people as spectacles and objects, whose existence and authenticity reside only in the myths that the visual media, including the postcard and Hollywood film, have created. One result of this kind of image making, of course, is that it denies any real understanding of the concrete experiences and conditions of Indian women in the past or present.

Notes

1. See Patricia Albers and Beatrice Medicine, eds., *The Hidden Half: Studies of Plains Indian Women* (Washington, D.C.: University Press of America, 1983), pp. 1–3.

2. For further discussion of the popularity of this image see John Ewers, "An Anthropologist Looks at Early Pictures of American Indians," *New York Historical Quarterly*, October, 1949, pp. 223–34; John Ewers, "The Emergence of the Plains Indian as the Symbol of the North American Indian," *Smithsonian Report*, 1964, pp. 531–44; Robert Berkhofer, Jr., *The White Man's Indian* (New York: Random House, 1979); Gretchen M. Bataille and Charles P. Silet, eds., *The Pretend Indians: Images of Native Americans in the Movies* (Ames: Iowa State University Press, 1980); Raymond William Steadman, *Shadows of the Indian: Stereotypes in American Culture* (Norman: University of Oklahoma Press, 1982).

3. Cf. Susan Sontag, *On Photography* (New York: Farrar, Straus and Giroux, 1973), p. 13.

4. This interpretive discussion is drawn from ibid. and from John Berger, *Ways of Seeing* (New York: Penguin Press, 1977); John Berger, *About Looking* (New York: Pantheon Books, 1980); John Berger, *Another Way of Telling* (New York: Pantheon Books, 1982).

5. For excellent critical analysis of photographs with Indian subjects see Joanna Scherer, "You Can't Believe Your Eyes: Inaccuracies in Photographs of North American Indians," *Studies in the Anthropology of Visual Communications* 2 (1975): 67–79; Margaret Blackman, "Posing the American Indian," *Natural History*, January, 1981, pp. 69–75; Christopher Lyman, *The Vanishing Race and Other Illusions* (New York: Pantheon Press, 1982); Erin Younger, "Changing Images: A Century of Photography on the Hopi Reservation," in Victor Masayesva, Jr., and Erin Younger, eds., *Hopi Photographers, Hopi Images* (Tucson: Sun Tracks and University of Arizona Press, 1983).

6. See also Patricia Albers and William James, "Tourism and the Changing Photographic Image of the Great Lakes Indian," in *Annals of Tourism Research*, special issue, Nelson Graburn, ed., *Anthropology of Tourism* 10 (1983): 123–48 (New York: Pergamon Press, 1983); and "The Dominance of Plains Indian Imagery on the Picture Post Card" in George P. Horse Capture and Gene Ball, eds., *Fifth Annual Plains Indian Seminar in Honor of Dr. John Ewers* (Cody, Wyo.: Buffalo Bill Historical Center, 1984).

7. Berger, *About Looking*, pp. 51–53.

8. Ibid., p. 52.

9. Cf. Albers and James, "Tourism and the Changing Photographic Image," pp. 131–33.

10. Albers and James, "The Dominance of Plains Indian Imagery."

11. Cf. ibid.

12. For an excellent analysis of the adoption of Plains and Woodlands costumes by California Indians see Craig D. Bates, "Dressing the Part: A Brief Look at the Development of Stereotypical Indian Clothing Among Native Peoples in the Far West," *Journal of California and Great Basin Anthropology* 4 (1982): 55–66.

13. Cf. Albers and James, "The Dominance of Plains Indian Imagery."

14. This contrasts with many postcard pictures produced in later years showing Indian subjects against definite scenic attractions, such as Yosemite Falls and the Grand Canyon. In these kinds of views the symbolic relationship between Indian culture and nature is reinforced.

15. Cf. Patricia Albers and William James, "Post Card Images of the American Indian: The Collectible Sets of the Pre-1920 Era," *American Post Card Journal* 7 (1982): 17–19.

16. While abstract labels are also associated with pictures of Indian men, such as

"chief," "brave," or "warrior," a greater number of postcards identify male subjects by their personal names.

17. The research for this article, including the estimations of trends in the kinds of pictures represented on postcards, is based on a collection of well over 10,000 different Indian postcards in the authors' possession. All postcards illustrated in this article are from this collection.

18. Cf. Rayna Green's excellent article "The Pocahontas Perplex: The Image of the Indian Woman in American Culture," *Massachusetts Review* 16 (1975): 698–714; Alison Bernstein, "Outgrowing Pocahontas: Toward a New History of American Indian Women," *Minority Notes* 2 (Spring–Summer, 1981).

19. Cf. Albers and James, "The Dominance of Plains Indian Imagery," and "Tourism and the Changing Photographic Image."

PART TWO Meetings

Western history began long before Euro-Americans explored and settled North America. It started with the American Indian and Hispanic people who already lived in what we now call "the West." The history of women in those societies is as much a part of western women's history as is that of the Euro-American women who migrated west in the 1840s and 1850s.

There is still much work to be done to recover the history of the earliest periods. Much valuable information is buried in anthropological data and is being reinterpreted by ethnographers. More remains to be excavated from older records and from archaeological sites.

While that work is going on, those of us who are not anthropologists can shift our focus away from an exclusive preoccupation with Euro-American settlers. We can recognize that American Indians and Hispanics were equal partners in a long and complex story of regional development and that they affected later settlers. We can read the work of anthropologists and ethnic historians which reveals portions of that history. Just as women have suffered from stereotyping, so have entire racial groups. Members of these groups, too, need to be seen as actors, rather than as objects, in the ongoing story.

As we suggested in the previous section, this change in perspective fundamentally shifts our thinking about western history. Euro-Americans become less important, and the story becomes a multidimensional one of contacts among people of different cultures. Although that process is commonly called culture contact, we should keep in mind that cultures do not contact. People do. The story of culture contact is therefore a quite complex one of many personal interactions. Euro-Americans recorded a great diversity of experiences with people of hundreds of American Indian tribes at different times. Similarly, each tribe had very different types of encounters with different groups: army officers, nuns, miners, and farmers.

The papers in this section explore whether gender had an impact on these relationships, whether women and men viewed people of different cultures differently. They show the directions in which a focus on culture contact can lead us. They also demonstrate that it is possible to study this history even with limited sources. In all three cases, while the sources are Euro-American, the authors are able to show us something of what the encounter looked like from the other side.

4

The Role of Native Women in the Creation of Fur Trade Society in Western Canada, 1670–1830

SYLVIA VAN KIRK

Sylvia Van Kirk provides a major example of how the understanding of history changes when women and minorities are treated seriously. In this article she highlights some of the findings from her pioneering study of the Canadian fur trade, Many Tender Ties. *As she shows, the Canadian fur trade was neither violent nor male-dominated, because the incoming Europeans needed the cooperation of Indians of both sexes for the trade to succeed. Van Kirk's explanation of the activities of Indian women is a model of the feminist scholar's art of "piecing together" information about women from male-focused and ethnocentric sources. Her account does not present a picture of the Canadian fur trade from an Indian perspective, but it does take a giant first step toward a multicultural history.*

The United States fur trade was much smaller and of shorter duration than the Canadian enterprise. American trappers seem to have depended more on their own resources and less on those of American Indians. However, many trappers married Indian women. Perhaps the American mountain man was not in fact the celebrated loner of legend and story. Because research on these questions is just beginning in the United States, it is still too early to tell.

In essence the history of the early Canadian West is the history of the fur trade. For nearly two hundred years, from the founding of the Hudson's Bay Company in 1670 until the transfer of Rupert's Land to the newly created dominion of Canada in 1870, the fur trade was the dominant force in shaping the history of what are today Canada's four western provinces.

This long and unified experience gave rise in western Canada to a frontier society that seems to have been unique in the realm of interracial contact. Canada's western history has been characterized by relatively little violent conflict between Indian and white. I would like to suggest two major reasons why this was so. First, by its very nature, the Canadian fur trade was predicated on a mutual exchange and dependency between Indian and white. The Indian not only trapped the fur pelts but also provided the market for European goods. Until very recently, the fur trade has been viewed as an all-male affair, but new research has revealed that Indian women played an active role in promoting this trade. Although the men

"At the Portage." The Indian family of a Hudson's Bay Company steersman watches while trade goods are being prepared for the portage at Grand Rapids, ca. 1882. From *Picturesque Canada,* vol. 1, edited by George Monro Grant, published by Belden Bros., Toronto, 1882.

were the hunters of beaver and large game animals, the women were responsible for trapping smaller fur-bearing animals, especially the marten whose pelt was highly prized.[1] The notable emergence of Indian women as diplomats and peacemakers also indicates that they were anxious to maintain the flow of European goods such as kettles, cloth, knives, needles, and axes which helped to alleviate their onerous work.[2]

The second factor in promoting harmonious relations was the remarkably wide extent of intermarriage between incoming traders and Indian women, especially among the Cree, the Ojibwa, and the Chipewyan. Indian wives proved indispensable helpmates to the officers and men of both the British-based Hudson's Bay Company and its Canadian rival, the North West Company. Such interracial unions were, in fact, the basis for a fur trade society and were sanctioned by an indigenous rite known as marriage *à la façon du pays*—according to the custom of the country.

The development of marriage *à la façon du pays* underscores the complex and changing interaction between the traders and the host Indian societies. In the initial phase of contact, many Indian bands actively encouraged the formation of marital alliances between their women and the traders. The Indians viewed marriage in an integrated social and economic context; marital alliances created reciprocal social ties, which served to consolidate their economic relationships with the incoming strangers. Thus, through marriage, many a trader was drawn into the Indian kinship circle. In return for giving the traders sexual and domestic rights to their women, the Indians expected reciprocal privileges such as free access to the posts and provisions.[3]

As a result of this Indian attitude, it was soon impressed upon the traders that marriage alliances were an important means of ensuring good will and cementing trade relations with new bands or tribes. The North West Company, a conglomerate of partnerships which began extensive trading in the West in the 1770s, had learned from its French predecessors of the benefits to be gained from intermarriage and officially sanctioned such unions for all ranks (from bourgeois down to *engagé*).[4] The Hudson's Bay Company, on the other hand, was much slower to appreciate the realities of life in Rupert's Land. Official policy formulated in faraway London forbade any intimacy with the Indians, but officers in the field early began to break the rules. They took the lead in forming unions with the women of prominent Indian leaders, although there was great variation in the extent to which the servants were allowed to form connections with native women.[5]

Apart from the public social benefits, the traders' desire to form unions with Indian women was increased by the absence of white women. Although they did not come as settlers, many of the fur traders spent the better part of their lives in Rupert's Land, and it is a singular fact in the social development of the Canadian West that for well over a century there were no white women.[6] The stability of many of the interracial unions formed in the Indian country stemmed partly from the fact that an Indian woman provided the only opportunity for a trader to replicate a domestic life with wife and children. Furthermore, although Indian mores differed from those of the whites, the traders learned that they trifled with Indian women at their peril. As one old voyageur explained, one could not just dally with any native woman who struck one's fancy. There was a great danger of getting one's head broken if a man attempted to take an Indian girl without her parents' consent.[7]

It is significant that, just as in the trade ceremony, the rituals of marriage à la façon du pays conformed more to Indian custom than to European. There were two basic steps to forming such a union. The first step was to secure the consent of the woman's relatives; it also appears that the wishes of the woman herself were respected, as there is ample evidence that Indian women actively sought for trade husbands. Once consent was secured, a bride price had then to be decided; this varied considerably among the tribes but could amount to several hundred dollars worth of trade goods. After these transactions, the couple were usually conducted ceremoniously to the post where they were now recognized as man and wife.[8] In the Canadian West, marriage à la façon du pays became the norm for Indian-white unions, being reinforced by mutual interest, tradition, and peer group pressure.[9] Although ultimately "the custom of the country" was to be strongly denounced by the missionaries, it is significant that in 1867, when the legitimacy of the union between Chief Factor William Connolly and his Cree wife was tried before a Canadian court, it was found to have constituted a lawful marriage. The judge declared a valid marriage existed because the wife had been married according to the customs and usages of her own people and because the consent of both parties, the essential element of civilized marriage, had been proved by twenty-eight years of repute, public acknowledgement, and cohabitation as man and wife.[10]

If intermarriage brought the trader commercial and personal benefit, it also provided him with a unique economic partner. The Indian wife possessed a range of skills and wilderness know-how that would have been quite foreign to a white wife. Although the burdensome work role of the nomadic Indian woman was somewhat alleviated by the move to the fur-trade post, the extent to which the traders relied upon native technology kept the women busy.

Perhaps the most important domestic task performed by the women at the fur-trade posts was to provide the men with a steady supply of "Indian shoes" or moccasins. The men of both companies generally did not dress in Indian style (the buckskinned mountain man was not part of the Canadian scene), but they universally adopted the moccasin as the most practical footwear for the wilderness. One wonders, for example, how the famed 1789 expedition of Alexander Mackenzie would have fared without the work of the wives of his two French-Canadian voyageurs. The women scarcely ever left the canoes, being "continually employ'd making shoes of moose skin as a pair does not last us above one Day."[11] Closely related to the manufacture of moccasins was the Indian woman's role in making snowshoes, without which winter travel was impossible. Although the men usually made the frames, the women prepared the sinews and netted the intricate webbing which provided support.[12]

Indian women also made a vital contribution in the preservation of food, especially in the manufacture of the all-important pemmican, the nutritious staple of the North West Company's canoe brigades. At the posts on the Plains, buffalo hunting and pemmican making formed an essential part of the yearly routine, each post being required to furnish an annual quota. In accordance with Indian custom, once the hunt was over the women's work began. The women skinned the animals and cut the meat into thin strips to be dried in the sun or over a slow fire. When the meat was dry, the women pounded it into a thick flaky mass, which was then mixed with melted buffalo fat. This pemmican would keep very well when packed into ninety-pound buffalo-hide sacks, which had been made by the women during the winter.[13]

But pemmican was too precious a commodity to form the basic food at the posts themselves. At the more northerly posts, the people subsisted mainly on fish, vast quantities of which were split and dried by the women to provide food for the winter. Maintaining adequate food supplies for a post for the winter was a precarious business, and numerous instances can be cited of Indian wives keeping the fur traders alive by their ability to snare small game such as rabbits and partridges. In 1815, for example, the young Nor'Wester George Nelson would probably have starved to death when provisions ran out at his small outpost north of Lake Superior had it not been for the resourcefulness of his Ojibwa wife who, during the month of February, brought in fifty-eight rabbits and thirty-four partridges.[14] Indian women also added to the diet by collecting berries and wild rice and making maple sugar. The spring trip to the sugar bush provided a welcome release from the monotony of the winter routine, and the men, with their families and Indian relatives, all enjoyed this annual event.[15]

As in other pre-industrial societies, the Indian women's role extended well beyond domestic maintenance as they assisted in specific fur-trade operations. With the adoption of the birch-bark canoe, especially by the North West Company, Indian women continued in their traditional role of helping in its manufacture. It was the women's job to collect annual quotas of spruce roots, which were split fine to sew the seams of the canoes, and also to collect the spruce gum, which was used for caulking the seams.[16] The inexperienced and undermanned Hudson's Bay Company also found itself calling upon the labor power of Indian women, who were adept at paddling and steering canoes. Indeed, although the inland explorations of various Hudson's Bay Company men such as Anthony Henday and Samuel Hearne have been glorified as individual exploits, they were, in fact, entirely dependent upon the Indians with whom they traveled, especially the women. "Women," marveled one inlander, "were as useful as men upon Journeys."[17] Henday's journey to the Plains in 1754, for example, owed much of its success to his Cree female companion who provided him with much timely advice about the plans of the Indians, in addition to a warm winter suit of furs.[18] The Hudson's Bay Company men emphasized to their London superiors the value of the Indian women's skill at working with fur pelts. In short, they argued that the economic services performed by Indian women at the fur-trade posts were of such importance that they should be considered as "Your Honours Servants".[19] Indian women were indeed an integral part of the fur-trade labor force, although, like most women, because their labor was largely unpaid, their contribution has been ignored.

The reliance on native women's skills remained an important aspect of fur-trade life, even though by the early nineteenth century there was a notable shift in the social dynamic of fur-trade society. By this time, partly because of the destructive competition between rival companies which had flooded the Indian country with alcohol, relations between many Indian bands and the traders deteriorated. In some well-established areas, traders sometimes resorted to coercive measures, and in some cases their abuse of Indian women became a source of conflict.[20] In this context, except in new areas such as the Pacific Slope, marriage alliances ceased to play the important function they once had. The decline of Indian-white marriages was also hastened by the fact that fur-trade society itself was producing a new pool of marriageable young women—the mixed-blood "daughters of the country." With her dual heritage, the mixed-blood woman possessed the ideal qualifications for a fur trader's wife; acclimatized to life in the West and familiar with Indian ways, she could also adapt successfully to white culture.

From their Indian mothers, mixed-blood girls learned the native skills so necessary to the functioning of the trade. As Sir George Simpson, governor of the Hudson's Bay Company emphasized in the 1820s: "It is the duty of the Women at the different Posts to do all that is necessary in regard to Needle Work,"[21] and the mixed-blood women's beautiful beadwork was highly prized. In addition to performing traditional Indian tasks, the women's range of domestic work increased in more European ways. They were responsible for the fort's washing and cleaning; "the Dames" at York Factory, for example, were kept "in Suds, Scrubbing and Scouring," according to one account.[22] As subsistence agriculture was developed around many of the posts, the native women took an active role in planting and harvesting. Chief Factor John Rowand of Fort Edmonton succinctly summarized the economic role of native women in the fur trade when he wrote in the mid-nineteenth century: "The women here work very hard, if it was not so, I do not know how we would get on with the Company work."[23] With her ties to the Indians and familiarity with native customs and language, the mixed-blood wife was also in a position to take over the role of intermediary or liaison previously played by the Indian wife. The daughters of the French-Canadian voyageurs were often excellent interpreters: some could speak several Indian languages. The timely intervention of more than one mixed-blood wife saved the life of a husband who had aroused Indian hostility.[24] Indeed, in his account of fur-trade life during the Hudson's Bay Company's monopoly after 1821, Isaac Cowie declared that many of the company's officers owed much of their success in overcoming difficulties and in maintaining the company's influence over the natives to "the wisdom and good counsel of their wives."[25]

In spite of the importance of native connections, many fur-trade fathers wanted to introduce their mixed-blood daughters to the rudiments of European culture. Since the place of work and home coincided, especially in the long winter months, the traders were able to take an active role in their children's upbringing and they were encouraged by company officials to do so.[26] When the beginnings of formal schooling were introduced at the posts on the Bay in the early 1800s, it was partly because it was felt to be essential that girls, who were very seldom sent overseas, should be given a basic education which would inculcate them with Christian virtue.[27] Increasingly, fathers promoted the marriage of their daughters to incoming traders, as the means to securing their place in fur-trade society. In a significant change of policy in 1806, the North West Company acknowledged some responsibility for the fate of its "daughters" when it sanctioned marriage *à la façon du pays* with daughters of white men, but now prohibited it with full-blooded Indian women.[28]

As mixed-blood wives became "the vogue" (to quote a contemporary), it is notable that "the custom of the country" began to evolve more toward European concepts of marriage. Most importantly, such unions were coming to be regarded as unions for life. When Hudson's Bay Company officer J. E. Harriott espoused Elizabeth Pruden, for example, he promised her father, a senior officer, that he would "live with her and treat her as my wife as long as we both lived."[29] It became customary for a couple to exchange brief vows before the officer in charge of the post, and the match was further celebrated by a dram of liquor to all hands and a wedding dance. The bride price was replaced by the opposite payment of a dowry, and many fur-trade officers were able to dower their daughters quite handsomely.[30] Marriage *à la façon du pays* was further regulated by the Hudson's Bay Company after 1821 with the introduction of marriage contracts, which emphasized the husband's financial obligations and the status of the woman as a legitimate wife.

The social role of the mixed-blood wife, unlike that of the Indian wife, served to cement ties within fur-trade society itself. Significantly, in the North West Company, many marriages cut across class lines, as numerous Scottish bourgeois chose their wives from among the daughters of the French-Canadian *engagés* who had married extensively among the native people. Among the Hudson's Bay Company men, it was appreciated that a useful way to enhance one's career prospects was to marry the daughter of a senior officer.[31] Whatever a man's initial motivation, the substantial private fur-trade correspondence which has survived from the nineteenth century reveals that many fur traders became devoted family men. Family could be a source of interest and consolation in a life that was often hard and monotonous. As Chief Factor James Douglas pointedly summed it up: "There is indeed no living with comfort in this country until a person has forgot the great world and has his tastes and character formed on the current standard of the stage . . . habit makes it familiar to us, softened as it is by the *many tender ties* which find a way to the heart." [32]

However, the founding in 1811 of the Selkirk Colony, the first agrarian settlement in western Canada, was to introduce new elements of white civilization that would hasten the decline of the indigenous fur-trade society. The chief agents of these changes were the missionaries and white women.

The missionaries, especially the Anglicans who arrived under the auspices of the Hudson's Bay Company in 1820, roundly denounced marriage *à la façon du pays* as being immoral and debased. [33] But while they exerted considerable pressure on long cohabiting couples to accept a church marriage, they were in no way champions of miscegenation. In fact, this attack upon fur-trade custom had a detrimental effect upon the position of native women. Incoming traders, now feeling free to ignore the marital obligations implicit in the "the custom of the country," increasingly looked upon native women as objects for temporary sexual gratification. The women, on the other hand, found themselves being judged according to strict British standards of female propriety. It was they, not the white men, who were to be held responsible for the perpetuation of immorality because of their supposedly promiscuous Indian heritage. The double standard, tinged with racism, had arrived with a vengeance!

Racial prejudice and class distinctions were augmented by the arrival of British women in Rupert's Land. The old fabric of fur-trade society was severely rent in 1830 when Simpson and another prominent Hudson's Bay Company officer returned from furlough, having wed genteel British ladies. [34] The appearance of such "flowers of civilization" provoked unflattering comparisons with native women; as one officer observed, "this influx of white faces has cast a still deeper shade over the faces of our Brunettes in the eyes of many." [35] In Red River especially, a white wife became a status symbol; witness the speed with which several retired Hudson's Bay Company factors married the English schoolmistresses after the demise of their native wives. To their credit, many company officers remained loyal to their native families, but they became painfully anxious to turn their daughters into young Victorian ladies, hoping that with accomplishments and connections, the stigma of their mixed blood would not prevent them from remaining among the social elite. Thus in the 1830s, a boarding school was established in Red River for the children of company officers; the girls' education was supervised by the missionary's wife, and more than one graduate was praised for being "quite English in her Manner." [36] In numerous cases, these highly acculturated young women were able to secure advantageous matches with incoming white men, but to some extent this was only because white ladies did not in fact make a successful adaptation to fur-trade life. It had been predicted that "the lovely, tender exotics" (as white women were dubbed) would languish in the harsh fur-trade environment,[37] and indeed they did, partly because they had no useful social or economic role to play. As a result, mixed marriages continued to be a feature of western Canadian society until well into the mid-nineteenth century, but it was not an enduring legacy. Indian and mixed-blood women, like their male counterparts, were quickly shunted aside with the development of the agrarian frontier after 1870. The vital role native women had played in the opening of the Canadian West was either demeaned or forgotten.

Notes

1. Sylvia Van Kirk, *Many Tender Ties: Women in Fur Trade Society, 1670–1870* (Norman: University of Oklahoma Press, 1980; Winnipeg, Manitoba: Watson and Dwyer, 1980), pp. 72–73.

2. The most outstanding examples of Indian women who, although not married to whites, were active peacemakers and diplomats, are Thanadelthur, a Chipewyan, and Lady Calpo, a Chinook. See ibid., pp. 66–71, 76–77.

3. The few cases of violent conflict, such as the Henley House Massacre of 1752, were caused by the traders' failure to respect this bargain. See ibid., pp. 41–44.

4. Ibid., p. 28.

5. Ibid., pp. 28–29, 41–42.

6. After an ill-fated venture in 1686, British wives were officially prohibited from traveling to Hudson Bay. It was not until 1812 with the Selkirk settlers that women were again officially transported to Hudson Bay. A French-Canadian woman in 1806 was the first and one of the few white women to come west in the North West Company canoes. See Van Kirk, *Many Tender Ties,* pp. 173–80.

7. *Johnstone et. al.* v. *Connolly,* Appeal Court, 7 Sept. 1869, *La Revue Legale,* 1:280 (hereafter cited as Connolly Appeal Case, 1869).

8. Van Kirk, *Many Tender Ties,* pp. 36–37. For a discussion of the motivation of the Indian women, see chap. 4.

9. This does not mean that sexual exploitation of Indian women was unknown in the Canadian West. Prostitution certainly existed, and the marriage relationship could be abused as in white society.

10. *Connolly vs. Woolrich,* Superior Court, Montreal, 9 July 1867, *Lower Canada Jurist* 11:230, 248.

11. W. Kaye Lamb, ed., *The Journals and Letters of Sir Alexander Mackenzie* (Cambridge, England: Cambridge University Press, 1970), p. 220.

12. Van Kirk, *Many Tender Ties,* pp. 54–55.

13. Ibid., p. 56.

14. Toronto Public Library, George Nelson Papers, Journal, 29 Jan.–23 June 1815. See also Van Kirk, *Many Tender Ties,* pp. 58–59.

15. Van Kirk, *Many Tender Ties,* p. 57.

16. Ibid., p. 61.

17. J. B. Tyrrell, ed., *Journals of Samuel Hearne and Philip Turnor, 1774–1792,* Champlain Society, vol. 21 (Toronto, 1934), pp. 252–53.

18. Van Kirk, *Many Tender Ties,* p. 64.

19. Hudson's Bay Company Archives, B.239/b/79, fols. 40d–41 (hereafter HBCA).

20. Van Kirk, *Many Tender Ties,* pp. 90–91.

21. R. H. Fleming, ed., *Minutes of Council of the Northern Department of Rupert's Land, 1821–31,* Hudson's Bay Record Society, vol. 3 (London, 1940), p. 378.

22. Public Archives of Canada, James Hargrave Correspondence, vol. 21, Hargrave to Christie, 13 June 1832.

23. HBCA, D.5/18, fols. 535d–536.

24. One of the most famous cases was that of James Douglas, a clerk in northern British Columbia, whose high-handed treatment so outraged the Carrier Indians that he might have been killed but for intervention of his mixed-blood wife Amelia and the wife of the interpreter. See Van Kirk, *Many Tender Ties,* pp. 111–13.

25. Isaac Cowie, *The Company of Adventurers* (Toronto: W. Briggs, 1913), p. 204.

26. Van Kirk, *Many Tender Ties,* pp. 97, 99, 106, 131.

27. Ibid., pp. 103–104.

28. W. S. Wallace, ed., *Documents Relating to the North West Company,* Champlain Society, vol. 22 (Toronto, 1934), p. 211.

29. Connolly Appeal Case, 1869, p. 286.

30. Van Kirk, *Many Tender Ties,* pp. 108, 115.

31. Ibid., pp. 108–109.

32. G. P. de T. Glazebrook, ed., *The Hargrave Correspondence, 1821–1843,* Champlain Society, vol. 24 (Toronto, 1928), p. 381.

33. Van Kirk, *Many Tender Ties,* pp. 153–56.

34. They also violated "the custom of the country" by callously casting aside their former mixed-blood partners after the fact. For a full discussion of this episode see Sylvia Van Kirk, "The Impact of White Women on Fur Trade Society," in *The Neglected Majority: Essays in Canadian Women's History* (Toronto: McClelland and Stewart, 1977), pp. 27–48.

35. PAC, Hargrave Correspondence, vol. 21, Hargrave to Charles Ross, 1 Dec. 1830.

36. Glazebrook, ed., *Hargrave Correspondence,* p. 229.

37. Ibid., pp. 310–11.

5.
_____

Beyond Princess and Squaw: Army Officers' Perceptions of Indian Women

SHERRY L. SMITH

In this article we see the range of attitudes that Euro-Americans, in this case Army officers, held toward American Indian women. Although swayed by cultural bias, many officers were careful and thoughtful observers of the lives of Indian women. They liked much of what they saw.

Sherry Smith uses a traditional source, army officers' observations, for a new purpose. Her examination of attitudes toward American Indian women yields double insights: into the actual lives of women, and into the extent and significance of the "cultural baggage" the army officers brought west with them. As this article shows, a focus on culture contact can tell us new things about both parties in the transaction.

In 1881, Capt. John Gregory Bourke visited the Santa Domingo Pueblo, in New Mexico. As he sauntered through the village, he watched, undetected, a pair of Pueblo lovers mending a quarrel through gentle touches and whispered words. The Indian man approached the woman, Bourke wrote, "and was received with a disdain tempered with so much sweetness and affection that he wilted at once, and, instead of boldly asserting himself, dared do nothing but timidly touch her hand." Finally, she took his grasp and "he, with earnest warmth was pouring into her ears words whose purport it was not difficult to conjecture." Bourke, who approached Indians not only with soldier's bayonet, but with ethnographer's notebook and pencil, thus presented an unconventional view of Indian people in a very human pose. He understood this view was rare. "So much stuff and nonsense have been written about the entire absence of affection from the Indian character, especially in the relations between the sexes," he commented, "that it affords me great pleasure to note this little incident, in which the parties acted with perfect freedom from the restraint the known presence of strangers imposes." [1]

While somewhat exceptional in relating such a positive view of Indian male-female relations, Bourke's assertion about Indian humanity after an encounter with an Indian woman was not uncommon. In fact, a study of officers' accounts indicates the worlds of Anglo-American military men and American Indian women were not as separate as modern readers might expect. And, in some respects, their worlds seemed closer than those of officers and Indian men.

Arapahoe women tanning deer hides. Courtesy Wyoming State Archives.

Clearly, many barriers between army officers and Indian women existed, including the officers' beliefs in the superiority of their culture and in their mission to subdue Indian resistance to Anglo-American occupation of their lands. There is evidence, however, that some army officers circumvented these barriers and created meaningful and genuine communication with Indian women; that some military men appreciated certain aspects of these women's lives; and that occasionally officers and Indian women attained a measure of mutual understanding that transcended assumptions about civilization and savagery or the roles of conqueror and conquered.

Army officers traveled west laden with a good deal of cultural baggage. Schoolbook stories, captivity narratives, and James Fenimore Cooper novels provided information, of sorts, about male and female Indians, with two basic notions prevailing. First, Anglo-Americans assumed it was possible to delineate general Indian characteristics without reference to tribal or cultural differences. Second, the dominant image of Indians was an ambivalent one, featuring both noble and ignoble qualities.

But contact and interaction with actual Indian women modified officers' attitudes. The women's reactions, responses, and relationships with officers, in turn, further changed the men's ideas about them. Some army officers, then, questioned prevailing images about Indian women and tried to record the reality, at least as they had experienced it.

Once on the frontier they learned that Indian women demonstrated friendliness, compassion, and affection. "In fact," Lt. Britton Davis wrote about Chiricahua and Warm Springs Apache women and men, "we began to find them decidedly human."[2] While they never dropped their fundamental concepts of savagery, civilization, and "Indian character," these officers gradually discovered that Indian women's actual experiences were richer, more diverse, and simply more human than the conquest mythology allowed or than most of their less informed countrymen might suppose.

Yet officers, for the most part, did not understand the anthropological truth about these women. Their comments reveal more about Anglo-American civilization's ideas of culture, savagery, and, in this case, woman's sphere than they do about the realities of American Indian women's lives and cultures. Nineteenth-century Americans, according to Roy Harvey Pearce, tended to define civilization in terms of savagery. This process "forced Americans to consider and reconsider what it was to be civilized and what it took to build a civilization. Studying the savage . . . in the end they had only studied themselves."[3]

Consequently, officers seemed compelled to compare Indian women to white women. For many, their women's ways of life set the civilized standard by which they measured Indian women's ways. They believed, for example, that native women's tendency to work out-of-doors, at a time when the prescribed civilized sphere for women emphasized home and hearth, reflected the Indians' savage state. On the other hand, a few praised the primitive virtues of a feminine outdoor life and criticized white women's customs. In either case, officers' comments about savage women often served as vehicles through which they reflected on themselves and their women.

Typically, then, army officers looked at Indian women in relation to themselves. The result was ambiguity. The noble Indian woman was the archetypal Indian princess, a Pocahontas type who was virginal, yet passionate. As Rayna Green noted, "Even Pocahontas [was] motivated by lust."[4] The Indian "princess" was childlike, naturally innocent, beautiful, and inclined toward civilization, Christianization, and to helping and mating with white men.

Conversely, the Anglo-American image of the ignoble squaw was of a squat, haggard, ugly, pappose-lugging drudge who toiled endlessly while her husband sported in the hunting fields or lolled about the lodge. She lived a most unfortunate, brutal life. Furthermore, she fought enemies with a vengeance and thirst for blood unmatched by any man. Such widely accepted ideas about Indian women made it difficult for officers to perceive them as real, individual humans. Both princess and squaw operated as depersonalized symbols, devoid of humanity.

It comes as no surprise that army officers' accounts of Indian women included these images. They acted as female counterparts to the images of males as noble savage and fiendish barbarian. However, officers discovered only occasional individuals who fit the princess image. Lt. C. A. Woodward, for example, identified a Comanche chief's daughter as "one of the most comely Indian maidens of the wild tribes I have met," noting she was beautifully garbed in bright colors and sat astride her horse "as only the queens of the forest can do." [5]

More typical was Lt. James W. Steele's description of the squaw—a repulsive, stoop-shouldered, wretched, toothless crone who "in all that is peculiarly Indianesque excels her master." He went on: "In cunning, hatred, and revenge, in the specialities of cruelty and the refinements of torture, she has no equal on earth or in Hades." Though extreme, Steele's sentiments represented many officers' reactions to native women. William E. Waters agreed that the legendary beauty of Indian women was a myth, noting that he had yet to see an Indian woman who bore the slightest comparison to Pocahontas. Rather, he felt, most were homely, not because of inherent racial features but because of their lives of drudgery.[6]

While officers criticized Indian men for supposedly enslaving their women, such treatment, they argued, was an inevitable condition of the Indians' savage state. In their eyes society's treatment of its women served as an important indicator of its level of civilization. Civilized people pampered women; savage people mistreated them. Most officers agreed with Brig. Gen. Richard Johnson that "the higher the human family rises in the scale of civilization, the more deference is paid to women. Among educated and refined people in America she is queen, and all men bow to her as they should." [7] Among Indians, the officers found, she was slave.

More unusual were officers who discarded these images. Some even expressed thinly veiled doubts about Anglo-American cultural superiority, asserting that Indian women had advantages over Anglo-American women. In fact, some claimed, the latter should emulate the former.

Even officers who emphasized the drudgery and degradation of Indian womanhood wrestled with a dilemma: Indian women did not despise their lives. Why were these women, living apparently brutal and desperate lives, happy? Why did they appear content with endless, wearisome servitude, and why did they submit to their fate without complaint? Admitting that "a happier, more light-hearted, more contented woman cannot be found," than an Indian woman, Col. Richard Dodge concluded her bliss was due either to ignorance of alternatives or to constant work, which kept her from reflecting on the horrors of her life. But Lt. Col. Albert Brackett offered a different explanation. While the Shoshoni and Ute women he met labored continually—pitching and packing tipis, carrying wood and water, cooking, and engaging in "all the drudgery of the camp"—he also declared their lives were "unquestionably far happier than the do-nothing, thankless, dyspeptic life led by a majority of American women." While one might be inclined to pity them for their lives of hard work, Brackett said, their health and happiness stemmed from living the outdoor life and taking plenty of exercise. These practices constituted the "main points in the pursuit of happiness." [8]

Other officers echoed Brackett's favorable comparison of Indian women to white women, particularly in matters of matrimony and maternity. In southwestern tribes some women lived in permanent villages and men shared the agricultural work, more closely approximating the Anglo-

American division of labor between sexes. Officers less frequently perceived these women as slaves and drudges. Beyond that, officers claimed, some southwestern Indian women had economic advantages, marital rights, and political privileges unknown to white women. Lt. William Woods Averell, for example, allowed that Navajo chiefs' wives' "voices were heard in the councils." Captain Bourke reported that Hopi women not only managed but owned their houses, and husbands could not sell household goods without their wives' permission. Even Steele spoke highly of Pueblo women as "creatures . . . whose dignity would not suffer by comparison with some of the queens of civilization." Furthermore, he believed, unlike white women who demanded rights but engaged in no productive labor, Pueblo women demonstrated that they had "rights all along because they engaged in manly labor" and so deserved them. He marveled at a Pueblo woman who sold piñons on an Albuquerque street corner while juggling her two-day-old baby on her hip. "Such women as these are alone physically competent to maintain rights," Steele pronounced.[9]

Outside the Southwest others reported that Indian women maintained marriage rights unknown to white women. Capt. Randolph Marcy claimed that among the Shawnee and Delaware the marriage contract was binding only as long as husband and wife wanted it so. If a woman left her husband she was authorized by tribal law to take all the personal property she possessed at the time of the marriage, and the husband had no claim upon it. Marcy found this practice very just, for it made a woman somewhat independent of her husband and probably deterred husbands from behaving tyrannically and abusing their wives.[10]

Dodge believed Indian women were virtually owned, like property, by husbands who could beat, even kill, them with impunity; yet, he wrote, "the domestic life of the Indian will bear comparison with that of the average civilized communities." Husbands were generally kind; wives generally faithful, obedient, and industrious. Moreover, Indian women could, according to Dodge, leave one husband for another and suffer no social stigma in the process. Rather than viewing this separation and remarriage process as barbarous, he regarded it as beneficial—a practice that probably ameliorated the conditions of Indian women. They could simply leave cruel husbands for kindlier ones. Civilized women did not have this option, or at least it was obtained less easily and at greater social cost.[11]

Army officers admired Indian women's vitality in childbirth and concluded, though with some hesitation, that the "Indian way" of bringing children into the world was preferable to the "civilized" way. Admiring their stamina, physical endurance, and capacity to continue working right up to, and then almost immediately after, parturition, a few perceived native women's apparent ease with childbirth as animal-like. While some thought white women should emulate Indian women on this matter, others feared it a sign of savagery, an indication they were closer to primitive nature than to the refinements of civilization.

Col. Philippe Régis de Trobriand, however, declared Indian women's childbirth practices "extraordinary." To him, working up to the onset of labor pains and returning to work the day after giving birth, was "natural" and appropriate. Civilization, he complained, had replaced this natural and easy process with "long torture, medical attendance, intervention of chloroform, puerperal fever, two weeks in bed, thirty days in the bedroom, and such precaution." Civilized people created artificial environments for themselves and their bodies and in the process, "physically and morally . . . corrupted the work of nature." As a result, white women weakened and often died, while Indian mothers gathered up their babies and vigorously went on their way.[12]

William T. Parker, a soldier who later became a doctor, also praised Indian women's stamina, especially regarding "womanly functions." A great admirer of their "fortitude, perseverance and unflagging devotion to womanly duty," particularly maternal duties, Parker attributed their ease in childbirth to large hips, "capacious" pelvises, and robust conditions. Unfortunately, he added, Indian women were beginning to consult white doctors and acquire white methods of childbearing—all to their detriment. "From an out-of-door life of activity with plenty of fresh game and wholesome food and clear water, with a healthful te-pee for home, the change has been made to log cabins with overheated close air." The result was deteriorating health and increasing numbers of miscarriages and diseases.[13]

Some military men praised women's physical endurance and capabilities in activities outside of "womanly functions"—in horseback riding, hunting, and even warfare. While these men were scandalized by white women riding astride mounts, rather than sidesaddle, they accepted, even admired, the practice among Indian women. Joseph Sladen thus rhapsodized about Apache women as they rode with their long hair dangling down their backs: "I have seldom seen a prettier picture than those of one of these young women sitting astride a horse and riding like the wind." Marcy admired Plains Indian women's equestrian expertise. Riding with one leg on each side of their horse, they were every bit as skillful as their men, he claimed. He was notably impressed with two Comanche women who lassoed several antelope with "unerring precision" from horseback.[14]

Indian women in warfare provoked more mixed responses from officers. Army officers were stung by eastern humanitarians' charges that they were brutal, bloodthirsty, ruffians of the border, and resented insinuations they purposefully killed women and children. The officers insisted these deaths were accidental rather than intentional, and that no one deplored these incidents more than the troopers. Others argued that Indian women took up arms against soldiers and consequently became fair game for troopers' bullets.[15]

In defending themselves from critics, officers frequently resorted to stereotype. Once a native woman became enraged, Capt. R. G. Carter explained, "[n]ot a gleam of pity entered her feminine breast. She was a cold-blooded, thirsty vulture, only intent upon her prey, as good as the warrior himself." He acknowledged that love and fear for their children's safety motivated Indian women to pick up arms, and that white mothers would certainly share this instinct. Yet, in an Indian woman, Carter insisted, maternal instinct partook more of "savage devotion and instinctive traits of the wild animals." When cornered, she fought with all the strength of her savage nature and with the "desperation of a tigress." [16]

Yet other officers openly respected Indian women who defended their homes and families. During the Gila Expedition of 1857, Col. John Van Deusen du Bois admired a native woman's valiant attempt to carry her wounded husband off the battlefield and was sickened when the troops killed them both. Cochise's sister, a fifty-year-old widow with "strongly marked, unprepossessing features giving evidence of a strong will," impressed Sladen. She was, he said, the "presiding genius" of an Apache outpost overlooking the road to Fort Bowie. While it was unusual for a woman to have such responsibility, Sladen wrote, Cochise had great confidence in his sister, and the army officer agreed that her "independence and force seemed to justify this faith in her ability." And Lieutenant Davis later recalled that while fighting Apache in 1882, he heard groans from a wounded enemy who was firing on troopers. Charging the sharpshooter's position, the soldiers discovered a young woman, shielding an infant. She drew her knife and fought the men until they overpowered her and disarmed her. She had a bullet-shattered leg, Davis remembered, but did not utter a single groan when her leg was amputated without anesthesia. "She stood it," he marveled, "without a murmur." [17]

Officers, then, found admirable qualities in the lives and characters of Indian women; some suggested that savage women lived healthier lives and had more rights, powers, and protections than white women. In addition, beyond making such generalizations about them, a few officers became friends, perhaps even intimates, with individual Indian women. The nature and frequency of these friendships, love affairs, or even sexual encounters is difficult to ascertain, however. Some men discussed friendships with native women but declined to elaborate on their level of intimacy, being exceedingly discreet about sexual matters. Furthermore, miscegenation was not condoned, and officers were not inclined to publicize any personal acquaintance with it.

There is evidence, however, that army officers and Indian women had romantic as well as sexual entanglements, although most official documents limit their remarks on these matters to enlisted men. Congress, disturbed over reports of miscegenation on the military frontier, convened the Banning Committee in 1876, to investigate the problem of "immorality" at frontier Army posts. The committee assumed the problem existed between enlisted men and Indian women and remained silent on officers. [18]

Exceptions to this official silence concerned officers who shamefully cavorted with prostitutes (white, Mexican, or Indian) in the presence of enlisted men and were consequently court-martialed. Officials preferred, however, to discourage documentation of such liaisons whenever possible. Capt. Nicholas Nodt finally succeeded, after a four-year effort, in reporting an incident at Fort Fauntleroy that involved officers' "favorite squaws." According to historian Anne Butler, officers at that post kept Navajo mistresses as a matter of course, and their commanding officer not only knew about the relationships but used the women as emissaries to others in their tribe.[19]

Perhaps the most infamous officer-Indian sexual relationship was the rumored affair between Lt. Col. George Armstrong Custer and a Cheyenne woman named Monasetah. Retired Capt. Frederick Benteen of the Seventh Cavalry, who despised Custer, claimed that, following the Battle of the Washita, Custer invited officers "desiring to avail themselves of the services of a captured squaw to come to the squaw round up corral, and select one!" Custer, Benteen charged, took first choice, Monasetah, and lived with her during the winter and spring of 1868 and 1869. Benteen also maintained that Army Surgeon Renick had "seen him not only sleeping with that indian girl all winter long, but [had] seen him many times in the act of copulating with her."[20] Benteen's obvious disregard for Custer, whom he labeled an "S.O.B. . . . murderer, thief, and liar," certainly undermined his objectivity and perhaps even his reliability on this matter. Since many nineteenth-century men maintained, at least in public statements, that sexual relations with Indian women degraded white men, Benteen may have intended to slander Custer's memory by making these accusations. However, whether or not Custer and Monasetah were actually lovers, rumors such as this one demonstrate such entanglements were not considered impossible.

Moreover, the potential for sexual intimacy between these men and women was clearly an issue of concern between officers and their wives. Several men mentioned Indian women in letters home, quickly adding that they had no interest in taking them as lovers. Lt. E. O. C. Ord, writing to his wife from Fort Walla Walla, Washington Territory, in 1858, said, " . . . tell Mrs. Hardie the capt. is looking extremely youthful & when any good looking squaws come along he looks toward them & sighs—for home." And, he added, "remember if Mrs. H takes this too hard—tell her Hardie is as anxious to get home—home, home! as your affectionate and devoted husband." Admiring the Crow at Fort Phil Kearny, Col. Luther Bradley wrote his fiance that "some of the women were even good looking." He hastened to add that such attractiveness was rare and that she "need not fear my falling in love with any of them, they are not in my style." Capt. Albert Barnitz also reassured his wife that he would not "fall in love with any of their dirty little squaws," referring to Cheyenne and Arapahoe. In a demonstration of his constancy, he claimed that, while he was at the 1867 Council at Medicine Lodge, Kansas, an Aarapahoe brought a young woman to be his companion for the night. Although she "was elegantly ornamented with vermillion, and seemed to have been especially gotten up for the occasion," Barnitz refused the offer. He showed the Arapahoe a picture of his wife and told him one "squaw" was enough.[21]

Time and again officers replayed, in letters and memoirs, Barnitz's scenario of Indian men offering Indian women to officers, who firmly, though graciously, refused, thus maintaining the highest moral standards. Some admitted they found Indian women tempting, but resisted either because they could not quite overcome their scruples about mixing with Indians, or they did not want to risk alienating spouses back home. Among the captives of the 1857 Gila River Expedition, Col. John du Bois was attracted to one woman—a princess, of course. Gracefully clothed in buckskin, with a sweet voice, curling lip, flashing eyes, and small hands and feet, she was "haughty as an Empress receiving homage. . . . By Jove—I could marry such a wildcat," he exclaimed, "if she lived on 5th Avenue & owned half a county." Whether he pursued a relationship with her, he did not say, although he commented, "*On dit* that the morals of the captives are not irreproachable."[22]

At least one officer acknowledged that Indian women took advantage of officers' attentions and sentimental or romantic inclinations. After their own families were wiped out by war, several Apache women, according to Davis, "practically adopted" army officers. A seven-year-old girl, with her mother's encouragement, became one officer's special protégé, acquiring finery at his expense:

These romantic friendships, Davis lamented, should have had the proper romantic ending—when the grateful Indian girl throws herself before the leveled rifles, à la Captain John Smith. But alas and alack! When the hostiles went out in the spring of 1885 the girl and the women went with them, seemingly not caring a trooper's damn whether I was filled full of lead or not.[23]

Officers' comments about women emphasized the romantic and ignored the more sordid implications of Benteen's charges against Custer. Most maintained, in public statements, that a sexual relationship or a marriage between "savagery" and "civilization" threatened the latter. While the Indian women would be elevated by the match, the white man would be lowered. One officer argued that white men were "naturally" demeaned by such liaisons because their personal cleanliness suffered, their clothing turned ragged, their self-respect was degraded, and they became indifferent to civilized life. "The moral and intellectual level of these bipeds (savages by choice)," de Trobriand maintained, "is more that of a brute than a civilized man." White officers treated their Indian wives like servants, did not communicate with their women since neither spoke the other's language, and had relationships "more bestial than human."[24]

If marriage or public acknowledgement of sexual mingling with Indian women was out of the question for officers, however, romance was not. In his novel, *An Apache Princess,* Capt. Charles King examined this possibility. Natzie, the princess—a "theoretical heathen, but a practical Christian"—fell in love with pale, genteel Lt. Neil Blakely. In Pocahontas-like fashion, she saved his life, but then learned that her love for Blakely was unrequited, for he loved the captain's eastern-educated daughter, Angela. While the genteel Blakely preferred hunting butterflies to drinking and gambling, his Army friends believed he encouraged Natzie's attentions in an ungentlemanly way. "Even women who could not find it possible to speak of her probable relations with Neil Blakely," King romanticized, "dwelt much in thought and word upon her superb devotion and her generosity. That he had encouraged her passionate and almost savage love for him, there were few to doubt." As King's novel demonstrates, an Apache princess was a suitable companion for a frontier flirtation and even a passionate affair. But, in the end, confirming the impossibility of any permanent commitment between an officer and an Indian, Blakely married Angela, and Natzie married a Chiricahua brave.[25]

King's fiction mirrored frontier reality. Though rare, such romances did occur. Officers' accounts, while vague about the nature of these relationships, revealed they were warm and of some consequence. Marriages, of course, were almost unknown, although Lt. D. H. Rucker of the 1st Dragoons married a "civilized" Cherokee woman. For most, the idea of marriage apparently was not seriously entertained.[26]

While never destined to achieve the respectability or sanctity of marriage, these relationships seemed to indicate that, if only for a short time, officers and Indian women could attain a level of communication, understanding, and affection that transcended concerns of savagery and civilization, of occupying army and overpowered native people. If one cuts through the imagery of hackneyed princess stereotypes, one can find indications of genuine human involvement.

For example, a Yuma beauty the soldiers named "Rose of the Colorado," charmed Lt. Thomas W. Sweeny. She had, according to Sweeny, beautiful black, dazzling eyes. Her face was soft and more intelligent, he believed, than any Indian face he had ever seen. But most impressive to Sweeny was "her form, which was almost nude, was truly magnificent, and would have been a glory to a young sculptor." Clearly attracted to her, Sweeny approached and, in time, they became friends. In one touching exchange, the Yuma woman asked Sweeny if white women were beautiful. He answered they were, but assured her she was every bit as handsome, although white men did not like women who painted themselves. Being painted, she looked rather sad at this and asked Sweeny if he felt the same way. He gently told her, it "is not wrong in you . . . for it is the practice of your people," but he added, " . . . believe me, you would look much handsomer without it."[27]

Similar warmth and affection characterized William Woods Averell's relationship with Ah-tlan-tiz-pa, a Navajo, who, he said, followed him into Fort Defiance, New Mexico Territory. He found her "undoubtedly the prettiest Navajo woman in the country." Averell admitted only that she was friendly and valuable to the army post, but it appears his interest in Ah-tlan-tiz-pa was more than professional. Upon hearing that he was wounded during the Navajo War, Averell related, Ah-tlan-tiz-pa ran into his tent and threw herself on the ground. "It was not until repeated assurances that I was alive and not fatally hurt that she partly raised herself and crept toward my bed." He made arrangements for her to freely enter the garrison and "so, to borrow the idiom of our ancient friend, J. Fenimore Cooper, the Indian maiden occasionally brought the breezy vigor of the piñon-clad mountains and the ruddy glow of savage life, unfettered by any conventionalities, into the quiet dead and alive cabin of the wounded paleface.'' Averell had several lovers during his stay in the Southwest, and Ah-tlan-tiz-pa was probably among them. The Navajo woman clearly demonstrated considerable feeling for the officer, and the relationship was of some import to both.[28]

The majority of officers uncritically adopted the myths and stereotypes that dominated Americans' ideas about Indian women. Yet a significant number of army officers in the trans-Mississippi West discovered that these stereotypes did not adequately describe the lives and experiences of Indian women. While they never abandoned their basic assumptions about savagery and civilization, they believed Indian women possessed admirable qualities and characteristics; these beliefs were grounded in reality rather than in the fanciful Pocahontas-princess image. These men discovered that Indian women had rights unknown to white women, and, in praising Indian women, they conversely criticized their own culture's treatment of women, its institution of marriage, and its methods of childbirth.

Furthermore, a few officers demonstrated a capacity to penetrate beyond notions of civilization and savagery, conqueror and conquered, to achieve close, perhaps even intimate, friendships with individual Indian women, without fully abandoning these notions or even experiencing an erosion of their potency. Although officers resorted to princess mythology in their accounts of these friendships, the use of princess symbols does not necessarily invalidate the friendships or emotional involvements. In a culture that frowned upon racial mixing, perhaps these myths provided the only acceptable means by which such men could comfortably write about romance with Indian women. In addition, by relating their interactions with these women, officers conveyed some sense of the Indians' curiosity about white culture, their generosity of spirit, devotion to family, courage under fire, and capacity for love, friendship, compassion, and forgiveness.

The result was that officers developed a more humanized view of Indians through examination of women. Why would women more than men elicit these reactions from officers? The officers may have been more inclined to see all women, regardless of race or culture, as more approachable, more emotional, and less inscrutable than men. Also, they defined Indian women in terms of their relations with others—husbands, children, the officers themselves—which reinforced concepts of the Indians as human. Further, although some women took up arms to defend home and family, officers did not seem to perceive them as the enemy, but believed their husbands, brothers, and fathers most directly threatened them. Finally, officers probably saw Indian women as more easily redeemed for civilization. Army men most likely accepted their culture's assumptions that white women were a civilizing influence on the frontier and perhaps assumed Indian women could play the same "gentle tamer" role in their own cultures.

Attitudes such as these, however, while demonstrating some change in perception based on experiences with actual Indian women, did not alter officers' actions. To acknowledge Indian women's humanity and their personal relationships with individuals could make their tasks as soldiers even more complicated, or even render them ineffective. For most officers, then, Indians remained, in the final analysis, inferior beings who obstructed civilization's advance across the continent. The officers' ultimate purpose was not to understand, communicate, and care for Indians but to clear the country-side of these obstacles—through peaceful means, if possible, through violent means, if necessary.

Notes

1. John Bourke, *The Snake Dance of the Moquis of Arizona* (New York: Charles Scribner's Sons, 1884), pp. 45–46. See also Lt. James Bradley, "Characteristics, Habits and Customs of the Blackfeet Indians," *Contributions to the Historical Society of Montana* 9 (1923): 270.

2. Britton Davis, *The Truth About Geronimo* (New Haven, Conn.: Yale University Press, 1929), p. 72.

3. Roy Harvey Pearce, *Savagism and Civilization: A Study of the Indian and the American Mind* (Baltimore, Md.: Johns Hopkins Press, 1967), p. v. Other studies of white attitudes toward Indians include Robert F. Berkhofer, Jr., *White Man's Indian: Images of the American Indian from Columbus to the Present* (New York: Vintage, 1978); Lewis O. Saum, *The Fur Trader and the Indian* (Seattle: University of Washington Press, 1965). The best studies on officers' attitudes toward Indians include Thomas C. Leonard, "Red, White and the Army Blue: Empathy and Anger in the American West," *American Quarterly* 26 (May, 1973); and William B. Skelton, "Army Officers' Attitudes Toward Indians, 1830–1860," *Pacific Northwest Quarterly* 67 (July, 1976).

4. Alison Bernstein, "Outgrowing Pocahontas: Toward a New History of American Indian Women," *Minority Notes* 2 (Spring–Summer, 1981): pp. 3–4; Rayna Green, "The Pocahontas Perplex: The Image of Indian Women in American Culture," *Massachusetts Review* 26 (Autumn, 1975): 703–704, 713.

5. Lt. C. A. Woodward, "Journal of an Expedition to Wichita Mountains from June 1 to July 13, 1863," in Benjamin Grierson Papers, Newberry Library, Chicago, Ill. See also General James F. Rusling, *Across America: Or, the Great West and Pacific Coast* (New York: Sheldon & Co., 1874), p. 116.

6. James Steele, *Frontier Army Sketches* (Chicago: Jansen, McClurg & Co., 1883), p. 84; William E. Waters, *Life Among the Mormons, and A March to Their Zion* (New York: Moorhead, Simpson & Bond, 1868), pp. 206–207. See also Randolph B. Marcy, *Thirty Years of Army Life on the Frontier* (New York: Harper & Brothers, 1866), pp. 21, 25, 28–29; Grant Foreman, ed., *Adventure on Red River: Report on the Exploration of the Headwaters of the Red River by Captain Randolph B. Marcy and Captain G. B. McClellan* (Norman: University of Oklahoma Press, 1937), pp. 157, 166–67; Col. Richard Irving Dodge, *Our Wild Indians: Thirty-three Years' Personal Experience Among the Red Men of the Great West* (Hartford: A. D. Worthington & Co., 1883), p. 193; Bradley, "Characteristics, Habits," p. 271; Rodney Glisan, *Journal of Army Life* (San Francisco: A. L. Bancroft & Co., 1874), p. 247; Capt. R. G. Carter, *On the Border with Mackenzie Or Winning West Texas from the Comanches* (New York: Antiquarian Press, 1961), p. 286; Rusling, *Across America*, p. 134; George Templeton, Diary, July 8, 1866 entry, Newberry Library, Chicago.

7. Brig. Gen. Richard Johnson, *A Soldier's Reminiscences in Peace and War* (Philadelphia: J. B. Lippincott, 1886), p. 144. For similar comments see Dodge, *Our Wild Indians*, pp. 345–46; Foreman, ed., *Adventure on Red River*, pp. 166–67.

8. Dodge, *Our Wild Indians*, pp. 204–205; Albert Brackett, "Fort Bridger," typescript, Colorado Historical Society, Denver, p. 11.

9. Edward K. Eckert and Nicholas J. Amata, eds., *Ten Years in the Saddle: The Memoirs of William Woods Averell* (San Rafael, Calif.: Presidio Press, 1972), pp. 154–55; Bourke, *The Snake-Dance*, p. 259; Steele, *Frontier Army Sketches*, pp. 188–89, 192.

10. Marcy, *Thirty Years,* pp. 88–89.

11. Dodge, *Our Wild Indians,* p. 215.

12. Ibid., p. 146.

13. William T. Parker, *Personal Experiences Among Our North American Indians From 1867 to 1885* (Northampton, Mass.: n. p. 1913), p. 101.

14. Joseph Sladen, letter to Mrs. Alice Crane, Oct. 26, 1896, United States Army Military Institute, Carlisle Barracks, Pa.; Foreman, ed., *Adventure on Red River,* p. 156.

15. For officers' comments on this issue see Dodge, *Our Wild Indians,* p. 466; John Fitzgerald as quoted in Abe Laufe, ed., *An Army Doctor's Wife on the Frontier: Letters from Alaska and the Far West* (Pittsburgh: University of Pittsburgh Press, 1962), p. 304. Some officers apparently suffered no remorse over deaths of Indian women during warfare. In his 1873 field journal Lt. Walter S. Schuyler matter-of-factly noted that his command discovered a rancheria containing three wickiups and eighteen Indians. "We got within 20 yards of them, and woke them up by firing into the houses. Two bucks and one squaw got away on account of the snowstorm." Demonstrating no apparent qualms about killing Indian women, Schuyler did prefer to "catch a squaw to use as guide." See "Notes of Scout From Camp Verde to McDowell and return, Dec. 1, 1873–Jan. 26, 1874," in Walter S. Schuyler Papers, Huntington Library, San Marino, Calif. For information on reformers' attitudes toward Indian policy and the military's role in Indian affairs see Robert W. Mardock, *The Reformers and the American Indian* (Columbia: University of Missouri Press, 1971); Francis Paul Prucha, *American Indian Policy in Crisis: Christian Reformers and the Indian, 1885–1887* (Norman: University of Oklahoma Press, 1976).

16. Carter, *On the Border,* p. 287. See also John Bourke, *An Apache Campaign in the Sierra Madre* (New York: Charles Scribner's Sons, 1886), pp. 90–91.

17. George P. Hammond, ed., *Campaigns in the West, 1856–1861: The Journal and Letters of Colonel John Van Deusen du Bois* (Tucson: Arizona Pioneers Historical Society, 1949), p. 30; Davis, *The Truth About Geronimo,* p. 26; Sladen letter to Mrs. Crane, USAMHI.

18. See Patricia Y. Stallard, *Glittering Misery: Dependents of the Indian Fighting Army* (Fort Collins: Old Army Press, 1978), p. 69–70.

19. Anne Butler, "Military Myopia: Prostitution on the Frontier," *Prologue,* Winter, 1981, p. 241.

20. Frederick W. Benteen to Theodore Goldin, 14 Feb. and 17 Feb. 1896, typescripts, Newberry Library, Chicago.

21. Lt. E. O. C. Ord to Molly Ord, 4 July 1858, E. O. C. Ord Papers, Stanford University Library, Palo Alto, Calif.; Luther Bradley to Ione Dewey, 10 July 1867, Luther Bradley Papers, USAMHI, Carlisle Barracks, Pa.; Robert M. Utley, ed., *Life in Custer's Cavalry: Diaries and Letters of Albert and Jennie Barnitz, 1867–1868* (New Haven, Conn.: Yale University Press, 1977), pp. 110, 111.

22. Hammond, ed., *Campaigns,* pp. 26, 28. See also Marcy, *Thirty Years,* pp. 49, 50.

23. Davis, *The Truth About Geronimo,* pp. 72–73.

24. Oliver O. Howard, *My Life and Experiences Among Our Hostile Indians* (New York: De Capo Press, 1972), pp. 525–26; Lucille M. Kane, ed., *Military Life in Dakota* (St. Paul, Minn.: Alvord Memorial Commission, 1951), p. 11.

25. Gen. Charles King, *An Apache Princess: A Tale of the Indian Frontier* (New York: Hobart Co., 1903), pp. 16, 282.

26. See Stephen Perry Jocelyn, *Mostly Alkali* (Caldwell, Idaho: Caxton Printers, 1953), p. 86.

27. Arthur Woodward, ed., *Journal of Lieutenant Thomas W. Sweeny, 1849–1853* (Los Angeles: Westernlore Press, 1956), pp. 68, 128.

28. Eckert and Amata, eds., *Ten Years,* p. 205.

6.
_____

Sharing Bed and Board: Cohabitation and Cultural Difference in Central Arizona Mining Towns, 1863–1873

SUSAN L. JOHNSON

This article compares two very different cultural patterns, the Mexican informal union and the Anglo double standard of morality, which co-existed in the Arizona goldfields of the 1860s. Both are examples of the persistence of earlier social forms, yet they became particular adaptations to boom town society, and their conjunction briefly produced something new.

Working from census records, Susan Johnson carefully reconstructs the lives of the Mexican women who lived in informal unions with Anglo or Mexican men. She effectively uses local folklore about two unusual Anglo women to explore Anglo attitudes toward race and sexuality. By tracing the two cultural patterns and analyzing their interaction, she widens our notion of culture contact as well as that of cultural persistence.

By the spring of 1864, nineteen-year-old Juanita Bachichia was well situated in a large, sturdy cabin on Lynx Creek, at the heart of central Arizona's burgeoning gold-mining districts. She had arrived only five months before, following close on the heels of the first prospectors. A native New Mexican, Bachichia cast her lot with George Clinton, a twenty-four-year-old miner and hotelkeeper from New York; their cabin soon became a boardinghouse where miners ate for two dollars a day. They were making final preparations for the new enterprise when the Reverend Hiram Walter Read approached the camp at Lynx Creek.

Like many of the first settlers, Reverend Read did double duty during the early months of the gold excitement. In addition to his religious role, as postmaster of the newly organized Territory of Arizona, he assumed responsibility for the census returns in the Third Judicial District. But Read, formerly a missionary in New Mexico, had more than census taking on his mind: "At Lynx Creek he fell in with George Clinton and Juanita Bachichia and a wedding was the consequence. The miners were quickly summoned, and the affair was conducted in an off-hand and truly Western manner. George was in his shirt sleeves and Juanita in her morning gown." Territorial Secretary Richard McCormick witnessed the bilingual ceremony, and remarked to the groom afterward that he "had as soon expected an earthquake as a wedding in the gulch." [1]

No clues are left to explain how the newlyweds met; why they decided to live together and, later, to consent to Read's makeshift marriage ceremony; how they shared the responsibilities and rewards of the boardinghouse. We know, however, that Juanita Bachichia was on her own again by the end of the decade. Clinton was killed in the spring of 1869, and the *Arizona Miner* concluded his obituary with the simple statement, "He leaves a Mexican woman."[2]

During her young adulthood Juanita Bachichia left her imprint on the historical record only three times—in the newspaper account of her wedding, in the 1864 territorial census, and in her husband's obituary. This stark outline of her existence suggests something of the character of life for most of the women who first responded to central Arizona's mining boom in the mid-1860s. Indeed, the largest group of women whom census taker Read identified in the spring of 1864 (almost half of the total number) were those sharing households in the Walker-Weaver mining area with men to whom they were not married. This essay, using census records and the few available accounts of individual lives, focuses on that subgroup of central Arizona women: those who, particularly during the heyday of the initial gold rush, lived informally with male companions.

By far the greatest number of these women were young and of Mexican descent, though a handful of Anglo women also cohabited with men. The experience of cohabitation, however, varied with the ethnicities of a woman and her companion. While Mexican working-class culture maintained a system of informal union which paralleled that of formal marriage, the dominant Anglo-American culture perpetuated a double standard of sexual morality that discouraged sex outside of marriage for women, but not, or at least not to the same extent, for men. As a result of this cultural difference, together with negative Anglo attitudes toward Mexicans in general, and with the imposition of Anglo dominance throughout the Southwest,[3] most Anglos condemned Mexican women who lived with men, while ignoring or rationalizing the behavior of the few Anglo women who cohabited. Finally, the incidence of Mexican women's cohabitation declined after the first turbulent year or two of the mining boom. This decline suggests that its earlier occurrence was not a simple reconstruction of Mexican culture in the gold fields, but rather an adaptation of cultural patterns to new circumstances where such patterns proved particularly appropriate.

MEXICAN WOMEN AND INFORMAL UNION

Census records gathered just months after a series of placer strikes are a valuable and uncommon primary source. When census taker Read made his rounds in central Arizona in 1864, however, he identified only forty women living in the area. Meanwhile, literary sources indicate that the actual female population far exceeded the numbers reported in the census. When one miner arrived at Weaver in September of 1863, for example, he found a population of about twenty Anglos (one of them a woman) and more than three hundred Mexican inhabitants, including "scores of Mexican women."[4] Despite this discrepancy in the sources, there is no reason to believe that the lives and circumstances of the women enumerated in the census differed significantly from those not counted. Thus, the reported female population can be taken as representative of the entire female population.

Seventeen (55 percent) of the thirty-one Mexican women enumerated by Reverend Read in 1864 lived with male companions.[5] Several probably came to Arizona from earlier territorial gold camps like La Paz and Pinos Altos, while others emigrated from various locations in New Mexico, southern Arizona, California, and the Mexican state of Sonora. Neither the census nor literary sources, however, reveal whether the women had accompanied their male companions to the diggings or became acquainted with them after arrival. Indeed, in many cases it is difficult to determine which woman lived with which man, as the 1864 census did not list residents by household. But Read saw fit to identify the occupation of almost all of the unmarried, Spanish-surnamed women as "mistress." Read's use of the term "mistress" may reflect his misconceptions of Mexican women's relational styles. First, if it is regarded as a sexual, and not an economic, term, then it reduces the phenomenon of informal union to its erotic component and, by selectively casting aspersions on the moral character of only the female partner, it lays full responsibility for cohabitation at the feet of the Mexican woman.[6] Second, the term suggests Read's ignorance of class differences in Mexican intimate relationships; while the Mexican middle and upper classes maintained a sexual double standard that permitted men to "take mistresses" (not unlike the one that characterized Anglo society), Mexican working-class culture tended to uphold, practically if not ideologically, a single standard in which the concept of a "mistress" had less prominence.[7]

The best documented of these informal heterosexual unions are those that existed between Mexican women and Anglo men. Juanita Bachichia's relationship with George Clinton is one case in point. The newspaper report of their marriage in April sheds no light on what Bachichia may have expected of the cohabitation. But her new husband seems to have been as much taken aback by the wedding as were the onlookers; the *Miner* insists that "he knew nothing of it himself two hours before." Invoking thinly veiled ethnocentrism, the editors then quip, "Despite his haste George has obeyed the Spanish maxim: 'Before you marry be sure of a house wherein you tarry.'"[8] The relationship between Pancha Acuña and Calvin Jackson is another documented case. Acuña was twenty-five when she came to central Arizona, though she had lived elsewhere in the territory for three years. She is listed along with her one-year-old daughter Faustina, in the 1864 census. Read recorded the young mother's occupation as "mistress."[9] By 1866 a county census taker in Prescott took down the name "Pancha Jackson," though it is unlikely that she and Calvin Jackson ever actually wed; neither the *Miner* nor the county legal records note any such marriage.[10] In fact, when Calvin Jackson died in the late

1870s, Pancha's name failed to appear in his obituary. The newspaper reports state only that Jackson had lost a wife in California in 1859 and that Faustina, his sixteen-year-old daughter, had "been his constant companion and nurse during his sickness." [11]

What became of Pancha Acuña is unclear. What *is* clear in this absence of records is the prevalent Anglo attitude toward informal unions between Mexican women and Anglo men. When an Anglo husband died and left an Anglo wife, obituaries never specified the woman's ethnicity, almost always gave her name, and generally ended with a laudatory statement about her actions or her character. [12] But Clinton's obituary, even though he eventually married Bachichia, concluded with the begrudging comment, "He leaves a Mexican woman." Pancha Acuña, perhaps because she did not marry her companion, fared even worse. When Jackson died, only the daughter of their union and a wife long since deceased were publicly recognized.

It did not take an event as solemn as a man's death to expose Anglo disdain for Mexican women and Anglo men who lived together. An Anglo woman vividly recalled a dinner she prepared for a dance sponsored by the Masons in Prescott in 1866. "One man living with a Mexican woman," she wrote, "was not invited to the dance. He supposed we had the inviting to do and he was very angry"—so angry, in fact, that he threatened to kill the Anglo woman's husband. [13] There is no record of the Mexican woman's response to the snub, but her companion, accustomed to the privilege inherent in being both Anglo and male, was outraged. [14]

While Mexican women's relationships with Anglo men are the most thoroughly documented in the literary sources (which were generated by Anglos), it was actually far more common for an unmarried Mexican woman who came to the gold fields to set up housekeeping with a Mexican man. But detailed accounts of these relationships are unavailable, due to both the paucity of Spanish-language source materials (there were, for example, no Spanish-language newspapers in the area) and the Anglo indifference to anything that occurred outside the boundaries of the Anglo community. Only the 1864 census reveals the preponderance of Mexican-Mexican informal unions. Although Reverend Read did not list residents by household, internal evidence in the census verifies that he did move from household to household, from neighborhood to neighborhood, and from camp to camp in an orderly fashion. Almost all of the Mexican women identified as "mistresses" in the census are listed within large blocks of Spanish-surnamed individuals, indicating that they lived with Mexican men in Mexican communities. Nineteen, or 61 percent, of the Mexican women enumerated lived with Mexican companions; this includes both the informal unions and five marriages. [15]

The recent focus on cross-cultural marriage in the Southwest, [16] then, may prove an inappropriate approach to the study of mining communities in their boom years. In central Arizona, at least, 55 percent of the Mexican women who followed the first prospectors cohabited informally with men; and 61 percent of those early female arrivals (including those few who were married) lived with Mexican men. If the more appropriate focus is on nonmarital relationships, particularly between Mexican women and Mexican men, it is important to investigate the meanings of such relationships to the participants. In the absence of self-reflective accounts by women who lived with men in the early years of central Arizona's gold excitement, secondary accounts detailing the significance of informal unions in Mexican culture are useful.

Scholars trace the Hispanic "folk custom" of informal union to its origins in European practices that were recognized by late Roman law; Spanish law on marriage essentially restated late Roman law.[17] In medieval Spain, the practice was called *barrangía*. Transported to Mexico with the sixteenth-century conquest, the Spanish custom rivaled the more official system of morality that required formal marriage. This was particularly true among those who could not afford the fees necessary to formalize a union and who, lacking wealth or access to public office, had little reason to concern themselves with issues of legitimacy and inheritance. Mexican Indians constituted an exception to this practice for a time; Christian missionary zeal and Spanish fiscal policy (the Spanish authorities exacted tribute from the Indians with the married couple as the fiscal unit) coalesced to encourage (that is, enforce) early marriage among the native peoples. But Mexican independence from Spain and, in particular, the reform movements of the 1850s and 1860s, led native Mexicans increasingly to adopt the practice of informal union that characterized the lower classes among Hispanicized Mexicans. These reforms, engendered in large part by conflict between church and state, included an 1859 law issued by Benito Juarez which declared marriage a civil contract that was valid only if made before and registered with civil authorities. The diminished influence of the church among Indians was accompanied by a sharp increase in the proportion of Indian births outside of civil marriage. Among Hispanicized Mexicans, the church-state conflict served to reinforce the already common practice of informal union. The legal reform, which occurred just four or five years before the central Arizona gold rush, seems neither to have reflected nor induced a change in Mexican couples' propensity to wed: women and men continued to live with one another, and those inclined to marry still tended to equate marriage with a religious, rather than a civil, ceremony.

These, then, were the antecedents of Mexican women's intimate relationships in the Arizona gold fields, where the absence of Catholic clergy must have augmented the trend. While this absence of clergy, and other factors, may have contributed to the substantial proportion of unmarried Mexican women cohabiting with men in the early years of the gold rush, it seems most reasonable—given the prevalence of informal union in Mexico, particularly among working-class and, later, native Mexicans—to view such unions not only as a response to specific mining frontier conditions, but also as a reconstruction of traditional Mexican culture in Arizona.

When a Mexican woman lived with a Mexican man in Arizona, it is likely that she and her partner came to the relationship with some like understandings of this tradition. But when a Mexican woman and an Anglo man shared a household, they may have approached the cohabitation with dissimilar notions about appropriate contexts for sexual intimacy and economic partnership. Unlike Mexicans, Anglo Americans did not maintain a system of informal union that paralleled the conditions of formal marriage. Anglos did maintain a sexual double standard that encouraged single women to be chaste and married women monogamous, while allowing men, married or single, considerably more latitude.[18] Anglos repeatedly ignored, discounted, and otherwise stigmatized relationships between unmarried Anglo men and Mexican women. In keeping with the prevalent double standard and the Anglo tendency to project unrestrained sexual expression upon those of other cultures and races, such censure fell disproportionately on Mexican women.

In Mexican-Anglo informal unions, then, intimacy occurred in the context of conflicting cultural conceptions of sexual morality. However, since all accounts of such unions originated with observers, rather than participants, one cannot determine the particular meanings that individual Mexican women and Anglo men attached to their relationships. One can only speculate that they brought their respective cultural beliefs to bear upon their actions. Thus, where both Mexican women and Anglo men must have seen potential for intimacy and economic partnership, the Anglo man may also have seen opportunity for sexual relations outside of marriage—opportunity less openly available in Anglo society, save with prostitutes. As for the Mexican woman, cohabitation with an Anglo man provided access to a standard of living otherwise closed to her; the 1864 and 1870 censuses reveal that Anglo household companions were far more apt than their Mexican counterparts to work in occupations of medium-to-high socioeconomic standing, and that male Anglo property values greatly exceeded those of Mexican men.[19] Still, a reductive analysis that imputes primarily sexual motivation to Anglo men and primarily economic motivation to Mexican women is inadequate. Anglo men must have benefited from the domestic labor performed by their companions, and there is no reason to believe that Mexican women did not also obtain erotic satisfaction in these informal unions. Certainly, both partners gained companionship in an otherwise unfamiliar, harsh, and chaotic environment.

ANGLO WOMEN AND INFORMAL UNION

Only a few Anglo-American women cohabited with men during the central Arizona boom; the households they maintained serve to delineate for us the boundaries of acceptable female behavior in the mining area.

One Anglo woman who seems to have moved with relative ease across those behavioral boundaries has captured the imagination of several writers concerned with the central Arizona gold rush; she was known variously as Mary DeCrow, Mary Brown, Mary Ramos, and Virgin Mary. She may have come to Arizona with a black Texan whom Anglos called "Negro Brown."[20] One source indicated that while a slave in Texas, Brown killed his master and fled to Arizona with the master's widow—and Mary DeCrow may well have been that widow.[21] But the partnership ended soon after Brown and DeCrow arrived in central Arizona in 1864. That year census taker Read identified seventeen-year-old Santa Lopez as the "mistress of Negro Brown" and found Mary "Brown" at Weaver with Cornelius Ramos, a twenty-nine-year-old, Mexican-born blacksmith.[22] At Weaver, DeCrow ran a tiny restaurant. By 1865, she and Ramos married, and she then kept a boardinghouse in Prescott before moving to Lynx Creek, where together she and her husband managed their goat ranch and looked after their placer claims.[23] One might expect, then, that if DeCrow would be remembered at all she would be remembered primarily as a woman of the dominant Anglo culture who flouted social boundaries, not only by entering into intimate relationships with men outside of marriage, but by establishing those relationships with men of color.

On the contrary, however, history and local lore have whitewashed the memory of Mary DeCrow to such a degree that it bears little resemblance to reality. Secondary accounts focus, first, on the origin of the name "Virgin Mary" and, second, on the competition between DeCrow's Prescott boardinghouse and that of another early entrepreneur. Storytellers generally agree that DeCrow's nickname came as a consequence of her kindness and generosity. Their explanations range from the simple "She received her nickname because of her benevolence," to the florid "None knew her name and none cared to. She was christened 'Virgin Mary' and when she passed away it was 'Virgin Mary has gone.' Her life was a beautiful exemplification of the Bible, . . . devoted to the wounded and distressed, and her purse and every farthing she could procure went in the same way."[24] Stories about the competing Prescott boardinghouse vary. All hold that Virgin Mary's establishment held the advantage of providing goat's milk for the miners' coffee. The proprietor of the other boardinghouse, however, is identified sometimes as a man named Jackson and sometimes as Negro Brown himself. One account maintains that Virgin Mary's competitor (in this case, Jackson) offered only stewed prunes to offset the coveted goat's milk,[25] while two other accounts focus on a female relative in the employ of the competitor. It was Brown's "buxom sixteen-year-old daughter" that lured miners away from Virgin Mary's establishment, according to a second chronicler.[26] A third explains how Jackson's boardinghouse, which featured chili at every meal, drew customers: "Jackson's step-daughter," the storyteller suggests, "was not so completely chilly as the menu."[27]

These local legends are curious for two reasons. First, they ignore Mary DeCrow's relational history, which more clearly sets her apart from the vast majority of central Arizona Anglo women than any other aspect of her life; that is, while it was not uncommon for Anglo women to gain reputations for generosity or to run boardinghouses, it was extremely unusual for them to enter into intimate unions with black or Mexican men. Second, the accounts oppose an image of womanhood that is white, Christian, and asexual to one that is primarily sexual. Thus, although the name

"Virgin Mary" could be seen as an ironic suggestion of actual misconduct (according to Anglo standards), the storytellers dissociate DeCrow from the erotic and identify her instead with a Christian image of the benevolent Virgin. In the origin-of-the-name stories, the sexual conception of womanhood is suggested mainly by its conspicuous absence and by the storytellers' obvious rhetorical attempts to steer readers away from such a conception. In the stories of the competing boardinghouses, furthermore, the opposing image of sexualized womanhood actually is embodied in the daughter (or stepdaughter) of the other proprietor. Given the Anglo propensity to associate unbounded passion with people of other cultures, and particularly with people of color, it is not surprising that in at least one version the erotic counterimage is a young black woman.

Virgin Mary shares the spotlight in central Arizona's local lore with another female figure whose cohabitation is documented in primary source materials. Mary Sawyer, otherwise known as Mollie Monroe, seems to have arrived in the area during the late 1860s, when she was scarcely twenty years old. She may have married one or more times as a young woman,[28] but the historical record links her most closely with an Anglo prospector named George Monroe. While Monroe and Sawyer probably never wed, in 1870 the census taker found them living together in Wickenburg.[29] Whatever the nature of their relationship, it is clear that Sawyer did not confine herself to a traditional wifely role. Early in the spring of 1872, for example, a newspaper correspondent from Wickenburg sent the following report to the *Miner* in Prescott: "The 'boys' were out last week prospecting. George Monroe, Joe Fuggit, Wm. Gellaspie, Tom Graves and Molly struck a galena lode, and styled it the 'Knock Down.'"[30]

Her name does not appear again in the historical record until 1877. On May 9 of that year the Yavapai County probate judge declared Sawyer insane and ordered her temporarily confined in the county jail. Arizona Territory did not yet have its own insane asylum, so the county board of supervisors decided to send her to the asylum in Stockton, California. Eventually, she was transferred to the insane asylum that was built in Phoenix, and it was there that she died in 1902.[31]

What remains unexplored in all accounts of Mary Sawyer's life is the nature of her "insanity"; not even the county probate records reveal anything about the behavior that led an acquaintance in 1877 to bring her into Prescott from a neighboring community, charging her with lunacy. Once she had been declared insane and sent off to Stockton, Mollie Monroe acquired notoriety in central Arizona. Local newspapers, which only casually noted her activities before 1877, began both to follow her condition closely and to recall in greater detail her early years in Arizona. Just months after her departure for California, the *Miner* reported that Sawyer had been transferred from Stockton to San Quentin Prison because she had become violent and "intent on burning the Asylum."[32] But within a year a California correspondent for the Yuma newspaper found her back at the asylum, "greatly improved mentally": she showed interest in old friends and in Arizona politics, and she stated firmly "that she had no longer any desire to drink." [33] In 1880, however, another correspondent held that Sawyer was "entirely devoid of any higher aspirations than to go back and resume the wild and dissolute life she led in the mountains of Arizona." She told her Arizona visitor that, although the doctors would tell him she was "crazier than ever," it was actually "only meanness in her. She said that she was the meanest thing on earth, and intended to be so until she was turned out and allowed to do as she pleased." [34]

Eventually Sawyer tired of waiting to be "turned out." By the late 1880s she had been transferred back to Phoenix, and in 1895, after almost twenty years of asylum life, she bolted the institution and set out across the desert on foot. For several days area newspapers reported on the sheriff's attempts to trail her through the hot sand and mountain rocks, reminding readers of her younger days in central Arizona when she "would invariably dress in male attire" [35] and "could ride anything with four feet, chew more tobacco and swear harder than any man" in the territory. [36] But it was not long before Indian men from the Maricopa-Pima reservation on the Gila River overtook her and turned her over to the sheriff, who in turn took her back to the asylum. A Phoenix newspaper reported that Sawyer was quite pleased with her adventure—that she "described it with eloquence and profanity," stating, " 'If I'd a' only had my breeches and my gun I'd a' been all right.' " [37]

By the time of Sawyer's death in 1902, Arizonans already had adopted a formulaic story that explained her behavior. Mollie Monroe, they claimed, was a New Englander who became engaged to a prosperous young man in the 1860s. Parental disapproval prevented the marriage, and the young man departed for the far West with plans for Mollie to follow soon thereafter. Follow she did, the story goes, but always clad in male apparel to elude pursuers. Yet when Mollie reached her destination, she found that her fiancé had been murdered. She searched in vain for the killer throughout the Southwest until finally, her hope for vengeance thwarted, she remained in central Arizona, becoming "addicted to liquor and finally to morals that are dissolute." Those who recounted Mollie Monroe's life story, however, also maintained that she invariably "assisted the needy," that "she was, with all of these faults, a noble and charitable woman." [38]

Questions about Sawyer's insanity, then, reflect a twentieth-century— and, in this case, feminist—concern with the nature and etiology of madness. The nineteenth-century Arizonan who followed Sawyer's story over the years and read the early reports of her activities did not ask, "What in this behavior makes officials conclude that Mollie Monroe is crazy?" but rather asked, "What drove Mollie Monroe crazy?" At least it is this second question that is answered in accounts of her life popular at the turn of the century. Sawyer's life during the boom years did indeed include participation in various mining ventures, dressing in male attire, heavy drinking (perhaps alcoholism), and informal unions with men. On the basis of this set of facts and perhaps others not disclosed in the primary sources, her contemporaries assumed her insanity and sought to explain its origins. And what better explanation for a woman's appropriation of the trappings of male privilege—masculine clothing, multiple sexual partners, men's work—than disappointment in heterosexual romance? This explanation also accounted for Sawyer's oft-mentioned generosity: she was, by Anglo sexual standards, a "good" woman who, through no fault of her own, had bad luck in romance. That failure, according to the story, quite literally drove her insane.

Mary Sawyer and Mary DeCrow are the only women from central Arizona's gold and silver boom years whose life stories have become local legends. They are also the only Anglo women whose nonmarital relationships with men can be thoroughly documented. These facts are not unrelated. The dominant Anglo culture was unlikely to move beyond its ethnic boundaries in recognizing and cultivating legendary figures—that is, Sawyer and DeCrow were much more likely candidates than Juanita Bachichia and Pancha Acuña. But what explains local lore's inclusion of two female figures—ethnicity aside—in the first place? The answer lies in the ways in which Sawyer and DeCrow defied the dominant culture's prescriptions of behavior for women.

DeCrow challenged Anglo notions of womanhood solely in her intimate relationships. She lived with two men to whom she was not married, one a black Texan and the other a Mexican immigrant. But, once the initial tumult of the gold rush subsided, she only partially persisted in her challenge; although throughout her years in Arizona she was involved with men of color, by 1865 she and Cornelius Ramos had wed. Still, the stories about Mary DeCrow represent Anglo attempts to take up the problem presented by her intimate life. Perhaps because of her apparent, if incomplete, bow to convention (her eventual marriage), and because of needed services she provided in the community as one of the first boardinghouse keepers, Anglo legend dealt with DeCrow's relationships by forgetting them and, what is more, by supplanting them with exaggerated accounts of her benevolence.

Mary Sawyer's "transgressions" were not so easily forgotten. In almost every aspect of her life she was the antithesis of Anglo womanhood—in her work, in her dress and other personal habits, in her relationships. True, her intimate attachments appear to have been heterosexual, and all of the men she chose may well have been Anglos. But her compliance with societal expectations stopped there. Furthermore, Sawyer never gave up her whiskey, her prospecting, or her men's apparel. Nor did she consent to a lasting marriage, not even when the boom years in central Arizona gave way to less turbulent times. The Anglo community, then, needed not only to control Sawyer's actions but also to explain them, and a charge of insanity served both purposes. In a single stroke the charge enabled officials, first, to restrain her and remove her from the area and, second, to account for her most unladylike conduct. As the years passed, storytellers delved deeper into their own powers of explanation and found as well a *cause* for Sawyer's lunacy. Thus, where the early story claimed simply that "she lived a man's life because she was crazy," later developments took the argument a step further: "she was crazy because she lost a male lover."

Mary Sawyer and Mary DeCrow, then, diverged in their attempts to resist their culture's behavioral prescriptions for women. DeCrow defied convention by acting more like the Mexican women in the community than like her Anglo neighbors. In contrast, Sawyer behaved primarily like an Anglo man. Both must have provoked incredulity in their contemporaries. But DeCrow was emulating individuals who were, structurally, members of the least powerful group in Arizona mining town society, and the dominant culture could afford to deal with her behavior by ignoring it. Sawyer, on the other hand, aspired to a higher position in that power structure. For that offense alone she could have received her just deserts—a lifetime in an asylum and a local legend that continues to discount her actions as those of a mad woman—though the historical record does not reveal the precise reasons for her asylum commitment. The lives of DeCrow and Sawyer indicate the struggle women faced in challenging the dominant culture's notion of Anglo womanhood. The legends of Virgin Mary and Mollie Monroe poignantly reveal the nature and extent of the ideological obstacles they encountered in that struggle.

CONCLUSIONS

Mary DeCrow's marriage to Cornelius Ramos in 1865, after a year or so of cohabitation, coincided with, and perhaps can be explained by, the start of a major shift in the ways central Arizona mining-town women conducted their intimate relationships and organized their households. That same shift helps to account for Sawyer's expulsion from the community in the 1870s. In 1864, just a year after the initial gold strikes, 45 percent of the forty women enumerated by the census taker lived with men, while another 18 percent lived without male companionship. Only 37 percent were married and living with their husbands.[39] By 1870 the female population had more than quadrupled to 170 women, and the percentage cohabiting with men had dropped to 4 percent. A full 43 percent were not economically bound to a husband or male lover. But in 1870 the majority, 53 percent, were married women who dwelled with their husbands. Among Mexican women the percentages differed: half were not living with husbands or male companions, while 42 percent were married and 8 percent still cohabited with men.[40] This shift did not reflect a wholesale movement toward marriage among those who formerly had cohabited with their companions, notwithstanding the case of Mary DeCrow. It reflected the exodus of early immigrants to the gold fields and the constant influx of new settlers.[41] The later immigrants created a new ethnic balance in central Arizona as well; the Mexican female population doubled between 1864 and 1870, while twelves times as many Anglo women appeared on the census rolls as were counted just six years earlier. By 1870, then, not only did the female population comprise a virtually new set of individuals; it was also now predominantly Anglo rather than predominantly Mexican.

What do these facts indicate about the women who lived with men in central Arizona between 1863 and 1873? First, the nature, meaning, and consequences of cohabitation differed according to a woman's ethnicity and that of her companion. For Mexican women, informal union existed as a cultural category in a way that it did not for Anglo women. Despite changes over time, then, Mexican women were always more apt than Anglos to set up households with men. When a Mexican woman moved in with a Mexican man, she could expect, first, to share with him a similar understanding of their partnership and, second, to move through her own ethnic community relatively free from public censure. When she lived with an Anglo man, however, in addition to intimacy and economic security, she may have encountered miscommunications (with her companion), hostility (from her Anglo neighbors), and resultant isolation, at least to the extent that her companion and neighbors perpetuated the dominant culture's racism and double standard of sexual morality. The tiny handful of Anglo women who cohabited with men flew in the face of that same double standard. Because there were so few such women and because their numbers did not change significantly over time, their relationships represent anomalous cases that probe the boundaries of Anglo prescriptions for female behavior.

Second, the decrease in the percentage of Mexican women who lived with men (from 55 percent in 1864 to 8 percent in 1870) indicates that the phenomenon of informal union was more than a simple reconstruction of traditional Mexican culture in central Arizona. By comparison, in Los Angeles between 1850 and 1880, the proportion of unmarried couples, taken as a percentage of all couples who lived together, held quite constant between 7 and 8 percent.[42] (If the central Arizona data are considered in this manner, one finds that in 1864, 65 percent of all unions involving a Mexican woman were informal, whereas in 1870, only 16 percent of them were.) The comparative data suggest that these nonmarital relationships, while grounded in Mexican cultural patterns, were especially well suited to the vagaries of mining-town life, particularly in the tumultuous months of the initial boom. The subsequent decline in the proportion of women who lived with men, and the accompanying increase in the proportion who married or lived without male companionship, came as a consequence of stabilizing conditions in the mining area and perhaps also as a response to the consolidation of Anglo dominance in the area. But the gold-rush phenomenon of widespread informal union among Mexican women represents their creative adaptation of a cultural tradition to circumstances where intimacy, economic security, and an ease of coming together were at a premium.

Notes

I would like to thank Estelle Freedman, David Gutierrez, Elizabeth Jameson, Mary Rothschild, and members of the women's history dissertation reading group at Stanford University—Sue Cobble, Gary Sue Goodman, Yukiko Hanawa, Sue Lynn, Valerie Matsumoto, Peggy Pascoe, and Linda Schott—for helpful comments on earlier versions of this paper.

1. *Arizona Miner* (Fort Whipple), 9 Apr. 1864. See also *Arizona Miner,* 20 Apr., 11 May, 6 July, 7 Sept. 1864; and *1864 Census of the Arizona Territory* (Territorial Copy), Department of Library and Archives, Arizona State Capitol, Phoenix (hereafter cited as *1864 Census*).

2. *Weekly Arizona Miner* (Prescott), 13 Mar. 1869.

3. On Anglo racism and the imposition of Anglo dominance in the Southwest, see David J. Weber, " 'Scarce More Than Apes': Historical Roots of Anglo American Stereotypes of Mexicans in the Border Regions," in David J. Weber, ed., *New Spain's Far Northern Frontier* (Albuquerque: University of New Mexico Press, 1979); S. Dale McLemore, "The Origins of Mexican American Subordination in Texas," *Social Science Quarterly* 53, no. 4 (1973): 656–70; Mario Barrera, *Race and Class in the Southwest: A Theory of Racial Inequality* (Notre Dame, Ind.: University of Notre Dame Press, 1979), esp. pp. 7–57; Rudolfo Acuña, "Sonora Invaded: The Occupation of Arizona," in *Occupied America: A History of Chicanos,* 2d ed. (New York: Harper & Row, 1981), esp. pp. 73–94; Richard Griswold del Castillo, *The Los Angeles Barrio, 1850–1890: A Social History* (Berkeley: University of California Press, 1979), esp. pp. 30–61; Albert Camarillo, *Chicanos in a Changing Society: From Mexican Pueblos to American Barrios in Santa Barbara and Southern California, 1848–1930* (Cambridge, Mass.: Harvard University Press, 1979), esp. pp. 33–78. On the exclusion of Mexican workers from California mining towns, see Leonard Pitt, " 'Greasers' in the Diggings: Californians and Sonorans under Attack," in *The Decline of the Californios: A Social History of the Spanish-Speaking Californians, 1846– 1890* (Berkeley: University of California Press, 1966), pp. 48–68. On discriminatory laws against Mexican miners in central Arizona, see Robert L. Spude, "The Walker-Weaver Diggings and the Mexican Placero, 1863–1864," *Journal of the West* 14 (October, 1975): 64–74.

4. Hayden Biographical Files ("Henry Augustus Bigelow"), Arizona Collection, Hayden Library, Arizona State University, Tempe (hereafter cited as Arizona Collection, Tempe).

5. *1864 Census.*

6. For a more thorough analysis of Anglo racist and sexist conceptions of Mexican women, see Beverly Trulio, "Anglo-American Attitudes Toward New Mexican Women," *Journal of the West* 12 (1973): 229–39.

7. See Woodrow Borah and Sherburne F. Cook, "Marriage and Legitimacy in Mexican Culture: Mexico and California," *California Law Review* 54 (May, 1966): 946–1008, esp. pp. 960–61; Ramon Arturo Gutierrez, "Marriage, Sex and the Family: Social Change in Colonial New Mexico, 1690–1846" (Ph.D. diss., University of Wisconsin—Madison, 1980), pp. 115–40.

8. *Arizona Miner* (Fort Whipple), 9 Apr. 1864.

9. *1864 Census.*

10. *Census of the Inhabitants of Yavapai County, Arizona* (April, 1866), Arizona Collection, Tempe (hereafter cited as *1866 County Census*).

11. Unidentified clipping (ca. 1879), Obituary Books, vol. 3, Sharlot Hall Museum Library and Archives, Prescott, Ariz. (hereafter cited as Sharlot Hall Museum, Prescott).

12. See, e.g., the obituary for Dr. Charles Leib, *Arizona Miner* (Prescott), 15 Feb. 1865.

13. Lois A. [Whitcomb] Boblett Reminiscences, Sharlot Hall Museum, Prescott, p. 25.

14. That there is no record of the woman's response does not necessarily indicate that she had none. If she did not respond, perhaps her experience with Anglo dominance, which included the imposition of Anglo social and sexual ideals, had taught her the futility of such violent reaction. At the same time, her connection with the Mexican community in Prescott may have minimized any importance she may have attached to the Anglo community's exclusive gatherings.

15. *1864 Census.*

16. See, e.g., Jane Dysart, "Mexican Women in San Antonio, 1830–1860: The Assimilation Process," *Western Historical Quarterly* 7, no. 4 (October, 1976): 365–75; Darlis A. Miller, "Cross-Cultural Marriages in the Southwest: The New Mexico Experience, 1846– 1900," *New Mexico Historical Review* 57, no. 4 (October, 1982): 335–59.

17. Borah and Cook, "Marriage and Legitimacy"; see also Gutierrez, "Marriage, Sex and the Family." The summary of Spanish and Mexican informal union is based on these studies.

18. Borah and Cook note that a similar double standard operated among the middle and upper classes in Mexico at least through the nineteenth century; pp. 960–62; see also Gutierrez. For a review of the literature dealing with the American double standard, see Estelle B. Freedman, "Sexuality in Nineteenth-Century America: Behavior, Ideology and Politics," *Reviews in American History* 10, no. 4 (December, 1982): 196–216.

19. *1864 Census; 1870 Census Population Schedules of Arizona* (Washington, D.C.: National Archives Microfilm Publications, 1965); hereafter cited as *1870 Census*.

20. What other blacks called Brown is unknown. The name "Negro Brown" appears in sources generated by Anglos, as does the name "Nigger Brown." Unidentified newspaper clippings in Biographical File and in "Tales of Prescott" Notebook, and Sharlot Hall's notes in Biographical File, Sharlot Hall Museum, Prescott; Biographical File, Benjamin Sacks Collection, Arizona Historical Foundation, Hayden Library, Arizona State University, Tempe (hereafter cited as Arizona Historical Foundation, Tempe).

21. An unidentified clipping from the *Tucson Star* in Scrapbook No. 1, Sharlot Hall Museum, Prescott, states that Brown slew his master in Texas and that "throughout all his wanderings . . . he was accompanied by his slain master's wife, . . . who is said to be yet living in the northern part of the Territory." DeCrow was indeed known as Mary Brown at one time, and she did hail from Texas; this evidence suggests, but is not sufficient to prove, that she was the wife of Brown's deceased owner. The *1864 Census* lists "Mary Brown" as a forty-two-year-old laundress from Texas. Her obituary (Biographical File, Sharlot Hall Museum, Prescott) states that she was born in 1819 and that her parents belonged to the Austin Colony.

22. *1864 Census*. The relationship between Santa Lopez and Negro Brown is the only documented union of a Mexican woman and a black man during this period. Directly below Santa Lopez's name Read listed an infant named "Mariana Bran"—perhaps a misspelling or mistranscription of Mariana Brown.

23. Sharlot Hall's notes and unidentified newspaper clipping in Biographical File, Sharlot Hall Museum, Prescott; *1866 County Census*. The name "Ramos" also appears as "Ramez" and "Reamis" in various sources. The historical record reveals little else about Mary Ramos, save a newspaper report that Indians had attempted to ambush her on the road, and another item detailing the Ramoses' sale of their ranch and mining property and their subsequent move to a spot farther up Lynx Creek. See *Weekly Arizona Miner* (Prescott), 13 Mar. 1869 and 4 June 1870.

24. See "Tales of Prescott" clipping; Charles H. Dunning and Edward Peplow, *Rocks to Riches: The Story of American Mining . . . Past, Present and Future . . . As Reflected in the Colorful History of Mining in Arizona, the Nation's Greatest Bonanza* (Phoenix: Southwest Publishing Co., 1959), p. 69; Orick Jackson, *The White Conquest of Arizona: History of the Pioneers* (Los Angeles: West Coast Magazine, 1908), p. 32.

25. "Tales of Prescott" clipping.

26. Glenn Chesney Quiett, *Pay Dirt: A Panorama of American Gold-Rushes* (Lincoln, Nebr.: Johnsen Publishing Co., 1971), p. 400.

27. Dunning and Peplow, *Rocks to Riches,* p. 69.

28. E.g., the *Arizona Miner* (Prescott), 10 Aug. 1867, notes that "Joe and Molly went to La Paz, got married, and are back in Wickenburg enjoying the honeymoon."

29. *1870 Census*.

30. *Weekly Arizona Miner* (Prescott), 23 Mar. 1872. Besides her prospecting work Mary Sawyer was also involved in financial aspects of mining in central Arizona. In 1871, for example, she sold two hundred feet in the Tiger Lode to two Anglo businessmen (*Weekly Arizona Miner,* 24 June 1871).

31. *Territory of Arizona* v. *Mary E. Sawyer or Mollie Monroe,* Probate Records Book 1a, pp. 378–79, Yavapai County, Prescott, Ariz. (1877); *Weekly Arizona Miner* (Prescott), 11 May and 18 May 1877; *Prescott Courier,* 27 Nov. 1902.

32. *Weekly Arizona Miner* (Prescott), 16 Nov. 1877.

33. *Arizona Sentinel* (Yuma), 2 Nov. 1878.

34. *Weekly Arizona Miner* (Prescott), 30 Jan. 1880.

35. *Arizona Gazette* (Phoenix), 28 Apr. 1895.

36. *Arizona Daily Star* (Tucson), 28 Apr. 1895.

37. *Arizona Republican* (Phoenix), 30 Apr. 1895. See also *Arizona Gazette* (Phoenix), 30 Apr. 1895; and *Arizona Daily Star* (Tucson), 1 May 1895. On cross-dressing women in the West, see San Franciso Lesbian and Gay History Project, *"She Even Chewed Tobacco": Passing Women in Nineteenth-Century America* (Berkeley, Calif.: Iris Films, 1983), slide-tape.

38. *Arizona Journal-Miner* (Prescott), 30 Dec. 1897, 24 Nov. 1902. An early version of this story appeared in the *San Francisco Mail* in 1877, just after Sawyer had been transferred to San Quentin. The *Mail* account (apparently written by a former Arizonan who knew Sawyer) states that Sawyer was from California and that "unrequited love drove [her] from her home . . . to seek refuge in the wilds of Arizona. In company with a party of prospectors she started for the Territory on horseback, dressed in male attire, and [from then on she] led a gypsy life." No copies of the *San Francisco Mail* for this date are extant. See clipping in Scrapbook no. 1, and Sharlot Hall's notes from that article in Notebook no. 2, both at Sharlot Hall Museum, Prescott. Comparison of the 1877 story with the 1897 and 1902 versions reveals the elaborate "Mollie Monroe" legend that Arizonans constructed between the time of her asylum commitment and her death.

39. *1864 Census*.

40. *1870 Census*.

41. In 1870, only ten of the fifty women and girls who had immigrated to central Arizona by 1864 (or eight of the original forty adult women) remained.

42. Richard Griswold del Castillo, *The Los Angeles Barrio, 1860–1890: A Social History* (Berkeley: University of California Press, 1979), pp. 67–68. Griswold del Castillo studies informal unions "as a percentage of the married couples in Los Angeles," while I focus on the proportion of women involved in informal unions as a percentage of all adult women. Thus, our statistics cannot be compared directly.

PART THREE

Emotional Continuities

When Euro-Americans settled in the West, how did they learn to live in the new and strange place in which they found themselves? Historians have developed two major theories. Frederick Jackson Turner claimed that the settlers adopted simpler modes of social organization than those they left behind, and finally evolved new, more democratic forms. In other words, the new environment forced them to adapt. The second, more recent theory, first argued by Earl Pomeroy,[1] maintained that the striking thing about Euro-American settlement was the absence of adaptation. Pomeroy asserted that settlers repeated the eastern patterns they left behind.

These two conflicting theories were formulated before women's history existed as a scholarly field. In both cases, male examples were used throughout for explanation and illustration. Doubtless, if they thought about it at all, Turner and Pomeroy intended their theories to include women as well as men. But do they in fact explain the experiences of western women? Conversely, what light does the experience of western women shed on the historical controversy between the two theories? It is not surprising that these topics are very much at issue among historians of western women, for the questions reflect the need to find the appropriate context in which to place pioneer women. What values and attitudes did women bring with them to the West? What did they hold on to, and what did they discard? What factors affected their choices?

We know, of course, that only a large number of specific and detailed studies will answer these questions adequately. As a starting point, the articles in this section focus on the attitudes that pioneer women brought to the West. The authors explore women's personal and emotional attitudes, with which conventional history has had little concern. And while traditional history commonly focuses on changes in the public sphere, these authors document both change and continuity in private life.

Historians of women frequently confront a paucity of information about women in customary historical sources. Increasingly we have found ourselves turning to diaries, letters, and women's literature. The authors in this section have found their source material in literature. The different literary techniques they employ in the following articles are all useful tools in the effort to understand the lives of women in the past.

Note

1. Earl Pomeroy, "Toward a Reorientation of Western History: Continuity and Environment," *Mississippi Valley Historical Review* 41 (March, 1955); 579–600.

7

Laura, Ma, Mary, Carrie, and Grace: Western Women as Portrayed by Laura Ingalls Wilder

KATHRYN ADAM

One of the warmest, most appealing portraits of a nineteenth-century western family we have was painted by Laura Ingalls Wilder in the "Little House" books. In this article, Kathryn Adam uses Wilder's fictional work as a historical resource to shed light on the role expectations and feelings of western women. Adam approaches the books straightforwardly, describing the attitudes of the different female characters. Not surprisingly, we find that "Ma" Ingalls embodies the virtues of the traditional domestic woman, while her daughter Laura, influenced by the sweep and beauty of the prairies, has a freer sense of woman's possibilities. This generational difference in attitude, so plain to see in this family-focused saga, has yet to be fully explored by historians of western women. It seems a fruitful approach.

Working from childhood memories, Laura Ingalls Wilder created a series of seven historical novels for children called the "Little House" books. They described pioneering in Wisconsin, Minnesota, Kansas, and South Dakota during the last quarter of the nineteenth century. Laura's family—her parents, the restless Charles Ingalls and the home-loving Caroline Ingalls, and their four daughters, Mary, Laura, Carrie, and Grace—made seven major geographic moves and countless shorter ones in an almost nomadic search for personal freedom and improved economic opportunity. They left Pepin, Wisconsin, in 1868 to homestead near Independence, Kansas, scene of *Little House on the Prairie*. In 1870 they returned to Pepin, the setting for *Little House in the Big Woods*, Wilder's first book. In 1874 they left Pepin again and settled in Walnut Grove, Minnesota, literally *On the Banks of Plum Creek*. After a series of misfortunes, including crop failures and the grasshopper plagues of the 1870s, the family moved in 1876 to Burr Oak, Iowa, to help run a hotel; the venture proved unsuccessful. En route to Burr Oak, an infant son, Frederick Ingalls, died; there is no Little House book covering this painful period in the Ingalls family history. In 1877 the family returned to Walnut Grove but enjoyed no greater prosperity; an additional blow in 1879 was the onset of Mary Ingalls's blindness, a complication of scarlet fever. When homesteading opened in Dakota Territory in 1879, the Ingallses followed the railroad-building crews

The Ingalls family in 1891. Seated, left to right: Caroline ("Ma"), Charles ("Pa"), and Mary. Standing, left to right: Carrie, Laura, and Grace. Courtesy The Laura Ingalls Wilder Memorial Society, Inc., DeSmet, South Dakota.

west into the new land and established a homestead at De Smet, D.T., in 1880, a period detailed in *By the Shores of Silver Lake.* Wilder's next book, *The Long Winter,* describes the harrowing winter of 1880–1881, when De Smet homesteaders, including the Ingallses, nearly starved to death because trains could not reach them through record cold and blizzards. The subject of *Little Town on the Prairie* was the physical and cultural growth of De Smet during the early 1880s, a period coinciding closely with Laura's own adolescence. The final volume of the series, *These Happy Golden Years,* describes Laura's early teaching experiences, the family's brief period of relative prosperity, and Laura's courtship and marriage to Almanzo Wilder. One other volume in the series, *Farmer Boy,* is a delightful account of Almanzo's childhood in upstate New York. There are also three posthumous publications of Laura Wilder's diaries and letters, *The First Four Years, On the Way Home,* and *West from Home,* but for the most part these fall outside the period and themes under consideration here.

During this entire erratic migration westward, Laura Ingalls was being reared by fairly conventional late-Victorian standards; however, in a family of sisters, she functioned by necessity (and often by preference) as her father's "right-hand man" in the arduous tasks of homesteading. The family's history and Laura's role in it meant that she lived a life in many ways typical of, and in a few ways unique to, western pioneer women. But Laura was singularly equipped to render for us an accurate historical and psychological portrait of the western woman's experience. Her artist's eye for the particular (honed by being "eyes" for the blind Mary) and her profound sense of place enabled her to articulate that experience as few others have. In Wilder's books we encounter women engaged in the rigors of homesteading, women building community and culture on the frontier, women working to preserve the family in the face of bitter adversity—all through her artful portrayal of a handful of women's lives in a series of vividly realized frontier landscapes. I propose to reacquaint you with Wilder's women, their characters, their concerns, and the homely details of their daily lives. It is also my contention, from a thorough study of the books and the extant scholarship on them, that Wilder viewed her frontier experience as essentially positive and intended her writing to convey a sense that her experience, though "hard" by some standards, was valuable, meaningful, and in some respects personally liberating. Exploring chiefly what we learn about women in the Little House books, I will occasionally add historical facts when such additions can enlarge our understanding. We will touch on most of the major themes, events, and issues of western pioneer farm women's lives, because Laura Ingalls Wilder so thoroughly re-created that world.

THE LITTLE HOUSE BOOKS AS HISTORICAL RESOURCES

Recent scholarship, most notably that by Donald Zochert and Rosa Ann Moore, suggests that the Little House books are, to a greater extent than was realized in the years immediately following their publication, works of fiction rather than pure autobiography. The historical facts, actual characters (often given real names), and real geographic localities of Wilder's life were created and shaped for definite literary ends by a conscious artist. Zochert's research, which culminated in a biography of Wilder,[1] has clearly shown, for instance, that the sequence of events in the Little House books is not always historically accurate and that events which an "objective" observer might have considered important have been excluded for one reason or another. Zochert was able to base his research on Wilder's hand-written memoir, a rough compilation of her experiences, from which she later fashioned her novels. Rosa Ann Moore, by comparing draft manuscripts of the books with the published versions, has ably illustrated the process by which the writer Wilder created fiction, that is, further distilled the "primary source" material of young-girl-Laura's raw experience: how characters were built by repetition of telling detail, how events were sequenced to build dramatic tension, how all that was extraneous in raw experience was pared away to obtain the desired effect.[2] This "desired effect" was twofold. The first, of course, was to tell some good stories well: "the story of Pa and the panther," "the story of Laura's first day at school," "the story of Nellie at Laura's party," etc. The second effect, more difficult to achieve, was the integration of these loosely related stories into a form that (1) showed the development of a set of characters over time, (2) traced threads of connection, or meaning, from event to event, and (3) left the reader with some sense of closure or wholeness at the conclusion. The "truth" achieved by such means is not the truth of verifiable historical fact, but the "truth" of fiction: what Wilder's daughter Rose Wilder Lane called "the meaning underlying facts." [3] Thus we cannot accept Wilder's accounts of her frontier experience in a totally literal fashion, but if we want to know what the experience felt like, what it meant to the women who lived it (and I suggest that is what we most especially *would* like to know), Wilder's fiction is an admirable source of data.

An additional level of complexity in using Wilder's fiction as resource concerns its authorship. One myth that must be laid to rest is that the Little House books were the naïve masterpieces of a literary Grandma Moses, a Laura Ingalls Wilder who sat down at her desk at age sixty-five and wrote eight perfectly graduated novels for children directly from her life experience. Both Zochert's and Moore's research has shown that, in fact, Rose Wilder Lane, a highly successful journalist and novelist, played an important collaborative role in the writing of the Little House books. Moore summarizes the evidence, from Wilder correspondence, of Rose's heavy artistic and editorial involvement in Laura's writing by saying, "The Little House books . . . are the legacy of a unique mother-daughter team, one providing the objectivity and the craft, the other bringing the life and the perspective." [4]

A final difficulty: Wilder wrote her books for children. We gain from this the freshness of viewpoint, the absence of sentimentality, and the beautiful simplicity of language that make these books classics. What we possibly lose is "adult" information about women's lives that we might have liked to have: we find no mention of sexuality, childbirth, or menstruation, for instance, in these stories of a family with five women in it. Yet it is doubtful that, even had she written for adults, a woman of Laura's generation and class would have discussed these topics.

In a personal correspondence women's studies scholar Elizabeth Hampsten has suggested to me that Wilder wrote for children so as not to upset her family with views and values of the pioneer experience that might be incompatible with their interpretation of it. I believe that this view contradicts the sense of Wilder's philosophy about pioneer life that we get from her books and from essays and letters in her collected works. Each book reaffirms her belief in the character-building qualities of the frontier experience for both men and women. She repeatedly shows the values of hard work, personal stoicism, courage, cheerfulness, family solidarity, and a positive outlook as both survival tools and sources of admirable character. Perhaps a brief quotation from Wilder's correspondence with Rose Lane during the writing of *By the Shores of Silver Lake* exemplifies the interpretation she characteristically applied to her experience. "On page 12 of

Silver Lake, as I wrote it, you will find the financial situation. Not 'poverty worse than ever' as you put it, but as I have said" (letter of 17 August 1938). Rosa Ann Moore comments on this statement:

"Poverty" is a word that the socially conscious New Yorker Rose might apply; it is a word used by outsiders to describe the material, social, and perhaps moral deprivation of some group of persons other than themselves; hence, its tone is condescending. Acceptance of its application to oneself is self-pitying. The young Laura would have seen none of these connotations in her own situation, nor would the older Laura have associated them with her earlier life.[5]

With these considerations as prologue, then, let us turn to Laura Wilder's western pioneer women.

"MA": CAROLINE QUINER INGALLS (1839–1924)

In an elegant study on "intimate immensity" as a theme of the Little House books, Dolores Rosenblum has said:

The basic "human" plot of all the narratives . . . is "to survive," that is, to learn the rules—and internalize them so that you can enjoy life as a civilized human being. . . . Wilder's central metaphor for the process of human survival and development always involves the problem of inhabiting space: how do you fill with your presence an emptiness that threatens to affect you? The narratives thus are organized around a variety of habitations constructed against and in compliance with the vast outer space surrounding the human figures.[6]

She goes on to say that the little house in the Big Woods—which the family leaves when Pa, a spiritual descendant of Daniel Boone in his quest for ever more "elbow room," begins to feel "crowded"—becomes the prototypical house for the Ingallses, the "mental diagram" of home that they will seek to re-create from the materials at hand wherever they go.[7]

It was chiefly Ma, Caroline Quiner Ingalls, who had to reconstruct that homelike place in the succession of log cabins, shanties, and little frame houses the Ingalls family inhabited as they moved westward. In every book we learn how red-checked tablecloths, bedsheet curtains, Ma's plump down pillows, and patchwork quilts made the most pinched and unlikely of habitations—for instance, the dirt-floored, one-room railroad shanty at Silver Lake—a home.

Wilder's symbol for Ma's homemaking function was the china shepherdess, a pretty knickknack that stood on a beautifully carved wooden bracket in the place of honor in each Ingalls house. The members of the family always knew that they were cosily settled when Ma asked Pa to nail up the bracket for the china shepherdess.

In Wilder's books her mother is almost invariably characterized as a personality of quiet strength. Ma's voice was usually soft and gentle; she tried to train her daughters to her own discreet murmur. In the early books it might be easy to see her as someone wholly dominated by her outgoing, adventuresome husband. "Whatever you say, Charles," "Whatever you think best, Charles," she responded when Pa consulted her about decisions involving the family. But it becomes clear as the books progress, and as Pa's itchy foot drove the family back and forth across the prairie, that Caroline Ingalls had a personal goal—the education of her daughters—that ultimately she would not see lost to Pa's hunger for new wildernesses to conquer. To Ma, who had been a teacher before her marriage, education was a prerequisite of civilization, a way for her daughters to participate in the larger world of the mind. She was adamant about not getting so far out on the frontier as to be beyond adequate schools.

The Ingallses' marriage, although clearly constructed along patriarchal lines, can be seen as a series of dynamic negotiations to maintain a mutually satisfying balance between his urge to go and her desire to stay put. Often the balance leaned more heavily toward Pa's side. Wilder describes Ma after they had left Plum Creek and were traveling by wagon, alone, to De Smet. The family had just narrowly missed being waylaid by a roving prairie gunman:

Ma looked back to see that her girls were all right, and she held Grace snugly on her lap. She did not say anything because nothing she could say would make any difference. But Laura knew that Ma had never wanted to leave Plum Creek and did not like to be here now; she did not like traveling in that lonely country with night coming on and such men riding the prairie.[8]

On another occasion, Ma had it her way, with an electrifying effect on the family. In a scene from *The Long Winter,* Pa proposed leaving the starving family to go out on the prairie and search for a man whose stored seed wheat crop could help the town survive the winter.

"I trust you aren't thinking of starting out on such a wild-goose chase, Charles," Ma said gently.

"A fellow might do it," Pa remarked. "With a couple of days of clear weather and a snowfall to hold up the sled, he ought to be able to make it all ri. . . . "

"No!" said Ma.

Pa looked at her, startled. They all stared at her. They had never seen Ma look like that. She was quiet but she was terrible.

Quietly she told Pa, "I say, No. You don't take such a chance."

"Why . . . Caroline!" Pa said.

"Your hauling hay is bad enough," Ma told him. *"You don't go hunting for that wheat."*

Pa said mildly, "Not as long as you feel that way about it, I won't. But . . . "

"I won't hear any buts," Ma said, still terrible. "This time I put my foot down."

"All right, that settles it," Pa agreed.

Laura and Carrie looked at each other. They felt as if thunder and lightning had come down on them suddenly, and suddenly gone. Ma poured the tea with a trembling hand.[9]

Wilder summed up in her memoir the working paradox of Ma and Pa's marriage: "Ma did follow Pa wherever he went, but Pa never went anywhere that Ma wouldn't follow."[10] This constantly negotiated equilibrium in a frontier marriage was perhaps unique; one gets the sense from many other accounts (cf. Fischer, Stratton, Schlissel[11]) that women were oftener than not dragged west by their husbands, silently hating it all the way.

But if the Ingallses were fairly unusual in their respectful negotiation of marital compromises, they were much like other frontier families in the way they assigned the tasks to be accomplished for the pioneer enterprise to succeed. Someone, preferably a woman, was needed to do the "woman's work" of cooking, homemaking, and child rearing and do it well. The success of Pa's efforts in farming, hunting, and building rested as surely on Ma's work as she depended on him for what he could provide. In Caroline Ingalls, Pa had found a worthy and willing teammate for this project. Ma grew and preserved all her own vegetables; made her own butter, cheese, brown sugar, sausage, and lard; sewed all her own and her children's clothes (without a sewing machine until 1885); knitted mittens, socks, and mufflers; made rag dolls; wove straw hats; cooked the daily meals over campfires, in fireplaces, or on woodburning stoves; kept the house clean whether the floor was dirt, puncheon logs, or wooden boards; and raised four daughters, one of whom was handicapped. We must also add that beyond "woman's work" Ma at one time or another in her pioneer career put out prairie fires, scared off wolves, placated hostile Indians, and helped build a log cabin.

The beautiful quality of the Ingallses' marriage, and surely part of the books' great charm, was that Ma and Pa regularly acknowledged one another's contributions in front of their children. Pa was quick with praise for Ma's housekeeping, for her endurance, for the way she could improvise in a tight situation. In the Ingalls family "woman's work" was seen as a matter of skill and achievement, and it could be a legitimate source of a woman's self-esteem. While it is true that Laura, for one, found a woman's traditional role limiting for someone of her energy and interests, at least womanly achievements were held in high regard by family and the larger community, not only because they signified the performance of an appropriate role but also because the things women knew how to do made a respected contribution to family and community life.

Ma's ability to improvise deserves some attention. Faced often, as were many pioneer women, with providing the necessities of life far from the conveniences of town, or when money was tight or weather hostile, Ma coped—with the ingenuity and pluck that so often marked the pioneer character. When blackbirds invaded the Ingallses' cornfield and ate the entire crop, Ma made blackbird pie from the birds Pa shot in an effort to control them.[12] In another year of sparse harvests, when an early blizzard prevented the garden's pumpkins from ripening, ma invented green pumpkin pie, which, by Laura's testimony, tasted exactly like apple pie and was a great treat for the family.[13] The "long winter" of 1880–1881 put Ma's ingenuity to its severest test. As the family's food supply slowly dwindled and trains could not reach the isolated town through endless blizzards, Ma fed her family on potatoes, served every possible way, and brown bread made by grinding hard wheat, one cup at a time, in the coffee mill. A small can of oysters in watery broth became a festive Christmas meal in

Ma's talented hands. When kerosene ran out, leaving the family without light in the evenings, Ma made a button lamp from axle grease, flannel, and a button, which provided a candlelike light for many nights.[14]

In this long, terrible winter, and in many that had preceded it, Ma's contributions to the family welfare were more than physical ones. Pa provided the fiddle music for singing and dancing on cold winter nights; Ma was a source of games to play, stories to hear read aloud, poems, speeches, and Bible verses to recite. Especially during the grasshopper years at Plum Creek, when Pa left for months to earn money working in the unspoiled harvests back East, Ma was the emotional as well as physical bulwark of the family. Such heroism took its toll—the stoic Ma wept openly when she had a letter from Pa saying that he would soon be home[15]—but Ma endured and brought the family through these lonely times.

Caroline Ingalls shared another characteristic with her frontier sisters. She was highly instrumental in the re-creation of community institutions and standards in the raw towns of the West. She and Pa were charter members of the Walnut Grove Congregational Church, and the first church services in De Smet were held at the Ingallses' temporary home on Silver Lake. She showed an interest in temperance, too. When Laura witnessed (and enjoyed) the antics of two happy drunks leaving one of De Smet's saloons, Ma bristled, "I begin to believe that if there isn't a stop put to the liquor traffic, women must bestir themselves and have something to say about it." [16]

Wilder left us with an image for her mother's character that goes far in conveying Caroline's essence. At the end of the "long winter" the family received a "missionary barrel" from back East with clothing for each member of the family. Among the items was a lovely shawl:

"Oh, Mary!" Laura said. "The most beautiful thing—a shawl made of silk! It is dove-colored, with fine stripes of green and rose and black and the richest, deep fringe with all those colors shimmering in it. Feel how soft and rich and heavy the silk is," and she put a corner of the shawl in Mary's hand.

"Oh, lovely!" Mary breathed.

"Who gets this shawl?" Pa asked, and they all said, "Ma!" Such a beautiful shawl was for Ma, of course. Pa laid it on her arm, and it was like her, so soft and yet firm and well-wearing, with the fine, bright colors in it.[17]

"LAURA": LAURA INGALLS WILDER (1867–1957)

Of course, Laura Ingalls Wilder portrayed herself with some consistency as the family rebel, although we must understand her rebelliousness within the rather narrow confines of the behavior expected of "nice" nineteenth-century children. Laura had energy, imagination, stubbornness, and passionate feeling; in her socially conventional family, where children were expected not to speak unless spoken to, to conceal emotion, especially tears, and to spend Sundays in quiet reading, Laura often experienced herself as "naughty." She also contrasted herself unfavorably with her sister Mary, who was temperamentally calm and quiet.

Laura realized that there were additional behavioral expectations placed on her because she was a girl. Quietness was especially prized in girls, because it meant they were appropriately ladylike. Throughout the books we find Laura chafing mildly at these restraints, wishing occasionally that she could do some of the things Pa did. But growing up among sisters, who were expected to behave as she did, may have neutralized the more intense feelings she might have had about these issues if she had had brothers, who would surely have known more opportunities for adventure and freedom than she.

As it was, Laura was the least passive of the four sisters, and makes a lively heroine in her stories. She waged a childhood-long battle against wearing sunbonnets, which were de rigeur for preserving a soft, pale complexion. As she entered her teens, waist-whittling corsets became mandatory, and Laura experienced these, too, as infringements on her freedom. In *Little Town on the Prairie,* as Ma and Laura tightened Mary's corset strings so the new dress they were making her would fit, Carrie commented:

"I'm glad I don't have to wear corsets yet" . . .

"Be glad while you can be," said Laura. "You'll have to wear them pretty soon." Her corsets were a sad affliction to her, from the time she put them on in the morning until she took them off at night. But when girls pinned up their hair and wore skirts down to their shoetops, they must wear corsets.

"You should wear them all night," Ma said. Mary did, but Laura could not bear at night the torment of the steels that would not let her draw a deep breath. Always before she could get to sleep, she had to take off her corsets.

"What your figure will be, goodness know," Ma warned her. "When I was married, your Pa could span my waist with his two hands."

"He can't now," Laura answered, a little saucily. "And he seems to like you." [18]

In spite of the constraints of feminine dress—which included not only sunbonnets and corsets but also in later years bustles, hoops, and knee-length hair to braid up daily—Laura was active and adventurous. She helped Pa in building the claim shanty, took care of chores for chickens and cattle, and carried wood and water for Ma. When the family had a dairy cow, she milked it and churned the butter. In spite of the exposure to "rough men" which it entailed, she talked Pa into taking her to watch the crews building the railroad; she was entranced by the spectacle of men and machines working in dusty harmony. [19] On a number of occasions she helped Pa with the fieldwork, although "Ma did not like to see women working in the fields. Only foreigners did that. Ma and her girls were Americans, above doing men's work." [20] Wilder's account of helping rake and load hay gives us some notion of the grit it took; after her first arduous day, Pa complimented her fine work and "Laura felt proud. Her arms ached and her back ached and her legs ached, and that night in bed she ached all over so badly that tears welled out of her eyes, but she did not tell anyone." [21] She continued to work proudly with Pa until the haying was done, and commented that her arms and legs "got used to the work and did not ache so badly."

Not all of Laura's joy in helping Pa make hay derived from a sense of duty; haying also put her out on the wide prairies that she and Pa both loved. Throughout the books, Laura identifies strongly with Pa's love of the spacious West, the open, untouched grasslands, the wide skies. Some of the most lyric descriptions in the novels are of this virgin land where the Ingalls family are only tiny human figures against a backdrop of endlessly rolling grass. Laura recognized, however, that the same great wilderness could engulf and destroy its human inhabitants—by blizzard and tornado, by its sheer size. Contrast Laura's feelings about the prairie in these scenes:

All around them, to the very edge of the world, there was nothing but grasses waving in the wind. Far overhead, a few white puffs of cloud sailed in the thin blue air.

Laura was very happy. The wind sang a low, rustling song in the grass. Grasshoppers' rasping quivered up from all the trees in the creek bottoms. But all these sounds made a great, warm, happy silence. Laura had never seen a place she liked so much as this place.[22]

And, on an afternoon when baby Grace disappeared from the yard for over an hour:

Laura ran on and on. Grace must have gone this way. Maybe she chased a butterfly. She didn't go into Big Slough! She didn't climb the hill, she wasn't there. Oh, baby sister, I couldn't see you anywhere east or south on this hateful prairie. "Grace!"

The horrible, sunny prairie was so large. No lost baby could ever be found on it.[23]

The rhythm of the Little House books carries Laura back and forth between town and prairie, civilization and wilderness, "stay" and "go"; in a sense she is the living embodiment of the central tension in her parents' marriage. However, we still find in Laura a stronger affirmation of the prairie's powerful beauty than many pioneer women seem to have brought away from the experience of confronting it. Whether this love of the land represents a unique personal strength of Laura's or was the product of her richly secure emotional upbringing it is difficult to say.

The family's economic circumstances plus the blow of Mary's blindness thrust Laura into early maturity. She assumed most of Mary's role as "responsible oldest daughter" in the family; in the later books we find Ma and Pa consulting Laura and planning the future with her as though she were much older. She got her first job, sewing shirts with a seamstress in De Smet, when she was fourteen. (She earned twenty-five cents plus dinner each day, for an eleven-hour day, six days a week.) Only a few months before this, the family had learned of a college for the blind in Iowa; Laura became fired with the idea of enabling Mary to enroll there. She took a number of part-time jobs to add to Mary's college fund. More importantly, she vowed to become a teacher, a goal she pursued relentlessly.

From a twentieth-century perspective, Laura became a teacher for all the wrong reasons: she wanted to please Ma, who had always dreamed that

Mary would become a teacher, and she wanted to earn as much money as she could. Laura hated the idea of being a teacher, but she felt that duty dictated her choice. It is interesting to observe how she lived out this difficult decision; perhaps it tells us a great deal about our foremothers and how they survived psychologically in their world of limited options. Once she had made her choice of profession, Laura determined to be the best teacher she could possibly be. She had found sewing equally onerous; she coped the same way: "She so hated making buttonholes that she had learned to do them quickly, and get it over with." [24] After several summers of intensive study Laura passed the teacher examination in 1882; a week later she began teaching. She was fifteen years old.

Her first frontier teaching experiences are both humorous and sobering to ponder. The efforts of the five-foot, two-inch teen-aged teacher to control her older, larger pupils gave her some bad moments; living conditions at the homestead where she boarded were actually dangerous.

The last books of the series show Laura coming to terms with the demands of nineteenth-century feminine maturity. She began to take an interest in fashion, although one has the refreshing sense that clothes interested her not just as personal adornment but also because she had earned the money herself to purchase beautiful things, and because she enjoyed observing the process which turned lengths of fabric into the intricate costumes of the 1880s. A brief scene in *By the Shores of Silver Lake* fixes on the poignant moment of transition between childhood and maturity as symbolized by clothing.

> Big girl as she was, Laura spread her arms wide to the wind and ran against it. She flung herself on the flowery grass and rolled like a colt. She lay in the soft, sweet grasses and looked at the great blueness above her and the high, pearly clouds sailing in it. She was so happy that tears came into her eyes.
>
> Suddenly she thought, "Have I got a grass stain on my dress?" She stood up and anxiously looked, and there was a green stain on the calico. Soberly she knew that she should be helping Ma, and she hurried to the little dark tar-paper shanty. [25]

Laura began to become interested in, and to receive attention from, young men; she seems to have greatly disliked sentimentality, and the conversations she reports with her eventual husband, Almanzo Wilder, display a rather charming detachment, wit, and humor. Laura married at eighteen, had a daughter, Rose, a year later, and began farming with Almanzo at De Smet.

It is instructive to follow Laura beyond these years, when she had done all that a late-nineteenth-century woman was supposed to do: teach, marry, and produce children. In the first four years after her marriage, Laura's house burned down, she lost an infant son to convulsions, Almanzo's crops failed in years of continuous drought, and Laura and Almanzo nearly died of diphtheria. Almanzo suffered a stroke during his convalescence and never recovered his full strength. After this siege of misfortune the young Wilders moved to Spring Valley, Minnesota, to live with Almanzo's family; then they moved, briefly, to Florida for the climate, but

returned to De Smet in 1892, almost penniless. They both got jobs—
Laura, sewing again—and eventually saved a nest egg of one hundred dollars. In 1894 they courageously loaded up a wagon and migrated to Missouri, where their luck finally changed. They bought a good piece of land;
after ten years of hard work (with Laura often behind a hammer or at one
end of a crosscut saw), they created a prosperous farm, with orchards,
fields, dairy cattle, chickens, and fine Morgan horses. They lived out the
remainder of their long lives there. For a time Laura administered a federal
farm-loan program in her area; she was responsible for handling more
than one million dollars in small loans in the twelve years she held the
job.[26] The final twenty-five years of her life were dominated by the writing,
publication, and attendant fame of the Little House books. All this after
the "happy ending" of marriage and motherhood!

There is much to see and ponder in Laura Wilder's life; there are few
easy generalizations. Her frontier experience, which could have spelled
only hard living conditions, cultural deprivation, and a limited career as
wife and mother, was tempered by the presence of an unusually close and
civilized family. Laura's identification with her adventurous and creative
father, and his mutual high regard for her and her abilities, was one source
of her confidence and self-esteem. Ma's steadiness and strength nurtured
Laura, too, and provided her with the continuity she needed in all the family's journeyings. Finally, there is a heroic dimension to the family's quest
for improved opportunity and their willingness to undergo extreme personal hardship in pursuit of that goal. In our more ambivalent age, with
our knowledge of the double-edged impact pioneering had, for instance,
on the American Indian population, or on the natural environment, or on
women, such heroism is perhaps less admired. Laura's character, for all
her charming rebelliousness and spunk, is thoroughly embedded in the
values of the white, American, male late-nineteenth-century—its expan-
sionism, optimism, and economic individualism. It would be the daughters of Laura's generation who would identify with the dark underside of
the pioneer woman's experience; who would point to its hardships, de-
privations, and inequalities; who would be dissatisfied with their mothers'
melioristic philosophies; and who would recreate their mothers' experiences in literature of a darker, more existential hue. (See, for instance,
Rose Wilder Lane's own reworking of Wilder's stories in her novels *Let the
Hurricane Roar* and *Free Land*.) But for Wilder herself, and probably for
most women who shared the homesteading experience, there was the
sense of having participated zestfully in the Great American Adventure.
Pioneering the frontier was, for Laura, a healthy and confidence-building
experience for a young woman; it required her to face challenges early in
life and to grow strong in meeting them.

"MARY": MARY AMELIA INGALLS (1865–1928)

Although Wilder somewhat exaggerated the portrait of her older sister,
Mary, in the Little House books, to provide a sharper literary contrast, it

seems evident that Mary *was* cut of a different cloth from Laura. Mary was a studious, obedient child; she loved to sew and embroider, to read and partake of indoor pleasures. Laura was occasionally able to draw her into enjoying such rowdy romps as jumping in Pa's carefully stacked straw (for which both girls got in trouble), but more often Mary calmly, and infuriatingly to Laura, tried to correct Laura's "wild" behavior. Mary wore her sunbonnet faithfully; her hair ribbons were always smooth; she always knew her Sunday school lesson. She dreamed of becoming a teacher, as Ma had been.

Fate singled out Mary, of the four sisters, to become blind at the age of fourteen. Though she would never become a teacher, of the four she was the most emotionally capable of the sedentary life of a handicapped nineteenth-century woman. In the years immediately following the onset of Mary's blindness, Ma taught her to navigate her surroundings by setting up the furniture in similar configurations in each house. Laura "saw" for Mary, providing running verbal descriptions of scenes and events as the family traveled, and on daily walks. (It was during these walks that Laura and Mary, as they reached womanhood, reconciled their childhood griev- ances against one another and developed an enduring sisterly love.) Mary learned at home to braid rag rugs. She could set the table by touch, and helped her mother by entertaining baby Grace in her rocking chair near the stove. Her parents encouraged Mary's strong religious faith; they ended by being almost awed at the courage and acceptance with which she met her hard destiny.

In 1881, after much family saving and sacrifice, Mary was enrolled at the Vinton, Iowa, College for the Blind. There, to the family's and Mary's own joy, she was able to study political science, literature, history, and mathematics, and to be trained in Braille, sewing, knitting, beadwork, and music. She spent eight years at Vinton, with occasional summer trips home, and graduated in 1889.

The remainder of Mary's life is a study in quiet endurance. She lived at home and occupied herself with reading, music, sewing, and housework. She was active in her church and often served as organist there. She seems to have maintained a cheerful attitude through most of her quiet life. Her mother's loving devotion to her surely contributed to her optimism; Ma's life seemed to revolve around Mary after Pa died in 1902.[27] Mary lived only four years after Ma's death, and died of a stroke in 1928, at the age of sixty-three.

"CARRIE": CAROLINE INGALLS SWANZEY (1870–1946)
"GRACE": GRACE INGALLS DOW (1877–1941)

Carrie and Grace, Laura's younger sisters, are less clearly portrayed in Wilder's books than are Mary and Laura, although we learn a great deal about the perils of raising children on the frontier in episodes involving them. Grace had to be watched constantly lest she wander away and be- come lost among the tall grasses of the prairie sloughs and hollows. Grace grew restless during the long winters spent in small houses; one can only imagine what it must have been like for Ma to live in essentially one room for four months at a stretch with a toddler and three grade-schoolers.

Carrie, three years younger than Laura, seems to have suffered from poor health, perhaps mild malnutrition, through a good deal of her childhood. Wilder often described her as "peaked," particularly after the "long winter," when the family had subsisted on little more than potatoes and brown bread for months. Early that same winter, Laura and Carrie had nearly been lost in a blizzard as they and their schoolmates tried to walk home from school at the beginning of the storm; the experience was especially hard on Carrie.

In spite of this inauspicious beginning, Carrie went on to lead a long and independent life. In her teens she trained as a typesetter at the *De Smet News,* and later she managed several newspapers in towns all across South Dakota. She homesteaded alone for a time; at forty-one she made a happy marriage with a widower with two children. Her life in Keystone, South Dakota, where the couple settled, was characterized by a high level of active civic involvement.[28]

MINOR CHARACTERS:
OTHER ASPECTS OF WESTERN WOMEN'S LIVES

Several women whose lives impinged on Laura's illustrate some other facets of the pioneer woman's experience.

When Laura took her first teaching job at a small settlement twelve miles south of De Smet, she lived for eight weeks with Louis and Lib Bouchie,[29] called "Mr. and Mrs. Brewster" in *These Happy Golden Years.* Mrs. Bouchie was the embodiment of the pioneer marriage contract gone bad. She had not wanted to homestead; the bleak landscape and winter weather unnerved her; she had no interest in keeping house under frontier conditions. In trying to get along with the sullen woman, Laura learned something that her happy home had not taught her: "that it takes two to make a smile."[30] The tension and misery at the Bouchies' culminated in a night when Mrs. Bouchie, "like a fugitive from *Giants in the Earth,*" says Rosa Ann Moore of this interlude,[31] threatened to murder her husband with a carving knife unless he took her back east. The incident highlights the extent to which a woman had to be committed philosophically to the pioneer experience if she hoped to survive emotionally.

Laura spent the summer of 1882 helping a Mrs. McKee and her small daughter hold down their claim near Manchester, about seven miles from De Smet. Among other provisions, the Homestead Act of 1862 stipulated that, to claim the "free" 160 acres to which a homesteader was entitled, someone had to live on the land at least seven months a year. As Mrs. McKee indignantly pointed out to Laura,

" . . . Whoever makes these laws ought to know that a man that's got enough money to farm, has got enough to buy a farm. If he hasn't got money, he's got to earn it, so why do they make a law that he's got to stay on a claim, when he can't? All it means is, his wife and family have got to sit idle on it, seven months of the year. I could be earning something, dressmaking, to help buy tools and seeds, if somebody didn't have to sit on this claim. I declare to goodness, I don't know but sometimes I believe in women's rights. If women were voting and making laws, I believe they'd have better sense." [32]

Finally, Mrs. Boast, a friend and neighbor of the Ingallses from 1879 on, best illustrates the qualities of a good pioneer neighbor. From the time the two families met at Silver Lake, Mrs. Boast, though many years younger than Ma, was a source of conversation, new ideas, and emotional support for her. Mrs. Boast gave Ma her first setting of chicks to begin a flock; she saved garden seeds for Ma's garden from the supply she brought from Iowa. For many years the Ingalls family and the Boasts celebrated Christmas at the Ingallses' and New Year's at the Boasts', replacing for one another the eastern relatives they would rarely, if ever, see again, the common situation of many pioneer families.

WILDER'S WESTERN PIONEER WOMEN

The lives of late-nineteenth-century western pioneer women as portrayed by Laura Ingalls Wilder shared elements of hard work, ingenuity, endurance, and a measure of personal independence. In these novels, family structures, ostensibly patriarchal and sex-role stereotyped, were flexible to an extent that we would perhaps not have recognized without accounts like Wilder's. (However, Katherine Harris's work, found elsewhere in this volume, corroborates this assertion based on hard historical data.) Wilder's books also depict Ma and the women of her generation working at parallel or cooperative civilizing activities with men in the community, albeit on projects that did seem to stem from womanly or domestic concerns (education, religion, temperance). Finally, the novels describe women engaged in a love-hate affair with the western landscape and climate; their responses often varied by individual personality and tended toward affirmation once some of the prairie's harshness had been blunted by innovation. Wilder's enduring portrait of these women acquaints us with the limitations under which they labored, and enlarges our vision of women's capabilities to act and to survive.

Notes

1. Donald Zochert, *Laura: The Life of Laura Ingalls Wilder* (Chicago: Henry Regnery Co., 1976).

2. Rosa Anna Moore, "Laura Ingalls Wilder's Orange Notebooks and the Art of the Little House Books," in Francelia Butler, et al., eds, *Children's Literature* (Philadelphia, Pa.: Temple University Press, 1975), 4: 105–19.

3. Rosa Anna Moore, "Laura Ingalls Wilder and Rose Wilder Lane: The Chemistry of Collaboration," in *Children's Literature in Education* 11 (Fall, 1980): 101–109.

4. Ibid., p. 108.

5. Ibid., p. 105.

6. Dolores Rosenblum, "Intimate Immensity: Mythic Space in the Work of Laura Ingalls Wilder," in *Where the West Begins: Essays on Middle Border and Siouxland Writings* (Sioux Falls, S. Dak.: Augustana College Center for Western Studies), p. 74.

7. Ibid., p. 75.

8. Laura Ingalls Wilder, *By the Shores of Silver Lake* (New York: Harper & Row, 1939), p. 66.

9. Laura Ingalls Wilder, *The Long Winter* (New York: Harper & Row, 1940), pp. 244–45.

10. Zochert, p. 104.

11. Lillian Schlissel, *Women's Diaries of the Westward Journey* (New York: Schocken Books, 1982); Joanna Stratton, *Pioneer Women: Voices from the Kansas Frontier* (New York: Simon and Schuster, 1981); Christiane Fischer, ed., *Women in the American West* (New York: E. P. Dutton, 1977).

12. Laura Ingalls Wilder, *Little Town on the Prairie* (New York: Harper & Row, 1941), p. 106.

13. Wilder, *The Long Winter*, p. 32.

14. Ibid., p. 197.

15. Laura Ingalls Wilder, *On the Banks of Plum Creek* (New York: Harper & Row, 1937), p. 226.

16. Wilder, *Little Town on the Prairie*, p. 54.

17. Wilder, *The Long Winter*, p. 324.

18. Ibid., pp. 93–94.

19. Wilder, *By the Shores of Silver Lake*, chap. 10.

20. Wilder, *The Long Winter*, p. 24.

21. Ibid., p. 9.

22. Laura Ingalls Wilder, *Little House on the Prairie* (New York: Harper & Row, 1935), p. 49.

23. Wilder, *By the Shores of Silver Lake*, p. 280.

24. Wilder, *Little Town on the Prairie*, p. 46.

25. Ibid., p. 271.

26. William Anderson, *Laura Wilder of Mansfield* (De Smet, S. Dak.: Laura Ingalls Wilder Memorial Society, 1974), p. 12.

27. William Anderson, *The Story of the Ingalls* (De Smet, S. Dak.: Laura Ingalls Wilder Memorial Society, 1971), pp. 24–26.

28. Ibid., pp. 26–29.

29. Zochert, *Laura*, p. 188.

30. Laura Ingalls Wilder, *These Happy Golden Years* (New York: Harper & Row, 1943), p. 23.

31. Moore, "Laura Ingalls Wilder's Orange Notebooks," p. 117.

32. Wilder, *These Happy Golden Years*, p. 119.

8

Violence Against Women: Power Dynamics in Literature of the Western Family [1]

MELODY GRAULICH

Here is a view of the western family horrifyingly at variance with the decent world of Ma and Pa Ingalls and their children. Yet there can be no doubt that wife and child abuse were as prevalent in the West as elsewhere.

"Somebody must say these things," and by saying them, Melody Graulich opens up an important topic for research. As she suggests, violence scars its victims not only physically but psychologically, causing permanent damage to daughters' views of the female role. The previous article suggested the usefulness of generational analysis; this article underlines that point and the need to consider all the relevant evidence, even the unpleasant. The importance of domestic violence as a theme in the literature of western women alerts us to look for its presence in other, nonliterary sources. As a result, we may rethink the theme of violence in traditional western history. Was there a connection between domestic violence, which remained hidden, and the celebration of rarer and more public displays of male violence?

"Somebody must say these things," wrote Mary Austin in 1932 as she prepared to give testimony about one of the most painful secrets of women's lives—violent abuse from a husband or lover. Recalling how a friend of her mother's came in the night "with a great bloody bruise on her face," Austin describes "the unwiped tears on [her] mother's face while the two women kept up between them the pretense of a blameless accident." [2] It is easy to understand why battered wives have kept up the pretense, why women have been reluctant to "say these things" to a society that has until recently covertly sanctioned wife abuse and has failed to listen to those women who did speak. But Austin is right when she suggests that though women may sometimes manage to intervene in individual acts of violence, as she did when she prevented a drunken husband from beating his pregnant wife, they will never stop woman abuse until they begin to speak about it and to analyze its causes.

Although recent data suggest that "more than half of all married women are beaten by their husbands," abuse of women has been an undercover subject in our society, an embarrassing "abnormality" to be concealed,

Jules and Mary Sandoz. Courtesy Mari Sandoz Estate.

and historical information has been difficult to find.[3] Yet isolated voices in
the wilderness, pioneer daughters like Austin, have realized the costs of
concealment and focused on violence against women in their autobiographical narratives, demonstrating its centrality to their understanding of
their mothers'—and their own—lives. I will examine four texts by western women writers which suggest that violence against women was commonplace in the American West: Mari Sandoz's *Old Jules* (1935); Agnes
Smedley's *Daughter of Earth* (1929); Meridel Le Sueur's *The Girl* (written

in 1939, published in 1978); and Tillie Olsen's *Yonnodio* (written between 1932 and 1937, published in 1973).[4] The radical conclusion of these writers—that violence against women is the result of patriarchal definitions of gender and marriage rather than of individual pathology—anticipates the analysis of the most recent feminist scholars.[5] Their books explore not only relations between women and men, but also how watching her mother become a victim of male aggression affects a daughter's complex identification with and resistance to her mother's life. They reveal the struggles women face growing up female in a world where women are victimized and devalued.

The four writers treat violence against women as the widespread and inevitable consequence of the common belief that men have the right to dominate women and to use force to coerce compliance with their wishes. Abuse of women appears as socially acceptable, rather than aberrant, behavior. Sandoz refers to wife abuse as "every husband's right" (p. 412). Le Sueur offers a chorus of male voices: "Thataboy, they shouted from inside, that's the way to treat her. A woman's got to be struck regular like a gong. . . . Knock it into her" (p. 81). Smedley describes how her protagonist Marie "hated [her father] for attacking a woman because she was his wife and the law gave him the right" (p. 106). In these books husbands who beat their wives are not presented as mentally ill, nor is their behavior motivated by events in their personal lives or by their wives' actions, though these may trigger violence. The causes for their brutality are embedded in their society's attitudes about women and marriage and in its sanctioning of male power and authority.

Sandoz conceived her biography of her father, a notorious "locator" in frontier Nebraska, as "the biography of a community, the upper Niobrara country in western Nebraska," and she focuses on her family as representative pioneers (*Old Jules*, p. vii). Exploring the unequal conflict between men and women in the West, Sandoz shows through repeated example that women are often the victims of the West's celebrated freedom. She presents her father as the archetypal frontiersman, whose desire for absolute free will and freedom of action makes him in some ways romantic and heroic, America's much-discussed and well-respected rugged individualist. The frontiersman is usually presented in literature as having only the barest and most stylized relations with women. Sandoz focuses on her father's marriages, and most readers finish the book shocked at his violent treatment of his four wives. When his first wife disobeyed an order, "Jules closed her mouth with the flat of his long muscular hand"; when his second wife asked why he did nothing, "his hand shot out, and the woman slumped against the bench. . . . [Later] he pretended not to notice [her] swollen lip, the dark bruises on her temple, and the tear-wearied eyes." When Sandoz's mother, Mary, asked Jules to help do the farm work, he responded: " 'You want me, an educated man, to work like a hired tramp!' he roared, and threw her against the wall" (pp. 5, 102, 199).

But Jules Sandoz is no more brutal than most other men in the book and is, in fact, most representative when he is beating his wives. Jules's conversations with his friends show that they believe women are to be used and controlled, their individuality of little consequence. The men mock and belittle women and make crude sexual comments. Sandoz makes it clear that Jules defines women as his society does: a woman is something to exploit; a man needs a wife to work, obey, and bear children. The laws and culture support his attitudes. Although the community knows which wives are victims of battering, it never interferes. The legal system, such as it is, sides with the male.

The economic system also helps institutionalize wife abuse by dictating women's dependence and forcing them to remain in violent marriages, as Smedley shows in *Daughter of Earth*. The "source of [Marie's] hatred of marriage" is her society's agreement that "a woman had to 'mind' her husband," primarily because he has "bought" her (pp. 66–67). Smedley focuses on the husband's traditional "property rights;" the marriage license is a certificate of ownership, giving men the right to beat and otherwise control their wives. Arguing that a woman's economic independence would give her some freedom, Marie describes a woman forced out of her "active, independent life" by her husband, who refuses to allow her to work and then abuses her when she is pregnant and unable to leave him. Marie believes (wrongly) that she can evade violence by remaining single. Yet she recognizes the economic pressures on women to marry and shows that it is nearly impossible for a woman to support her children alone. Comparing marriage to prostitution, Smedley sees the causes of violence in the unequal distribution of economic power within capitalist society and within patriarchal marriage.

Like Smedley, Le Sueur is a socialist, and in *The Girl* she creates representative working-class characters from pioneer backgrounds who have moved to the city. Le Sueur's women see violence as an inevitable part of sexual relations, a belief she suggests they inherit from their pioneer mothers. "Their experience of this world," she says in an autobiographical piece, "centered around the male as beast, his drunkenness and chicanery, his oppressive violence."[6]

Olsen, the fourth writer, presents family violence as the norm in her society, as her proletarian family moves from mining camp to tenant farm to the Chicago stockyards. Her most graphic and representative scene describes a sexual assault. Marital rapes also occur in the other books: Jules rapes his third wife, a mail-order bride who had met him only that day; the mother of *The Girl's* unnamed narrator is attacked by her husband when she refuses to sleep with him; and after overhearing her mother talking about a woman who was "forced," Smedley's Marie worries about the "hard, bitter weeping" she hears behind her parents' locked bedroom door (p. 78). Olsen makes the husband's expectations most explicit; the point of view belongs to the nine-year-old protagonist, Mazie:

What was happening? It seemed the darkness bristled with blood, with horror. The shaking of the bed as if someone were sobbing in it, the wind burrowing through the leaves filling the night with a shaken sound. And the words, the words leaping.

"Dont, Jim, dont. It hurts too much. No, Jim, no."
"Cant screw my own wife. Expect me to go to a whore? Hold still."[p. 91]

Jim believes, as do the other husbands, that he has sexual rights to his wife upon demand, and he uses violence to achieve these "rights." Later Mazie finds her mother lying in blood on the kitchen floor. Four months after bearing her youngest child, Anna has miscarried.

In these books, women are victims of individual men, but in the larger sense they are victims of social and economic institutions, of gender expectations. The male characters are by no means wholly unsympathetic; they are often creative, energetic, and sometimes likeable. The writers are well aware that men are shaped by patriarchal expectations, that they too are victims of gender roles and of economic exploitation. But none of the authors forgets that her mother's life and character is far more circumscribed than her father's, and her mother's physical victimization is one of the most powerful results of the unequal power men hold over women.

Although the writers may briefly question whether a woman in any way "provokes" her husband's violence, they soon dismiss this possibility. They explore the mother's life not to discover the causes of violence— which they locate in patriarchal institutions and assumptions—but to show how it affects her character. Like all victims of violent attack, the women feel intimidated, vulnerable, and helpless. Their daughters describe the constant fear, the drudgery leading to illnesses and early death, the anger buried under compliance. Each daughter sorrows over her mother's lost beauty, that perennial symbol of a woman's value.

After years of having their personal dignity and control over their lives forceably taken from them, the mothers believe they possess no value. Their sense of self effaced, they become unable to acknowledge, let alone assert, their own needs. Le Sueur's narrator's "mama" has a "small frightened face"; she behaves "as if apologizing for everything, . . . as if she didn't want to bother anybody" (p. 35). Mazie's mother, Anna, whose husband "struck [her] too often to remember," becomes paralyzed, disappearing behind "the shadow curtaining her . . . eyes" (p. 15). Smedley's Ellie Rogers seems to her daughter to disappear, saying "I don't need nothin'. I don't go nowhere and I don't see nobody" (p. 113). Economically dependent women who are beaten for "demanding" household money from a husband who legally controls the family finances soon learn to reduce their needs, but Smedley also implies that the threat of violence causes Ellie to conclude that she herself is "nothing."

The beatings threaten the women with spiritual and literal death. Ellie's voice is "lifeless" when she speaks of her husband's threat to hit her with a rope, adding, " 'Marie, . . . if he hits me, I'll drop dead!' " (pp. 105–106). Mary Sandoz tries to take control of her life through suicide:

Mary avoided crossing him or bothering him for help in anything she could possibly do alone. But there were times when she must have his help, as when the roof leaked or the calves had to be castrated. It took weeks of diplomatic approach to get him to look after the two bull calves before they were too big for her to handle at all. And when she couldn't hold the larger one from kicking, Jules, gray-white above his beard, threw his knife into the manure and loped to the back door. "I learn the goddamn balky woman to obey me when I say 'hold him'" He tore a handful of four-foot wire stays from the bundle in the corner of the shop and was gone towards the corral, the frightened grandmother and the children huddled at the back window.

They heard the banging of the gate. Jules's bellow of curses. Then Mary ran through the door, past the children and straight to the poison drawer. It stuck, came free, the blood dripping from her face and her hand where she had been struck with the wire whip, the woman snatched up a bottle, struggled with the cork, pulling at it with her teeth. The grandmother was upon her, begging, pleading, clutching at the red bottle with the crossbones.

Jules burst in. "Wo's the goddamned woman? I learn her to obey me if I got to kill her!"

"You!" the grandmother cried, shaking her fist against him. "For you there is a place in hell!"

With the same movement of her arm she swung out, knocking the open bottle from the woman's mouth. . . . Then she led Mary out of the house and to the brush along the river. [p. 230–31]

Saved from death by her ties to her mother and her children, Mary manages to encourage Jules to mellow by giving up her own needs and choosing another kind of self-destruction. Even when Jules stops beating her, he has the power in the family: he controls the money; he refuses to consult her in any decision; he harasses her constantly; and he will not work. Without him, Mary possesses the strength to be independent but, married to him, she must squelch her character and her ambitions; she must bend to his authority and find ways to circumvent his power.

Like Ellie, who feels "silence settling more and more about her," Mary learns silence, as do the others (p. 113), including Olsen's Anna. "Once Anna had questioned [her husband] timidly concerning his work; he struck her on the mouth with a bellow of 'Shut your damn trap'" (p. 15); later he thinks "just let her say one word to me and I'll bash her head in" (p. 76). When a man responds to his wife's efforts to talk about family needs and problems only with verbal aggression and violence, this *is* a mode of communication. He "teaches" the woman who controls the relationship and shows her how problems will be "solved," and tells her what to think about herself. Powerless, separated from others, unheard, she has no way to validate her feelings. She has been successfully intimidated. The husband maintains his power over his wife through enforced isolation and silence, which contribute to her self-doubts and her sense of shame.

Like most historians of pioneer women, these writers suggest that the isolation is increased by the western way of life, where frequent moves and distant neighbors made bonds difficult to establish. Marie Rogers describes how her sister "went into the silence where all pioneer women had gone before her" (p. 92). The authors demonstrate women's recognition of their need of each other: most turn at some point to women friends and to their daughters or mothers, who are sometimes able to help. But the women often have few friends who might share their problems and let them know they are not crazy, as they are often called, or to blame; those few who are willing to help are usually powerless and poor, like Marie's Aunt Helen. Isolation not only exacerbates their loss of selfhood; it also seems to increase their victimization. The West's dogged resistance to any interference with individual "freedom" and the western myths of individualism and violence may have further fueled the belief in the "sanctity" of the patriarchal family.

The authors stress the women's lack of alternatives to their entrapment by economic considerations and social attitudes. Mary Sandoz, "brought up in a tradition of subordination to man," has been rendered economically dependent, like the other mothers (p. 187). She has no money, and she has children; she cannot leave her husband. She also believes that divorce is shameful and that her children need a father; her culture has taught her that a violent home is preferable to a broken one. Ironically, it is husbands who often threaten to leave their wives—and do. Ellie cannot support herself and her family, and time and again her daughter watches her respond to her husband's abuse by begging him not to abandon them. Economically dependent and socialized to find satisfaction and value in ties to others, the wives struggle to make their relationships work. The women in *The Girl,* afraid of being left, attempt to bond men to them by sacrificing themselves; like the girl's mother, they have internalized society's dictum that the woman is responsible for creating a "happy" family and satisfying others' needs.

The writers imply that social expectations that women marry, become dependent, and bear and take primary responsibility for children lead to wife battering. Says Jules: "Women got to have children to keep healthy" (p. 110). Mazie's father, Jim, wonders "what other earthly use can a woman have" (p. 10). Although Mary tries to avoid pregnancy by nursing each baby for several years and the women in *The Girl* have many health-destroying illegal abortions, there is no effective birth control. Their husbands force sex upon them, then refer to the children as "your kids" and abuse them. While the fathers vary in their attention to the children, they do not take any major responsibility for their care, nor are they attached to them by bonds as strong as the mothers'. Some men leave the children without providing for them, but no woman considers this option, though without a man she often cannot provide for them herself. Their devotion to their children chains the women to abusive husbands and adds to their feelings of inadequacy and shame.

Like most researchers who believe that "both victims and perpetrators of family violence were often exposed to similar violence in their childhoods," these writers show that the children are shaped by violence, though it is difficult to separate the effects of wife abuse and child abuse.[7] Certainly fear dominates their children's family lives. "Hidden far under the bed," the Sandoz children watch their father attack their mother and "cower . . . like frightened little rabbits, afraid to cry" (p. 231). Mazie's brother Will cries out in his sleep, " 'dont hit me, Poppa, dont" (p. 24). Le Sueur's girl's mother wants her daughter to marry a "good" man like papa, who spent his life brutalizing his family, and the girl does notice that the man she picks is "like papa." Some daughters learn to hate men: after watching her mother being beaten, the girl's sister Stasia decides that she will never marry. Marie Rogers comes to the same conclusion.

As family violence teaches girls what to expect from men, it also influences boys' attitudes about and behavior toward women. One of the grisliest scenes in *Old Jules* concerns Mrs. Blaska, whose husband uses her love for her sons to coax her back after she dares to leave him. After she is found dead, "stripped naked, in the open chicken yard," her husband admits he whipped her. "She started to run away again, and handicapped by his crutch, he sent her sons to bring her back. They held her while he pounded her." (p. 412).

The Blaska boys, like many of the sons in these works, suffer from what Talcott Parsons has called "compulsive masculinity," characterized by aggression toward women who "are to blame."[8] By the end of *Yonnondio,* Mazie's brother Will becomes "sullen" and "defiant," having learned "a lust to hit back, a lust not to care" (p. 71). The books demonstrate that violence is circular: society's devalued view of women and implicit support of male domination cause violence, while men learn to further devalue women through watching them being beaten. Recent feminist theorists who argue that gender identity is based on a child's relationship to the mother show how traits that these earlier writers link to violence are formed in childhood. Carol Gilligan has suggested that, because boys must separate from their mothers to develop a masculine gender identity while femininity is defined through attachment, "male gender identity is threatened by intimacy while female gender identity is threatened by separation."[9] The boys learn to reject women, but the books reveal a good deal more about how the girls attempt to deal with identifying with a victimized woman.

Sandoz, Smedley, Le Sueur, and Olsen focus on how the daughters resist, reject, and come to understand themselves through their mothers' lives. Some suffer from what Adrienne Rich calls "matrophobia": the fear "of becoming one's mother, . . . the splitting of the self, in the desire to become purged once and for all of our mothers' bondage."[10] Rich argues that daughters often see their mothers as standing "for the victim in ourselves," as "having taught compromise and self-hatred," as "the one through whom the restrictions and degradations of a female existence" are passed on (pp. 238, 237). While the authors do not find wholly adequate solutions to this blurring and overlapping of their own and their mothers' personalities, they also do not resemble the daughters Rich describes who find it "easier by far to hate and reject a mother outright than to see beyond her to the forces acting upon her" (p. 237). Partly by identifying these forces, the daughters in these books resolve their feelings about their mothers in various ways. In a sense, each book bears testimony to the daughter's inability to separate herself from her mother and to her belief that her mother's life had value.

The daughters find themselves torn between their attraction to their fathers, whom they see as creative and colorful figures, and their recognition of themselves as women who may be destined to occupy their mothers' roles. Describing their characters' fascination with their fathers' storytelling, each author writes of key moments in her childhood when her father chose her as audience. Says Sandoz, " . . . the most impressive stories were those told me by Old Jules himself," and she believes these stories helped create her own narrative skill (*Old Jules*, vii–viii). Marie Rogers thinks she is her "father's daughter," partially because "he told me stories when I sat by his side. . . . [To] him, as to me, fancy was as real as sticks and stones. . . . [but my mother] never believed in imaginin' things" (p. 57). Loving her father's stories, Mazie thinks that "daddy knowen everything" and tries to model herself on him by listing what she's "a-knowing": "words and words" (pp. 16, 12). The daughters often associate their own creativity with their fathers.

While these writers present working-class men as possessing limited power, they nonetheless connect the fathers with traits traditionally ascribed to the western male—and to men in general: independence, power, defiance, activity, cockiness, individualism, even freedom. Jules came west seeking "free land, far from law and convention," where he could "live as he liked," and Sandoz presents him as " 'a big man—crazy maybe, but big' " (pp. 4, 398). Marie Rogers admires her father for daring "what no one else dared. . . . He was the living, articulate expression of their desires" (p. 23). "To be like him," she thinks, "was my one desire in life" (pp. 12–13).

And yet the daughters know they cannot be "like him" because they are women, as their fathers teach them. Jules says to his daughter, " 'There is nobody to carry on my work. . . . If [Mari] was a man she might—as a woman she is not worth a damn' " (p. 418). Mazie tries to "force [her father] into some recognition of her existence, her desire, her emotions" (p. 16). Rejected by her father after his first son is born, Marie learns that there is "something wrong with me, . . . something too deep to even cry about" (p. 12). Judged inadequate because of their sex, these girls have difficulty developing self-respect.

They come to judge their fathers' lives in various ways; Le Sueur's girl, for instance, believes her "papa was a failure and mean" (p. 43), though she falls in love with another mean failure. All eventually see that the male's "superiority" carries with it traits and values they reject. The girls are drawn to the male world not so much because it is attractive as because they see their mothers' worlds as so limited and constricted; they do not want to grow up to be women. Marie Rogers thinks, "I would not be a woman, I would not" (pp. 148–49). Seeing as the central difference between her parents that her mother "preferred the smaller, the more familiar things, while her Jules saw only the far, the large, the exalted canvas," Sandoz presents her mother as possessing a qualified heroism, subordinate to Jules' visionary power (p. 191). She respects her mother who, like other pioneer women, "made the best of the situation," but the mother's life was filled with situations to avoid, not to aspire to.[11]

Many violent and sexual incidents suggest to the girls what it means to be a woman and demonstrate their ties to their mothers. Sandoz recognizes that she is identified with her mother and realizes what womanhood will bring her when Jules, unable to beat the pregnant Mary, "whipped [Mari] until he was breathless" (p. 279). She is confronted with the powerlessness of her sexuality when she is attacked by a convict her father boards; the father hides the man's offense, sexual assault on young girls. After witnessing her mother's rape, Mazie comes to realize her own sexual vulnerability. Some boys intimidate her from jumping with them onto ice trucks by making up a rhyme about how they see her "pants" and her "pie," and so Mazie becomes "clumsy": "No more for her that lithe joy, that sense of power" (p. 127). Marie Rogers describes how she first experiences her tie to her mother when they face together her father's assault: "A bond had at last been welded between us two, . . . a bond of misery that was never broken" (p. 107). Loving, pitying, and supporting her mother, who dies in her arms, she learns from her life the costs of sexuality: "Sex meant violence, marriage, or prostitution, and marriage meant children, . . . unhappiness, and all the things that I feared and dreaded and intended to avoid" (p. 181).

Perhaps because of the violence associated with marriage and sexuality, the daughters also associate children with entrapment, and they resent being forced to take responsibility for child care. (Le Sueur has quite a different point of view on this issue, to which I will return shortly.) "Never Jules or James, always Mari," thinks Sandoz, and she eventually confronts her mother: " 'I should think you'd be tired of having babies—I'm tired of watching them—' (pp. 296, 341). Mazie has a similar encounter with her mother:

"Why is it always me that has to help? How come Will gets to play?"
"Willie's a boy."
"Why couldn't *I* get borned a boy?" [p. 142]

Thus, the daughter sometimes comes to feel that her mother is forcing her to take on her own devalued role. Faced with her subordinate status, she turns against herself; Marie Rogers "hated [herself] most of all for having been born a woman" and hated her brothers and sister for existing and making her feel responsible for them (p. 137).

Marie is so damaged by witnessing what it is to be a woman that she rejects positive traits associated with womanhood. "Love, tenderness and duty belong to women and to weaklings in general," she thinks, planning to "have none of them!" (p. 136). Yet Smedley suggests that such declarations are defenses against her feelings of guilt for "deserting" her siblings after her mother's death, and her guilt is evidence that she cannot escape her womanhood. She suppressed "the desire for love" because of the "perverted idea of love and sex that had been ground into [her] being" (pp. 182, 194). Marie believes that women's values lead inevitably to the powerlessness of her mother's role. "Love and tenderness meant only pain and suffering and defeat" (p. 148).

Like Smedley, Le Sueur explores the consequences of women's capacity for emotional involvement with others and contrasts women's values with those of men, but the girl's conclusions about her mother's life differ markedly from those of Marie. Believing she will discover truths about her own identity through understanding her mother's experience, she goes to see her, hoping "she would tell me something" (p. 40). And she comes back "a different person":

I was into my mama's life for the first time, and knew how she all the time, chased like a pack of wolves, kept us alive, fierce and terrible. . . . Mama had a secret. She let me feel it, let me know it. [p. 45]

The girl thinks repeatedly of her mother throughout the book; her "secret," what she "has felt" and helps the girl feel, is her "fierce" attachment to others. When the girl realizes that her own ability to give birth and nurture life is her "treasure," she thinks, "I felt like mama" (p. 134).

In *The Girl,* Le Sueur creates a community of women whose united voices assert that women's devalued strengths—nurturance, vulnerability, interdependence—can and will prevail. Yet in reclaiming women's values and mythologizing their relationships with each other, based on the mother-daughter bond, Le Sueur denies the girl any radical analysis of the limitations in her mother's life, and she herself evades some problematical issues. As I have shown, there are serious threats in mama's lessons, drawbacks in her life. The girl's relations with men mirror her mother's, and Le Sueur can achieve her visionary end only by killing off her male characters, all of whom abuse women. But she does not envision women living without men, and, in fact, her women are obsessed with establishing relations with men and with having babies. She cannot empower women's values in a world in which male values dominate, so she cannot resolve a central issue her book raises: how to stop the abuse of women.

All of the daughters in these books are left with more questions than answers. *Daughter of Earth* ends with Marie still struggling with her profound sympathy and love for her mother and her rebellion against her role. After writing a woman's history of the West, hidden within a biography of her *father,* Sandoz turns, in her later histories, to the classic masculine West and its themes, to what she calls "the romantic days." Unable, perhaps unwilling, to identify with her mother's West, interested in heroism, individualism, and power, and encouraged by the historical establishment to write "epic" history, she never again gives a woman a starring role in her histories. Like the other writers, Sandoz presents a radical analysis of power dynamics in the western family, but she can find few solutions, in her work or in her life.

"Her tears, . . . they embittered my life!" says Marie Rogers (p. 32). "Mama wept all night," says the girl (p. 31). Mazie sees her mother's "head bent over her sewing in the attitude of a woman weeping" (p. 16). This is the image the daughters carry of their mothers. Seeking to break out of the eternal mold of the weeping woman, they nonetheless find that they cannot—and will not—separate themselves from their mothers, whom they associate with life, with their very selfhood:

The fingers stroked, spun a web, cocooned Mazie into happiness and intactness and selfness. Soft wove the bliss round hurt and fear and want and shame—the old worn fragile bliss, a new frail selfness bliss, healing, transforming. Up from the grasses, from the earth, from the broad tree trunk at their back, latent life streamed and seeded. The air and self shone boundless. Absently, her mother stroked; stroked unfolding, wingedness, boundlessness. [p. 119]

Although she sees her mother's life as "so cruel, . . . so ugly," Mazie comes to feel the beauty in the world through Anna's nurturing. Olsen grows up to write a famous story, "Ironing," in which a mother meditates about her love for her daughter and her guilt over her inability to protect her from the pain of being a woman. It is a measure of the power and influence of their mothers that these authors attempt to re-examine, re-tell, and re-claim their lives.

Although some knew each others' work, Sandoz, Smedley, Le Sueur, and Olsen were not well-known authors before the feminist resurgence of the 1970s. As Dale Spender suggests, feminist writers throughout the century have analyzed and criticized the social structure, but their work has been largely overlooked (or worse, suppressed) by mainstream literary and social historians.[12] As woman abuse was invisible in our society, so was it absent from our literary canon. Few Americans have been willing to believe that the frontiersman or pioneer was a woman abuser; that the real Davy Crocketts, Natty Bumppos, Virginians, and Ben Cartwrights took for granted a patriarchal authority that sanctioned woman abuse; that the frontier's cherished freedom and individualism, which helped shape American history and culture, might encourage the violent domination of women. These four works implicitly demand a reassessment of western experience and the myths our culture has invented to explain it. Literature not only verbalizes the author's view of social reality,but it also may shape cultural attitudes. Had these women, who dared to break the silence about violence in women's lives, been heard and believed, wife abuse might have been recognized as a serious social problem long before the 1970s.

As many feminist critics have said, women cannot fully understand their own lives until they see their experiences explored in literature. Sandoz, Smedley, Le Sueur, and Olsen dared to write about their mothers' lives and their own because they knew their experiences were not unique; their books can help wives and daughters see the real causes of the violence in their lives and realize their ties to each other. To demonstrate this point, and to conclude my essay, I have chosen an unusual form: a personal digression.

I learned to digress from my grandfather, who may have learned it from Twain's Jim Blaine. Born in the Badlands of South Dakota, my grandfather drifted throughout the West. He rode buffalo, dated a girl named

Duckfoot Sue, and was a descendant of Geronimo—or, on alternate days, Sitting Bull. When accused, never by me, Gramps would say that while he never lied, it might be that he sometimes "pre-va-ri-cated"—and he would stretch out the word for its full ten-dollar value.

Wandering with me in the western mountains, telling his tall tales, my grandfather was the larger-than-life star in my childhood melodrama. As I grew up and recognized his failings and his alcoholism, I came to see him as a flawed visionary, trampled on by a seedy conformist society; as, in short, a quintessential western hero. His freedom-seeking, rebellious footprints led me directly to the field of American studies.

A few years after my grandfather died, my mother drank a little one night and told me some family stories I had not heard before. The climactic one chronicled what she said was a frequent occurrence in her childhood: my grandfather beating my grandmother. As she described, in detail, several beatings she remembered, she told me how she had felt responsible, powerless, embarrassed. It was awful to hear this. Pieces of me tore apart jaggedly and settled into new, uncomfortable relations to each other. The next day when I saw my grandmother, I was appalled to discover that I could not respond to my new information about her. I could not identify with her suffering. I felt only that I needed to understand what could have caused my beloved grandfather to do such a thing, and to find a way to explain and excuse him.

It was at least two painful, unresolved years later that I discovered *Old Jules*. Coming to understand Sandoz's confusion about whether to identify with her father or with her mother gave me, I thought, a way to explain my own feelings about my grandfather. I wrote an essay on Sandoz, and I presented papers in which I told about my family, thinking all the while of how "I learned to digress from my grandfather."

But I missed the point. My mother had told me secrets she and my grandmother had kept for thirty-five years, yet I used these secrets not to understand their lives, but to explore my grandfather and my identification with him. I did not conceal the story but, like Sandoz, I thought it was about the man, and I did not see that perhaps the story was really about the teller, "her father's daughter," my mother. Although I am a feminist, I rendered my mother invisible and thoughtlessly covered up her knowledge of the real costs of woman abuse. Sandoz, Smedley, Le Sueur, and Olsen showed me this, and I am grateful.

Notes

Portions of this article were written with the aid of a CURF grant from the University of New Hampshire.

I would like to dedicate this article to my mother, Gloria Graulich, and to my grandmother Mae Wilkerson.

1. This article is a condensation of a longer and more theoretical unpublished piece. Two other articles treat individual writers in more depth: "Every Husband's Right: Sex Roles in Mari Sandoz's *Old Jules*," *Western American Literature*, May, 1983, pp. 3–20;

" 'For what is one voice alone': Separation and Connection in Meridel Le Sueur's *The Girl*" (conference paper).

2. Mary Austin, *Earth Horizon* (New York: Houghton Mifflin, 1932), p. 142.

3. Reported in *Boston Globe* (6 June 1982), p. 17. See also Murray A. Straus, "Wife-Beating: How Common and Why?" in Murray A. Straus and Gerald T. Hotaling, eds., *The Social Causes of Husband-Wife Violence* (Minneapolis: University of Minnesota Press, 1980), where Straus claims that "the true incidence for violence in a marriage is probably closer to *50 or 60 percent of all couples*" (p. 31). While some nineteenth-century feminists certainly attempted to expose the widespread practice of wife abuse, it was not until the feminist resurgence of the 1970s that the subject received sustained attention. Recent western historians have looked for information about what Julie Roy Jeffrey calls "power dynamics" within the family, but they have discovered, as John Faragher says, that some "human concerns [are] too dangerous to commit to paper" (*Frontier Women: The Trans-Mississippi West, 1840–1880* [New York: Hill & Wang, 1979], p. 63; and *Women and Men on the Overland Trail* [New Haven, Conn.: Yale University Press, 1979], p. 47). In "Women and Honor: Some Notes on Lying," Adrienne Rich has argued that women "have been complicit, have acted out the fiction of a well-lived life, until the day we testify in court of rapes, beatings, psychic cruelties, public and private humiliations" (*On Lies, Secrets, and Silences* [New York: Norton, 1979], p. 189). This feminist attack on the mythology of domestic tranquility is supported by researchers like Straus. I will adopt Rich's description of abuse as my definition.

4. Mari Sandoz, *Old Jules* (Lincoln: University of Nebrasks Press, 1962); Agnes Smedley, *Daughter of Earth* (Old Westbury, N.Y.: Feminist Press, 1976); Meridel Le Sueur, *The Girl* (Minneapolis, Minn.: West End Press, 1978); Tillie Olsen, *Yonnondio: From the Thirties* (New York: Dell, 1974). Page numbers follow quotations in text. These authors frequently use irregular punctuation; it will not be noted. Rosemary Whitaker's "Violence in *Old Jules* and *Slogum House*," *Western American Literature* 16, no. 3 (November, 1981); 215–24, discusses violence in Sandoz's works without considering the implications of woman abuse.

5. See, for instance, R. Emerson and Russell Dobash, *Violence Against Wives* (New York: Free Press, 1979), pp. 33, 24, where they argue that "to be a wife meant becoming the property of a husband, taking a secondary position in a marital hierarchy of power and worth, being legally and morally bound to obey the will and wishes of one's husband, and thus, quite logically, subject to his control even to the point of physical chastisement and murder," and that "men who assault their wives are actually living up to cultural prescriptions that are cherished in western society—aggressiveness, male dominance, and female subordination—and they are using physical force as a means to enforce that dominance." See also Wini Breines and Linda Gordon, "The New Scholarship on Family Violence," *Signs* 8, no. 3 (Spring, 1983): 490–531; Susan Schechter, *Women and Male Violence* (Boston: South End Press, 1983); and Diana E. H. Russell, *Rape in Marriage* (Riverside, N.J.: Macmillan, 1983), in which she claims that, of the women she interviewed, one out of seven reported at least one incident of rape by her husband. Without the insights of these scholars I might have overlooked important issues within the texts I discuss.

6. Meridel Le Sueur, "The Ancient People and the Newly Come," in Elaine Hedges, ed., *Ripening: Selected Work, 1927–1980* (Old Westbury, N.Y.: Feminist Press, 1982), p. 44. While *The Girl* is less strictly autobiographical than the other texts, this quotation suggests that Le Sueur created her universalized female characters from her own experience.

7. Breines and Gordon, "The New Scholarship on Family Violence," p. 516. Schechter believes that this is an oversimplification of a complex issue and presents some objections. It is true that some of the women in these books resort to violence. As our society has implicitly sanctioned wife abuse, it has also encouraged child abuse through the faith in "spanking" as essential to childrearing. As the wives and children in these books learn, violence works; it is an effective method of intimidation and control over those who possess less power.

8. Straus, "Wife-Beating," p. 88.

9. Carol Gilligan, *In a Different Voice: Psychological Theory and Women's Develop-*

ment (Cambridge, Mass.: Harvard University Press, 1982), p. 8. Gilligan bases her conclusions on the research of Nancy Chodorow, *The Reproduction of Mothering: Psychoanalysis and the Sociology of Gender* (Berkeley: University of California Press, 1978).

10. Adrienne Rich, *Of Woman Born* (New York: Bantam, 1976), pp. 237–38. Subsequent quotations in text are followed by page numbers in Rich.

11. Mari Sandoz, "Pioneer Women," unpublished essay excerpted in Mari Sandoz, *Hostiles and Friendlies,* ed. Virginia Faulkner (Lincoln: University of Nebraska Press, 1959), p. 59.

12. Dale Spender, *There's Always Been a Woman's Movement in This Century* (Boston: Pandora Press, 1982). Of course, some historians and critics have argued for the inclusion of materials on women. David Potter is only one such example.

9.
_____

Lena Olmstead and Oscar Phillips: Love and Marriage

ELIZABETH HAMPSTEN

Few things are more commonplace than love and marriage. Here is a late-nineteenth-century western version, preserved in the letters of Lena and Oscar (Phill) Phillips, of North Dakota and Minnesota, exchanged before their marriage. This illuminating analysis by Elizabeth Hampsten appears deceptively simple at first glance. But she gives a careful and attentive reading to letters that many persons would regard as uninteresting. She insists that we must treat these mundane letters from ordinary people as seriously as we do letters judged "great literature," and read them seriously, patiently, and in their entirety (see her Read This Only to Yourself: The Private Writings of Midwestern Women, 1880–1910 *[Bloomington: Indiana University Press, 1982]). When we do so, we gain glimpses into the lives of ordinary people who are otherwise inaccessible to us. Hampsten's approach demonstrates a way to understand women's nontraditional literature—letters, diaries, and reminiscences. As we seek to explore the lives of ordinary women, we must learn to understand them in their own terms.*

All the world loves lovers: we are charmed, bemused, and moved by events and emotions that take on overwhelming importance for the principals in a romance. Most of us have been through something like it ourselves (the number of love-story plots is limited). Private writings about love and marriage carry psychological interest, because in a state of heightened emotion people are apt to express themselves with more vigor than usual, and their gender-specific language may interest feminist linguists. The letters described in this article, composed at the turn of the century, display both the whimsy of well-requited love, and a pronounced linguistic difference between the male and female writers. But my primary interest in them is neither historical nor linguistic.

Rather, I should like to present these nonpublic, nonprofessional writings by ordinary people as literature, whose fullest meanings can be revealed through the kind of analysis that is appropriate to literature. For I am convinced that to be fair to letters, diaries, and other private writings by both women and men, we are obliged to pay attention to vocabulary, grammar, tone, and style, just as we are with poetry or fiction. All these

Lebanese wedding couple. Eighteen-year-old John Attey and his fifteen-year-old bride, Sarah George, Salt Lake City, 1909. Courtesy Utah State Historical Society.

forms are created primarily in imagination; they depend on experience, on talent, and on an audience. They may well, of course, also contain discrete information—names, dates, reports of events—but the first purpose of private writing, as of professional imaginative literature, is less to persuade or inform than it is, in the words of the sixteenth-century critic Sir Phillip Sidney, to "strike, pierce, and possess the site of the soul"—words particularly apt to our present subject.

Lena Olmstead and Oscar Phillips were married December 10, 1890, at Comodale, Minnesota, near St. Paul.[1] For exactly three months before the wedding they were apart, she at her home in Bartlett, North Dakota, and later in Comodale, and he in Larimore, North Dakota, tending a farm-implement dealership and arranging their housing. The letters they wrote to each other every few days show them preparing to be happy by earning the approval of the people they knew. Neither hints at criticism or rebellion against what is expected of them; each assumes that the reward for pleasing the other will be social, as well as personal, happiness. Their accommodations to these expectations were not entirely effortless.

There are eighteen letters from Oscar to Lena between September 10 and December 7, 1890, and five from her to him. Lena's first letter is dated November 23, though she had been writing to Phill (as he was called) from the start; there appear to be no gaps among his. Phill's letters consist of declarations of love for Lena, local news and gossip, reports on his progress in buying and furnishing a house, and his daily activities. He goes to council meetings, makes "collections" on farm implements, visits and dines with friends, goes hunting, and writes letters. He is interested in Democratic party fortunes in the national elections, reports on opera in Grand Forks and Larimore, and is on the "management" committee of a ball to celebrate the dedication of the Larimore City Hall. Lena's letters tell of her shopping and visiting, her family, and neighbors.

While the correspondence is primarily given to reporting "news," it conveys also information about the writers' more emotional perceptions, their expectations of themselves and of each other. There is, for instance, the matter of their being teased by friends for their love affair. Lena writes as though she is amused, possibly flattered, and on the whole tolerant; she appears to take comfort in such attention. Phill betrays no humor; he evades his friends' impertinances, he is impatient, even angry that he might be thought ridiculous, and he rebukes Lena for appearing to collaborate in the teasing. Their intimacies are most closely revealed in decision-making powers. Phill has ostensibly proposed the marriage, but Lena is setting the date, time, place, and guest list. Phill buys and furnishes the house because he happens to be at hand, but a difference over carpeting shows him backing off. Several times he finds cause to rebuke Lena on the propriety of her behavior; then he apologizes, although nothing in her letters would indicate strong chagrin. She is inclined to mock herself, he never.

These currents in the emotional level of their correspondence run through the otherwise very detailed and circumstantial content of the letters, yet emotional intimacy is not a subject addressed directly in any of their writing. Phill's language comes in three modes: straight reportage, avuncular instruction, and affected and artificial flights on the subject of love; of these, the rebukes are his closest approaches to intimacy. Lena's tones are chatty, and where she risks revealing herself to him she is humorous. She laughs at herself for being teased, for being too fat, and for having by accident cut her bangs too short. But nowhere do they write about the subject of sexuality, which surely must have also been on their minds. Only in reference to the birth of a child of Lena's father is there a hint of sexuality, and it is disapproved of. Her father, in fact, appears to represent an exception to Tolstoy's assertion that "Happy families are all alike."

Phill's first letter opens in his reportorial style, "I just returned from council meeting 9:30," then changes abruptly to the literary.

As the sky is overcast and the deep toned thunder is rolling along in the distance and the vivid flashes of lightning flash across the heavens and rent asunder the dark hanging mass of clouds, opening up as it were the flood gates of heaven for just at this moment, the rain drops begin to patter on the roof. And I all alone am writing to the darling of my heart. As I just came down the streets and looked up to the landing, all was dark and still, no light in the window or sweet strains of music to beckon me on to the side of her I love. So I am going to sit down and talk with you anyway.

Then he returns to the reporting manner:

To begin with must tell you what I have been doing. Monday did not do much, felt all broke up with my cold. Came home early, took some quinine and had a big shot of whiskey sling and went to bed at 9 o'clock. Up Tuesday morning, worked some, visited with two or three travelers, went hunting at 4 p.m., returned at 8, shot 8 chickens. Had a nice trip and a very pleasant drive. Mr. George Fadden went with me.

Several paragraphs later (Phill's letters average three or four handwritten pages), he addressed her directly, but rebukingly, his language bending again to the bookish:

Well Darling I was somewhat disappointed in not getting a letter from you tonight. Think you might of found time to have written me you arrived all safe. Presume you have been quite busy viewing the stock, farm improvements, grand scenery, and different places of amusements and interests since your arrival. Trusting that the novelty of it has worn off, and you will devote a portion of your time to describing the places and things of interest that have passed under your observance since your departure from this little city which seems to be devoid of interest the last evening or two.

Lena was with her father, whom Phill regarded with no particular warmth: "What is the Governor doing, and Mrs. Nella also. Give them my regards" (September 10).

Lena had written the same day as Phill, whose second letter sounds even more annoyed that Lena should be thriving so cheerfully apart from him. He disapproved of her family, her friends, and her making her own plans.

Your looked for letter of 10th instant came to hand. Glad to hear that you arrived all safe, and find things so different from what you expected. So you are quite infatuated with country life and don't know when you will return but expect it will be a long time. All right my dear, enjoy your visit as long as you can; rather lonely here of an evening though. . . . As to you associating with Miss Ovick use your own Judgment My Dear, but remember that you may meet her at places where you don't wish to associate with her so you want to use a little tact in the matter. . . . Well you interviewed your Pa on the subject I see and he thinks the plan all OK. We will talk the matter over in regard to St. Paul, but the other matter is entirely out of the question my dear.

Her sense of humor also irritated Phill, especially when it was displayed in combination with an intimacy over which he had no control: her relationship with her father's new wife, a woman presumably not much older than Lena:

So you and Nella seem to get some enjoyment out of playing Jim as you call him. All right my dear, if you can find any real enjoyment in teasing an illiterate half silly fellow as I imagine Jim is, or he would see through your schemes. You are different from what I think you are. And as he seems to be more industrious since your arrival, your papa may not want to part with you, and then my suit would be a struggle.

Phill was uneasy, lonely, and at loose ends; Lena appeared not to recognize the claim he felt he ought to have on her. Sounding stern was his way of trying to touch her more intimately, and his letter ends, "This is a very fine day, a little chilly but a fine fall day. If you were here I would be tempted to ask you to take a drive this afternoon. . . . It is dinner time and will close. Expecting to get a letter this evening train, I am Truly Yours, Phill." As for Jim and Nellie he does not let the matter drop:

So you were surprised at my last letter and could not make out my meaning. Well I meant just what I said, that if you and Nellie were teasing Jim I did not think it right. As far as you changing I did not think of that dear, it never entered my head. . . . And I am very sorry I made you feel bad by causing you to think I doubted your love for me. Nor I did not think you cared for Jim, not but what he is worthy of some one's love, but not yours for that belongs to me. [September 18]

But for all his apologies, Phill did not resist lecturing Lena. She invited him to a party ("As for myself I have declined your kind invitation") but he reminded her how to behave: "It is perfectly proper that you should not want to go with either of the parties mentioned unless your escort should be your Papa. Trusting you will have a pleasant time, and get home at reasonable hours" (September 18). She evidently ignored the advice, for a week later he writes:

Sorry to hear that the dance had such a bad effect on you. Hope that you have fully recovered by this time, and next time be more moderate in your dancing my dear and you will not suffer the consequences that follow an overindulgence. And so time flies rapidly with you and you are happy as can be. All right darling stay just as long as you like, but don't think I don't want to see you for I do and think of you every hour of the day. [September 24]

There was an edge to his desire for letters from her:

Well darling if I did get a letter last Sunday to keep me from getting cross none came this, and I will admit I was somewhat disappointed, although at the breakfast table, when the mail train went by I said letter or no letter from my dear. I thought no letter as I felt just that way, and sure enough no letter it was. And I will expect a great long one written today to make up for it. [November 23]

Keeping him from being cross, Lena must have known by then, would be a fairly constant preoccupation.

Their closest approach to a quarrel was over carpeting, a difference which also reveals the contrast in emotional language between the two of them. Phill had been reporting in exhaustive detail about a house he had thought to rent, then did not, and a second one he was buying and preparing to furnish.

I called on Mr. and Mrs. F Monday eve. . . . Did not make any purchases but took the prices under advisement. They want $15 for the front room carpet, a fair Brussels but somewhat worn. . . . Am waiting for the samples you were to send. [November 19]

Lena wrote on the twenty-third:

Did you get the samples of carpet and how do you like them and can't you do as well to buy new. I should think so. Justine only paid $60 for their ingrain here and it doesn't cost but very little to have them all sewed, 5¢ per yard or less I believe.

Her letter crossed with Phill's of the same day in which he reported the Fagens as again urging him to buy their carpets, and in addition:

I received the samples of carpets from the St. Paul house and I received a day or so before a lot from a Minneapolis house I had written to, and as you have left the matter entirely with me to furnish and fix up the house, I will either buy theirs or send and have some shipped up.

Two days later her letter had reached him, and he wrote:

I was very much pleased to get it and read it at once, and note what you say as to the new carpets and the cheapness of furniture, but you are a little late Dear in making up your mind, as you told me in one of your previous letters that you would leave it all to me, and now you say that you think we could do better in St. Paul. I was afraid you were placing too much confidence in my ability to furnish a house. Am sorry you did not tell me sooner, but I will just blame myself, as I should of investigated the matter farther.

He will let her, he says, "pick the ballance of the furniture." Phill's cross temper was a poor match to Lena's sanguine one, and his elaborations affect her like so much water off a duck's back: "Now Phil stop your worrying about the old carpets, stoves and furniture you have got, for I'm sure it is all right. You are just talking anyway."

He also rebuked her for a matter involving some money Phill sent her to spend on wedding preparations, which she returned. He wrote on the same as she had written of the carpet quarrel:

Yes Darling I regret very much that you told Mrs. Hendrickson that I sent you the money. And I truly believed I could trust you with our *private* affairs. I do not reproach you for this dear, but freely forgive you, but can't forget that I have been sorely disappointed and sincerely hope we may never have cause to refer to a matter of this kind again. For I love you dearly, Darling, and don't want anything to occur to mar our happiness for I could take you in my arms now dear and shower kisses on you and forget all our little unpleasantness. For I know dear that I have faults that loom up as big black clouds as compared with the light ethereal ones of yours [November 30]

Three days later, before she had replied, he wrote again:

I thought of the first part of my last letter to you, how harsh and cruel it must of seemed darling when you read it. Forgive me dear for it, I should of waited and told you with my arms around you dear for I did not write it darling because I was mad or wanted to hurt your feelings. No darling I wrote it just as I would of told you darling and would of kissed you, but I know that it must of looked harsh on paper. Write and tell me dear that you forgive me, and I will never be guilty of such an act again.

He closed:

And it is just one week from today darling that I am to see you and call you my own sweet darling Lena, for I do truly love you and when one more week rolls by I am to claim you as my own darling to protect and love through life.

His "claim" to her appears to be the basis of his anxiety and irritation, for his strongest outbursts are connected to Lena's allegiances to others: to her father and stepmother in the case of teasing Jim and going to the dance, and to the Hendrickson family for telling them of the money and for just being close to Lena ("So I am no stranger to the Hendrickson family. Well it amounts to the same thing to me as if I were, as they are total strangers to me" [November 30]). Even though each rebuke was followed by an apology of sorts, another scolding came soon after. Lena referred to the matter only very briefly in what she called a "third addition" to her last letter to him on December 7. "And the other matter certainly I forgive, but as far as that I'd just as soon you wrote it as to tell it."

Oscar Phillips' querulous tone was also his most intimate expression; her "light ethereal" faults stimulated direct and forceful language. Phill's habit of mind on many topics is plain and detailed. Stoves, carpeting, and window curtains elicited painstaking expertise, and so did gossip about acquaintances. But when he addressed "love," virtually all his words were ones he had read somewhere else. He could be writing about anyone, and seemed not to know of any other way to express his feelings. On September 26 he was expecting Lena's return to Larimore from Bartlett:

Do I miss you darling? Ask of the withered flowers after the hot sun has parched and made to droop their heads if they would miss the cool refreshing dews of evening. Or the tender plant just pushing forth from mother earth in the cool damp spring if it would miss the warming rays of the sun. Your presence dear is like the refreshing dews of evening to the parched and withered flower, and your love dear shot from those eyes I love to gaze into has an influence on me that warms up my cold and wintry nature. And if your presence is so dear to me, why your question is answered.

A week later, when she had left for Minneapolis, he was in the midst of office work and council meetings:

But just remember that I love you and think of you every hour of the day and long for the day to come when I can take you in my arms and kiss you once more. Yes I did kiss you in the car and as you think, it will have to last you a long time. Now about myself. . . . [November 4]

The next day he was "pondering over the political situation," thinking of her shopping and sightseeing in the city, and bemoaning the weather and "continual round of dull monotony as is prevalent in Larimore the year round." He pictured her "completely carried away with the country and its surroundings." The thought of her vitality made him nervous, and the vague and dreamy scene he comforted himself with harnessed all his anxieties:

And no doubt that cold bleak winter will soon be upon us. But I am comforted with the thought that it will not be long before we are sitting around our own pleasant fireside where we will be warm and cozy within, and our lives will be radiant with the love we bear for each other. [November 5]

This is a particularly long letter about politics (national elections had resulted in Democratic party gains in various states, though not in North Dakota), about business, gossip, and wedding plans, interwoven with his imaginings of their life together:

I saw Mr. Swan this evening and I thought of the drives we had out to his place over the prairies, and thought that the happiest moments of my life had been spent in your company. Just to think darling of the pleasant drives of the last two years, down on the river at our old Trysting place, and to think we never went there once this summer. And last summer of all the places we went to, that was the place we loved best. And then I allow my thoughts to penetrate into the future, and see a little house neatly furnished and neatly kept, and when my day's work is complete and I wend my way homeward with a brisk step knowing that my darling awaits my coming with one of the sweetest kisses imaginable. And then to sit down and talk of the day's duties that have just been done. And listen to you my dear as you sit at the Piano and play some of my favorites. And thus the evenings of the cold bleak winter that is before us will pass away. Evenings that will be what we make them and that will be pleasant ones for how could they be otherwise—two—us two who look forward to making each other happy.

Oscar Phillips wrote to Lena also of his dreams, whose details were not very different from his waking reveries. His many-paged letter of November 9 moved him to remark on its length: "if I don't stop soon I will not have anything to write next time, unless it be a love letter":

And I will begin it now. I dreamed I was floating down the placid stream the banks lined with trees from which came the sweet song of birds. The perfume of thousand of beautiful flowers was wafted over the water. I liked not these, for you my dear was in the boat. And I was gazing in those wondrous eyes of yours that shot forth flames of love. That was penetrated my cold gloomy nature and made me see that life was all a blank without some loved one to cheer you on.

He wrote more, about her voice "like the riple of silver waters," and about the "liquid depths of those glowing eyes" that had made him "a target for cupid's bow that drives the arrow of love." Then, like a dreamer waking, he abruptly changed scenery by changing language, but it is difficult to decide whether he meant any humor:

It was thus I dreamed as I floated down the stream, and of wandering through sunny fields, shady groves and with my loved one by my side. We talked of the future, and of how happy we would be, and how it thrilled me with joy when you put your hand in mine and we wandered back to the river. Well dear I woke up here and found that you were in St. Paul. And that I only have a two cents stamp to post this with and that if I wanted it to carry it, I had better stop.

Phillips indicated that he thought of passages such as these to be deliberate composed set pieces, for the next day he wrote again of carpeting and papering, and added a postscript:

I believe I started the last letter very abruptly and not with very endearing terms. When I started to write I could not think of any term endearing enough and thought would leave it and finish and start the letter afterwards and it strikes me that in the rush to get it mailed I forgot to start it right but it was an oversight dear and not premeditated and will try and make up for it in the future.

His letter of November 16 praised one he had received from her: "And how I would like to see you if but for a short time say this evening. I can almost feel your hot breath on my cheek now as if I was going to receive one of the sweetest kisses man ever received. But it is not so," and he kissed her picture instead "for I haven't the original to kiss and have to make the shadow answer." He had little patience, however, with dreams and fancies of others:

And tell Mrs. Hendrickson that I think she thinks more about getting rid of you than I do of coming down, or else she would not of drempt of it as it is said that the thing that fills one mind, or the thing dwelt on the most is the thing apt to be reproduced in one's dreams, and so far I think I have one on her. [November 25]

For Oscar Phillips literary phrases were the most personal expressions he could risk in approaching Lena Olmstead. He depended on them to express his love and to calm his various anxieties. When he tried to make amends after rebuking her for having told Mrs. Hendrickson that he had sent her money, and he wanted to cure his faults, he said,

for everything must be as pleasant and calm in our cozy little home as a clear summer day in June with no clouds to mar its brightness. The clouds if any must float away before our wedding day, as the damp mist flee from the rising sun on a foggy morning. [November 30]

He returned to the cozy home waiting for him in the last letter of the series. About the wedding, to take place three days later, he wrote that the beginning of my dream will be realized. And the balance will depend largely on my self as to its complement. But with your love to carry me along the dark clouds if any will clear away and all be bright and lovely.

Phill was deeply self-absorbed. He thought of Lena almost entirely in relation to himself, as a wife he would protect. When he occasionally was obliged to notice that parts of her life had nothing to do with him, he became confused and angry. He did not imagine her point of view; it did not occur to him to be curious about it. As a result he was at least once left in the dark, on the seemingly trivial question of setting the wedding day. From the onset of the correspondence both took it for granted that they were to be married; the question was precisely when. Other people's convenience does not appear to have been a factor: Lena's father and stepmother in Bartlett, while not opposed, were not being included in plans, and a brother and sister whom Phill mentioned were not involved either. The Hendricksons were ready to help find a clergyman to carry out a simple ceremony. Yet for Lena, deciding on a particular day was difficult, and Phill did not understand why that should be. She wrote to him from St. Paul on November 23, the first letter of hers in the series:

This is a beautiful day. Wish you were down here with your trotter (only a little better broken). Wouldn't we have fun. Well I think I'd be satisfied if just you were here, but one consolation, you will be soon. I suppose you often wonder when that will be and so do I. I had hoped it might be about the first of December, but now I am almost afraid it won't be, am quite sure of it in fact, for that is only a week hence. Of course we must be married on a Wednesday. I live in hopes it may be by the 10th of December anyway, but I can not tell anything about it. I am very sorry, but it is not my fault. Oh I often think how happy I will be when it is all over with and I am all yours. I expect to be in my seventh heaven when you are my *lord* and *master,* don't I? I never think of you that way though only just as my only love, my *dearest* darling Phil.

Lena teases about the term "lord and master" (it is rather close to the way Phill thinks of himself). Phill, meanwhile, had been chairman of a committee to plan a ball celebrating the dedication of the Larimore city hall, and for which a date also was to be set. The two events, marriage and ball, were logistically a single problem for Phill:

And we just had a meeting since I rec'd your letter and read it, and we set the date the 12th of December '90. It is to be a grand affair and I will feel quite disappointed if you are not able to attend for my enjoyment as it will depend greatly on your attendance. And I hereby beg of you to allow me the pleasure of acting as your escort and protector on that eve. Don't understand darling that I wish to hurry you up for I do not. You state the fault is not yours, that you are not ready. Whose is it dear, you are ready as far as I am concerned any time. I know you will want to attend the dance, and don't let any foolish ideas deter you from it, if I can help you (not that I think you have any). But if it depends on your Pa, write him and tell him the facts in the case, and that you must attend the dance. So you want to be married on a Wednesday. December 3rd comes on Wednesday, and that would give plenty of time in St. Paul after the wedding to select furniture and household goods such as we should buy, and get home in time for the Ball. [November 25]

Lena's wanting to be married on a Wednesday may have been a private superstition, but her vacillation among the weeks in December, I assume, though Phill did not, was because she did not want her wedding to coincide with her next menstrual period. The vague quibble over "fault," her lack of explanation when everything else she spoke about was so detailed, and her not alluding to the subject again, all suggest reserve but not crisis. Menstruation was still a taboo subject in 1890; it was hardly spoken of in public until after World War I when the Kotex Company began advertising its new invention, disposable sanitary napkins. But for Lena Olmstead, predicting her next period was not evidently a subject she could mention to a man like Oscar Phillips, even though she intended to marry him.

There is no overt mention of sexuality in these letters, no word even about children to share the coziness of their well-appointed home (though before long they had two daughters). There is a good deal in the letters, however, to suggest that the subject in some form was never far from their minds. Lena's humor toward herself, her fairly relaxed acceptance of other people, her practical and cheerful good sense and tactful kindness, all express a certain canny wisdom about what she is getting into. Phill is more solemn, humorless, anxious, deliberately evasive. Two topics in particular show each of them trying to cope with the unmentionable: the family affairs of Charles Olmstead, Lena's father, and the teasing Lena and Phill receive.

Lena felt both exasperation and affection toward her father. Once married and back in Larimore, she wrote to him on December 29, "Dearest Papa and Nellie and baby, I now address you as Mrs. O. H. Phillips, settled in Larimore all nice and cozy." She alluded enthusiastically though without details to the wedding, a week of shopping and theater in St. Paul, the house, her father's expected visit. "Oh Papa, I am just as happy as ever I can be. I wouldn't go back as I was for anything. I always thought I was happy then, but I am ever so much more so now." And then the more troublesome matter: "Well how is that wonderful baby getting along and have you named it yet. It seems so queer that I have a little brother. I am very anxious to see him." "Queer" with a touch of malice is the primary emotion the birth had elicited from Phill. He told her in the letter of November 19:

No Dear the folks have not shown up yet. Last eve five of us fellows were in to call on Sprague and Will said I had a little brother. I said of course I had a small brother or two, and nothing more was said. Have you heard? That is all I know, but don't give it away. How is that for my predictions.

Lena reacted sanguinely:

No, I was not aware that you had a little brother. Well that's great if it is so, isn't it. I just thought all the time that they wouldn't get down to Larimore. I'll bet Nell is disappointed if they aren't coming for she was bound to go. Actually I don't know of anyone who can be more provoking than Pa. I get so provoked at him sometimes I could fly. Now don't get scared Phil, for you are not one bit like him so of course you know I couldn't fly mad at you, why the very idea makes me smile, but

I know you would not blame me, for you know something about him. I would like to know if that is so. Wonder how Will heard. I haven't heard anything about them. [23 November]

Phill's letter of November 25 confirmed matters: "Yes it is true that the folks at Bartlett have a son, born two or three weeks since. Your Pa was down this week and went home today. Said the folks were getting on nicely, expect to move down in a few weeks at most." And on the thirtieth: "I don't know what your Pa intends to do, or when he will be down. I had very little talk with him except in a business way, and know nothing of his future plans," and more criptically several pages later: "Yes darling you have a half brother, but how do you mean he might of done you harm by appearing earlier?" If Lena was visiting her father's family in Bartlett in mid-September, and the child was born the first week of November, she surely must have been aware that her stepmother was pregnant, especially since she and Nellie appeared to have been on friendly terms, given the episode of teasing the hired man, Jim. It is possible that she may not have known; in any case, no mention evidently was made to Phill.

Charles Olmstead's apparently improper behavior; Phill's own "wintry" temperament, together with his financial and social ambitions; Lena's combined ingenuous good humor and inviolability, all made nervous days for Oscar Phillips before his wedding. He was not a good man to tease. He morbidly dreaded gossip about himself, but filled his letters with the private events of other people: "Mrs. Minnie Wall went to St. Paul last week, and I was told 'confidentially' (but it is all over town) that she had joined Mr. Wall her husband and everything was lovely once more. What do you think of that, ha" [September 17]. By late September Phill still had not told his friends that he intended to marry; moreover, he still denied it:

Oh yes a party came in the office today and held out his hand saying Phillips allow me to congratulate you, and I said certainly many thanks, and will you be so kind as to tell me the cause of this outburst of good wishes etc. Why he said, I was told you were married. Oh is that all I said, I thought perhaps I had fell heir to a fortune (and I had when I gained your love but I did not tell him so). But you are a little previous on the matrimonial subject. Come around later in the fall when chestnuts are ripe.

Phill defended his dignity in the literary mode, but the thought of "talk" nagged him:

Don't people talk about us. Well not a great deal to my knowledge. I guess they think it is a settled thing, and a sure thing has no charm for the gossipers, as they like to talk and invent things that are uncertain. Of course some times I am asked when it is to come off. I say what? or anything to suit the occasion. I see the papers quotes me as buying the Fagen house but I don't know where they get their authority as I told no one, but Mr. Miller and Wells as they were in a position to know but they said mum was the word but I don't care.

Lena, more relaxed and amused, entered into the joke:

When we got the Larimore paper where you had bought the house, how Messrs Hendrickson and Paish did talk all the time about the little house west of the church, the turtle doves and oh! I don't know what all. [November 23]

Lena's impatience with teasing had a more practical basis than Phill's, yet she showed none of his fear:

Received a letter from Mrs. Thompson Friday. I asked her how I should get into the house etc. She said if Mr. Fagen knew when I was coming he might make arrangements about the key or else I might come after it, or probably would find some *willing messenger*. Guess she doesn't imagine I will walk right to *our* own little home. What do folks think anyway, do they think I'm coming home and then—or don't they think at all. Surely they must, or what will happen? I was thinking what if Mr. H should tell Mrs. Stolz and then she tell Mr. S. Perhaps Mr. Hendrickson doesn't know that we intend to be married here but I shouldn't won-der, for one evening Erb was asking him where to get a license. He said he knew. He got Mr. S. and it doesn't cost anything. They are the biggest teasers here you ever saw. I expect they will give you a great rigamarole when you come. They have something to tell you 40 times a day. [November 30]

Phill regarded none of this with amusement: "So I am no stranger to the Hendrickson family. Well it amounts to the same thing to me as if I were, as they are total strangers to me. And Mr. Al Hendrickson wishes I was there so as to make fun for him. Well dear I have never posed as a char-acter of that kind and don't propose to now, especially to a stranger" [November 30]. Eventually he did make his intentions public, grudgingly:

So you want to know what people say about our marriage. Well dear they don't say very much to me about it. Someone will say that things look suspicious. I reply well I don't know that there is anything suspicious in my actions, for I am going to be married and am just fixing up the house so as to move in, so they let me alone.

His landlady invited him to supper on his last night in Larimore before the wedding:

This was offered in her motherly kindness and not for the purpose of teasing or gussing me. I thanked her heartily and said as arrangements wanted completion she might have a chance to befriend me yet, but would let her know in time. So you see dear that there are some folks that take an interest in my case out of pure kindness. [December 3]

But most of the interest he did not take kindly. Four days before the wed-ding, as he getting ready to leave Larimore, Mr. Wells

remarked that he supposed we would be married about the first, and inside of a month be settled there. I remarked that it was merely a supposition of his and required no answer. So that is the talk I occasionally hear, but I don't care who knows. [December 7]

How difficult it was for this couple to maintain privacy, what with the prying and spying, the reluctance conflicting with the desire to be known. Adding to the complications was their indecision about selecting their se-crets, separating what other people might as well know from what they truly wanted to keep to themselves. That separation was the more difficult to make because there was so little that Lena and Phill could permit themselves to be intimate about; they said so little to each other that was different from what they said to the world at large. The reticence, the brake on intimate disclosure, rested, in the letters, more heavily on Phill. At numerous times Lena risked exposing herself to him, and he reproved her every time: for staying out too late at a dance in Bartlett, for telling Mrs. Hendrickson that he had sent her some money, for prevaricating on setting the date for the wedding, for giving her opinion on the market for carpeting in St. Paul. He would have heard none of these small injuries from another source, and she did not need to tell him any of them, but, generously, she did. Doing so was her manner, her language of private rapport.

Oscar Phillips's private language runs to affected rhapsodies on love. He appeared suspicious and a little fearful, perhaps at her making herself vulnerable to him, since he neither shared nor recognized her sense of humor about herself. She could be funny at her own expense, as in this, four days before she was to be wed:

Oh Phil. I am the *maddest* girl tonight. I could cry if it would do any good. I went to have my bangs trimmed and curled today, they cut them too short. Oh I just look *horrid,* and just now when I wouldn't for anything. Of course it just makes me sick almost. You'll just be ashamed of me I know, for I am of myself. I surely thought they knew what they were about. Perhaps it won't be so bad when the curl gets out. It's curled as tight as wool. Oh I look sweet. . . . When I was so mad tonight I just wished I had you. I'd cry it out in your arms then (for I know you love to have me cry so well). . . . Good night. I'm going to dream of bangs now, or you. I hope you. Lena.

Her recovery was not prolonged, and the next day she told him:

I'm just a little better natured this morning, although I've made up my mind to cut my own hair after this. I'm horrid enough without becoming any worse. I'm afraid you'll disown me when you come. Guess I'll wear a mask or some such thing. I've heard of such cases in novels. [December 7]

And so the correspondence closed between Lena Olmstead and Oscar Phillips.

Neither Phill nor Lena visibly quarreled with prevailing social values, and in many respects they can be seen as "typical" of their time and class. They had the makings of a happy family. Phill, typically, was a rising young man. His business was prospering and well established, he had civic importance and the attention of numerous acquaintances—men for hunting and dining, women for dances and calls. His landlady was fond of him. It is true that he belittled the idea of living in Larimore and that he spoke of no relative or single acquaintance as a close friend. He expressed no passionate interests or ideas. His punctuation meanders and his spelling of words with double consonants is no better than chance. But other

than admitting to a "wintry" disposition, Oscar Phillips at the close of the
year 1890 could be judged a happy man, to the extent that he was unen-
cumbered by specific sorrows. The world, such at it was, was all before
him. And he was newly endowed with both house and wife. For him and
other men of his time who were rising in the middle class, unexplored
options were open. If he were dissatisfied with selling farm implements
in Larimore, he presumably could have earned a similar living elsewhere, and if Lena were not willing to marry him, there clearly were other
women glad of the chance. Other than voting Democratic in a Republican
district, Oscar Phillips behaved himself about as unobtrusively as anyone
could ask.

Lena also conformed to expectations. Even her complaints that she was
getting fat and growing a double chin are usual for attractive young
women. She was cheerful, good-natured, competent, loyal to her father
and his wife, and companionable with friends. But apart from marrying
Phill, she mentioned no other opportunities—no job or profession she was
foregoing for marriage, or other partners she might turn to if he defaulted.
Nevertheless, she was unafraid; the trip to Minneapolis, shopping and
travel, maneuvering her own wedding, to say nothing of furnishing her
house—none of these logistics appeared to worry her unduly.

The letters between Lena Olmstead and Oscar Phillips document also
the omissions upon which this Tolstoian happiness depended. Both of
them wrote fluently and with verve on the surface of things, showing catty
tones of voice, the stops and starts in conversation, and, Lena particularly,
an almost joyous self-deprecation. They poured their words on what was
safe—the price of carpeting and window sash—and these nearly profli-
gate details took the place of what they could not write about explicitly:
the eroticism compellingly evident around them. They said little of women
friends who schemed for dances; of other young women and men either
anxious for their futures or relieved, like the recently married McFs,
"happy as turtle doves also"; or of Matt Burgett whom Lena saw at church:
"He came down to get married also, introduced me to his wife, was married
last Wed., is going back next Wed. Catching isn't it?" [December 7]. Not
only was their own wedding on their minds, with the attendant gossip,
teasing, and rivalries of anxious competitors, but the less attractive example of Charles and Nellie Olmstead also was before them. For these
darker but interesting parts of their lives, Lena and Phill had few words.
Lena almost certainly knew about her impending half-brother, and said
nothing. Phill first wanted to deny the birth as he denied that he was to be
married, and shrugged them both off as past history. "Love" when he
wrote of it was a hazy literary dream, sleeping or waking. The careful and
polite cooperation and energetic competence that both gave to buying and
furnishing a house became their erotic speech with one another; it was
their way of agreeing to a domestic life together. Their exchange of letters
illustrates that this language worked not too badly for them, and doubtless
for many others.

Note

1. Phillips Family Correspondence, 1890–1919. Orin G. L. Libby Manuscript Collection, University of North Dakota Libraries. Contributed by Josephine Linscott, of Larimore, N. Dak.

PART FOUR

Coming to Terms with the West

After Euro-American women came west, did their behavior and attitudes change? Did the western experience help transform sex roles and perceptions of acceptable behavior for women and men? Historians interested in these questions have wrestled with the assumptions found in the older western history and those of the newer women's history as well. We have long debated the impact of the western frontier on American culture, since Frederick Jackson Turner suggested that the frontier provided an area in which to form new institutions and values. In 1959, David Potter closely examined employment opportunities on the frontier and questioned whether the assumed individualism and freedom associated with the West applied to women.[1] That question has influenced explorations of western women's lives ever since and several answers have been suggested. Recently Sandra Myres suggested that Turner was right, that for women, as for men, the frontier supported innovations in roles and behaviors, and that women realized the promise of expanded opportunities on the frontier.[2] But many scholars see little real transformation in sex-roles on the frontier.

Feminist historians who want to know how the West changed women's lives have also been influenced by new scholarship in women's history, and particularly by Barbara Welter's important article "The Cult of True Womanhood," which defined the four cardinal virtues of piety, purity, domesticity, and submissiveness that a "true" woman of the nineteenth century was supposed to embody.[3] Implicit in the ideology of True Womanhood were the assumptions that men and women occupied "separate spheres," that women's worlds were private, and that public action belonged to men. Dee Brown, who wrote the first major book on western women, The Gentle Tamers,[4] reinforced the image of the Victorian civilizer in the West. Brown maintained that women were the vehicles of east-

ern culture on the frontier where their mission was to re-establish civilized society. Supporting the argument of some western historians that there was more continuity than innovation on the frontier, Brown made women the agents of that continuity.

Recently, feminist historians have explored the extent to which the Victorian Cult of True Womanhood was adopted or changed in the West as one indication of whether the frontier was liberating for women. Julie Roy Jeffrey, for instance, found that many western women tried to live up to the precepts of the cult; in her view this mentality indicated a lack of innovation or liberation in western women's lives.[5] Others, like Katherine Harris, whose article appears in this section, think that the notion of separate spheres empowered women by presuming their superiority in certain areas of daily life. We need more work to understand how deeply and in what ways Victorian ideology affected westerners and how sex roles were adapted to western life. The articles in this section are an important start.

These articles explore the questions of how women came to terms with the West, and how older roles were preserved or changed. Certainly, women had to make many adaptations in a new land. Older forms of housekeeping and childrearing, of friendship and social life, were changed in a new and unfamiliar environment. By exploring how work roles, family roles, and community participation were defined during the frontier period and after, we may begin to understand how sex roles changed, and the parts westerners played in changing them.

Notes

1. David M. Potter, "American Women and the American Character," a lecture presented in 1959 at Stetson University, in Don E. Fehrenbacher, ed., *History and American Society: Essays of David M. Potter* (New York: Oxford University Press, 1973), pp. 277–303.

2. Sandra L. Myres, *Westering Women and the Frontier Experience, 1800–1915* (Albuquerque: University of New Mexico Press, 1982).

3. Barbara Welter, "The Cult of True Womanhood: 1820–1860," *American Quarterly* 18, no. 2 (Summer, 1966): 151–74.

4. Dee Brown, *The Gentle Tamers: Women of the Old Wild West* (Lincoln: University of Nebraska Press, 1958).

5. Julie Roy Jeffrey, *Frontier Women: The Trans-Mississippi West, 1840–1880* (New York: Hill and Wang, 1979).

10.

Women as Workers, Women as Civilizers: True Womanhood in the American West

ELIZABETH JAMESON

In this article, Elizabeth Jameson questions whether Frederick Jackson Turner's frontier thesis and the Cult of True Womanhood are useful start-ing points for examining changes in the lives of western women. Imposing the images either of frontier liberation or of genteel womanhood, she says, distorts women's lives and makes women passive objects of their own history. More explicitly than in any other article in this book, Jameson shows the methodological consequences of making women the actors in their own stories. Once we do this, we can look through western women's eyes at the contrast between their private lives and their public images. Jameson goes on to offer a number of suggestions for getting past the stereotyped images to the realities of how women shaped continuity and change in their own lives. She provides useful guideposts for judging the meaning of the western experience from the perspectives of the women who lived it.

I lived the history that I can tell. And of course the history today in books that's written a lot is not really the true thing, as it was lived.[1]

May Wing, who spoke these words, was born in Leadville, Colorado, in 1890. A daughter, wife, and mother of miners, she spent her life in Colo-rado mining towns. I do not think that May Wing would recognize herself in much of the scholarship on western women, which has been influenced by the assumptions of both traditional western history and the Victorian Cult of True Womanhood.[2] Assuming that men's and women's worlds were separate, that men's lives were public and women's were private, that men were active and women were passive, historians have created a number of polarized images of western women. Common stereotypes divide them into good and bad women, either genteel civilizers and sunbonneted help-mates, or hell raisers and bad women.[3] Recently some historians have dis-tinguished class divisions within prostitution and have begun to provide a more complicated sense of "bad women's" lives and options.[4] But our understanding of all women's roles has been shaped by prescriptions for female respectability in Victorian America, and I want to concentrate here

Home in the Rockies, December, 1896. Courtesy Amon Carter Museum, Fort Worth, Texas.

on interpretations of the lives of most western women, who were married and therefore "good."

Understandings of these "good" women's lives have been influenced by the polarized images of the genteel civilizer and the helpmate (or the oppressed drudge). The civilizer was projected from Victorian prescriptive literature, which reflected and taught the cardinal virtues of "true womanhood": piety, purity, domesticity, and submissiveness to male authority. Women were to shape national morality from the privacy of their family hearthsides, leaving public action to men. The assumption that women behaved as they were told influenced early works on western women, beginning with Dee Brown's *The Gentle Tamers* in 1958.[5] He portrayed an image of western woman as the reluctant pioneer who, while her man tamed the physical wilderness, gently and passively tamed the man and brought civilized culture to the frontier. Although civilization and culture were, perhaps, laudable goals, the problem with the genteel civilizer was that she did nothing active to achieve them. Historians countered this passive image by emphasizing the hard work women did, but this approach led to equally one-dimensional views of the heroic feats and stoic endurance of oppressed wives. Both the genteel civilizer and the oppressed drudge can be found in recent works.[6]

These dichotomized images are rooted in the presumed separation of public spheres as places for men only and private spheres for women only. Yet in the West women entered the public arena of the voting booth before their eastern sisters did. By 1914 women could vote in the Territory of Alaska and eleven states. All but Illinois were west of the Mississippi, and in Canada suffrage was first won in three western provinces. Influenced by Frederick Jackson Turner's frontier thesis that the West was a liberating and innovative environment, historians accepted the belief that the frontier liberated women. Then they debated whether men "gave" women the vote because they valued women's civilizing influence or because they recognized women's contributions as workers. Recently, feminist historians like Julie Roy Jeffrey have questioned the significance of suffrage, pointing out that political emancipation does not necessarily mean sexual or social emancipation, and have looked instead for transformations in the Cult of True Womanhood and in women's work roles as evidence of women's liberation in the West. While the assumptions of a public literature which sharply differentiated women's and men's roles and spheres have been a starting point for most of this history, there are important questions we need to raise about how accurately that literature reflected western women's lives. We need to think carefully about what different sources tell us about the work, daily concerns, and public actions of western women.

The use of prescriptive literature assumes literacy in English and adherence to upper-class Euro-American values, an assumption which excludes virtually all American Indians, Hispanics, blacks, Asians, and many European immigrants, and fails to explore class differences among Euro-American women. When historians find evidence of Victorian values in western women's writing, we need to remember who *wasn't* writing. By virtue of class or ethnicity, most western women did not fit the prescriptions of True Womanhood. Moreover, ideology does not describe behavior. We need only to reflect on the prescriptive literature which surrounds us today, from *Cosmopolitan* to *Ladies Home Journal,* to realize that there is often a difference between what a culture tells us we *ought* to do and what we in fact *do.*

Our problems of interpretation of western women's lives have been at least partially problems of sources. Historians went first to prescriptive literature and the writings of prominent people because those were the easiest sources to locate. Such documents are saved in archives. The census and other demographic materials provide descriptions of some important factors: the ratio of women to men, the ethnic composition of an area, female literacy, the number and spacing of children, who kept boarders, and so on. Such materials, though they have not yet been used extensively in western women's history, have much to tell us. But they cannot provide a subjective entry into women's lives, nor are they helpful in describing the variety of women's work, which, with the exception of keeping boarders, was rarely noted by census takers. We need additional sources to provide accurate, three-dimensional pictures of western women.

I began thinking about how our images are related to our sources through my work on women in the Cripple Creek, Colorado, mining district. The public literature I consulted, including male working-class newspapers, defined men by their work roles, but defined women by their relationship to morality, as either "good" or "bad." This literature, so pre-occupied with female gentility, virtually ignored women's work.[7] But my oral-history interviews with mining-town women revealed a women's community and a female culture which revolved around the female life cycle and around women's work. I began to question some of my earlier interpretations and to contrast the public image of mining-town women with the images they drew themselves.

In questioning others' interpretations of western women, then, I am not denigrating the often-important work of historians who have used the conceptual frameworks of prescriptive literature, but am trying to describe a historiographic journey in which we are all engaged. I have used the work of other historians in this article to include women outside the scope of my own research. I have included Canadian materials because western women in the United States and Canada did similar work, received similar messages about appropriate domestic roles, and were granted the vote before eastern women.

Most of the documents we have used to explore the lives of western women have been public documents. These include newspapers and other male sources, and also women's diaries, which were often intended to be shared as family history, as guidebooks for the western journey, or for publication. Some were copied before they were given to archives or to family members.[8] They often omit women's private concerns, although they are sources for accounts of daily activities and were more frequently outlets for emotions than were men's diaries. What sources, then, round out the picture of women's lives in the West? We are not, to use an over-worked concept, dealing with histories of the "inarticulate." We are trying to hear what women *have* articulated, but which has not been heard, either because their words are not found in archives, or because they speak of things which until recently we haven't defined as the stuff of history. Two excellent sources through which to approach the daily lives of western women are oral histories and private writing, some of which is in historical collections, and more of which can be gleaned from family attics. Elizabeth Hampsten, who has published the letters of North Dakota women, made some important observations about the language of women's sources. She emphasized that nineteenth-century language instruction "strongly advocated rising class expectations," so that public documents use more formal and genteel language and are more likely to reflect pre-scribed cultural values. "I have found," she wrote, "that this language of composition differs markedly from the conversational talk encountered in the letters and diaries of working women," and she noted the "highly oral" and less formal language of these sources, which is similar to the language of oral history interviews.[9] While public language sometimes supported notions of female submissiveness, purity, and leisured domesticity, the women's informal talk frequently does not. Understanding the contexts of public and private language, we may begin to transcend the dichotomized spheres and see women whole. We can consider what different sources tell us about women's image as reluctant pioneer, about their daily work, and about the supposedly widely separate worlds of private sexuality and public community involvement.

Although historians differ about the impact of the westward journey on women's roles, most agree that the decision to move west was made by men.[10] The image of women as reluctant pioneers is derived partly from women's diaries and letters from the Overland Trail, which indicate that many women felt torn about the western journey or joined their husbands under protest. An example is the frequently quoted Abby Fulkerath, who wrote: "Agreeable to the wish of my husband, I left all my relatives in Ohio . . . & started on this long and somewhat perilous journey. . . . it proved a hard task to leave them but harder still to leave my children buried in graveyards."[11] Responding to her pain at leaving her family and dead children, we may too easily reduce her to a reluctant pioneer. But what did she mean by "agreeable"? Did she genuinely agree with her husband's desire to move, but feel torn at the same time by what she left behind? A more complicated reading of such sources may replace the images of adventurous men and passive women with a more complex understanding of the competing emotional and economic reasons each had for staying or leaving. Women's pain at going west is expressed primarily in terms of leaving family and women friends. Some, of course, may have been able to prevent the move west, and we don't know how many vetoed the journey. More importantly, for many women such concerns did not apply, because they brought their families with them. Nearly half "of all emigrant families traveled in larger-than-family groups based on kin," most often in extended family groups. At least 40 percent of the households listed in the 1850 Oregon census had kinship ties with at least one other household,[12] and after the first settlement of an area, people often migrated to reunite families, an entirely different emotional proposition from leaving kin. Since many diarists wrote for family and friends left behind, they may not accurately represent the feelings of all women emigrants.

Another factor that affected a woman's enthusiasm was her point in the life cycle. Lillian Schlissel found that Overland Trail diaries reflected that newlyweds and single women liked the journey more than did women of childbearing age. Sheryll Patterson-Black found considerable enthusiasm for establishing homesteads among women who moved to western Nebraska or eastern Colorado from areas slightly further east, from single women and widows, and from independent women homesteaders.[13] We need to sort out the relative importance of the length of the journey, closeness of women and kin, life cycle, previous farming experience, and family status in women's feelings about the move west. Beyond these distinctions, we need to remember that experience sometimes overcame initial reluctance, and diaries written during the journey did not represent women's reactions after they were settled. The image of the reluctant pioneer illustrates the need to be careful about assuming that our images represent women's real experiences.

DAILY REALITY

The daily realities of western women's lives were shaped by work and by family concerns related to childbearing and childrearing. These two areas were not unrelated. A woman's work multiplied as her family did, and women did not therefore make as sharp a separation between work and sexuality as the public culture implied. Although some historians have questioned whether the frontier was a liberating environment for women because traditional divisions of labor were not abandoned, the *existence* of work roles rather than their persistence should encourage us to rethink the significance of the Cult of True Womanhood in the West. While some of its ideals were expressed by some western women, the roles it prescribed could be attained only by leisure-class urban women. Definitions of Victorian womanhood arose from the changing realities of an elite who did not perform productive labor and who were valued for their very economic uselessness. That ideal was far from the reality for homesteaders or for working-class women in mining towns or urban areas.

Women as civilizers were presumed to be dependent on male labor and submissive, therefore, to male authority. Yet the homestead family was an interdependent economic unit. Work was divided, as in most cultures, along gender lines. Men plowed, planted, and cared for the sheep, horses, and pigs. Women raised and processed vegetables, kept the dairy and the poultry, made clothing, cared for the sick, and did housework. In mining towns, where the male-dominated work structure created the greatest possibility for achieving idealized work roles, women's wage work consisted mostly of domestic labor—cooking, sewing, keeping boarders, waitressing, doing laundry, and prostitution. Married women frequently tended vegetable gardens and small livestock, made clothing, did housework, and provided income by keeping boarders, cooking, or doing laundry at home. The existence of separate work roles does not tell us how women perceived or valued their labor. Moreover, the spheres, if separate, were permeable. Men could and did cook, do housework, care for the sick and dying, even deliver babies. Women could and did plow, plant, and harvest.[14] And all western women knew periods when they had full responsibility for managing family economic fortunes. Male homesteaders left to earn money. Mormon men went on missions, and Mormon women assumed primary economic responsibility. The wage work available to black men, especially on the railroads, took them away from their families.[15] In mining towns, shutdowns, strikes, and accidents, if they didn't leave a woman a widow, left her responsible for family welfare for a time. And a man's death left a woman responsible for wage work or fieldwork as well as "women's work."[16] In any of these circumstances, family survival depended on flexibility and interdependence in work roles. One consequence may have been that men and women understood the labor involved in each other's work and respected one another for it. As one man who briefly agreed to cook on the Overland Trail wrote, "I have given up the office of chief cook and take my turn with the rest and my portion of other duties. I had rather do it as it is more slavish work than I had anticipated and by far the hardest post to occupy." [17]

The public image of women's work, however, was often idealized. The public literature said, for instance, that "the interior of the home of the average industrious miner of the Cripple Creek district . . . would be a revelation. . . . Their homes are neatly furnished, carpets on the floor, kitchens furnished with all the conveniences a good housewife is so proud to own." One Cripple Creek woman wrote that a workingman should be able to come home to a "rosy wife" who could "sing at the wash tub" and find "nothing under the sun that makes her as merry as housecleaning." [18] The reality was harder and more mundane. For all the talk of "modern conveniences," no woman I interviewed had a washing machine before 1915, and few had running water. Cooking on coal or wood stoves; hauling water for cooking, cleaning, and washing; sometimes hauling and heating water for baths for men on different shifts; doing the family baking; raising and processing vegetables at high altitudes, were more than full-time oc-cupations. One woman I interviewed baked fifteen loaves of bread twice a week. Leslie Wilkinson remembered clearly how hard his mother worked.

Bake day, mending day. A certain day for a certain thing. That's what I remember, those special days that my ma had. Ironing, cooking, and washing, every day. Then her day, Friday, was mending day. She always sat down and mended every-thing that had to be mended. . . . Oh, it went on to maybe 11 o'clock at night, my mother'd be ironing, the door wide open.

Kathleen Chapman described how much housework had changed from the days when she scrubbed clothes on a washboard, and hauled fuel in and ashes out. She said her mother "never was idle. I never knew Mama to be idle." [19]

Since children added to women's workloads, it should not surprise us that private sources reveal women sharing information about the various stages of their life cycles, including how to avoid pregnancy. Perhaps no-where is the difference between public assumptions about women's nature and private reality more pronounced than in the expectation that "true women" were "pure," that is, asexual. The strains of childbearing and the work involved in caring for small children formed an important difference between male and female experience. As one woman told me, " . . . one thing that was nice, after you went through menopause, you didn't have to worry. You don't have to figure on a calendar and figure up so many days, you know." And John Ise wrote that his home was "pleasanter" after his mother stopped having children, that she became "gentler and mellower" after she was released "from the strain of bearing and caring for the babies." [20]

A rich and largely private world of women sharing information about contraception, pregnancy, birth, and menopause is beginning to be documented from a number of places. In contrast to the more careful prose of public life, women wrote privately about excreting and "farting"; they discussed, often with humor, concerns about sexuality, contraception, and pregnancy.[21] Although a number of birth-control techniques were described in print before 1873, the passage of the Comstock Laws made it illegal to mail contraceptive information and pushed this aspect of women's culture even further underground. Yet the women of the nineteenth-century West were less prudish than prescriptive literature would lead us to expect. The first woman I interviewed about birth control was by far the most uneasy. She told me that she didn't know how her mother "kept from having more than she did," because when her mother's friends visited, the children were locked out of the parlor while the "woman talk was going on." [22] Although she was barred from the "woman talk," it was harder to maintain such innocence in a one-room house, and many children must have been aware of sexuality.[23]

Whether or not a woman's mother explained the facts of life to her, some older woman usually offered advice. One woman said her mother-in-law told her how to douche.[24] Another told me:

Well, usually when a girl was going to be married, these old ladies would tell them. I imagine if my mother had been alive, she would. But my second stepmother, she used to talk to us girls a lot. And then they was a lady that lived next door. When she heard I was going to be married, she asked me over to tea one day. She asked me if I knew anything, and then she told me a lot of things.[25]

The variety of suggested contraceptives demonstrates women's determination to find something that worked.

Well, they had different things that they would use. Now, I know, when I was married, the older women, they used Vaseline a lot. They said a greased egg wouldn't hatch. And then a lot of them used salt. They would use this, you know, that they put in ice cream, this rock salt. . . . I never did use the rock salt. Because we were told that it wasn't a good thing to use—it affected the mind. . . . And then, of course, we were more or less a little bit careful. I suppose the Catholics called it the rhythm, you know, and we were taught on that. Well, of course, we were always told as long as you nursed a baby, you wouldn't conceive. You see, you wouldn't menstruate. So I didn't, I nursed Bob until he was 18 months old. . . . [T]he older women, they would get out of bed right away, and in that way they claimed that they could help themselves. Of course, we had chambers at that time, and they would just go there, and of course they thought that they had lost everything. They was a lady that come through one time, and she asked us if we used birth control, and she had a recipe, or a receipt, whichever you'd call it. She took cocoa butter, and you took a shoebox, with the top on it, and then you put holes in it. Then you put this melted cocoa butter in it. Then there was something else she used to put in it—what was it? . . . Boric acid. So much boric acid with so much cocoa butter. And you made these—they'd be a little cone, like, and you'd use those. We made them together, this [friend] and I; we met the lady and we used to make them together. Yes, it worked. And in later years, in the magazine, you saw where there was a rubber kind of a thing, that you would insert in your vagina. Like a diaphragm.[26]

The same list of possibilities crops up in sources from different places. The cocoa butter recipe, for instance, is spelled out in greater detail in an unsigned letter addressed to "Dear Momma," included in Violet McNaughton's papers in Canada, and the recipe was accompanied by a batch of the suppositories, in this case cut into squares like fudge. In Canada, women's sections of agricultural newspapers carried requests for contraceptive information. In both countries, references to attempts to miscarry can be found, even in published sources.[27] These glimpses of a widespread folk tradition shared by Victorian women suggest a history of private concerns that knit women's lives together. We might document this more fully through private literature and oral histories.

While women shared information about contraception, childbirth, and menopause, sex was a slightly different matter. One woman told me that "Our sex life was secret," and denied that women talked about sex, even though she could tell me the birth-control strategies of each of her friends. My small number of interviews about sex revealed different feelings about sexuality and who controlled it. Most women said they were ignorant of sex before marriage, but one woman suggested that men were ignorant, too. She said that she was married two weeks before her husband touched her, which surprised her because "I had been told, you know, how some men, how—they were." She said that she was happy with being kissed and held "because I didn't know any different. But after I realized what sex was, why, it was different." She said, "I suppose somebody maybe at the store told him what he was to do—what that thing was for!" This woman said that she enjoyed sex and experienced orgasm. "As I've told so many, you've got to find a man knows how to handle a woman in sex, for you to enjoy it." But, she said, "I could take it or leave it and be happy either way. . . . I never married a man for sex, or I don't think I ever married a man for love, either. More for security." She felt that it was not proper for her to initiate sex, and that she could not refuse. "I felt that that was my duty, to be available. They were making a living for you. . . then you should please them." She reflected the Victorian notion of wifely duty, but her experience of sexuality was more complex. While this woman felt sexually subservient because she was financially dependent, a contemporary expressed the opposite view. She said, "Sex wasn't your main life, as it is today," because women worked harder in the past and "most men respected a woman if she was tired"; consequently, women initiated sex. She added, "I had a good man. Now some of them weren't that good. They were demanding. Didn't make any difference how a woman felt."[28] It is clear from her generalizations about "most men" and "some men who were demanding" that women discussed at least that aspect of sexuality. At the same time, it is important to hear the tension in these statements between women's beliefs about what ladies *should* talk about and the reality of what women *did* discuss. Further, most of the evidence we have for women's private concerns about sexuality is from the late nineteenth and early twentieth centuries; we don't yet know whether we are documenting the transformation of women's attitudes, or conversations that existed earlier but can no longer be recorded.

If women discussed sexuality in private, their talk did not change public portrayals of female purity. Although western women were most concerned with daily reality, they also wanted to appear respectable. They publicly denied some private concerns, and they desired the nicer things that ladies could have. Some adolescents, like Laura Ingalls and Anne Ellis, resented the discomfort of ladies' clothing and resisted wearing corsets. Others desired respectability more than comfort. Beulah Pryor was taken out of school to help her mother do laundry and run a boardinghouse to support the family, after her mother threw her husband out of the house for beating her. Beulah saved every cent for years to buy a much-coveted corset and a pair of high-heeled shoes; she did hard work in this uncomfortable clothing because it represented so much to her. The corset may have contributed to an early hysterectomy after carrying heavy buckets of coal ruptured her ovaries.[29] Trying to do heavy labor in the trappings of a "lady" is a highly material sign of the contradiction between upper-class ideology and working-class reality. Similarly, the distance between women's private letters and conversations and the public image suggests that daily life was "corseted" into genteel language for public respectability.

PUBLIC LIFE

It is not surprising that much of women's private talk remained private. It is more difficult to grapple with the fact that much of their public work remained similarly invisible to historians. Women's family concerns were extended to establishing communities and building schools, churches, and social groups. But women received less credit than men for their community service, and the public recognition system has enforced the distinction between public spheres for men and private spheres for women. Julie Roy Jeffrey wrote, for example, that in Roseburg, Oregon:

as elsewhere, it was the men who usually established the political, social, and economic institutions which would help to integrate the community and who founded its official cultural groups like lyceums and debating societies. *At least they took credit for these activities.* [italics added][30]

But many women knew otherwise. One Canadian woman described how the Women's Institute started hospitals and libraries when no one else would, and then municipalities took the credit after they were established. "That happened again and again. The Institute started something and then it was taken over by the people who should have done it in the first place." Another said, "The women . . . did just as much to make this western country as any of the men did. They were just taken for granted. . . . Women sat in the background while the men got praised."[31]

Occasionally women were recognized, as in emergencies when they performed "male" roles. In mining towns, women received public notice for their toughness during strikes, much as women workers have been valued during wartime. During strikes, women and children could yell at the militia, throw stones at soldiers, distribute strike relief, and do other things for which men would have been jailed or shot. They received public praise for these actions, but the public accounts again differ in tone from the women's own voices. The *Miners' Magazine* wrote during the Cripple Creek strike, for instance:

Mrs. James Prenty and Mrs. Blixer, both prominent in the women's auxiliary . . . were in custody, though not under arrest, for about an hour today. They were charged with having indulged in insolent criticism and denunciation of the military. They were allowed to sit on the stairs leading to the bullpen for a while and were then taken before Provost Marshal McClelland, who gave them a lecture on the necessity of using caution in their public speech.[32]

There is a sharp contrast between the "insolent criticism and denunciation" of public discourse, and women's more earthy accounts of the strikes, which connect family concerns with public action. One woman told me how her mother wrapped her firstborn in a blanket and went with her husband to mill around Bull Hill to convince the sheriff's deputies who were coming to end a strike that they were outnumbered. She dated the strike in family time: "In 1894 Tom was born, and that's when the Bull Hill strike was." Another told me how the women in her family protected their homes from the militia.

I did have an uncle that lived in Goldfield. His name was Ed Doran. And Grandma was there, Aunt Mary was expecting. So Uncle Ed, of course, got out. Well, he got word that they were going to raid the house. Of course the militia had the way of doing, in the middle of the night they'd come after the men and take 'em to the bullpen and then they'd send 'em out. But Uncle Ed got word that they were going to come that night, so he left. Grandma never said just exactly where he went or where he hid. But she was there when they came, and they tore that house to pieces! They even looked in the breadbox. Well, that got Grandma's goat. And she said, "Shure'n he's not little enough to put in the breadbox! Now every God-blesset one of you get out of this house and leave this woman alone!" She said, "You can see what condition she's in. Now," she said, "git!"
    Then I had another aunt that lived there. Her name was Hannah Welch. . . . And she had two great big butcher knives, and she kept those knives razor sharp. And she always said if one of those militia men ever come in her house in the middle of the night, they'd leave with less than they brought in![33]

The women saw the connection of public action with family needs, and seem to have known how hard they worked and what they contributed. As Nellie McClung, the Canadian feminist, said during World War I:

Women have been discovered more or less since the war began. You know we always knew ourselves that we were here; we always knew that we had hands to work and brains to think and hearts to love; we always knew that we were a National asset but there were some people that had not just realized it yet, statesmen particularly.[34]

There are two related issues here. The first is whether men recognized women's contributions, and what the differential rewards were for men's and women's community service. The answers will illuminate the question of whether some public options, like the vote and access to higher education, were extended to women at least partially because their work was valued. The second issue is how women themselves valued their daily work and community activities, and the extent to which they organized in their own behalf. Jeffrey argued that women did not act for themselves and that the recognition they received was based in conservative beliefs about sex roles:

A careful study of the two territories granting suffrage to women in 1869 and 1870 reveals, first of all, that the vote was offered to women, not because women thought to ask for it, but because it suited a minority of men to give it, and second, that the arguments made in favor of granting women the suffrage were conservative. Women were to vote not because they were the same or equal to men, but because they were different from men. The domestic conception of women provided the basis for the suffrage defense.[35]

The passivity of western women about suffrage has recently been challenged in two ways. Some new studies, like Carolyn Stefanco's, which appears in this book, document suffrage coalitions in the various western states. Other historians argue that women may have influenced politics in private, and criticize histories that focus on legislative debates and public arenas from which women were excluded before they could vote. Virginia Scharff, for instance, suggested that women's rights advocate Julia Bright probably influenced her husband, William, who introduced the suffrage bill in Wyoming.[36] At the first Wyoming legislative session, the lawmakers passed bills for suffrage, married women's property rights, and equal pay for male and female teachers. If as Jeffrey suggested there was no women's movement in Wyoming in 1869, it was perhaps because there were not enough women for a movement, but feminists like Julia Bright and Esther Morris influenced the legislation. Wyoming is an exception in western suffrage, however, which generally was achieved after the frontier period, when women were more numerous and more organized. After the frontier period, workloads lightened, neighbors were nearer, and contacts among women which led to organized reform increased.[37]

In Utah part of the support for suffrage came from the desire to insure a solid Mormon voting majority when non-Mormon settlement increased after the transcontinental railroad was completed. Additional factors included the existence of strong women's groups, the belief that granting suffrage would help hold onto a faction in the Church that favored it, and the desire to refute critics who believed polygamy enslaved women. For forty years after they were enfranchised, Mormon women published women's newspapers, organized suffrage groups, and campaigned for suffrage in other western states with Mormon settlement.[38]

There is considerable evidence in both the United States and Canada that women organized in their own behalf, and that their participation in rural reform movements, organized labor, and partisan politics contributed to suffrage victories. After the Civil War, large numbers of women were active in farm protest movements for the first time. They participated in the Grange, the Farmers' Alliance, the Populist Party, and later in the Socialist Party and the Farm Union. In both countries, women joined the pro-suffrage Women's Christian Temperance Union, not only in defense of morality, but also in defense of homes they had helped build and which they feared were threatened by male expenditures for alcohol. The genteel temperance movement took women out of their prescribed sphere and into the public arena. Smashing up saloons was hardly genteel behavior, however civilizing it may have been.[39]

The Grange and the Farmers' Alliance were unusual among male-dominated organizations in admitting female members, officers, and convention delegates. The Grange lodges provided services for women, like sewing-machine cooperatives; adopted women's issues, like opposing margarine as a substitute for their cash product, butter; and endorsed political rights for women. The Populist Party supported women as organizers, theorists, delegates, and candidates for public office. The Farmers' Alliance argued that women should be active because they had a direct economic interest in reform. That those direct economic interests were tied to regional and family economies does not make the argument conservative, but concrete. Some western women became interested in politics when they realized that the farms and homes they had helped build were endangered by public policy or could be sold by their husbands without their consent.[40]

The suffrage coalition included all of these groups, and could combine their moral and egalitarian arguments. The conservative arguments for suffrage were also used in the East but didn't work there, and both women and men tended to emphasize Victorian ideals in the public arena. Western women organized suffrage campaigns, circulated petitions, and lobbied for the vote. Male support seems to have come less from the genteel upper classes than from farmers and miners who endorsed political philosophies that supported equality. In the 1890s, Populists achieved suffrage in Colorado and Idaho, and in California and Kansas the countryside voted for suffrage, but urban voters defeated it.[41] In Colorado, the first state to enfranchise women by a vote of the male electorate, the strongest support before it was adopted correlated with the Greenback vote from 1878 to 1884, and with the Union-Labor vote in 1888. When it passed in 1893, the major support came from Populist metal miners.[42] While middle-class women were most visible as suffrage leaders, the influence of farm women and miners' wives on the vote needs to be considered.

The process was similar in Canada. In 1916 Manitoba, Alberta, and Saskatchewan became the first three provinces to enfranchise women. Again, the suffrage movement was related to female participation in agrarian reform. The Women's Institute was a forum and a meeting place, and by 1914 farm women with overtly political aims organized through the United Farm Women of Alberta and the Women Grain Growers' Association. The western women's movement began in Manitoba, where Icelandic women organized a suffrage league in the 1890s and the WCTU championed the cause before 1893. The Winnipeg (later the Manitoba) Political Equality League was founded in 1912 with support from the WCTU and the Manitoba Grain Growers. Manitoba women gathered 40,000 signatures on a suffrage petition before winning the vote on January 28, 1916. The Saskatchewan WCTU and Grain Growers Association petitioned for suffrage in 1912, and the Provincial Equal Franchise Board collected 10,000 signatures before women were enfranchised March 14, 1916. Alberta followed suit on April 6, after six years of lobbying by the WCTU, the UFWA, the Equal Franchise League, Women's Canadian Clubs, and Women's Institutes. The leadership of the WCTU and support from farm and labor movements characterized suffrage organizing in all three provinces.[43] Women in the western United States and Canada were not the passive recipients of male generosity regarding votes for women.

Western women voted as western men did after they were enfranchised. Perhaps their politics were shaped by family economic options rather than by abstract ideals about special female roles and values. We need a more complicated history to explain the connections between western women's daily lives and their public activism. Western women's history allows us to explore the reshaping of gender ideologies by people for whom leisure-class roles were not possible. Such a history cannot begin with the assumption that traditional cultural beliefs determined behavior. If they did, the belief systems would never change. The interaction between ideology and behavior makes history dynamic and reveals people's roles as historical actors who help shape social life.

The interplay of gender, family roles, and economics which shaped western women's options is more complicated than the images we have imposed on them. The Women's West Conference was an important step in the process of questioning older interpretations. Our evidence is still too scattered to suggest a new synthesis of western women's history, but new hypotheses are emerging.

It is fairly easy to criticize the traditional images of western women for their racial and class bias, and for the incredible passivity of the "gentle tamers." The emphasis on the helpmate's hard work was an important corrective to the utterly passive civilizer, but the helpmate led too easily to the one-dimensional drudge who was the passive victim of male oppression. Neither the civilizer nor the helpmate was an actor who helped to shape her own history, and thus neither image explains how beliefs and work roles changed. Despite notions of genteel womanhood that promised respectability, despite a patriarchal family system, and despite the fact that men got more public recognition than women for their work, women created a female community which supported them and they helped to shape communities and politics in the West.

How can we best explain western women's history? First, we need to stop assuming that all westerners believed in the Cult of True Womanhood. Instead, we need to define the beliefs about sex roles that westerners of different classes, races, and ethnic backgrounds expressed. Even when they publicly espoused some Victorian values, we need to examine the context and remember that they may have done so to lend respectability to beliefs and movements that challenged genteel assumptions. Thus, conservative arguments could lead to suffrage victories. As we document more concretely the variety of gender ideologies held in the West, we can explore whether contacts among people with different heritages, experiences, and beliefs created new understandings of sex roles.

If our research shows that some westerners internalized genteel sex roles, then we will need to look at how the Cult of True Womanhood was changed in the West. The possibilities include that change occurred because the belief system clashed with daily necessity, that internal inconsistencies within the belief system itself were heightened, and that change occurred over time through different generations' responses to the West and to larger social and economic changes. Let me comment briefly on each of these hypotheses.

First, the Cult of True Womanhood contained a widely recognized internal contradiction: women had to leave the domestic sphere for public action to achieve the moral authority they were told they should exercise. As women became more active in public arenas, their initial preoccupations with morality and culture could lead to sharper analyses of social issues, including the restriction of women to the private sphere. For example, Frances Willard, president of the WCTU, turned to socialism in the last years of her work, saying that she had thought people were poor because they drank, but that she had come to understand that they drank because they were poor. Sarah Platt Decker of Colorado, as president of the General Federation of Women's Clubs, helped shift her organization from a primary focus on culture to working for suffrage.

Just as involvement in "civilizing" activities could lead to political consciousness, daily experience may also have modified women's beliefs. Our genteel western foremothers learned to take off their gloves and cook with buffalo chips, however distasteful they found it. We need to explore further how such necessary acts modified genteel expectations, and then we need to look at frontier women's daughters, who appear to have been more receptive to new roles than their mothers were to the western journey.

These approaches need to be set in the context of larger economic and social changes that affected western women and their families. The West of traditional western history was the last frontier, both because Euro-Americans reached the western shores of the continent and, more importantly, because the development of national transportation, markets, and manufacturing transformed the West as Euro-Americans settled there. By the late nineteenth century, western agriculture was affected by new technology and by access to national markets, and mining had changed from the first excitement of the boom days to dangerous labor for a daily wage.

Families in farming and mining areas confronted growing urban and corporate control of their lives. On the farm, some of women's cash products were threatened, as butter was by margarine. Families were hard-pressed to buy machinery to grow cash crops for distant markets, and frequently felt threatened by banks, railroads, and grain elevators. Family security in mining towns was endangered by accidents, shutdowns, and strikes, and mine owners and the militia became tangible enemies to working-class families. The perception of common enemies may have emphasized the interdependence of family members and what women and men shared more than what separated them. Such common understandings may help explain women's entry into public life through reform and protest groups and partisan politics. Thus, outside forces may have helped transform genteel beliefs about appropriate behavior in the West.

Until we explore what beliefs and values men and women shared, we cannot assume that they inhabited totally different spheres. John Faragher found, for instance, that midwestern farm men and women were both concerned about practical economic considerations,[44] which may have been a major factor in couples' shared decisions to move west. The popular notion that women would civilize the West was really propaganda to encourage family settlement. Rather than assuming that western men were mythic rugged individuals whom genteel women were to civilize, we need to explore whether both sexes shared desires for stable households and communities. This will require that we look at men's private beliefs and concerns as well as women's, and one contribution of this new history may be that we will begin to look at the connections between public and private life for both men and women.

Rather than classifying women as civilizers or workers, and dividing the world into public and private spheres, exploring the connections of family and public concerns will show how women contributed in both arenas. One scenario is that women overcame loneliness by forming friendships and sharing work and private concerns. Then they joined together to build schools and churches, and entered public life to accomplish goals connected to family needs, which the public culture considered appropriate for women. In Colorado, for instance, women received the vote in school elections in 1876, and then the full franchise seventeen years later. At the same time, economic change stimulated the growth of populist and labor movements, which appealed to women's interests and which supported political alliances that contributed to suffrage victories.

Western women expected and found lives shaped largely by family responsibilities and hard work. Their understanding of family needs helped them transcend the dichotomized world the Cult of True Womanhood prescribed. They did not see themselves as passive civilizers or as uniquely oppressed, as wholly private or public. They understood that they performed valuable work for their families and their communities, and that these efforts were intertwined. One example is May Wing, who entrusted me with what she wanted said at her funeral. She did not talk about her hard work or her civilizing mission, but she wanted people to remember

that she had run the Victor Museum for twenty years (from age seventy to
ninety), that she had helped start the hot school lunch program in Victor,
that she had organized a boys' chorus, and that she had helped found and
had taught in a multidenominational Sunday School in Goldfield. She
worked hard all her life, and the connection of family with schools and
churches helped stimulate and support her community involvement, but
imposing the image of either civilizer or helpmate on her would falsify the
way she described her life and options. May Wing valued her work and
wanted recognition for it. "And these things I'm kind of proud of," she
said. "You can give it to the preacher and he could preach the story of
my life."[45]

We need to approach western women's history, not through the filters of
prescriptive literature or concepts of frontier liberation and oppression,
but through the experiences of the people who lived the history. The documents are hard to find, and until recently historians have not looked for
them. But we need to remember that western women "always knew ourselves that we were here." As we approach women's lives anew, we need to
let new questions come from their experience. The daily details of work,
family survival, and relationships dominate their words. Given the pre-
dominance of daily and personal experience, we might even ask whether
the question of public recognition is the most important starting place. We
may be accepting a male belief in the superior merit of public recognition
in conferring status, which needs to be balanced by the daily recognition
and support from family and women friends. Our foremothers may have
known that the details of daily survival and human touch dominate our
lives, not brief moments of public recognition or a few minutes in a voting
booth. If that is true, their emphasis on daily detail may be an important
contribution to feminist history. It may say that a history of daily life, in
which women were important actors, is more important than a history of
battles, dates, and kings.

I am not certain where our historiographic journey will take us next, but
our starting point must be western women's lives as they experienced
them. The challenge was issued by May Wing and by Nellie McClung,
who wrote, "I grew indignant as I read the history and saw how little the
people ever counted. . . . When I wrote I would write of the people who
do the work of the world, and I would write it from their side of the
fence."[46] Before we can usefully interpret western women's histories, we
need to accept their challenge. We need to listen to the many voices of the
women who lived the history that they can tell us, and then we need to
write it from their side of the fence.

Notes

I am indebted to many people, especially to the authors cited in this article, including
those whose conclusions I have questioned. Changing interpretations are healthy in a developing field, and everyone's work has been important in enabling us to raise new questions.
Elizabeth Hampsten, Maureen Ursenbach Beecher, Diane Sands, and Elliott West provided

useful comments for rewriting this article. I am particularly grateful to Susan Armitage for playing devil's advocate in ongoing conversations that have stimulated my questions and helped me rethink the topic.

1. Interview with May Wing, Colorado Springs, Colo., 16 Feb. 1979.

2. Barbara Welter delineated the prescriptions of the Cult of True Womanhood in her important article "The Cult of True Womanhood: 1820–1860," in *American Quarterly* 18, no. 2 (Summer, 1966): 151–74. An example of recent work that was influenced by older western history is Sandra Myres, *Westering Women and the Frontier Experience, 1800–1915* (Albuquerque: University of new Mexico Press, 1982), which emphasizes the themes of individualism and of the frontier as an arena for adaptation and liberation for women.

3. Beverly Stoeltje delineated the stereotypes in "A Helpmate for Man Indeed: The Image of the Frontier Woman," *Journal of American Folklore* 88, no. 347 (January–March, 1975): 27–41. For a discussion of challenges to the stereotypes see Joan M. Jensen and Darlis A. Miller, "The Gentle Tamers Revisited: New Approaches to the History of Women in the American West," *Pacific Historical Review* 49 (1980): 180–85.

4. See for instance Mary Murphy, "The Private Lives of Public Women," in this volume and "Women on the Line: Prostitution in Butte, Montana, 1878–1917" (Master's thesis, University of North Carolina at Chapel Hill, 1983); Paula Petrik, "Capitalists with Rooms: Prostitution in Helena, Montana, 1865–1900," *Montana The Magazine of Western History* 31 (April, 1981): 28–41; Marion S. Goldman, *Gold Diggers and Silver Miners: Prostitution and Social Life on the Comstock Lode* (Ann Arbor: University of Michigan Press, 1981).

5. Dee Brown, *The Gentle Tamers: Women of the Old Wild West* (Lincoln: University of Nebraska Press, 1958).

6. Julie Roy Jeffrey, *Frontier Women: The Trans-Mississippi West, 1840–1880* (New York: Hill and Wang, 1979), argues that women were civilizers who were strongly identified with the Cult of True Womanhood. Lillian Schlissel, *Women's Diaries of the Westward Journey* (New York: Schocken Books, 1982) emphasizes the image of woman as reluctant pioneer. Examples of the oppressed drudge or helpmate are most often found in local histories but are suggested by Schlissel and by Joanna Stratton, *Pioneer Women: Voices from the Kansas Frontier* (New York: Simon and Schuster, 1981).

7. Elizabeth Jameson, "Imperfect Unions: Class and Gender in Cripple Creek, 1894–1904," *Frontiers* 1, no. 2 (Spring, 1976): 89–117; also in Milton Cantor and Bruce Laurie, eds., *Class, Sex, and the Woman Worker* (Westport, Conn., and London: Greenwood Press, 1977), pp. 166–202.

8. The diary of Mollie Sanford, for instance, published as *Mollie: The Journal of Mollie Dorsey Sanford in Nebraska and Colorado Territories, 1857–1866* (Lincoln: University of Nebraska Press, 1959), was taken from a holographic copy which Mollie Sanford produced before bequeathing it to her grandson.

9. Elizabeth Hampsten, *Read This Only to Yourself: The Private Writing of Midwestern Women, 1880–1910* (Bloomington: Indiana University Press, 1982), pp. 50–51, and *To All Inquiring Friends: Letters, Diaries, and Essays in North Dakota, 1880–1910* (Grand Forks: Department of English, University of North Dakota, 1979), p. 1.

10. Schlissel, *Women's Diaries of the Westward Journey,* p. 10; John Mack Faragher, *Women and Men on the Overland Trail* (New Haven, Conn., and London: Yale University Press, 1979), p. 171; Jeffrey, *Frontier Women,* pp. 63–64.

11. Quoted in Lillian Schlissel, "Mothers and Daughters on the Western Frontier," *Frontiers* 3, no. 2 (Summer, 1978): 30.

12. Faragher, *Women and Men,* p. 33; Jeffrey, *Frontier Women,* p. 76.

13. Schlissel, "Mothers and Daughters on the Western Frontier," pp. 29–33; Sheryll Patterson-Black, "Women Homesteaders on the Great Plains Frontier," *Frontiers* 1, no. 2 (Spring, 1976): 67–88.

14. See William D. Haywood, *Bill Haywood's Book: The Autobiography of Big Bill Haywood* (1929; reprint, New York: International Publishers, 1974), pp. 38–39, 45, for examples of a man delivering a child and doing housework; and John Ise, *Sod and Stubble*

(1936; reprint, Lincoln: University of Nebraska Press, 1967), pp. 29, 83–84, 109, for examples of women doing fieldwork and of men nursing the sick. Other examples abound in the primary literature.

15. Ruth Flowers interview by Theresa Banfield, quoted in Sue Armitage, Theresa Banfield, and Sarah Jacobus, "Black Women and Their Communities in Colorado," *Frontiers* 2, no. 2 (Summer, 1977): 46.

16. See, for example, the account of Maria Duran Apodaca, quoted in Joan Jensen, *With These Hands: Women Working on the Land* (Old Westbury, N.Y.: Feminist Press; New York, St. Louis, and San Francisco: McGraw-Hill Book Co., 1981), p. 121.

17. Quoted in Faragher, *Women and Men*, p. 82.

18. "Business Prosperity Depends on Labor," *Cripple Creek Daily Press*, 23 Apr. 1901, p. 4; Augusta Prescott, "The Kind of a Woman a Workingman Should Marry," *Cripple Creek Daily Press*, 15 Feb. 1903, p. 12.

19. Interview with May Wing, Victor, Colo., 21 Oct. 1978; interview with Leslie Wilkinson, Cripple Creek, Colo., 7 Sept. 1975; interview with Kathleen Chapman, Wheat Ridge, Colo., 27 Apr. 1979.

20. May Wing interview; 21 Oct. 1978; Ise, *Sod and Stubble*, p. 274.

21. For examples see Hampsten, *To All Inquiring Friends*, pp. 34, 44, 15–16, 18–19, 30, 39; and Linda Rasmussen, Lorna Rasmussen, Candace Savage, and Anne Wheeler, *A Harvest Yet to Reap: A History of Prairie Women* (Toronto: Women's Press, 1976), p. 72.

22. Interview with Clara Stiverson, Golden, Colo., 29 July 1975.

23. I began thinking about children's awareness of sexuality on the frontier in 1972, when I was in Nulato, an Alaskan Athabaskan village. One day a small boy asked me where moose came from. Like most children in Nulato, he lived in a one- to three-room house. As I struggled with my limited knowledge of the mating habits of moose, his face suddenly lit up with recognition. "Oh," he said. "They got boy moose and girl moose!"

24. Interview with Beulah Pryor, Colorado Springs, Colo., 6 May 1979.

25. Interview with May Wing, Boulder, Colo., 6 Mar. 1976.

26. Ibid.

27. See Rasmussen, Rasmussen, Savage, and Wheeler, *A Harvest Yet to Reap*, pp. 27, 74; Anne Ellis, *The Life of An Ordinary Woman* (1929; reprint, Lincoln and London: University of Nebraska Press, 1980), pp 193–94; Faragher, *Women and Men*, pp. 123, 235; Jeffrey, *Frontier Women*, p. 58.

28. Although I have been granted permission, through signed release forms, to share this information, I have elected not to identify the narrators in this section. All were women born in the 1890s.

29. Beulah Pryor interview.

30. Jeffrey, *Frontier Women*, p. 85.

31. Quoted in Rasmussen, Rasmussen, Savage, and Wheeler, *A Harvest Yet to Reap*, p. 142; Inez Henderson, Hythe, Alberta, interview 1974, quoted in ibid., p. 44.

32. "The Situation in Colorado," *Miners' Magazine*, 16 June 1904, p. 9.

33. Kathleen Chapman interview; May Wing interview, 21 Oct. 1978.

34. Nellie McClung, ca. 1917, quoted in Rasmussen, Rasmussen, Savage, and Wheeler, *A Harvest Yet to Reap*, p. 116.

35. Jeffrey, *Frontier Women*, p. 190.

36. Carolyn Stefanco, "Networking on the Frontier: The Colorado Women's Suffrage Movement, 1876–1893," in this book; and Virginia Scharff, "The Case for Domestic Feminism: Woman Suffrage in Wyoming" (paper presented to Western History Association, Phoenix, Ariz., 1982).

37. See Carol Hymowitz and Michaele Weissman, *A History of Women in America* (New York: Bantam, 1978), p. 184.

38. Beverly Beeton, "Woman Suffrage in Territorial Utah," *Utah Historical Quarterly* 46 (1978): 100–20.

39. Jensen, *With These Hands*, p. 144.

40. Ibid., pp. 45–46, 145.

41. Ibid., p. 147.

42. James Edward Wright, *The Politics of Populism: Dissent in Colorado* (New Haven, Conn., and London: Yale University Press, 1974), pp. 116, 190, 203.

43. Candace Savage in Rasmussen, Rasmussen, Savage, and Wheeler, *A Harvest Yet to Reap*, pp. 122, 174–75.

44. Faragher, *Women and Men,* p. 15. In an analysis of the diaries of twenty-two men and twenty-eight women, Faragher found that two-thirds of their concerns overlapped in the areas of "a natural aesthetic, hard work, good health, and practical economic considerations." The remaining one-third of the content was distinguished by women's concern with family and relational values, while men emphasized aggressive values.

45. May Wing interview, 21 Oct. 1978.

46. Nellie McClung, *Clearing in the West,* epigraph in Rasmussen, Rasmussen, Savage, and Wheeler, *A Harvest Yet to Reap.*

11

Homesteading in Northeastern Colorado, 1873–1920: Sex Roles and Women's Experience

KATHERINE HARRIS

In this article, Katherine Harris describes the sharing and respect for women expressed among homesteading families in northern Colorado. This mutuality seems to contradict the distinct sex roles inherent in the Cult of True Womanhood, which most historians have seen as restricting women's opportunities in the West. Harris suggests that the western emphasis on the role of helpmate gave women more opportunities than they had had before because they had a greater share of responsibility and decision-making in the family. Above all, she shows the economic importance of women's activities in the homesteading period.

Historians debate what preceded the Cult of True Womanhood. Some believe that white women in colonial America had a greater range of options than their nineteenth-century descendants, that women had higher status in the colonial period because their labor was essential. Other historians, however, question the notion of women's opportunity during the colonial period, saying that earlier agricultural families were extremely patriarchal. These scholars, like Harris, see the Cult of True Womanhood as liberating compared to earlier patriarchal family roles. Whichever view one prefers, Harris's work indicates that a restrictive ideology did not determine the lives of homesteading women in Colorado in the late nineteenth century, and reminds us again to look beyond prescriptive literature to the actual circumstances of people's lives.

Much of the recent historiography describing women on the agricultural frontier has produced a bleak picture of their condition. According to these interpretations, women were coerced and exploited participants in a venture undertaken primarily for the benefit of men.[1] My study of homesteaders in Washington and Logan counties in northeastern Colorado does not support this conclusion.[2] In the years between 1873 and 1920, thousands of individuals and families worked to establish claims under the homestead laws. Women were significantly represented among the land entrants, and their success rate was approximately the same as men's.[3] Among the female population, however, only spinsters and widows were eligible to enter claims, so that other parameters of the homesteading experience must also be explored to gain a broader understanding of its

Grandma Pryor, Pryor Homestead, near Kit Carson, Colorado. Courtesy Colorado Historical Society.

effect on women. One of these, the impact of pioneering on gender-linked work and behavior patterns, is the subject of this paper.[4]

For the white, native-born Americans making up the bulk of those migrating to northeastern Colorado, culturally prescribed rules for behavior derived from nineteenth-century eastern, urban, middle- and upper middle-class models of propriety. A historian of American women, Barbara Welter, has labeled this ideal the Cult of True Womanhood and noted its emphasis on the role of women in maintaining harmonious relations between the sexes. Yet the cult was prescriptive for men, as well. Both sexes ideally confined their activities to separate spheres. Women were to occupy themselves with the moral and practical issues relating to the nurturance of children and the management of the home. They were also to cultivate personal qualities of purity, piety, domesticity, and submissiveness to better meet the needs of husbands, fathers, and children. Men, on the other hand, were to restrict their actions largely to the world of wage work and public affairs. They were expected to be aggressive and competitive, yet not too concerned with moral issues, for men were generally thought to possess spiritual natures intrinsically inferior to women's.[5]

There is some question when, where, and how completely the Cult of True Womanhood was assimilated by native, white agrarians. A study of mid-nineteenth-century midwestern migrants on the Overland Trail found no evidence of the cult's penetration into their lives. Instead, these families were organized along pre-industrial, patriarchal lines with women dominated by men in nearly all aspects of their lives.[6] Nonetheless, the evidence is strong that during the latter half of the nineteenth century, midwestern farm families became well acquainted with the cult's ideals. Popular magazines, books, and newspapers with a wide circulation through much of rural America carried countless articles and advice columns stressing women's domestic responsibilities as mothers of children and helpmates to husbands.[7] It was this role of helpmate that made the urban Cult of True Womanhood compatible with the farm economy. As their husbands' helpers, women could work outside their proper sphere and still maintain the integrity of the ideal.

There is little doubt that northeastern Colorado's homesteaders were familiar with the behavioral prescriptions broadcast by the popular press. Most of the immigrants' families of origin were midwestern agrarians. Those with urban roots were even more likely to have assimilated these ideals. Eastern social customs and styles were evident in the way many settlers lived. And eastern-based churches, clubs, and lodges distinguished town life at an early date.[8]

While it appears certain that homesteaders were familiar with eastern notions of propriety, how completely they acted on them before migrating west is open to question. It it, however, possible to discover how women, men, and children related to each other after they arrived in Colorado. The weight of the evidence indicates, first, a large measure of mutuality, or sharing, between the sexes, and implies a relaxation of culturally determined barriers dividing men and women. And, second, it reveals a pattern of childrearing that imposed many responsibilities on children, regardless of gender, yet allowed them a great deal of freedom as well. Both in the community and in the family, the homesteading experience enhanced female status and autonomy.

Among notheastern Colorado's homesteaders, role-sharing between the sexes was more likely to occur in relations with neighbors than within the family. But the performance of some community obligations remained strongly gender-linked. Women, for example, nearly always had the task of dispensing hospitality by feeding and bedding down visitors to the homestead. And childbirth, an event involving both family and community, was usually an exclusively female occasion, when women friends and relatives provided both emotional support and their skills as midwives to the expectant mother. Women also tended their communities' ill and injured, frequently sharing the task of helping a stricken family.[9]

Yet ministering to the infirm was by no means a wholly feminine role. Martin Skiles, according to his daughter, "would sit up with sick people" and "was also called to doctor sick horses and cows." Other men, too, served as nurses for their sick and dying neighbors. And during the crisis caused by the influenza epidemic of 1918, perhaps as many men as women tended the stricken.[10]

Just as men sometimes assumed the role of nurse and care-giver usually reserved for women, women might undertake "male" duties when death followed illness or injury. Sarah McDonald "quite often conducted funeral services of neighbors" in the vicinity of Fleming where for some time there was no minister.[11] And according to an early-twentieth-century resident of Logan County, one woman "made coffins . . . , buried people, and did everything that could be done, other than preaching the sermon."[12]

The shared responsibilities of men and women were also evident in the process of establishing schools and churches. The first community building to be erected in any neighborhood was nearly always a school. The time between settlement and the construction of a schoolhouse varied widely, depending on the perceived needs of homesteaders in a given locale and their ability to finance the undertaking. In a Washington County community settled largely by Danish bachelors, no school was built for at least ten years after their arrival in the mid-1880's. Even where families with school-age children were more concentrated, tax money might be insufficient to support a teacher.[13] If money were available, it was often barely adequate, so that school terms were typically short, often only three months. Pupils sometimes attended sessions in two districts at different times of the year. Where there were no schools, children might be tutored by their parents, with either the mother or the father assuming this responsibility.[14]

The construction of churches lagged behind that of schools; the presence of families again was a determining factor. (Those same Danish bachelors had no church services, either.) An important practical consideration, of course, was the availability of the schoolhouse, or even settlers' homes, to serve secondarily as places of worship.[15] Also, the fact that homesteaders represented many different denominations delayed, although it did not necessarily prevent, the members of the community from working together to build a church. Many congregations had a notably ecumenical makeup, including not only a variety of Protestants but sometimes Catholics as well. For this reason, churches were crucial to the process of community building by uniting people from diverse religious backgrounds.[16]

Organizing Sunday schools, as religious meetings were known when no preacher was presiding, was primarily the work of women. But men also showed their eagerness to attend by the fact that families often traveled many miles, sometimes on foot, to meetings. In the absence of a minister, services consisted of classes taught by both women and men.[17] With or without a minister Sunday was a high point. No matter how lonely, dull, or difficult the rest of the week might be, homesteaders could look forward to the Lord's Day as a time for resting from some kinds of work, for sharing religious feelings, and for visiting with other families. Indeed, the social aspects of religion can hardly be overemphasized. Families routinely shared Sunday meals with each other, and on those occasions when a revival was under way, they might spend as long as a month together.[18]

Community-wide family attendance characterized the secular as well as the religious gatherings of homesteaders. Dances, picnics, box suppers, spelling bees, baseball games, card parties, "literaries," and other events involved the whole family. The mixed attendance at literaries was, in fact, contrary to the practice of the closest parallels to these events in towns: "ladies'" Fortnightly Club meetings. Among homesteaders, literary nights were occasions for individuals of all ages and both sexes to take turns performing before their neighbors. Debating at these functions was apparently a male preserve, but it was not without hazard to masculine prestige. One man remembered his feelings of astonishment when, as a boy, he discovered that "grown men could be afraid to get up and speak before a group of their friends."[19]

A leveling effect was not the only consequence of shared social experience. Another was the relatively weak development of female networking. Women did, of course, seek out each other's company. After the turn of the century some women organized more or less formal groups, such as the Merrie Minglers Sewing Club and the Sunshine Club, to provide more opportunities for female sociability. But frequently when these groups met, the husbands came along and visited with each other or played cards, checkers, or horseshoes.[20]

The extensive mingling of the sexes, as well as the degree to which gender roles were muted in all areas of community life, can largely be attributed to the simple fact of geography. Homesteads were more or less isolated from one another. But distances were usually not extreme, and homesteaders were able to meet relatively frequently.[21] Still, for reasons of safety, convenience, and the desire to communicate with someone outside the family, settlers' gatherings generally included everyone.

Beginning in 1893, woman suffrage may have had a subtle effect, making many women less eager to segregate themselves in female groups, and stimulating a greater mutuality between the sexes. In both Logan and Washington counties the measure passed by nearly two-to-one, a considerably greater margin of victory than it received state-wide. The strength of the favorable vote by men implies that women and men had already shared some decision-making powers. Moreover, there is evidence that women themselves worked in behalf of their enfranchisement, suggesting a self-image in disparity with legal constraints.[22]

The muting of gender-role distinctions, evident in homesteaders' community activities, also affected the division of labor between males and females in families. Necessity frequently required men and women to assume each other's tasks, leading to the development of unfamiliar skills, especially among women. Children grew up with fewer constraints on their behavior and work patterns than their parents had known. A few even acquired a conscious recognition of equality within the family circle.

Among the routine chores, hauling water, gathering cow chips for fuel, and milking were relatively free from gender connotations. In a given family either the husband or wife might perform these tasks, although the responsibility often shifted to the children as they grew older.[23] Churning cream to make butter, on the other hand, was a job reserved for women, and children under their supervision. Butter production, along with eggs from the chickens women raised, were important elements of the domestic economy, for money received from their sale was sometimes the only cash income a family had. Women sold their butter locally, or shipped it to Denver, and even to the East, earning from ten to thirty cents a pound for as much as fifty to one hundred pounds produced every week. For comparison, at a time when butter brought twelve cents per pound (in the late 1880s and early 1890s), eggs sold for five cents a dozen and corn for seven cents a bushel.[24]

Women's other work within homesteading families encompassed those tasks traditionally assigned to their sex. They "kept house"—cooked, canned (meat, fruit, and vegetables), sewed, washed, and ironed. They tended very young children and usually kept a garden. Toward the end of the nineteenth century, mechanization had begun to produce changes in the nature of some jobs. One of the most important acquisitions for domestic work on a homestead was a sewing machine. As one matron commented, "only women who have struggled along sewing by hand can realize what a sewing machine meant to me."[25] A second device, the hand-operated washing machine, ameliorated what was perhaps the most arduous task of all, doing the family laundry. Its basic mechanism was simply a paddle with a handle for manually agitating the wash. The principal labor-saving feature of the machine was that children could readily be assigned the task of operating it, thus relieving their mothers from the backbreaking job of scrubbing clothes on a washboard.[26]

Men had no day in their weekly routine to compare with women's washday. Their labor was more seasonal, with intense periods of activity during planting and harvest. Through the rest of the year, their work probably had less variation than women's, centering largely on the care of stock and occasional construction and repair jobs.[27] An important though understated side to men's work was their role in parenting. In many families, children of both sexes started doing fieldwork and cross-country errands by age nine or ten. Their chores included helping with the planting, hoeing, and harvesting; herding cattle; hauling feed, fuel, and water; trading at local stores; and taking crops to market.[28] In performing these tasks, children were often supervised by their fathers. This nurturance implies a paternal influence on daughters who may have internalized male role models to some extent. This may have been enhanced by the competition between brothers and sisters performing the same "masculine" jobs.[29]

In some families girls, as well as boys, continued to perform additional farm duties as they grew older. Most assumed jobs out of necessity: perhaps they had no brothers old enough to do the work. Thus the Middlecoff sisters cut and shocked corn with their father; and the Nelson girls drove the family's cattle the twenty-five miles to the Sterling winter feedlot. Eva Morris assumed the farming when her father was absent. In her case, however, an unusually clear statement illuminates her attitude toward men's work. As one family member related, "farming and working with animals was her main love—housework was for girls, not for Eva."[30]

In many, if not most, homesteading families work was in such demand that the gender of the laborer was relatively unimportant. Pioneering, nonetheless, had a different impact on daughters than on wives and mothers. While most daughters were expected to learn "household duties,"[31] they appear to have had greater scope for their behavior than married women, probably because girls' sexual identities were often incidental to their contributions to the family. Wives and mothers, on the other hand, had fewer opportunities to alter gender-role patterns because their sexual identities defined their work in the family. Whether acting out of necessity or preference, they generally performed nontraditional tasks in the context of helping husbands and children.

Disregarding those cases where women and girls apparently preferred nontraditional over "female" domestic pursuits, we may ask to what extent the helpmate role may have been a device for exploiting women's labor.[32] Although there is no unequivocal answer, the subject may be approached obliquely by looking at instances where men did jobs ordinarily assigned to women.

Women's work did not have the same prestige as men's. The boys in one family, for example, helped their sisters sew carpet rags only as a punishment. Moreover, the record shows many more girls and women transcending gender-defined work roles than boys and men. Males probably did less nontraditional work than females, but another factor was men's reluctance to mention the "female" tasks they performed. Thus, Clark Woodis never recorded in his diary the fact that he washed dishes and cleaned the house, although entries for the same dates by his wife, Ruth, indicated that he did these chores.[33]

Clark's motivation for performing domestic tasks was the same governing many, if not most, women who labored in the fields: necessity. Ruth suffered from a heart condition, and she was often unable to work. Men also helped their wives when the need to do so could not be described as dire. To be sure, Orrin Hall carried water to fill the washtub and irrigate the garden for his wife, Ruth, who, by her own description, was not a strong woman. Yet he also ironed her clothes (including the artificial bosom of starched ruffles worn under Ruth's "full chested shirt waist") during the period she taught school—a job that provided their household with much needed cash income.[34] The evidence certainly is not conclusive, but the fact that some men filled the helpmate role argues against wholesale exploitation of wives' labor.

Part of the vital work associated with homesteading was the earning of cash income. Everyone except the smallest children might contribute to the family cash economy, but each member did so in ways that ordinarily varied in relation to age and gender.

While the primary source of married women's cash income was from marketing the surplus butter and eggs, some women also marketed their garden vegetables or other domestic products such as bread, sausages, and cheese. Most cash-producing jobs matrons performed were carried on in the home environment, or at least did not take them away from the homestead for extended periods. Commonly, women took in boarders (usually teachers, but also railroad workers), charging them at the rate of ten dollars per month for food, accommodations, and such additional amenities as washing, ironing, and mending. They also washed, ironed, and sewed for local bachelors, worked as dressmakers for their neighbors, and served as postmistresses.[35]

Daughters sometimes took over the domestic chores to give their mothers the time to earn money. But daughters also earned wages. Some found employment in the hotels of nearby towns; a few even owned and operated restaurants. Others worked as domestics in private homes. Salaries for housework were low—about two dollars a week in the 1890s. Teaching, on the other hand, paid three or more times as much and was therefore, considerably more desirable. Many wage-earning daughters, of course, lived with their families. Certainly, their role in helping to support their families was important, although the portion of income they kept for their own use is unclear. Another class of daughters—those who entered homesteads to expand family holdings—probably had more control over their wages. Lois Ervin, recalling her experience as a homesteading daughter, said the money she received from teaching was her own. Amy Dickinson Worthley, on the other hand, said her earnings and those of her siblings were pooled to pay for their education. She added, however, that she thought this practice was unusual.[36]

Young unmarried men, like young women, probably kept some or all of the money they earned. Many young males taught school because the salaries were relatively high: twenty-five to forty dollars a month around the turn of the century.[37]

The amount varied according to the affluence of the school district, the date, and probably the number of students. But there is no evidence that the sex of the teacher affected the pay. Nevertheless, men made up only a small percentage of teachers,[38] in part because males had many more kinds of work available to them than did females.

Male settlers held a nearly endless variety of jobs, even discounting those who owned businesses and homesteaded as a sideline. They not only worked weekdays in town, but they also traveled, sometimes hundreds of miles, to secure employment for months at a time.[39] These absences had a significant impact on women and children, increasing their workloads and their importance.

The contribution of women and children to the family economy of the homestead was acknowledged in the degree to which they could direct the allocation of resources. Children received material assets in accordance with whatever parents could spare. Indeed, one way parents recognized their children's increasing autonomy was to allow them to keep a larger proportion of their earnings as they grew older. Another was through the gift of livestock. One father gave each of his sons and daughters a heifer calf; the issue of that animal was also the child's property. In time, the growing herd provided income for clothing, tuition, and school supplies. Another family provided each of twelve children with a filly. When these daughters and sons left home as young adults, they took with them their own herd of horses, in addition to a milk cow given as a kind of "going-away" present.[40]

Within marriage, decisions for allocating resources appear to have been shared. This finding contradicts studies indicating women's second-class status in farm families, a conclusion based on investment of capital in additional land and farm machinery rather than in domestic labor-saving devices or improvements to the home.[41] In the native-born white families of northeastern Colorado, there were many examples of husbands spending time and money for the well-being of wives. But women also played an active role in determining how sizeable sums of money were to be spent. When Ollie and Willis Barden moved to their homestead in 1903, they lived in a "half dug out." Three years later they moved into a three-room frame house. Meanwhile, Willis used a walking plow that someone had given him for breaking sod. Orrin and Ruth Hall had a bumper wheat crop in 1917. They invested their profit in a four-bedroom frame house with indoor plumbing. Ruth eagerly anticipated "all this luxury after eight years in the little sod house." But Orrin was in no hurry to move, thinking their new quarters should "cure for a while." Ruth strongly disagreed, and she got her way: "the wildlife could have the soddy. I was getting out. So we moved into our new house in April 1918." Amy Dickinson Worthley's mother inherited money which she used to buy a farm next to the Dickinsons' place in Nebraska. When the family moved to Logan County, the sale of her land helped buy the new farm. But Mrs. Dickinson was distressed at losing title to her own real estate, so her husband made her a co-owner of the Colorado property.[42]

Wives' power to command resources and direct expenditures was evident in many other circumstances. When Mary and Samuel Wright decided to buy new furniture, one of their purchases was a sewing machine; Mary Hayes bought a sewing machine and lace curtains with money she earned from taking in boarders; Jessie Hassig Challis had title to her own cattle, and her own brand.

At least some wives retained control of property they had acquired before marriage. Lois Ervin had proved up a claim in her own right. Using the $1,600 from the sale of her homestead, she bought a second quarter section. In 1925 this land sold for $4,000 and ten years later Lois invested the money from this venture in her son's trucking business.[43] Typically, she used her resources to promote her family. Nonetheless, within the constraints of habit and custom governing female behavior, the decision to do so was hers.

The foregoing examples strongly suggest women's considerable status within the family. Men and women generally had different roles to play, but the mutuality between the sexes enforced by the needs of homesteading expanded women's power to negotiate and win. Inevitably, the strength of women's position affected the power dynamics of the whole family; this conclusion is supported by an uncompromising statement from a man whose mother and father homesteaded in 1908. He wrote, "our parents taught us [children that] . . . each member of a family is equal." [44] This does not mean, of course, that equality actually existed in homesteading families. But the fact that it occurred even as an ideal is significant.

The high status that at least some women homesteaders experienced was sometimes overshadowed by painful feelings associated with changing roles and disrupted relationships caused by the move to Colorado. Usually, those who felt most disoriented were middle-aged or older; a few were used to an urban environment. Yet the loneliness some women felt was inconsistent with an objective evaluation of their lives. Women were generally in daily contact with family members. They saw neighbors once a week or oftener, and homesteaders of both sexes made regular trips to town. [45] Women's close personal friendships with other women formed much of the meaningful fabric of their former lives. These rich emotional relationships, with their associations of place and time, had no easy substitutes. New relationships of similar intensity were necessarily slow to develop and in the meantime, some women experienced an intense sense of isolation. Yet for other women this same emotional vacuum seems to have encouraged a closer rapport with men.

Unreserved enthusiasm for homesteading was almost always associated with youth. Jessie Nolan, who was fifteen when her family came to Colorado, reported that she and the other children were "jubilant" about the move. Ollie Barden, a bride in 1902 when she and her husband settled near Haxtun, wrote, "we lived and were happy, had good neighbors and we were One Big Family." Young single women often viewed homesteading as a personal, romantic adventure. An excerpt from Mary Anderson's autograph album illustrates this point. In 1886, Mary and a friend, Bee Randolph, homesteaded adjoining quarter sections and shared a shack built over the property line. Mary's wedding the following year caused some melancholy for Bee, who composed the following:

Dear Mame—Here we are in our little preemption home for the last time together, at least for some year [sic] to come. But I hope sometime we may visit it again. We cannot be happier than we have been here, although we may have wealth and other great pleasures. Can you not almost remember every day from the first, what has happened? Our laughing, singing, playing, working, our company, etc. [46]

For these young women, one of the essential attractions of homesteading was the independence that proving up a claim offered. Self-determination was not an option generally available to their sex. Yet homesteading held out that possibility, sanctioned by laws whose original intent was to encourage settlement by families and, thereby, social and political stability on the agricultural frontier. Moreover, the legal right of single women to patent government land had an unforeseen result. The elevated status and autonomy of this very visible group in the local female population served

as an inspiration to all women and especially to girls, who were most receptive to novel ways of acting. To be sure, the labor shortage and the
relative isolation of the family unit, which forced its members to greater
reliance on each other, also played a part in promoting mutuality between
the sexes. But the possibility of acquiring land raised the expectations of
all females in the homesteading community. "Why can't I have some [gov-
ernment land], too?" was a question that surely more than one spinster
asked herself.[47] And while wives could not enter claims, they probably
acquired some psychological benefit from the unprecedented opportunities
for land ownership available to their daughters and to others of their sex. It
is true that for some women, the climate of enhanced freedom of action
and elevated economic status was not worth the disruption of well-defined
sex roles and the physical hardships pioneering imposed. But for those of
a more resilient disposition, homesteading in northeastern Colorado had
much to offer.

As I noted earlier, my findings of high status and opportunity for women
on a portion of Colorado's agricultural frontier conflict with the conclusions reached by many recent studies of westering women. The explanation for this disagreement does not lie solely in the evaluation of the data.
Several factors relating to time, place, the nature of women's economic
role, and the focus of research on a particular phase of the pioneering process may account for differences in interpretation.

The variable of time is clearly responsible to a large degree for women's
high status among northeastern Colorado homesteaders. Other studies
have considered events predating the first settlement of Logan and Washington counties by as much as four or five decades. Agrarians of these
earlier generations were unlikely to have yet emerged from the rigid patriarchy characteristic of pre–industrial and colonial families. Indeed,
John Faragher specifically identified his subjects as living under this kind
of family organization.[48] The homesteaders of northeastern Colorado, on
the other hand, had assimilated the Cult of True Womanhood and its eleva-
tion of women within their proper sphere.

It is probable, too, that distinct family types not only evolved over time,
but became geographically segregated, as well. One historian has classified within pre–industrial patriarchy three family patterns based on the
relative power exercised by the eldest male. In the most rigidly hierarchical families, which he called "evangelical," the father's power was limited
only by his obedience to God. This type of family was threatened by even
the modest power sharing that occurred within "genteel" and "moderate"
families; therefore, evangelicals tended to remove themselves from contact
with other groups.[49] In the nineteenth century, family variations probably
became even more complex with the development of companionate marriages arising out of the Cult of True Womanhood. Further, although the
shift over time has generally been away from hierarchical and toward more
companionate family styles, both styles have continued to coexist. The
historian studying white, native-born women on the agricultural frontier

must, therefore avoid generalizing. What may be true for one population may not accurately describe another, because family organization with its consequences for women probably varied significantly over the American West.[50]

Finally, the oppression of women described by some historians may be related to frontiers where women were, for some reason, constrained from entering claims. In addition, studies that look only at the migration[51] necessarily exclude women's entrepreneurial activities during settlement and focus instead on a part of the pioneering process likely to have inflicted the greatest physical and psychological pain. As a frontier business enterprise, homesteading was probably unique because of the relatively large numbers of women who directly participated by acquiring land patents, and because of the rising expectation their success generated among others of their sex.

Further study of women on homesteads and in other agricultural settings is needed to explore variations in women's status on the farmers' frontier. Nevertheless, in the light of recent publications, the data from northeastern Colorado suggest that the experience of pioneer agrarian women was more diverse and complex than might previously have been suspected.

Notes

1. John Mack Faragher, *Women and Men on the Overland Trail* (New Haven, Conn.: Yale University Press, 1979); Julie Roy Jeffrey, *Frontier Women: The Trans-Mississippi West, 1840–1880* (New York: Hill and Wang, 1979); Joan Jensen, *With These Hands: Women Working on the Land* (New York: Feminist Press and McGraw-Hill Book Co., 1981); Lillian Schlissel, *Women's Diaries of the Westward Journey* (New York: Schocken Books, 1982); Christine Stansell, "Women on the Great Plains, 1865–1890," *Women's Studies* 4 (1976): 87–98. Exceptions are Glenda Riley, *Frontierswomen: The Iowa Experience* (Ames: Iowa State University Press, 1981); and Sandra L. Myres, *Westering Women and the Frontier Experience, 1800–1915* (Albuquerque: University of New Mexico Press, 1982)

2. This paper is based on a larger study of homesteading women. See Katharine Llewellyn Hill Harris, "Women and Families on Northeastern Colorado Homesteads, 1873–1920" (Ph.D. diss., University of Colorado, 1983). The research was directed by Lee Chambers-Schiller and Ralph Mann, who were the first and second readers, respectively.

3 As many as 18 percent of the land entries in the period after 1900 were made by women, and 55 percent of these entrants patented land. Figures for homestead land entries in Logan and Washington counties were compiled from the land office tract book records available on microfilm from the Bureau of Land Management.

4. Although oral histories provided important evidence, written reminiscences comprised the bulk of the source materials for this study. See especially the family histories collected in the following volumes: Washington County Museum Association, *The Pioneer Book of Washington County, Colorado* (Denver: Big Mountain Press, 1959), hereafter cited as *PBWC;* Washington County Museum Association, *The Pioneer Book II of Washington County, Colorado* (Fort Morgan, Colo.: Print Shop; Aurora, Colo.: Rocky Mountain Press, n.d.), hereafter cited as *PBWC II;* Dorothea Safford and Helen Taylor, eds., *No Fuss and Feathers—Crook: A History of the Crook Community* (Fort Collins, Colo.: Crook Historical Society, Economy Printing, 1977), hereafter cited as CHS, *No Fuss and Feathers;* Fleming

Historical Society, *Memories of Our Pioneers* (Iowa Falls, Iowa: General Publishing and Binding, 1971), hereafter cited as FHS, *Memories*. The homesteading women of Washington and Logan counties did not leave a rich legacy of letters and diaries. This lack is particularly regrettable because of the tendency of the memory to suppress whatever was stressful and to recall, sometimes in embellished form, the pleasanter aspects of an experience. I have tried to keep this phenomenon in mind when weighing statements made years after the events they describe.

5. Barbara Welter, "The Cult of True Womanhood, 1820–1860," *American Quarterly* 18 (Summer, 1966): 151–74.

6. Faragher, *Women and Men on the Overland Trail*, p. 244 n.5, pp. 119, 138–40.

7. Norton Juster, *So Sweet to Labor: Rural Women in America, 1865–1895* (New York: Viking Press, 1979). Mary P. Ryan placed the beginnings of widespread dissemination of the cult after 1830, the year low-cost printing technology was invented. See her *Womanhood in America from Colonial Times to the Present* (New York: New Viewpoints, 1975), p. 143, cited in Faragher, *Women and Men on the Overland Trail*, p. 244 n.5.

8. *PBWC*, pp. 70, 223, 276, 278, 324, 367, 369–70, 379; CHS, *No Fuss and Feathers*, pp. 49–50; *PBWC II*, p. 207.

9. *PBWC*, pp. 31, 324; *PBWC II*, p. 426; CHS, *No Fuss and Feathers*, p. 49.

10. *PBWC*, pp. 222, 73, 163; *PBWC II*, pp. 126–27, 181, 381, 396, 427, 585.

11. FHS, *Memories*, pp. 50–51.

12. Opal Covington, tape-recorded interview with Margaret Cooley, Akron, Colo., 15 May 1975; *PBWC*, pp. 163, 190, 222.

13 *PBWC*, p. 56; FHS, *Memories*, p. 238.

14. *PBWC II*, pp. 49–50, 139–40; *PBWC*, p. 220; FHS, *Memories*, pp. 76, 242.

15. *PBWC*, p. 379.

16. Ibid., pp. 352, 175, 195–96.

17. Ibid., pp. 27–28, 45, 141, 379, FHS, *Memories*, p. 180; *PBWC II*, p. 355.

18. *PBWC II*, pp. 230–31; *PBWC*, p. 137

19. Glen R. Durrell, "Homesteading in Colorado," *Colorado Magazine*, Spring, 1974, p. 105. Durrell's reminiscences date from 1908 to 1916 in neighboring Lincoln County (*PBWC II*, pp. 349–50).

20. *PBWC*, pp. 198, 356, 380; PBWC II, pp. 275–76, 451, 515.

21. *PBWC II*, pp. 44, 396, 523.

22. Across Colorado, 55 percent of the voters approved woman suffrage. State of Colorado, *Abstract of Votes Cast for State Officers at the General Elections of the Years 1892–1900 Inclusive* (Denver: Smith Brooks Printing Co., 1901), p. 7.

23. *PBWC*, pp. 322, 117, 345, 362; *PBWC II*, pp. 354, 410, 426, 601; FHS, *Memories*, p. 206. Collecting chips was usually a job for women and children on the Overland Trail. Myres, *Westering Women*, p. 105.

24, Eggs, butter, and cream were often simply traded for groceries and other items. *PBWC II*, pp. 252, 515, 601; *PBWC*, pp. 43, 64, 167–70; FHS, *Memories*, p. 159. The importance of butter and egg production as a source of cash income has been noted for other parts of the agricultural frontier. See, for example, Glendy Riley, *Frontierswomen: The Iowa Experience* (Ames: Iowa University Press, 1981), pp. 86–87.

25. *PBWC*, pp. 353, 131; *PBWC*, pp. 325, 529; FHS, *Memories*, p. 31.

26. *PBWC II*, pp. 111, 353, 553; *PBWC*, pp. 131, 382.

27. Diaries of Ruth and Clark Woodis, *The Story of a Colorado Homestead, 1913–1928* (n.p., 1976). Ruth and Clark Woodis homesteaded near Deertrail, west of Logan and Washington counties. Ruth's chores appear to have been much more varied than Clark's.

28. *PBWC*, pp. 31, 42–43, 117, 322; FHS, *Memories*, pp. 104, 216.

29. This hypothesis is supported by Teresa Jordan's oral history of modern ranch women. See her *Cowgirls: Women of the American West* (New York: Anchor Press, Doubleday and Co., 1982), pp. 24–25, 39–41, 50–51, 66–67.

30. Eva Morris was born in 1898. FHS, *Memories*, pp. 195–96, 204, 246; *PBWC*, pp. 149, 173, 259, 342; *PBWC II*, pp. 66, 197.

31. *PBWC II*, p. 460; FHS, *Memories*, p. 216.

32. In support of the idea that men exploited women's labor on the agricultural frontier, see especially Stansell, "Women on the Great Plains," p. 93; and Faragher, *Women and Men on the Overland Trail*, pp. 59–65, 115, 183–87.

33. Diaries of Ruth and Clark Woodis, 5 May 1918 and 5 March 1919.

34. Ruth Schooley Hall, *Soddie Bride* (Fort Collins, Colo.: Robinson Press, 1973), pp. 34, 70, 80.

35. *PBWC*, pp. 138, 147–48, 160, 163, 170, 192, 350; *PBWC II*, pp. 20, 125–26, 231, 354–55, 426, 695; FHS, *Memories*, p. 167.

36. Lois Ervin, tape-recorded interview with Katherine Harris, Sterling, Colo., 7 June 1980; Amy Dickinson Worthley, tape-recorded interview with Katherine Harris, near Sterling, Colo., 7 June 1980; Helen Alishouse, tape-recorded interview with Margaret Cooley, Akron, Colo., 12 Nov. 1975; *PBWC*, pp. 87, 173, 248, 264.

37. For comparison, ranch hands at the turn of the century earned about fifteen dollars a month (*PBWC*, pp. 29, 88, 265); *PBWC II*, p. 183.

38. *PBWC*, p. 60.

39. Ibid., pp. 160, 162, 177, 192, 258, 284–85, 321, 359–60; FHS, *Memories*, pp. 41, 126–27, 161, 175, 194–95, 201, 207; *PBWC II*, pp. 18, 101, 125–26, 348–49, 396, 449, 588; Nell Brown Propst, *Those Strenuous Dames of the Colorado Prairie* (Boulder, Colo.: Pruett Publishing Co., 1982), pp. 77–78.

40. *PBWC*, pp. 150, 380

41. Stansell, "Women on the Great Plains," p. 91; Mary W. M. Hargreaves, "Women in the Agricultural Settlement of the Northern Plains," *Agricultural History* 50 (January, 1976): 187.

42. Mrs. Dickinson was native of Denmark, but her husband was American-born. Worthley, interview; Hall, *Soddie Bride*, pp. 122–23; FHS, *Memories*, pp. 30, 216; *PBWC*, p. 176.

43. Ervin, interview; *PBWC*, pp. 157, 163, 353.

44. FHS, *Memories*, pp. 206–207, 209. The family consisted of a father, mother ("who could keep up with a lot of men when it came to . . . [doing any] . . . homestead job"), two sons, and a daughter.

45. Ibid., pp. 131, 214; Hall, *Soddie Bride*, p. 95; Clara Watson, "Homesteading on the Plains," *Colorado Magazine*, April, 1961, pp. 142–43; *PBWC II*, pp. 175, 201, 585, 596. For a similar observation concerning women of the Iowa frontier, see Dorothy Schwieder, "Labor and Economic Roles of Iowa Farm Wives, 1840–80," in Trudy Huskamp Peterson, ed., *Farmers, Bureaucrats, and Middlemen: Historical Perspectives on American Agriculture* (Washington, D.C.: Howard University Press, 1980), p. 165.

46. *PBWC*, pp. 159–60; *PBWC II*, pp. 398–99; FHS, *Memories*, p. 31.

47. *PBWC II*, p. 673.

48. Faragher, *Women and Men on the Overland Trail*, p. 244 n.5.

49. Philip J. Greven, *The Protestant Temperament: Patterns of Childrearing, Religious Experience, and the Self in Early America* (New York: Alfred A. Knopf, 1977), pp. 12–18, 25–28, 124–40. Recently Joan Jensen pointed out geographically distinct differences in the agrarian experience, in an unpublished paper given at the Sex/Gender Division of Labor: Feminist Perspectives Conference, 13–15 May, 1983, University of Minnesota, St. Paul campus. See her "The Sexual Division of Labor on American Farms: 1750–1850."

50. One of the diarists in Schlissel's *Women's Diaries*, p. 78, hinted at the difference in family organization when she unfavorably compared Missourian with Yankee husbands. Further suggestive evidence is the early granting of the vote to Colorado women, which may have been related, in part, to a high concentration of companionate families in the state.

51. Schlissel, *Women's Diaries;* Faragher, *Women and Men on the Overland Trail*.

12.
_____

Beyond Baby Doe: Child Rearing on the Mining Frontier

ELLIOTT WEST

While women homesteaders performed many essential economic tasks, women in urban areas were more commonly dependent on male wages. Did this mean they were more likely to conform to the Cult of True Womanhood than were their rural contemporaries? In this article Elliott West looks at housekeeping and childrearing to explore how women in hard-rock mining towns adapted their understanding of appropriate female behavior. West makes the important point that creating healthy environments for their children was harder for urban working-class women and single mothers than for the wives of the wealthy elite. The difficulty of creating a domestic haven amidst poverty and the bawdy life of the red-light district presented what West calls a "cruel dilemma" for mothers. They often had to work for wages, which took time and energy they needed to meet their high standards as homemakers and mothers. This exploration of how women juggled their ideals about home life in such difficult circumstances is important to our understanding of western families. West's careful attention to class differences is especially valuable. Values and beliefs may appear more constant when viewed through the eyes of a small elite who could afford to follow them than from the perspective of working-class women who had to work much harder to achieve their ideals. Their compromises with reality were one way that women changed their roles.

Who were they? In photographs of early gold- and silver-mining towns, they stand along the muddy streets, looking enigmatically at the camera, clothed turtlelike in bonnets and ankle-length dresses that show only their faces and hands. There is a fitting irony here, for histories of the era have left the women of the mining frontier similarly unrevealed. Most of the story of the mining West tells of the efforts of men to discover precious metals and deliver them from the earth. The main characters are scruffy prospectors, engineering wizards, entrepreneurial buccaneers, and political kingpins. If women appear at all in these accounts, they typically match crudely drawn stereotypes, particularly that of the prostitute cavorting in a saloon or plush brothel of Deadwood or Silver City.[1]

In fact, the vast majority of women on the mining frontier were not hurdy-gurdy girls or "soiled doves" but wives and mothers. Their central

Maud Park, 1905. Courtesy Colorado Historical Society.

concern was the establishment of homes and the rearing of children—another group woefully neglected by historians. This lack of attention is somewhat puzzling because libraries and archives of western history are bulging with useful, revealing material on the family, much of it from the hands of mining-town mothers. It is a diverse and complex body of evidence. Until we bring it into our picture of western life, we will be left with traditional, male-oriented images that make up a distorted and incomplete portrait of frontier society.

Women typically made up less—often far less—than 20 percent of all adults in the mining camps. From the male perspective, women were rare commodities indeed, and it is part of frontier folklore that miners greeted the first of them with whooping, boot-stomping enthusiasm. A sourdough in an early piece of gold-rush fiction reacted this way:

Whoora! for a live woman in the mines. What'll the boys say? They'll peel out o' their skins for joy. A live female woman in the mines! Turnpikes and railroads come next and steam engines! Whoora for Pike County! Wheat bread and chicken fixins now—hoe cakes and slapjacks d———d—whoora![2]

We know that men sometimes rewarded the earliest female arrivals with food, lumber, and even free town lots.[3]

The reactions of these men, however, tell virtually nothing about the daily lives and feelings of the women. More important, the men's enthusiasm can easily give a false impression. Women did receive some special favor and respect, but it does not follow that they found exceptional economic and social opportunities on the mining frontier. In fact, men looked upon the women as symbols of respectability and a traditional social order, not as full partners in the western venture, and they fully expected these new arrivals to behave and work much as their sisters did elsewhere in Victorian America.

The picture clears somewhat if we go beyond the miners' colorful, raucous greetings to the facts shown in the manuscript censuses taken in the camps.[4] Of the women listed in these censuses, at most about one in ten appears to be an independent wage earner. Among them were some hotel-keepers, teachers, and restaurateurs, but most of this minority worked in lower-paying jobs traditionally reserved for women—seamstresses, washerwomen, cooks, and domestics. The great majority of women, at least according to the census alone, were not a part of the public work force. Usually 90 percent or more were described as "keeping house," a catchall phrase for all the activities of maintaining a family household, and most of these had children living with them. Of the 103 adult women in Virginia City, Montana, in 1870, for example, ninety-five were listed as "keeping house," and seventy-six of these had children.

There is little evidence, then, of more flexible attitudes toward a women's role in the frontier community. The study of most women in mining towns narrows sharply to the study of housewifery and child rearing, their possibilities and limitations. Women themselves have described their lives, but the choice of testimony can distort the picture. Most significant in the variety of women's experience is the question of class. More so than on the farming, ranching, and most other frontiers, mining-camp society was sorted out rather quickly into crude but easily distinguished economic levels. The mines could produce a lot of money quickly. They often demanded the skills of well-educated, fairly well-to-do managers, engineers, and other specialists, and these men often brought their families with them. Though they accounted for only a few of those living in the towns, this better-schooled financial and social elite left behind more documents about their feelings and ways of living than the poorer, less articulate majority living around them. It is tempting to rely on what this group has written, but to do so is risky.

For instance, social class affected women's emotional responses to their new homes, and these emotions determined in part how mothers dealt with the demands of childrearing on the frontier. Women of the social elite typically complained, sometimes bitterly, about what they found in the mountain settlements. Mary Hallock Foote, author, illustrator, mother, and engineer's wife, found Leadville, Colorado, a "senseless, rootless place," and to her friend and fellow writer Helen Hunt Jackson the Cloud City was "unnatural. Grass would not grow there, and cats could not live." [5] These women found few friends of their own background and interests, and few of the amenities they had taken for granted at home. Louise A. K. Clappe, a doctor's wife who as "Dame Shirley" wrote a series of letters describing life in the California gold fields, asked her sisters to imagine trying to live with:

no newspapers, no churches, lectures, concerts, or theaters; no fresh books; no shopping, calling nor gossiping little tea-drinkings; no parties, no balls, no picnics, no tableaus, no charades, no latest fashions, no daily mail . . . , no promenades, no rides or drives; no vegetables but potatoes and onions, no milk, no eggs, no *nothing*. [6]

Deprived of these things and isolated from like-minded women of their social class, mothers of this sort looked on childrearing with misgivings. Foote remembered that "in the back of my mind always . . . was a secret quake when I thought of our little boy." [7]

Social historians, however, need to ask whether these sentiments accurately reflected the feelings of most women of that time and place. To be sure, women of all classes sacrificed some things when they moved west. In recent writing on women's history it is commonplace to read that wives and mothers in the more settled parts of America found comfort and aid in networks of kinfolk and tested friends. Such a system provided emotional support, an outlet for frustrations, and help in the daily tasks of homemaking. [8] It is just as obvious that for many women migrating westward shattered that supportive network. Those who tried to reestablish those bonds in the mining towns faced two formidable problems. First, there were few women with whom to form new relationships, especially in the early years of a town's life. Second, the mining camps were among the most unstable and transient human gatherings in the history of the unsettled young republic. In towns in which ninety of every one hundred persons typically moved on within ten years, women did not always find it easy to weave together a new fabric of trusted friends.

Consequently, wives and mothers of the elite were not the only ones to feel a loss of social network. "I never was so lonely and homesick in all my life," a prospector's young wife wrote from Denver in 1863, and another cried out in her diary: "My sweet *sweet* home! Why did I ever leave you in the stranger's land to dwell?" A Nevada mother of three, after following her restless husband to that parched frontier, regularly filled her journal with terse, bleak comments: "lonely day," "very lonesome," "town dull & everything lonesome." [9]

These comments were heard most frequently from the women who had arrived most recently in the mountains. In time, women, particularly those of working-class families who remained in the West for more than a few years, may have worked out more comfortable accommodations with their new homes. After moving frequently from town to town over a period of years, a woman was likely to know some people anywhere she settled. The special conditions of motherhood in those mountain towns, moreover, appear to have created a sense of community based not on place but on shared experiences and difficulties. One study shows that women in California during the years after the gold rush generally could depend on help from friends in times of personal trials. Another indicates that miners' wives in Cripple Creek, Colorado, found a measure of emotional support and material aid through the labor associations they helped establish. [10] This sort of evidence, inconclusive but intriguing, suggests that the support systems that played an important part in child rearing may well have been more resilient and adaptive than previously appreciated. For those working-class mothers who remained in the mining West, life may not have been quite as emotionally isolated as the elite and the earliest arrivals testified.

Regardless of her personal circumstances, a mother arriving in a mining town had to turn quickly to her first responsibility—the establishment of a physical residence. The special conditions of the mining frontier made this task particularly difficult. Construction materials, household furnishings, and the tools of homemaking were scarce and expensive in the mountains. When his wife wrote to say she hoped to join him, a Montana merchant sent her an inventory of what he considered necessities that had to be carried in from the outside. This list included bedding, carpets, chairs, bookcase and books, cooking and heating stoves, and a sewing machine with needles, thread, and varieties of cloth. [11]

If such was considered the basis of a household, only the reasonably well-to-do could afford it. By the time the wives of professionals, managers, and successful merchants arrived, their husbands could often provide them with roomy and comfortable houses. In the most flourishing towns they built Victorian showplaces, painted outside, plastered and wainscoted within, with covered porches, bay windows, marble fireplaces, and other contemporary symbols of success. In one such place in a Colorado silver town, five children grew up with camel's-hair wallpaper, a solarium, and a nine-seater outhouse with a servants' entrance. These wealthier mothers also had resources to furnish their houses to their tastes. An editor's wife bought three dozen yards of carpet on her way up the Missouri to Montana, and others of her economic level imported mahogany pianos, upholstered furniture, crates of books, and a variety of Victorian house-stuffings.[12]

In maintaining these homes and caring for their children, wealthier mothers usually could afford the help of domestics. The servant of an Idaho family saw to the shopping, cleaning, washing, ironing, and cooking, and a Montanan admitted to her mother: "I don't think there is any need for anybody to waste any pity on me for living on the 'outskirts of civilization.'" No wonder. A day maid and night nurse saw to the chores and the care of her two children, while her husband sent out the cleaning and took her to dinner every evening.[13] From this sort of evidence it seems that the sons and daughters of the mining elite, at least in their immediate surroundings, lived much as did others of their class elsewhere in Gilded Age America.

For most mothers, however, making and keeping a house was quite different. They arrived with much less and faced the same high prices, but even in the best of times the family's income barely covered expenses. Furthermore, in the erratic mountain economy of booms, busts, and seasonal slumps, a husband's income was unpredictable. The making of a household budget must have been quite a frustration.

One group of mining-town mothers is virtually invisible in the usual descriptions, and for them making a home was more difficult still. In those mountain settlements were a surprisingly large number of single mothers. The census shows that they presided over about one family in twelve in Pinal County, Arizona, for instance; about one in eight in Lake County, Colorado; and one in five in Globe, Arizona.[14] Some of these women were widowed and others abandoned, but many may well have chosen to care for their families on their own. The record in California, at least, indicated many women there expressed a spirit of independence by seeking divorces or simply walking away from unfulfilling marriages.[15] In Colorado, when one restless husband announced that the family would once again be moving on, his wife dug in her heels and dissolved the union:

Ernest, you can move on if you have to, but I've dragged two boys and a houseful of furniture just as far as I'm going to. First it was Ohio, then Michigan, then the Peninsula, then Minnesota, Michigan again, then Denver, Weaver, and Creede, and right here I'm going to stay.[16]

She may have spoken for many others.

The poorer wives and single mothers had to make and maintain their homes with a few unreliable resources; outside observers, judging them by standards of the day, sometimes were shocked by the result. "In all my travels on the American continent, I have never yet beheld a scene so thoroughly degrading," an Englishman wrote of a cramped, stuffy Idaho roadhouse run by a single woman with six "infidel imps." In Gregory's Diggings in Colorado, the heart of a new arrival went out to the mothers he saw there: "The hardest sight . . . is to behold four or five women with families of little children washing and cooking in the broiling sun and obliged to gather and cut their own wood." [17]

The journals of these women do contain moments of irritation and despair. One arrived in Gold Hill, Colorado, to find a one-room, dirt-floored, drafty cabin with a few tin cups and plates, and a bed and table made of pine boughs. "I fear I shall sink under this burden," she wrote. "It is not what my fancy pictured it." [18] At best these mothers found quarters in clapboard houses of two or three rooms. Many brought their children to cabins of little more than one hundred square feet with dirt floors, a low door, no windows, and sometimes only a canvas roof. "Snug is the only word I can think of that properly describes our condition," a child said of such a house. [19] Furniture was at a premium. Anything beyond makeshift beds, a table, and a few chairs or stools was considered a luxury. In the corner might sit a water bucket and dipper, and on a shelf above the cook stove, some coffee, salt, dried beans, and flour. The list of cooking gear usually was short—an iron pot, dutch oven, frying pan, and coffee pot. [20]

These mothers put remarkable effort into making these places "homelike" by Victorian standards. They lined the walls with cheap cotton cloth, then covered it with wallpaper. A mother of three in Summit, Montana, laid a small piece of Brussels carpet on her dirt floor and hung printed shades on the log walls to show her youngsters where the windows should have been. Another used sheets of canvas to divide a single room into bedrooms, kitchen, and parlor. At considerable effort and risk, almost all brought west some piece of china, a chromo (lithographed colored picture), a delicately framed photograph, silver caster, or lace tablecloth. [21] Besides being the main arena of child rearing, in a land where so much had been left behind the home became a depository of traditional culture. With these artifacts and icons of domesticity, mothers tried to give their children a sense of the "proper" life.

Mining-town mothers faced a regimen of work not much different from that of midwestern farm wives, though conditions in the camps made these chores even more difficult. Besides washing and cooking, they hauled water, cared for family animals, chopped wood, swept wooden floors and sprinkled dirt ones, and made and mended clothes. At appropriate times during the year they also saw to gardening, canning, slaughtering, curing, and the making of candles and soap. [22] Older children helped with all these jobs, but for the many younger wives just starting families, infants and toddlers meant more work. Wives also sometimes helped their husbands at the mines by clerking and even freighting and shoveling gravel at the sluices, but men seem to have taken on the traditional chores of women only in emergencies. Normally the "doctrine of the two spheres" held firm. The few surviving diaries kept separately by husband and wife for the same period, show a clear division between the workaday worlds of men and women. [23]

The contribution of women's labor to the economy of both the family and the community deserves more attention than historians have yet allowed

it. Mothers not only maintained their dwelling places; they also added indirectly to family income by producing food and clothing that otherwise
would have to be bought.[24] Beyond that, many poorer wives and virtually
all single mothers had to bring in additional money by seeking out other
work. Most of them did for others what they did for their own—washing,
sewing, and cooking for the many unattached men in the diggings. "A
wife of the right sort," a Californian called the sixty-eight-pound spouse
of a tavern-keeper. "She earnt her *old man* . . . nine hundred dollars
in nine weeks, clear of all expenses, by washing."[25] In this sense such
women retained some of their aura of domesticity even as they edged into
the public work force.

The mining frontier posed an array of special problems for the mother's
most important responsibility—the physical, ethical and educational care
of her children. "To be raised in a mining camp means an experience as
full of thrills and wounds and scars as going to the war," recalled one man
who had grown up near the Comstock Lode. "You who have tried it and
have survived its perils deserve service medals."[26] Surely most mothers
would have agreed. The fouled water, streets strewn with garbage and
offal, and the crowded living conditions encouraged the spread of cholera,
diphtheria, influenza, measles, and other child killers. When epidemics
struck, mothers tried to isolate their young but with only limited success.
Disease could devastate a family. Helen Hunt Jackson visited a Colorado
mother who had lost two children in as many months to scarlet fever and
meningitis; her third and last was sick with fever. In 1879 all three children
of a Caribou, Colorado, couple died in four days.[27] The gap between the
rich and the poor narrowed in combating disease. The elite could afford a
better diet and healthier housing, and they could pay for what doctoring
was available, but their understanding of the prevention and treatment of
diseases was often little better than that of their poorer neighbors. Among
the four households of the prominent Fisk family of Helena, Montana, two
children died in half a year.[28]

Then there were accidents. From the time they could walk, boys and
girls might tumble into mine shafts or swift-running streams. On the
streets children could stray into the path of horses or heavy ore wagons;
nearer to home they might swallow lye or other poisons, be thrown from a
horse, or be wounded in hunting accidents or target practice. The poorest
mothers with the heaviest burdens of work—and so the least time to keep
close watch over their young—lived in the most congested and dangerous
parts of town. It is little wonder, then, that one woman wrote from Rich
Bar, California: "This is an awful place for children, and nervous mothers
would 'die daily.'"[29]

Similarly, the mining towns seemed to some mothers to threaten the
moral well-being of children. In late-nineteenth-century literature on family life and education, a set of definite ideas about the proper methods and
goals of child rearing emerged. The new urban, industrial, fast-paced
America offered youth a variety of temptations, from the open degradation of the corner saloon to the subtler bondage of materialism and need-

less comforts. Parents, it was said, should rely upon a child's natural goodness and have faith in the powers of affection and reason to promote the
traditional virtues of sobriety, reverence, diligence, and respect for authority, learning, and the welfare of society. Daughters should learn to be
efficient and virtuous keepers of the hearth, sons to be aggressive but honest lords of the marketplace. This ideal of child rearing was most firmly
established among the middle class in the cities of the Northeast, but it
apparently was spreading to an ever greater portion of the nation's families
by the end of the century.[30]

How deeply were these beliefs entrenched among parents in the mining
towns? If we listen mainly to those at the top of the economic and social
order, it again will be easy to leave with a distorted impression. In general
the elite held to these standards of proper child nurture; and consequently,
in the gold and silver camps they found much to alarm them. Here, more
than practically anywhere else in the country, vice was widely visible and
practically unavoidable. Mining towns "openly wear the worse side out,"
as an observer put it.[31] Saloons, bordellos, and dance halls thrived among
the crowds of young working men. Youngsters walking the streets would
be exposed not only to drinking and whoring but to gambling, smoking,
brawling, and an assortment of social blights. And the language! More
formally educated parents worried not just about the bald obscenities but
also about the colorful slang that was so much a part of westerners' conversations. A "you bet" or "hankering" or "I licked him" brought further
shudders. "Must my little girl soil her sweet mouth with such words and
expressions?" worried an editor's wife. This vernacular would be the first
step, she feared, toward her child's becoming a "fast western woman."[32]
Almost everywhere they turned, there seemed to be something to alarm
such fastidious parents. "On this score[morality], it is impossible to be too
severe," a new arrival in California wrote home, and an Idaho mother
agreed: "This is the hardest place to live upon principle I ever saw, and the
young are almost sure to be led away."[33]

The wealthiest mothers at least could try to keep their children within
the fold. They frequently lived in isolated residential sections where, as
a judge's daughter in Deadwood remembered, children might live lives
"as sheltered as the courtyard of a convent."[34] More important, these
mothers were freed from much of the work that consumed the days of their
poorest neighbors. They had the luxury of time to spend looking after
their youngsters.

The children of the elite tell us something about the results. According
to the diary of eleven-year-old Edna Hedges, daughter of a wealthy lawyer
and politician of Helena, Montana, she was expected to work at home, but
not too hard and only at the traditional tasks of womenfolk. She sewed,
"held the baby," dusted, swept, and occasionally washed dishes. Only
once in a year, when she walked to a bakery, was she asked to run an er-
rand alone outside the house. Though she had to set aside time for music
lessons and memorizing Bible verses, she had plenty of time for play;
these hours at her own house or those of friends were well supervised. She

enjoyed tea parties, croquet, skits, and rounds of "tin tin," "cross questions and crooked answers," and other parlor games. She also spent time
with her parents. She worked and visited wih her mother, and her father
wrote Latin epigrams in her autograph album and took her for walks. Her
thoughts hint she was internalizing the hundreds of lessons in the training
of a proper young lady. "I am trying to be good and not snap as much,"
she wrote one evening. She worried about being "mean," then about gig-
gling, and once scribbled in frustration: "Oh! I do wish I could be decent." [35] By the standards of her time and class she was well on her way.

To the great majority of mothers and children, however, that kind of
close scrutiny and direction must have been all but unimaginable. Bur-
dened with the rigors of housework, and often sewing and cooking for
others as well, working-class mothers could give their sons and daughters
only what time was left over. Though boys had somewhat more freedom
than girls, the reminiscences of both sexes tell of working and playing in
ways that brought them into the mainstream of town life. They panned
along the placers, ran errands, sold cakes and pies and cats, and hung
about the stores, mines, and dance halls, all the time taking in the colorful
words and ways of the men who worked and lounged there. [36] They often
took part in the almost continuous gambling on the streets. Schoolchildren
in Cripple Creek passed daily by a local bordello, and they knew the names
of the women who waved to them from its windows. Young Anne Ellis of
Bonanza, Colorado, spent pleasant evenings reading "Peck's Bad Boy" with
Lil, a local "notorious woman." Anne also could have told Edna Hedges
what a saloon ("strong, sickening") and a whorehouse ("sweet") smelled
like. There is little evidence that the mothers of these children thought
much about the dangers of slang and the virtues of Latin epigrams. [37]

This does not mean, however, that these young persons grew up without
any of the widely accepted benefits of proper child rearing. If nothing
else, they often found affection and some ethical guidance from childless
adults who missed children and young relatives they had left behind. In
their own homes even the busiest parents could find time at the end of the
workday for family entertainments. Group readings were especially popular, as well as singing and playing guitars and violins. The parents of two
boys taught them to recite "The Burial of Sir John Moore" and scenes
from Shakespeare and then pitched them nickles at the end of perfor-
mances. Still, childhood was not entirely lighhearted. "The juniors were a
part of the family circle and shared in the discussion of plans, projects and
problems with their elders," a boy from southern Montana recalled. [38]
Guardians of traditional morality might have been shocked by some parts
of their lives, but these children of the working class certainly shared a
bond of affection and attention with the parents.

Many children were educated at home. Prescriptions of the day held
that the mother should teach her youngsters the basics of reading, writing,
and ciphering—a responsibility even more urgent in fledgling towns where
formal schooling was erratic at best. As expected, mothers among the
well-to-do found it easier to perform these duties. They set aside time dur-

ing the day for lessons and paid for private tutors. In their spacious houses libraries of impressive breadth provided curious children the basis of a liberal education.[39]

But more remarkable in their way were the wives of placer miners, drillers, muckers, common laborers, and small merchants who achieved the same goals with less time and fewer resources. They were aided by a revolution in publishing that brought a great array of printed material within their reach. Women usually carried a few cherished volumes to their new homes, and in time they bought or sent for others. They pinched pennies to subscribe to periodicals, some of which served double duty. Two travelers a thousand miles apart found lowly cabins papered, respectively, by *London Illustrated* and the *Phrenological Journal*.[40] With the help of this dearly bought literature, fathers and especially mothers found time to drill their sons and daughters in the "three R's," plus history and science. This instruction typically was laced with moral and cultural lessons of the day. Coming as it did in the evenings behind the doors of working-class families, the private education of children went largely unnoticed by the social elite and by literary tourists who paused briefly to look and cluck their tongues at the degeneration of culture and learning in the camps.

These activities—schooling, making and maintaining a home by its physical and cultural definition, and nurturing children's health and spirits—filled much of the days of most women living on the mining frontiers of the far West. Through it all ran a common theme in the world of western women—a conflict between the roles expected of their sex and the realities of life in this new land.[41] In the mining towns the underlying social ideology of the Victorian era survived largely intact. It taught that a woman should use her life to make and preserve a proper home: a safe harbor of rest and support for her husband and a school of strength and virtue for her children. Men cheered "the first live woman in the mines" precisely because her arrival meant to them that this process would begin. To these men, she heralded the first real rooting of civilization. If anything, therefore, a woman in the camps faced a heightened pressure to carry out her traditional mission of Victorian wife and mother.

These women, however, were not "gentle tamers" who brought civilization with their simple presence. The prescriptions of Victorian womanhood demanded skills, experience, and effort at least equal to that of a miner, assayer, or dry-goods merchant. The women who hoped to approach these goals could do so only with dedication and creativity. Frontier conditions, moreover, made such ideals even more difficult to achieve. The move west deprived many women of the friends and relatives who could have given them help and comfort. The isolation, harsh environment, and high cost of living posed serious problems in making a home and keeping children healthy, while social conditions tempted the young from the proper paths. At the same time, a wife's economic role was expanded, thus subtracting still more from the invaluable time and energy needed to keep up with her family responsibilities.

Historians need to describe more fully the many facets of this cruel dilemma. To do so, they surely should go beyond traditional sources to listen to the women themselves. In sorting out the voices of these pioneer women, I have stressed the obvious distinctions of economic and social class, but it is necessary to ask other questions as well. What ethnic or regional heritage did a particular woman bring with her? Was she a newlywed, a young mother with infants, or one with a houseful of older sons and daughters? How long had she lived in the West and under what conditions? Had she established bonds with local institutions such as churches, reform groups, or labor organizations?

The testimony is there, but only when much more has been gathered and studied with a respect for the diversity of women's experiences can historians begin to speak with much confidence about the thousands of wives and mothers who lived in Virginia City, Spanish Bar, or Slumgullion Gulch. There still is much to discover about the figures who look at us from those fading photographs.

Notes

1. To cite only one example, in 252 pages of text in his otherwise excellent survey of the social history of the mining frontier, Duane A. Smith devotes 7 to prostitution and 2 to the everyday lives of wives and mothers. *Rocky Mountain Mining Camps: The Urban Frontier* (Bloomington: Indiana University Press, 1967), pp. 187–89, 227–34.

2. Alonzo Delano, *A Live Woman in the Mines: Or, Pike County Ahead!* (New York: S. French, 1857), p. 9.

3. C. Haskins, *The Argonauts of California* (New York: Fords, Howard and Hulbert, 1890), p. 107; Louise Amelia Knapp [Smith] Clappe, *The Shirley Letters from California Mines in 1851–1852* (San Francisco: T. C. Russell, 1922), p. 49.

4. For surveys of mining-town societies based on census data, see Elliott West, "Five Idaho Mining Towns: A Computer Profile," *Pacific Northwest Quarterly* 73, no. 3 (July, 1982): 108–20; Ralph Mann, *After the Gold Rush: Society in Grass Valley and Nevada City, California, 1849–1870* (Stanford, Calif.: Stanford University Press, 1982); Duane A. Smith, "The San Juaner: A Computerized Portrait," *Colorado Magazine* 52, no. 2 (Spring, 1975): 137–52.

5. Rodman W. Paul, ed., *A Victorian Gentlewoman in the Far West: The Reminiscences of Mary Hallock Foote* (San Marino, Calif.: Huntington Library, 1972), p. 179.

6. Clappe, *Shirley Letters*, pp. 100–101.

7. Paul, ed., *Victorian Gentlewoman*, p. 179.

8. Carroll Smith-Rosenberg, "The Female World of Love and Ritual: Relations Between Women in 19th–Century America," *Signs* 1, no. 1 (Fall, 1975): 1–29.

9. Sarah Hively journal, 30 Aug. 1863, Western History Collection, Denver Public Library; Mollie Dorsey Sanford, *Mollie: The Journal of Mollie Dorsey Sanford in Nebraska and Colorado Territories 1857–1866* (Lincoln: University of Nebraska Press, 1959), p. 141; Marvin Lewis, *Martha and the Doctor: A Frontier Family in Central Nevada,* ed. B. Betty Lewis (Reno: University of Nevada Press, 1977), p. 102.

10. Robert L. Griswold, "Apart but Not Adrift: Wives, Divorce, and Independence in California 1850–1890," *Pacific Historical Review* 49, no. 2 (May, 1980): 275–79; Elizabeth Jameson, "Imperfect Unions: Class and Gender in Cripple Creek, 1894–1904," in Milton Cantor and Bruce Laurie, eds., *Class, Sex and the Woman Worker* (Westport, Conn.: Greenwood Press, 1977), pp. 177–78.

11. Thomas Conrad to Mary, 1 Jan. 1865, Thomas Conrad Papers, no. 30, box 1, folder 8, Montana Historical Society.

12. Cornelius Hedges to parents, 18 July 1868, Hedges Family Papers, no. 33, box 2, folder 9, Montana Historical Society; James L. Thane, ed., *A Governor's Wife on the Mining Frontier: The Letters of Mary Edgerton From Montana, 1863–1865* (Salt Lake City, Utah: Tanner Trust Fund, 1976), p. 63; Emma Shepard Hill, *A Dangerous Crossing and What Happened on the Other Side* (Denver: Press of the Smith-Brooks Co., 1914), pp. 47–8; Kathryn DePew, "William A. Hamill, Early Colorado Pioneer of Georgetown," *Colorado Magazine* 32 (October, 1935): 266–79; Elizabeth Fisk to mother, 17 Sept. 1871, Fisk Family Papers, no. 31, box 6, folder 5, Montana Historical Society.

13. "Reminiscences of Early Days in Boise," Carolyn H. Palmer Collection, MS2/24, Idaho Historical Society; Margaret F. Ferris to mother, 21 July 1878, Mrs. Eddy F. Ferris Collection, Montana State University Library.

14. These figures are based on my own calculations from the 1870 and 1880 manuscript census tables.

15. Griswold, "Apart but Not Adrift," pp. 265–84.

16. Edwin Lewis Bennett, *Boom Town Boy* (Chicago: Sage Books, 1966), pp. 25–26.

17. C. Aubrey Angelo, *Sketches of Travel in Oregon and Idaho, with Map of South Boise* (New York: L. D. Robertson, 1866), p. 165; Harry Faulkner diary, 14 June 1859, Western History Collection, Denver Public Library.

18. Sanford, *Mollie,* p. 137.

19. Owen P. White, *A Frontier Mother* (New York: Minton, Balch, 1929), p. 57.

20. Clarence W. Kellogg, "Early Life in California Mining Camps," pp 33–34, typescript, Bancroft Library, University of California, Berkeley; Mary L. Boatman reminiscence, SC444, Montana Historical Society; Mrs. John H. Smith reminiscence, California Historical Society; Elizabeth E. O'Neil reminiscence, Mary Ann Busick Collection, Montana State University Library; Sallie Davenport Davidson reminiscence, SC606, Montana Historical Society; Lizzie Moore Sisk reminiscence, Idaho Historical Society; Lewis, *Martha and the Doctor,* p. 63.

21. Louisa Walters to "Dear Friends," 17 May 1865, Louisa Walters Letters, MS2/312, Idaho Historical Society; Francis D. Haines, Jr., ed., *A Bride on the Bozeman Trail: The Letters and Diary of Ellen Gordon Fletcher, 1866* (Medford, Ore.: Gandee Printing, 1970), p. 82; Anne Ellis, *The Life of an Ordinary Woman* (Lincoln: University of Nebraska Press, 1980), pp. 81, 102–103; Angelo, *Sketches of Travel,* p. 143; Harriet Fish Backus, *Tomboy Bride* (Boulder, Colo.: Pruett Press, 1969), pp. 197–98.

22. Kellogg, "Early Life in California Mining Camps," Bancroft Library, University of California, Berkeley; "Reminiscences of Early Days in Boise," Carolyn H. Palmer Collection, MS2/24, Idaho Historical Society; Lizzie Moore Fisk reminiscence, Idaho Historical Society.

23. See, for instance, James and Emily Galloway diaries, 1862–1866, Bancroft Library, University of California, Berkeley.

24. Susan H. Armitage, "Household Work and Childrearing on the Frontier: The Oral History Record," *Sociology and Social Research* 63, no. 3 (April, 1979): 467–74.

25. Clappe, *Shirley Letters,* pp. 72–73.

26. John Taylor Waldorf, *A Kid on the Comstock: Reminiscences of a Virginia City Childhood* (Palo Alto, Calif.: American West Publishing Co., 1970) p. 50.

27. Helen Hunt Jackson, *Bits of Travel at Home* (Boston: Robert Brothers, 1887), p. 269; David H. Stratton, "The Rise and Fall of Caribou," *Colorado Magazine* 30 (April, 1953): 118.

28. Elizabeth Fisk to mother, 19 Aug. 1875, Fisk Family Papers, no. 31, box 6, folder 10, Montana Historical Society.

29. Clappe, *Shirley Letters,* p. 75.

30. Bernard Wishy, *The Child and the Republic: The Dawn of Modern American Child Nurture* (Philadelphia: University of Pennsylvania Press, 1968).

31. Quoted in Rodman W. Paul, *Mining Frontiers of the Far West, 1848–1880* (New York: Holt, Rinehart and Winston, 1963), p. 166.

32. Elizabeth Fisk to mother, 5 Feb. 1871, Fisk Family Papers, no. 31, box 6, folder 4, Montana Historical Society.

33. Louisa Walters to "Dear Friends," 17 May 1875, Louisa Walters Letters MS2/312, Idaho Historical Society.

34. Estelline Bennett, *Old Deadwood Days* (New York: J. H. Sears and Co., 1928), p. 6.

35. Edna Hedges diary, 19 Sept., 7 Oct., 15 Oct., 4 Nov., 13 Nov., 12 Dec., 31 Dec., 1878; 17 Mar., 23 Mar., 16 Apr., 17 Apr., 19 Apr., 25 Apr., 26 Apr., 28 Apr., 1879, Hedges Family Papers, no. 33, box 11, folder 27, Montana Historical Society.

36. John Moses interview, no. 211, Pioneer Foundation Collection, University of New Mexico Library; Raleigh F. Wilkeson reminiscence, SC983, Montana Historical Society; Erasmus L. Anthony reminiscence, SC364, Montana Historical Society; Bennett, *Boom Town Boy*, p. 48; Theodore T. Johnson, *Sights in the Gold Region* (New York: Baker and Scribner, 1849), p. 183; Martin G. Wenger, *Recollections of Telluride, Colorado, 1895–1920* (Mesa Verde, Colo.: Gilbert R. Wenger, 1978), pp. 23–25.

37. Mabel Barbee Lee, *Cripple Creek Days* (Garden City, N.Y.: Doubleday, 1958), p. 27; Ellis, *Life of an Ordinary Woman*, pp. 40–41, 45–46.

38. White, *Frontier Mother*, p. 87; Charles H. Draper reminiscence, SC642, Montana Historical Society; Kellogg, "Early Day Life in California Mining Camps," pp. 47–49, Bancroft Library, University of California, Berkeley.

39. Mary Edgerton to [?], 7 Jan. 1864, in Thane, *A Governor's Wife*, p. 72; Elizabeth Fisk to mother, 22 Mar. 1875, Fisk Family Papers, no. 32, box 6, folder 10, Montana Historical Society; Margaret F. Ferris to mother, 10 Sept. 1880, Mrs. Eddy F. Ferris Collection, Montana State University Library.

40. Stella Fairlamb interview, no. 139, Pioneer Foundation Collection, University of New Mexico Library; Bennett Seymour reminiscence, 9, Bennett Seymour Collection, no. 563, Colorado State Historical Society; Lewis, *Martha and the Doctor*, p. 148; Mrs. John H. Smith reminiscence, 4, California Historical Society; Isabella L. Bird, *A Lady's Life in the Rocky Mountains* (Norman: University of Oklahoma Press, 1960), p. 157; Alden Brooks diary, 8 June 1860, California Historical Society.

41. Lillian Schlissel, "Frontier Families: A Crisis in Ideology," in Sam B. Girgus, ed., *The American Self: Myth, Ideology, and Popular Culture* (Albuquerque: University of New Mexico Press, 1981), pp. 155–65.

13

The Private Lives of Public Women:
Prostitution in Butte, Montana, 1878–1917

MARY MURPHY

The Cult of True Womanhood excluded one important group of western women—prostitutes. They had left the "private sphere" to become the most public of women and left it for sexual commerce, while "true women" were supposed to be asexual. This belief was reflected in the Butte, Montana, statute Mary Murphy cites in this article, which differentiated "women" from "lewd and dissolute female persons." Western mythology softened this distinction by creating the "whore with the heart of gold," who had all the gentle virtues of proper women. Murphy's study of prostitution in Butte takes us beyond these stereotypes to look at why women became prostitutes, what their private lives were like, and the people who helped or hurt them. Murphy finds no whores with hearts of gold, but she does find women whose lives were as much affected by economic circumstances and emotional needs as other women's.

Because mining towns had many more men than women, they supported large red-light districts and made "private" life fairly public. These circumstances may have led to a more open recognition of the reality of sex. We don't know yet if this recognition included more realistic acknowledgements of female sexuality than the Cult of True Womanhood would suggest. The impact of public sexuality on standards of "normal" male and female behavior merits further investigation. Murphy takes us beyond polarized images of "good" and "bad" women, and helps us rethink an important chapter in the history of "private" life.

The prostitutes who worked in Butte, Montana, before 1917 were daughters of the nineteenth century, yet they violated every tenet of Victorian "womanliness." They were hardly temperate with regard to social or sexual intercourse, they were impious and impure, they lived without true homes or families, and they were anything but submissive. They aggressively sought customers, fought publicly, and cursed not only among themselves but with patrons and the police.[1] Between 1878, when its first hurdy-gurdy house opened, and 1917, when its red-light district closed down, Butte was the temporary home of hundreds, perhaps thousands, of prostitutes. They lived and worked in a one-block area where most of the vices of the nineteenth century were available for a price. The red-light district was

Crapper Jack's Dance Hall and Saloon, Myers Avenue, Cripple Creek, Colorado. Courtesy Glenn Kinnamon.

their home, the demimonde their family. In the world of prostitution the division between public and private, which was so central to nineteenth-century women's lives, was virtually nonexistent. Sexuality, a most private and intimate concern for most people, became blatantly public for prostitutes. Their husbands or lovers were often pimps, and family or lovers' squabbles were regularly reported in the paper as battles among the "denizens" of the district. Prostitutes' clothing and language, even their shopping places, became issues of public policy and regulation.

Prostitution was a highly stratified occupation. Each woman's status was determined by a combination of race, ethnicity, education, sociability, and sexual skill and was reflected in the place in which she worked. Parlor houses, such as Butte's elaborately furnished Windsor and the Irish World, were the top of the line; they functioned as social centers as well as brothels. Madams hired attractive women, usually white, who dressed well, acted like ladies, and played the parts of companions as well as sexual partners. These houses were few, however, and many more prostitutes worked in shabby brothels decorated with brewery calendars and whiskey-stained chairs rather than gilt-framed mirrors and brocade couches. A few prostitutes acquired the resources to work on their own in small cottages on the fringes of the red-light district. But the vast majority of prostitutes in Butte, women of all ages and races, were "everynight workingman's whores" who lived and worked in the cribs lining the streets and alleys of Butte's tenderloin.

Only those women who were private mistresses, served clients in the large parlor houses, or worked out of their own cottages managed to retain a degree of privacy. They catered to a middle-class clientele for whom publicity was undesirable. In return for discretion these women received protection from the police, public censure, and the violence of street life. However, for prostitutes who worked on the street or in cribs, public display was part of the trade. They could not afford both a public and private life.

Prostitutes had no place within the ranks of true womanhood. They were "public women," belonging to all men, not one man, and therefore not quite women at all. The Butte city council expressed this position in its ordinance concerning vagrancy, which drew a distinction between "women" and "lewd and dissolute female persons." These "female persons" were subject to arrest if they conducted themselves in an "improper, profane or obscene manner" within the sight or hearing of women.[2]

The consequences of occupying this position outside "womanhood" were mixed. On the one hand prostitutes were freed from maintaining the facade of middle-class respectability. They were expected to curse, drink, and smoke in public; they frequented saloons and gambling halls where even the most curious of respectable women dared not enter. But the costs of flouting the image of true womanhood far outweighed the pleasures of drinking and smoking in public. The arrival of "true" or "good" women on the frontier brought into sharp relief the bad women of town and exaggerated their outlaw character. Persons who lived through the early days of mining towns recalled prostitutes as "real women beneath their coldly-warm exterior . . . not . . . the hard-shelled harlots they have all been pictured."[3] Such a sympathetic view changed when respectable "real" women established themselves in the West. Prostitutes then forfeited the public courtesies due women, though not all Butte residents were able to recognize a lady when they saw one. In 1909 a man was fined ten dollars for insulting a woman on West Park Street, and the court delivered a lecture on the evils of men loitering on the sidewalks and street corners making "improper remarks to ladies."[4] Prostitutes complied with the new code of manners and used it to their advantage when they were outside the district. One miner observed: "They knew how to act like ladies when away from the district—and did it too. I seen one of them up and give a poke in the face to a masher on Park Street one afternoon, when he . . . tried to flirt with her."[5] Prostitutes tended to exact retribution more directly than did ladies. Operating outside the boundaries of "womanhood" had graver consequences than the loss of courtesy. Because of their status prostitutes enjoyed little protection from insult or violence. In 1881 a man was fined ten dollars for disfiguring a prostitute, the same fine a woman paid when convicted of vagrancy.[6]

The public nature of their lives often denied prostitutes the private comforts of home and family. Though each woman cherished the few possessions which distinguished her crib from every other, nothing could disguise the fact that her bedroom, often her only quarters, was a place of business. A few prostitutes managed to keep a room apart from their cribs, sometimes sharing it with a husband or "secretary," a euphemism for "pimp" apparently used only in Butte. Although a few prostitutes formed long-term relationships with men who had nothing to do with their business, most of their liaisons were with "secretaries" and were rarely formalized by marriage.[7] The lack of legal bonds in their partnerships again denied prostitutes legitimacy in the eyes of respectable society.

The relationship between prostitutes and pimps was the most complex in the demimonde. Some prostitutes considered pimps parasites and would have nothing to do with them. One independent Frenchwoman commenting on the district in 1902, declared, "There are at least twenty-five secretaries on this street who live on the fat of the land because foolish girls will give them their money."[8] Pimps unquestionably exploited prostitutes, living off their earnings and often treating them viciously. But some women willingly allied with pimps. Whatever emotional support, physical protection, sexual satisfaction, or illusion of romance these men "of fancy dress and patent leather shoes" provided seemed to offset the abuse with which they treated their lovers.[9] John Day was arrested for stealing fifty dollars from a woman whose crib he had shared for some time. However, once his lover had him arrested she never came forward to testify against him. May Raymond was "beaten almost into insensibility" by William Beierman, her paramour of eight months, but she did not press charges. In one of the most tragic stories of Butte's tenderloin, Mollie Scott, a young woman employed in a dance hall, was murdered by her husband, "the man whom she had cheerfully supported from the gains of her arduous calling," in a trivial argument about whether she could visit another dancing saloon.[10]

Many prosititutes demanded faithfulness from their paramours, and when they suspected infidelity, they took action. One night at a party Laura Evans decided that her "beau," Arthur, was dancing too frequently with another woman and knocked him through a plate-glass window, nearly cutting his throat. Dolly Arthur lived with one man for twenty-six years. After witnessing his repeated affairs, she told him they could continue living together "but you must never put your hands on me again."[11]

In many respects prostitutes' relationships with pimps were similar to those with madams. Both pimps and madams procured customers, protected prostitutes from violence inflicted by others, and established an emotional bond of some permanence. Yet in the popular culture madams became romanticized, often admired figures, while pimps were always despised. By some criteria madams fit the nineteenth-century ideology of womanliness. They kept a house; they played the role of mother to their "girls"; they wielded influence and used their sexuality behind the scenes, rarely making overt use of what power they may have had. Pimps, however, violated every tenet of nineteenth-century manliness. Men of all classes derived their identity from their work, and pimps did neither "honest" nor "manly" work. They were supported by women; worse, they exploited women's virtue. In an age when men fought for wages that would keep their families "from the soup house and the brothel," pimps, who pushed women into vice, could only be despised.[12]

Middle-class Victorian ideas of manliness and women's lack of passion fated pimps to condemnation and again made prostitutes' lives subject to public scrutiny. While repulsed by prostitution, many Victorians were sympathetic to prostitutes, imagining them to have been trapped by white slavers, driven to sexual commerce by dire economic need, or seduced, abandoned, and then "honor-bound" to take the only course left open to a ruined woman. That women had some choice or might enjoy their work was beyond their understanding, or perhaps threatening to their own sexuality. The possibility that a woman could voluntarily associate with a pimp was unthinkable, and thus women's own needs and motives were ignored in the public campaigns to rid western towns of pimps. During one of the repeated attempts to cleanse Butte of secretaries, Judge Donlan settled the maximum fine of three hundred dollars on one man arrested for vagrancy and censured him for carrying on "the lowest and vilest business that could possibly be imagined for a human being."[13]

Just as prostitutes' relationships with lovers were jeopardized by their work and by public policy, so were their attempts at motherhood. Few prostitutes were wives in the traditional sense, and children had little place in a brothel. In several frontier communities, when children were discovered living in the red-light district they were taken from their mothers and placed in the county poor farm. Prostitutes' appeals to place them in private homes went unheeded.[14] For this reason prostitutes frequently left their children with relatives or paid families to take them in. Many mothers desired to protect their children from the environment of the red-light district and recognized that the transience of their occupation often precluded good care. Many Butte prostitutes had borne children, but only a few lived with them.[15]

Prostitutes could hardly practice the most common forms of nineteenth-century birth control, abstinence and withdrawal, although women undoubtedly made use of pessaries, vaginal sponges, suppositories, and douches. They also resorted to abortion, a decision often painfully calculated.[16] Madeleine Blair, who started working as a prostitute at seventeen had borne two children by the time she was twenty-one. Her daughter died at birth, and she was determined to rear her second child, a son. Intending to save enough money to start a legitimate business, she left him with a nurse and went to Winnipeg to work for the summer. She returned and reclaimed her son, but, not having made enough to start her business, she continued to work as an occasional prostitute. Madeleine soon found herself pregnant again. While she was debating whether to have an abortion, her son died of pneumonia. In grief and anger at the thought of bearing another fatherless child she performed a self-induced abortion in her fifth month. She nearly died from peritonitis but recovered to mourn "with strange perversity and inconsistency" for the child she had "deliberately destroyed."[17]

In Butte between 1900 and 1917, twenty-three women died as a result of abortions. They ranged in age from seventeen to thirty-nine; they were married, single, divorced; black and white. It is unclear how many were prostitutes. These deaths only hint at the number of abortions performed in the city in the late nineteenth and early twentieth centuries. In Montana prostitution was considered a misdemeanor, but having an abortion carried a one-year jail sentence. Because of its illegality only unsuccessful procedures, revealed by sickness or death, were reported, and hundreds of successful abortions went unrecorded.[18]

Creating a home or family was only one of the problems faced by prostitutes. Prostitution was a competitive business in both the parlor houses and the cribs. Although in parlor houses madams often tried to distribute customers equally among the workers, the women vied for men. Since prostitutes split each fee with the madam, it was in their own interest to have as many "callers" as possible, and they tried to build up a regular clientele. Down on the street there was no mediating factor like a madam. Prostitutes posed in the doors and windows of their cribs "as if [they] were a part of a live-stock exhibition."[19] The term "lost sisterhood" which has been applied to prostitutes is apt, for the fierce competition for customers gnawed at any bonds of solidarity. One pimp wrote of the competition among prostitutes, "In rivalry they eat the flesh skin off one another alive."[20]

Rivalry often led to the violence endemic in the district. Women fought with each other verbally and physically, sometimes quarreling over a customer, more often over pimps. They frequently joined in the general brawls that erupted in the saloons and dance halls. Sometimes they fought out of sheer spite. When one prostitute placed the skins of some plums on her neighbor's doorstep rather than in the garbage can, her neighbor attacked her with scissors and inflicted a severe scalp wound.[21]

Although prostitutes occasionally availed themselves of the courts to redress a wrong, more often they acted immediately and personally—and often ended up in court as the accused. When a peddler somehow provoked two "Park Street women," they assaulted him with cayenne pepper and beer bottles. Laura Evans, who bore the scars to prove it, testified that when she and her lover were angry at each other they fought with knives. When a drunken man in the Royal parlor house struck Emma Robinson in the face, she stabbed him.[22]

Prostitutes were much more often on the receiving end of violence, frequently from unpredictable customers. On May 21, 1907, under the headline "Woman of Lower World Is Stabbed by Italian Tamale Vendor," the *Butte Miner* reported in unusual detail an assault in the red-light district. Teodosio Campanelli had given Gussie Clark a dollar, stood outside her crib talking for some time, and then asked for the dollar back. Clark, who had come from Seattle only two days before, called to her neighbor Mollie Quinn, who told her not to return the money. Campanelli pulled a knife; Quinn seized him, permitting Clark to escape while Campanelli stabbed Quinn in the abdomen. Quinn's husband arrived on the scene as she was being placed on a stretcher. As he stood by her side, an elderly woman emerged from the crowd, shook her fist, and cursed him: "You have disgraced your dead father in the boneyard. You told me years ago that you had quit her. Yet here you are . . . May you die the death that woman is dying. And she deserves it, for you were a good boy till you took up with Mollie Quinn." Another prostitute who had witnessed the scene muttered to a reporter, "That's your Christianity." [23]

Denied protection enjoyed by "true women," prostitutes often had only each other to rely upon in times of danger or crises; at such moments some tenuous bonds of sisterhood emerged. The common hazards prostitutes faced sometimes brought them together; abortion, the death of a child, assault by a customer, or attempted suicide suspended the daily competition. There were many incidents like Campanelli's attack on Gussie Clark, and women like Mollie Quinn were often the only defenders other prostitutes had. When a prostitute was killed or committed suicide, it was fellow members of the lost sisterhood who buried her. [24]

Amid the atmosphere of spite and rivalry, and hidden in the dismal quarters of the district, was a corner of the nineteenth-century "female world of love and ritual." Not all prostitutes were like Dolly Arthur, who claimed she "never had a good girlfriend in [her] life." [25] Prostitutes frequently traveled in pairs and sought jobs together. There are many allusions to lesbianism in brothels, and it is likely that women often turned to each other for the love and comfort lacking in their relationships with men. [26]

Sometimes, however, women's pride kept them apart. Laura Evans's friend Spud Murphy left her to set up her own business, which prospered for many years. But as she grew older, she became an alcoholic, lost her house, and ended up as a washerwoman in another red-light district. Evans went to offer her a home with her for the rest of her life, but Spuddy refused to see her, ashamed of the way her life had turned out. She continued to reject any help from Evans and died alone. [27]

Women joined the fast life for a number of reasons, but it did not always lead to what they expected. Investigators from the mid-nineteenth century through the Progressive Era sought to explain why a woman turned to commercialized sex. They posited as causes abuse as a child or wife, poverty, early sexual experience, alcoholism, emotional deprivation, "keeping bad company," or abandonment by a man. All these factors were undoubtedly contributing influences in particular cases. But there were other reasons, too. Some women decided that prostitution would provide them with fancy clothing, a desirable social life, sexual freedom, or simply a better standard of living. [28] Other women joined the sisterhood out of despair, expecting nothing better than the life they had been leading, and probably worse. Some women found the luxury and excitement they desired; others experienced a brief period of financial success, enjoying a standard of living beyond the means of most working-class women. But the constant travel, the threat of arrest, violence, betrayal, and immersion in a world of alcohol, drugs, and disease debilitated women emotionally and physically. Contrary to white-slave tracts, which portrayed women following the path to ruin after visiting an opium den or becoming an alcoholic, it is far more likely that prostitutes turned to opiates and alcohol to numb themselves once they discovered that the fast life was not all they had hoped or was even worse than they had expected.[29]

Alcohol and drugs were a part of the tenderloin culture and addiction only sucked prostitutes more deeply into the life. Alcoholism and drug abuse united members of the demimonde and drew yet another line between them and Butte's respectable citizenry. A Butte bard wrote an epic poem describing a dance attended by Butte's demimonde in 1898. Several verses illustrate the community involved and suggest the widespread use of a variety of drugs.

> All the junkies were invited,
> Yes, every gink and muff,
> Not a single one was slighted
> If they were on the stuff.
> Invitations were presented
> To every hustler and her man.
> They even sent up invites
> To the hopheads in the can.
>
> "But, before they play the grand march
> Let each dancer have a shot;
> It will act as stimulation,
> And should make the dancin' hot."
> So from scores of hiding places
> Guests brought forth their hypo gats;
> From sleeves, brassieres and bustles,
> Some even hid them in their rats.
>
> Not all the cokies used the needle,
> Some from their opium pipes did whiff;
> Others drained their paregoric,
> A few of "happy dust" did sniff.
> Opium pills or hasheesh
> Came forth from many a sock,
> And some twist from China Alley
> Brought out her old yen hok.[30]

Prostitutes used anodynes other than alcohol and drugs. Some women became addicted to gambling, viewing it as their only chance to create a new life, but more often they only dug themselves more deeply into debt.[31] Others married. In 1882 the *Butte Miner* reported a "matrimonial epidemic" on Park Street when several prostitutes married.[32] Perhaps they hoped for stability if not a total escape from the life. It is impossible to know how many achieved that stability, although western folklore says that many prostitutes wed and vanished happily into the ranks of respectability. Many women, however, could not shed their pasts and either returned to prostitution or chose another alternative.[33]

Suicide was a drastic solution to the despair of prostitutes' lives, but it was often attempted. Some women shot themselves or used arsenic or chloral; more commonly they took overdoses of opiates, which were easily obtained in drugstores.[34] The coy prose with which newspapers usually reported prostitutes' attempted suicides masked the desperation that led to such acts. Lottie Ables had come to Helena in the 1870s. She was nick-named "Sorrel Mike" after a racehorse that arrived in the territory about the same time. While she was in Helena, she attempted suicide several times. Around 1879 she moved to Butte, where she married a saloonkeeper named Pickett, and apparently continued to work as a prostitute while dancing in Pickett's saloon. But married life was no balm, and two weeks after her wedding she again attempted suicide by drinking a phial of laudanum. Once more she was revived. Ables's life got no easier; a few months later a man was convicted of assault and battery on her. She continued to live and work in Butte, attempting suicide again in July 1880. At some time that year her husband vanished, and her sister moved into the small house she occupied just south of Park Street. In December 1881, Lottie Ables finally died, but not by her own hand. After quarreling with her lover, she went out and found another man. When he left the house without paying for the wine he had drunk, she reputedly drew a pistol. In the ensuing struggle Ables was shot in the abdomen and died the next day. The newspaper reported her age to be around thirty, but she was only twenty-two.[35]

The undeniable tragedy of many prostitutes' lives has led some historians and feminists to cast them in the role of hapless victims of society and male exploitation. In this respect we are as short-sighted as the Victorians who reduced them to one-dimensional caricatures of "bad" women. Butte's prostitutes were victims—victims of a tangled sexual ideology that advocated "passionlessness" in women but recognized the need for prostitution to absorb the "excess lust" of men; victims of a city government that exploited their vulnerable legal position to fill the city treasury; victims of madams and pimps who exploited their emotional vulnerability and need for physical protection and security; and victims of men who denied them any personal dignity, treating them only as sexual objects. Yet, just as women exercised some choice in the process of becoming prostitutes, they sometimes exercised power in their trade and had some pride in their accomplishments. Prostitutes like Dolly Arthur were proud of their popularity, of running a "clean" house where men had a good time and did not have to worry about being robbed. They enjoyed men, they enjoyed their work, and they considered the money they were paid a flattering reflection of their worth. While they disbursed their share of bribes and fines, they also used skill and charm to play upon men's vanities and to protect themselves from the courts, the police, and difficult customers.

In a parlor house a man paid for companionship, entertainment, and a semblance of romance, as well as for intercourse, but in poorer brothels and cribs, no such illusion existed. Prostitutes often had several customers each night, and they reduced sexual intercourse to a mechanical process. One worker described his experience:

She'd lay on her back and get you on top of her so fast, you wouldn't even know you'd come up there on your own power. She'd grind so that you almost felt like you had nothing to do with it. Well, after that, she had you. She could make it get off as quickly as she wanted to, . . . and she didn't waste any time, I'll tell you, . . . I'd say the whole thing, from the time you got in the room until the time you came didn't take three minutes.[36]

Women in the cribs were not selling romance, and unless a man lingered to drink there was no profit in prolonging the engagement. Prostitutes like Madeleine could not reconcile themselves to the fact that some men wanted more than their bodies:

I could not make a demonstration of affection over men nor any pretense or response to their caresses. For the life of me, I could not understand why they should expect it. They had only bought my body. I could not see why they should want more. My love was not for sale, piecemeal, to every man who had the price to pay for my body.[37]

The relationship between prostitute and client was a marketplace transaction, and, as in any other commercial exchange, the customer sought to get as much as he could for his money. Much of the violence directed against prostitutes occurred when a man thought he had purchased more than a woman was willing to give. Because of crib women's low status they were especially fair game for cheating and abuse. Several bloody altercations in the district occurred when women tried to get payment from parsimonious customers. For the most part, however, women controlled what happened in their cribs and in their beds, "turning a trick" on men who thought they had bought "the right to handle [them] at will." [38]

When a man became a nuisance or blind drunk, prostitutes often "made a touch." Some whores felt that it was "against their religion" to let a man get away with a penny in his pocket, and they were not choosy about the means they used to get it. Men who were robbed were frequently reluctant to make a legal complaint for fear of publicity. Dozens of men, including a sheriff from another part of Montana, claimed that they were robbed in Beryl Hasting's house on Mercury Street, but none would swear out a complaint, much to the chagrin of the police.[39]

Although Butte prostitutes exerted some personal power in their individual lives, there is little evidence that they, or any other member of the tenderloin, ever acted collectively to improve their lot. Madams may have used their influence on important men in the city, and individual prostitutes may have had some sway over a policeman or official. But the examples of Denver, where prostitutes formed an organized voting block, or Cripple Creek, Colorado, where dance hall girls founded the Dance Hall Girls Protective Association and called a strike to protest a reduction in their percentage of liquor sales, are absent, or still hidden, in Butte's history.[40]

Perhaps prostitutes' greatest source of power was society's need for them. The prostitutes of the demimonde were indeed residents of a half-world with little legal and no moral standing since they had, in effect, been read out of the ranks of "true women." But prostitutes and their madams, pimps, and liquor and drug suppliers weathered many storms of reform, for they knew there was an enduring demand for their services. Power is exercised in subtle ways by oppressed groups or members of an under-class, many times by giving those in power the illusion of submission. The members of Butte's demimonde, for all their flamboyance, knew how to play a subtle game. They were able to protect themselves by giving some-thing to everyone, even reformers.

In May 1905, Christian reformers invaded the red-light district of Butte. The Reverend C. L. Bovard and the Salvation Army band, accom-panied by a thousand men, women, and children, held a revival meeting and then marched through the district singing, "Where Is My Wandering Boy Tonight?" Later that evening the evangelist William Biederwolf ad-dressed the crowd, calling Butte "the lowest sinkhole of vice in the west." The week-long revival culminated in a meeting in the district. The mana-ger of the Casino Theater opened his doors to the evangelist. The or-chestra pit was jammed with "gamblers, rounders and male habitues" of the district; the boxes were filled with "women in flimsy garments" ac-companied by their secretaries and paramours. For thirty-five minutes Biederwolf addressed the crowd; when he asked those who desired to do better to raise their hands, everyone did. After Biederwolf departed, the bar reopened, the orchestra struck up a tune, and the women went back to work. Someone asked the manager of the Casino whether he intended to give up the liquor trade. He looked up in amazement and said, "Me? I guess not."[41]

Business returned to normal in the district. Prostitutes continued to ply their trade, to be picked up for vagrancy, fined, and released to be arrested the following month. In 1915 the *Miner* reported that the district had a larger population than ever and business was booming. But prosperity was short-lived. The wave of reform that swept through America during World War I touched Butte as well. In 1917 the city attorney declared war on houses of ill repute. The Copper King saloon and hotel, the financial heart of the district, was described as "a haunt for some of the most disreputable characters in the city," and it was closed in the first battle of the campaign against vice. Butte joined two hundred other American cities that shut down their red-light districts by 1920.[42]

The closing of Butte's red-light district did not end prostitution, just as Prohibition which came in 1918, did not end the sale and consumption of liquor. But the two events changed the structure of vice. Earlier in the cen-tury when Butte attempted to shut down its district, one prostitute re-sponded by saying that she would merely go into the lodging houses or "rustle" in the streets.[43] That is what happened in 1917. Vice moved underground as prostitutes dispersed through the city and speakeasies re-placed corner saloons. Prostitution was a firmly established business in Butte, and prostitutes continued to demonstrate persistence and flexibility in pursuit of their trade. The closing of the red-light district ended a particular form of commercialized vice, affecting both the public and private lives of prostitutes, but it certainly did not extinguish Butte's demimonde.

Notes

1. *Butte Miner,* 11 Sept. 1880, 16 March 1881, 22 Sept. 1881.
2. William E. Carroll, comp., *The Revised Ordinances of the City of Butte* (1914), pp. 460–61.
3. Frank A. Crampton, *Deep Enough: A Working Stiff in the Western Mine Camps* (Denver: Sage Books, 1956), p. 50; reprint (Norman: University of Oklahoma Press, 1982).
4. *Butte Miner,* 20 Aug. 1909.
5. Federal Writers' Project, *Copper Camp* (New York: Hastings House, 1943), p. 181.
6. *Butte Miner,* 6 March 1881; Butte City Ordinance no. 824, 1914.
7. Madeleine Blair maintained a relationship with one man for several years. He was a protector and lover but never acted as a pimp. Other women continued working as prostitutes while they were married to men who had nothing to do with their business. Pearl Heflin for instance, who worked as a prostitute in Butte in 1900, was married to a day laborer.
8. *Butte Miner,* 19 Jan. 1902.
9. Martha Louise Black, *My Ninety Years* (Anchorage: Alaska Northwest Publishing Co., 1976), p. 48.
10. *Butte Miner,* 27 May 1907, 19 Aug. 1909, 5 Aug. 1880.
11. Forbes Parkhill, *The Wildest of the West* (Denver: Sage Books, 1951), p. xiii; June Allen, *Dolly's House* (Ketchikan, Alaska: Tongass Publishing Co., 1976), pp. 20–21.
12. Peter G. Filene, *Him Her Self; Sex Roles in Modern America* (New York: Harcourt Brace Jovanovich, 1974), see chapter 3, "Men & Manliness"; Elizabeth Jameson, "Imperfect Unions: Class and Gender in Cripple Creek, 1894–1904," *Frontiers* 1 (Spring, 1976): 101.
13. *Butte Miner,* 23 July 1910. In 1905 a "crusade" was begun to rid the city of men known as "red-light vagrants." One of the tactics was to arrest and fine prostitutes, presumably with the hope that if deprived of their income, the men would move on. *Butte Miner,* 26 July 1905.
14. Margaret H. Davis, "Harlots and Hymnals: A Historic Confrontation of Vice and Virtue in Waco, Texas," *Mid-South Folklore* 4 (Winter, 1976): 92.
15. "Tenth Census," 1880, vol. 1, "Montana" (manuscript); "Twelfth Census of the Population," 1900, vol. 9, "Silver Bow County" (manuscript). Two children were living with prostitutes in 1880; in 1900 no children were recorded in the red-light district, but the census revealed that prostitutes had borne twenty-six children, twelve of whom were living.
16. Marion S. Goldman, *Gold Diggers and Silver Miners: Prostitution and Social Life on the Comstock Lode* (Ann Arbor: University of Michigan Press, 1981), p. 126.
17. *Madeleine: An Autobiography* (New York: Harper and Brothers, 1910), pp. 196–202.
18. Butte Mortuary Records, 1900–17; *Revised Codes of Montana,* 1907.
19. *Madeleine,* p. 216.
20. U.S. Cong., Senate, *Importing Women for Immoral Purposes: A Partial Report from the Immigration Commission on the Importation and Harboring of Women for Immoral Purposes,* 61st Cong., 2d sess., doc. 196 (Washington, D.C.: Government Printing Office, 1909), p. 59.
21. *Butte Miner,* 4 March 1880, 17 March 1880, 26 May 1880, 5 Oct. 1881, 21 Aug. 1909.
22. *Butte Miner,* 20 Feb. 1881, 26 May 1880; Parkhill, *The Wildest of the West,* p. xiii; *Butte Miner,* 16 Oct. 1903.
23. *Butte Miner,* 21 May 1907.

24. *Butte Miner*, 5 Aug. 1880, 11 Nov. 1881.

25. Dolly Arthur, interview by John Grainger, Ketchikan, Alaska, n.d.

26. Ruth Rosen, *The Lost Sisterhood: Prostitution in America, 1900–1918* (Baltimore: Johns Hopkins University Press, 1982), pp. 104, 163; Paula Petrik, "The Bonanza Town: Women and Family on the Rocky Mountain Frontier, Helena, Montana, 1865–1900" (Ph.D. diss. SUNY-Binghampton, 1982), p. 194; Goldman, *Gold Diggers and Silver Miners*, pp. 116–21.

27. Parkhill, *The Wildest of the West*, p. xv.

28. For a discussion of why women turned to prostitution and an analysis of the many vice commissions, see Rosen, *The Lost Sisterhood*, chap. 8.

29. Parkhill, *The Wildest of the West*, p. xv; *Madeleine*, pp. 228–312. Regular use of opiates also caused disruption or cessation of menstruation; thus it is possible that prostitutes used opiates as a form of birth control. David T. Courtwright, "Opiate Addiction in America, 1880–1940" (Ph.D. diss. Rice University, 1979), p. 93.

30. Federal Writers' Project, pp. 272–73. *Gink* means a fellow or "guy"; *muff*, prostitute; *gat*, pistol or revolver; *rat*, pad with tapering ends over which a woman's hair is arranged; *cokie*, drug addict, cocaine user; *happy dust*, cocaine; *twist*, woman with loose or "twisted" morals.

31. Lucie Cheng Hirata, "Chinese Immigrant Women in Nineteenth Century California," in Carol Berkin and Mary Beth Norton, eds., *Women of America, A History* (Boston: Houghton Mifflin, 1979), p. 232; *Madeleine*, pp. 233–38.

32. *Butte Miner*, 8 Feb. 1882.

33. Crampton, *Deep Enough*, p. 50; Petrik, "The Bonanza Town," pp. 194–99; Anne Ellis, *The Life of an Ordinary Woman* (1929; reprint, Lincoln: University of Nebraska Press, 1980), pp. 222–23; James Gray, *Red Lights on the Prairie* (Toronto: Macmillan, 1971), pp. 179–80.

34. Alfred R. Lindesmith, *Addiction and Opiates* (Chicago: Aldine Publishing Co., 1968), p. 210; Goldman, *Gold Diggers and Silver Miners*, pp. 134–35; *Butte Miner*, 20 Feb. 1880, 26 May 1880, 6 Oct. 1881, 11 Nov. 1881, 7 Aug. 1883, 6 Apr. 1884.

35. *Butte Miner*, 28 Aug. 1879, 7 Oct. 1879, 31 July 1880, 16 Dec. 1881; *Tenth Census*, 1880.

36. Rosen, *The Lost Sisterhood*, p. 96.

37. *Madeleine*, p. 71.

38. *Madeleine*, p. 82.

39. Parkhill, *The Wildest of the West*, p. xii; Anne K. Butler, "The Tarnished Frontier: Prostitution in the Trans-Mississippi West, 1865–1890," (Ph.D. diss., University of Maryland, 1979), p. 119; *Butte Miner*, 5 Oct. 1881, 7 May 1905, 27 May 1907, 20 Feb. 1909, 20 Aug. 1909.

40. Parkhill, *The Wildest of the West*, pp. 23–24; Ruth Rosen, "The Lost Sisterhood: Prostitution During the Progressive Era," (Ph.D. diss., University of California, Berkeley, 1976), p. 132; Jameson, "Imperfect Unions," p. 101.

41. *Butte Miner*, 5 May 1905, 11 May 1905.

42. *Butte Miner*, 16 July 1915, 11 May 1917; Mark Connelly, *The Response to Prostitution in the Progressive Era* (Chapel Hill: University of North Carolina Press, 1980), p. 26.

43. *Butte Miner*, 19 Jan. 1902.

14

Essential Servants: Immigrant Domestics on the Canadian Prairies, 1885–1930

NORMA J. MILTON

To a woman the meaning of "frontier opportunity" depended partly upon the real alternatives she had had elsewhere. In this article Norma J. Milton explores the lives of women who immigrated to the West from other countries, in this case European women who were recruited to be domestic servants on the Canadian prairies. Certainly, their lives were affected by domestic ideology, and they worked in the domestic sphere, as did most other women wage earners in the West. For the Canadian government, they were "gentle tamers" of sorts, who would help to equalize the ratio of women to men and who would re-create stable families and farm life on the frontier. For the women themselves, Canada promised greater economic mobility than they could expect in their old homelands. Some married and helped build family farms. For these women, families and homesteads may not have been traditional choices; marriage and property were not always available to working-class women in their countries of birth. They may have elected domestic roles not so much from allegiance to genteel beliefs as because domesticity promised enhanced status and economic improvement. Milton shows us how the same option may have meant mobility or stability to different individuals, depending on the eyes through which one viewed it. The promise of the frontier depended on the options women had elsewhere.

The Canadian prairies offered the promise of a better life for many unmarried immigrant women during the period from 1885 to 1930. The promise, however, masked the loneliness, isolation, hard work, and harsh conditions of being a domestic servant. At the time, Europe and Britain offered little economic security, social position, or educational opportunity to the single woman. Thus, many chose immigration to Canada as a domestic servant over poverty, social ostracism, and unemployment in their homelands. Whatever their motive, an estimated 250,000 British and European single women migrated to Canada as domestic servants between 1885 and 1930, about one-half of them taking positions in the homes of prairie Canada. These young women have remained almost anonymous in Canadian history, yet they were an essential element in developing the economic potential envisioned when Canada purchased the prairies from the Hudson's Bay Company in 1869.[1]

URGENT!

Thousands of nice girls are wanted in THE CANADIAN WEST.

Over 20,000 Men are sighing for what they cannot get—WIVES! Shame!

Don't hesitate-COME AT ONCE. If you cannot come, send your sisters.

So great is the demand that anything in skirts stands a chance.

No reasonable offer refused They are all shy but willing. All Prizes! No Blanks.

Hustle up now Girls and don't miss this chance. Some of you will never get another.

Special Application Card from

Poster recruiting young British women to come to Canada. The only legal entry available to unaccompanied females was as domestic servants. Courtesy Glenbow Museum, Glenbow-Alberta Institute.

The period from 1869 to 1896 saw the development of the economic and social infrastructure of prairie Canada. The land was surveyed and studied to determine its farming potential; the Canadian Pacific Railway was built; the native peoples were settled on reservations, and eastern Canadians moved westward, many taking with them Victorian social values, which became established as the norm for prairie society. World economic recession from 1873 to 1896 inhibited prairie development, but migrants arrived, established farms, and helped towns and cities grow and prosper. A few immigrant domestic servants came during this period, but most arrived between 1896 and 1930.[2]

Domestic servants were one of only three occupational groups welcomed under federal immigration legislation; the others were farmers and farm laborers. Servants were also sought to relieve some of the workload of farm housewives and to lend prestige to middle-class households in towns and cities, where the Victorian values of the society were most often expressed. Canadian immigration department records contain numerous requests for immigrant domestic help and for the immigration of single women. The *Daily Nor' Wester,* a Winnipeg, Manitoba, newspaper, reported in 1896 that a CPR land commission had stated:

. . . the great want of the North west is more women. The bachelor farm is, . . . the greatest drawback to this prairie country. His home is unkempt and his life unsweetened by human companionship save that of his own stern sex.[3]

The report went on to urge the federal government to encourage the migration of young women of marriageable age. Similar sentiments were often expressed in newspaper editorials and letters to the editor. The occasional classified advertisement appearing under "Domestic Servants Wanted" could be interpreted as seeking a wife more than a housekeeper. For example, the *Regina Leader Post* published this advertisement in March, 1923:

Wanted—Housekeeper by Canadian bachelor on ¼ section; age 42. Close to school, six miles from town. Good home. Permanent position if suited. Apply stating wages, particulars and nationality. Box 141, Chapin, Sask.

As a result of public demand for domestics and a recognition of the need to overcome the male-female imbalance in the population, the federal government seriously began recruiting domestic servants in 1899. Canadian representatives selected domestics, then escorted them to their new locale, and supervised their placement in Canadian homes. Although variations occurred over the next thirty years, most domestic servants who arrived in Canada before 1930 came through this process.[4]

Some of their experiences have been recorded in the records of the Canadian immigration department and the files of the Canadian Pacific Railway, but few diaries or letter collections recording domestics' personal experiences have emerged. Thus with few exceptions the evidence of their part in the society and economy of the Canadian prairies is sparse.[5]

One of the exceptions is a series of letters from an anonymous young British woman, who signed her letters with the initials B. A. S. and is known to us as BAS. These letters described her life as a domestic servant and farm wife from 1909 to 1914.

BAS arrived in Canada in 1909 intending to visit her brother, who was homesteading in Alberta, and to experience the adventure of living and working in the Canadian Northwest. She first worked on a chicken farm near Edmonton, Alberta, where she helped prepare meals for five hired men. She described the environment as "a happy go lucky place" where they "lived most extravagantly." By January, 1910, she was employed in the MacPherson household in Saskatoon, Saskatchewan, which she described as the home "of a real Highlander, . . . a second son making his fortune in the colonies." There BAS learned how to cook and was treated as part of the family. "So far I haven't regretted my venture, but of course there are times when I would like to fly [home], just for one peep and back again." Despite her enthusiasm for prairie Canada she missed the spring flowers of home. She did not like "Western Canadians at all—they dress most outrageously and their accent is fierce." To hear "some bumptious, very self-made & very uneducated Canadian talk against England" made her angry. BAS found the countryside "dreary" but thought that Canadian cookstoves were more convenient than English stoves.[6]

By September, 1910, BAS was planning a trip back to England and had left her position in Saskatoon to go to her brother's farm near Bassano, Alberta. Her 1910 Christmas letter wistfully stated: "I am spending another Xmas in this cold country. . . . we are quite removed from civilization here & mail day on Wednesday is *the* day of the week." In the letter BAS described hauling water from a coulee for household use and told her friends, "Count your blessings my dears, and each tap in the house is equal to six blessings!!" She also described her brother's house of tarpaper, wood, and sod; how she and her brother dug coal at a burned-out mine fourteen miles away; and how they became lost in a snowstorm on their way home: "We wandered from ridge to ridge of this blessed prairie looking in vain for a shack that we knew." On the more positive side BAS mentioned skating, sleighing, and surprise parties, where she had a "gay time."[7]

Perhaps it was at one of these parties that BAS met her future husband. By June, 1911 she was writing from Stoppington, Alberta, to tell her friends that she was married. BAS had married a widower with a teenage daughter and an eight-year-old son who, in her words, "seems to have taken a great fancy to his new mother." She also described helping her husband and two hired men line a well. She was called on to hold a prop during this operation. The prop slipped and fell on her, breaking her collarbone. "This is no place for an invalid—no visitors, no flowers, no books to read, no anything."[8]

June, 1913, found BAS expecting a baby at the end of July and being cared for by a German neighbor woman who was a qualified doctor. Despite her pregnancy BAS cooked and cleaned for three hired men during spring work because she was unable to hire help. Instead her stepson helped with the work. BAS said that he was going to Youngstown, the nearest town, to mail her letter and would bring her a present of bananas if he could find them. Isolation had been reduced somewhat by the time she wrote her next letter in January 1914, because a new town, Baraca, was only four miles away. That letter, the last in the collection, was a description of her son and her new life with the baby.

BAS, the adventure-seeking domestic of 1909, became the busy farm wife envisioned by the writers of literature promoting immigration. In the process, she changed. Her former dislike for Canadians became admiration when she wrote of her stepdaughter's marriage to a man she described as "another of the excellent breed of males with which this country abounds!" Her past dislike of cold weather was transmuted to fear that her husband would be caught in a blizzard when he went to town, some eighty miles away, before Baraca existed. Although she had not learned to cook until she arrived in Saskatoon, she wrote of a busy summer growing and harvesting her vegetable garden, and preserving fruit, vegetables, fish, meat, and chicken; but she commented, "as for cherries, currants, plums, pears, I forget the look of them." She started to describe changing customs regarding threshing crews but stopped": . . . this won't interest you." In matters of dress the change was significant. The young BAS of 1910 who ordered a green evening gown from a fashionable London department store for a party in Saskatoon became the farm wife of 1912 whose husband thought of going to Calgary for Christmas, "but I'm not keen on it—ones clothes are out of date [t]here."[9]

Similarly, her enthusiastic plans for a visit to England in 1910 became a thought that "if I don't come soon, I'll be withered & grey." Her perception of the countryside as being "dreary" changed to one of enthusiasm because she found it "awfully interesting watching the new places develop." Days of "work, heat & storms" while working for others became busy with gardening, pickling, and preserving for her own family. Although maturity undoubtedly contributed to some of these changes, others resulted from her greater stake in the land and her labor.[10]

BAS had an adventurous life in Canada, but perhaps not the sort of adventure she had anticipated or desired. On the other hand, BAS represents the ideal envisioned by immigrant promoters and government immigration policymakers. She worked as a domestic for two years, learned the ways of prairie housekeeping, married a farmer, and became the mother of a new citizen.

While BAS was becoming the epitome of promotion literature's prairie farm wife, some women's groups in Britain questioned the promises of Canadian promotion literature. One such group, the British Women's Press Club, commissioned journalist Ella Sykes to investigate Canadian conditions firsthand. Sykes worked as a domestic servant in western Canada for six months in 1911 to discover what British girls and women might expect if they emigrated. She recorded her experiences in *A Home Help in Canada,* published in 1912.

Sykes assumed her role of domestic servant on arrival in Winnipeg, Manitoba, where she stayed at the Girl's Home of Welcome, a women's center similar to the YWCA, and registered for employment. Her first offer was to cook, clean, and wash for six adults, milk three cows, and make butter. Not knowing how to milk a cow or make butter, she rejected the first offer and another for the same reasons. However, she accepted a job cooking, cleaning, and laundering for two men and a woman, where the mistress helped with the work. After ten days at this job she was fired because she refused to close her bedroom window at night.[11]

Sykes then moved to Calgary, Alberta, where she stayed in the Women's Hostel. She found that the YWCA acted as a women's employment bureau and that advertising for a position through the newspaper often brought indirect marriage proposals. During this period Sykes also found she "greatly disliked being unemployed." Finally a Frenchwoman who lived on a ranch twenty miles from the railway offered her a job. Because Sykes spoke French and the wage offered was above average, she accepted the position. However, the job did not materialize because the woman disappeared. Sykes suspected that the woman was a madam seeking brothel inmates.[12]

Primitive conditions and lack of privacy characterized Sykes's next job, on a dairy farm near Calgary, where she was a companion to the housewife. She lived in a small room with thin walls and only a thin curtain for a door. Although her work was light, her only free time was after seven o'clock each evening. After a few weeks in this job Sykes chose to move to British Columbia.[13]

There she found a position as a home helper with an English couple who had a small child. She requested to be treated as a member of the family because the position offer indicated sharing the workload with the mistress. However, during her first dinner with the family Sykes forgot her "inferior position" in some way and was refused further participation in family meals. Subsequently she ate alone after the family had finished their meal. Her sparsely furnished room had no chair and only a few nails for hanging her clothes. She was given a detailed set of written instructions for each day's work and found that much of her agreed free time was taken up by babysitting. Soon the loneliness and social isolation of the position drove Sykes to seek a job in a town.[14]

The expectation of more social contact in town was not fulfilled; Sykes was ignored by most of the townspeople and spoken to only by her employer and the tradesmen with whom she dealt. Her accommodation in a guest room, however, was luxurious by comparison to others she had experienced. The job, on the other hand, was less than desirable. She found herself a "fetch and carry" on a first-name basis with her employer. She described her mistress as "a curious mixture of kindness coupled with a desire to get the last cents worth of work out of anyone whom she employed . . ." Sykes left this position after two weeks with the "sensation of being utterly friendless."[15]

Work on a Saskatchewan farm during harvest season did little do dispel the negative impressions of domestic service for Sykes. To help care for ten people she was up at 4:30 A.M. to prepare breakfast, washed the kitchen floor every day after the noon meal, and worked side-by-side with her mistress canning, pickling, and cooking. Her only rest break was an hour in the afternoon and she often worked until 8 P.M. When she left this job, her last before returning home, Sykes stated:

I felt half ashamed of myself for feeling so delighted to be leaving them all, but the life was by now becoming intolerable to me, . . . I had felt like a prisoner cooped up in the little house, and now I was my own mistress again, and would have a room to myself where I could shut the door and be quite alone.[16]

Despite her misgivings about her own experiences, Sykes advised energetic and resourceful British women and girls to emigrate if they did not have good positions or were unemployed. She still believed life in Canada for many young women was preferable to life in overcrowded England.[17]

Technically, Sykes was only playing the role of an immigrant domestic, yet her experiences of long hours, loneliness, lack of privacy, poor accomodations, and employer indifferences were common among immigrant domestic servants.[18]

While British domestics were most acceptable under Canadian immigration policy, young European women were also recruited. Most of them came through the promotion efforts of the Canadian Pacific Railway and under the Railways Agreement of 1925. The records of the CPR Colonization Branch contain letters from employers regarding their employees and a few letters from the more assertive European women. A German woman wrote the CPR Women's Colonization Board stating she wanted to leave her place of work because "she [her employer] doesn't understand a word of German and hates Germans. . . . I would like to go somewhere where things are managed properly. Here things are done in any old fashion."[19] The board advised her to give notice and said that it would find her another position. Many problems related to health or the language barrier and the resulting misunderstandings. Reporting health problems sometimes had serious consequences for the young immigrant women. For example, an employer advised the CPR Women's Colonization Board of her domestic's eye problem. The board's medical inspector investigated and recommended deportation of the woman for a serious eye infection and stated that the woman appeared to be on the verge of a nervous breakdown. Most health problems were resolved, however, without a serious effect on the women's immigration status or threat to their ability to earn a living.[20]

Female domestic servants risked sexual assault in the homes in which they were employed. Placement agencies tried to protect them from this possibility by requesting references from all employers and by refusing to send domestics to homes where there were no adult females. However, evidence exists that sexual assaults occurred. When an assault was reported, placement agencies and immigration authorities acted quickly to remove the domestic and find her an alternative position. Also the government Immigration Department, CPR immigration offices, and other placement agencies were advised not to send domestics to specific homes. However, no other assistance was offered to the victim.[21]

Indeed, little assistance was available for domestics with personal or work-related problems. Except for temporary shelter, occasional language classes, and social events offered by women's hostels and the YWCA, most domestic servants were dependent on their own resources to overcome language barriers, loneliness, homesickness, or frustrations related to work and new work methods.[22]

Personal economic difficulty was an ever-present risk for domestic servants employed in an economy dependent on the world market for wheat. Because they were not essential to a household's economic survival, they were frequently victims of the "last hired, first fired" cycle of low-status, low-paying service occupations during periods of economic fluctuation. The immigrant domestic's role in Canadian society was to assist the overworked farm wife, or to be a visible indicator of success for an urban businessman's home, and eventually to become mistresses of their own homes. They were not economically essential until they became housewives themselves. As the life stories of a few immigrant domestics indicates, most fulfilled society's expectations. However, during the periods between trying to fulfill their own expectations and those of society, the immigrant domestic often faced economic hardship.[23]

The first economic trial for an immigrant domestic was often the repayment of passage money advanced by her employer or an immigrant loan granted by an organization such as the British Women's Emigration Society. This debt was usually discharged by the employer withholding up to one-half her monthly wages to keep or to send to Canadian authorities designated to collect loans on behalf of immigration agencies. Few young women defaulted on their loan repayments, largely because of the follow-up contacts made with them and their employers. Those who did default were vigorously sought and often prosecuted. Inherent in default and prosecution was the possibility of deportation as an undesirable, but this option was rarely exercised by Canadian authorities and remained mainly a threat.[24]

A second threat to economic survival for immigrant domestics was not being paid by their employers. Available evidence suggests that few employers refused to pay their servants. However, because only English-speaking and the occasional assertive non-English-speaking domestic servant contacted immigration authorities with their problems it is impossible to estimate the frequency of this problem. When contacted regarding outstanding wages, immigration agencies attempted to collect these and were frequently successful. Friends and other employers of domestics also assisted young women in collecting wages from former employers.[25]

Farm households that employed immigrant and Canadian-born domestics often cut their wages during the winter months when there was little work to be done. The employers considered this an act of generosity; the young women would still have a home, a job, and a small wage. Most domestics reluctantly accepted this wage cut as being better than unemployment and homelessness during the coldest months of the year. Reduced wages during the winter were sometimes offset by higher wages at harvest season when meal preparation for threshing crews significantly increased the workload of farm wives and hired servants.[26]

Despite wage problems and the fluctuations of the grain economy, most immigrant domestics improved their economic status significantly by migration. One way to improve their lot was to seek work in hotels or hostels. These opportunities, though less readily available than work in farm or city households, provided independence, regular hours of work, and wages regulated by legislation after World War I. Even before minimum-wage legislation came into being in Alberta in 1921, the female employees of the All Saints Home for Girls in Edmonton worked regular hours and were paid from twenty to twenty-five dollars per month. However, only a small range of occupational alternatives existed for those skilled only in domestic service.[27]

The difficulties, both economic and social, of being a domestic servant increased with growth of industrialization. Domestic work was increasingly seen by the public as nonproductive and was not officially considered part of the national economy, though industrialization and urbanization brought a demand by the expanding middle class for trained domestic servants. At the same time, reformers recognized the precarious economic position of the domestic servant and attempted to form associations, similar to trade unions, to protect domestics from employer exploitation and provide courses to upgrade their skills.[28]

The Calgary Housekeeper's Association formed in 1916 grew out of a Sunday afternoon Bible study group for domestic servants sponsored by the YWCA. Its objectives were to achieve "a better recognition of the dignity of the position of housekeeper; to obtain for them proper conditions of work including a standard wage and maximum day; to defend its members against unfair treatment by employers." The association printed a standard employment contract form for members; offered a course in household science with certificates given for successful completion; set a maximum day of ten hours and minimum wage of fifteen dollars per month; and chose a uniform dress, which included distinctions between certified and uncertified members. An overtime rate of fifteen cents per hour was also set. The standard contract form read in part:

I shall have every Sunday evening free after half-past six o'clock, unless otherwise mutually agreed upon. The employer will speak of me as her "Housekeeper" and shall address me as "Miss." The privilege of entering or departing by the front door shall be accorded to me, . . . also the use of a suitable room one evening a week in which I may entertain my friends until ten o'clock. . . . I will make it a rule to be in my employer's house at 11 P.M. . . . Proper board and comfortable and sanitary lodgings shall be provided for me by my employer.

Either party could terminate the contract at any time by giving two weeks' notice, and it would terminate immediately if any of the conditions were violated. The scant evidence of the existence of this association, unfortunately, gives no indication of its success or of whether employers accepted the contractual obligations. However, the first annual report indicates a membership of forty-five; the sponsorship of twenty lectures on domestic science and cooking, twenty-four general interest lectures, one picnic, two socials, and three dances among the year's activities.[29]

Wages and working conditions for women in manufacturing, retail shops, offices, and restaurants were legislated in 1917 in Alberta, and in 1919 in Saskatchewan and Manitoba, but in all provinces domestic servants were explicitly excluded. No legislation changes occurred until after at least 1936, when the Domestic Workers League of Calgary, together with national representatives of the YWCA and Local Councils of Women, sought legislation to specify hours of work and wages for domestic servants.[30]

Despite the social and economic problems of adjusting to new surroundings, pioneer conditions, a different society, and, for the European women, learning a new language, most immigrant domestics stayed. They married, raised children, and helped the farm communities, towns and cities of prairie Canada grow and prosper. They also proved to be essential elements in the households of leaders of the temperance and suffrage movements. By freeing assertive, ambitious, elite women from household chores and child care, domestic servants enabled them to work for the improvement of women and of society as a whole. Domestic servants helped many thousands of farm wives care for the needs of seasonal farm labor crews and families. They served the needs of the society, while seeking to fulfill their personal expectations of a better life. Not all succeeded in their quest, but most apparently made the necessary compromises.

Notes

1. *Census of Canada,* 1921 and 1931, in M. C. Urquhart and K. A. H. Buckley, *Historical Statistics of Canada* (Toronto, 1965). Census data are relatively unrefined in the categories of occupation and ethnicity. A category change from "birthplace" to "origin" in 1931 includes the Canadian-born immigrant parents, making it difficult to determine accurate numbers.

2. Eugene C. Black, ed., *Victorian Culture and Society* (New York: Walker and Co., 1974); Joseph A. Banks, *Feminism and Family Planning in Victorian England* (Liverpool: Liverpool University Press, 1954); Frank E. Huggett, *Life Below Stairs: Domestic Service in England from Victorian Times* (London: John Murray, 1977); E. J. Hobsbawm, *The Age of Capital, 1848–1875* (London: Weiderfield and Nicholson, 1975); Richard Allen, *The Social Passion: Religion and Social Reform in Canada, 1914–1928* (Toronto: University of Toronto Press, 1971); James H. Gray, *Red Lights on the Prairies* (Toronto: Macmillan of Canada, 1971); James H. Gray, *Booze* (Toronto: MacMillan of Canada, 1972); James H. Gray, *The Roar of the Twenties* (Toronto: MacMillan of Canada, 1975); N. E. S. Griffiths, *Penelope's Web: Some Perceptions of Women in European and Canadian Society* (Toronto: Oxford University Press, 1977); Michael B. Katz, *The People of Hamilton, Canada West: Family and Class in a Mid-Nineteenth Century City* (Cambridge, Mass., and London: Harvard University Press, 1975).

3. Glenbow Alberta Institute Archives (hereafter GAA); Canadian Pacific Railway Papers (hereafter CPR Papers); Public Archives of Canada (hereafter PAC) Immigration Papers, RG76. *Calgary Albertan, Calgary Herald, Edmonton Journal, Regina Leader Post, Winnipeg Free Press, Grain Growers Guide.*

4. PAC, RG 76, vols. 45, 48, and 113.

5. Mary Hall, "A Lady's Life on a Farm in Manitoba," in Susan Jackel, ed., *A Flannel Shirt and Liberty: British Emigrant Gentlewomen in the Canadian North West, 1880–1914* (Vancouver and London: University of British Columbia Press, 1982). Brief mentions of domestic service experiences are contained in several local Alberta histories; for example, *The Lantern Years* (Hughendon Women's Institute, n.d.), p. 87; Jessie T. Campbell, ed. *Chatter from Beaver Dam Creek* (Castor: Old Timers Association, 1974), p. 472; Kew Priddis and Bragg Creek Historical Society, *Our Foothills* (Calgary, 1975), pp. 303 and 356; Helen D. Howe, ed., *75 Years on the Red Deer River* (Calgary: D. W. Friesen, 1971), p. 62; Marie F. Campbell, ed., *Still God's Country* (Byemoor Historical Society, 1975), p. 127.

6. Provincial Archives of Alberta (hereafter PAA), Letters from BAS, acc. 78:79, quotations from letters dated 18 Sept. 1909, 11 Jan. 1910, 8 Apr. 1910.

7. Ibid., quotations from letters dated 9 Sept. and 10 Dec. 1910. Her emphasis.

8. Ibid., quotations from letters dated 11 June and 10 Oct. 1911.

9. Ibid., quotations from letters dated 28 Jan. 1912, 4 Dec. 1912, 8 Aug. 1910, 4 Dec. 1912, 11 June 1911.

10. Ibid.

11. Ella C. Sykes, *A Home Help in Canada* (London: G. Bell & Sons, 1912), pp. 60–65.

12. Ibid., quotations from p. 89.

13. Ibid., pp. 95–96.

14. Ibid., pp. 111–15.

15. Ibid., pp. 177–78.

16. Ibid., quotation from p. 221.

17. Ibid., chap. 13.

18. Interviews: Mrs. George Murray, March 1982; Mrs. Agnes Wight, November 1981; GAA, CPR Papers, box 149, file 1463, letter November 1928; box 186, file 1866, letter April 1928 and April 1930.

19. GAA, CPR Papers, box 186, file 1866, translated letter July 1925.

20. GAA, CPR Papers, box 186, file 1867.

21. PAC, RG76, vol. 347.

22. PAC, RG76; CPR Papers.

23. W. A. Mackintosh, *Economic Problems of the Prairie Provinces,* vol. 4, W. A. Mackintosh and J. L. Joerg, eds., Canadian Frontiers of Settlement Series (Toronto: Macmillan Company of Canada, 1935); A. W. Currie, *Canadian Economic Development,* 4th ed. (Toronto: Thomas Nelson and Sons [Canada], 1960). For detailed analysis and discussion of economic development in western Canada, see also W. T. Easterbook and Hugh G. J. Aitken, *Canadian Economic History* (Toronto: Macmillan Company of Canada, 1956), chap. 20.

24. PAC, RG76.

25. GAA, CPR Papers, box 186, file 1866; box 149, file 1469; Nellie McClung, *The Stream Runs Fast: My Own Story* (Toronto: Thomas Allan, 1945).

26. GAA, CPR Papers, box 186, file 1866, interview with Agnes Wight, November 1981.

27. *Statutes of Alberta* 1921 established a minimum wage for women which applied in towns and cities only and excluded domestic servants in private homes; PAA, Dingwall Collection.

28. Genevive Leslie, "Domestic Service in Canada." in Janice Acton et al., eds., *Women at Work* (Toronto: Canadian Women's Educational Press, 1974).

29. GAA, Pamphlet *Club Womens Record,* (n.d., n.p.); unpublished summary of history of Calgary YWCA; *Calgary Albertan,* 10 June 1916.

30. *Statues of Alberta,* 1917; *Statues of Saskatchewan,* 1919; *Statues of Manitoba,* 1919; *Calgary Herald,* 6 Feb. and 12 June 1936.

15.

Waitresses in the Trans–Mississippi West: "Pretty Waiter Girls," Harvey Girls and Union Maids

MARY LEE SPENCE

Like the domestic servants on the Canadian prairie, the "waiter girls" of the United States provided the comforts of home for single men and new settlers in developing western communities. Such work provided some opportunity for young women to be independent without forsaking the domestic definition of womanhood. Mary Lee Spence demonstrates the need to be specific about what such opportunities meant for women by looking at three groups of waitresses whose adherence to the domestic ideal varied enormously. Waitresses in dance halls and saloons did not behave like "proper" domestic women, but waitresses in the paternalistic Harvey Houses did. The "union maids" who organized women's labor unions challenged some domestic precepts by acting in their own behalf in the public sphere. These differences in behavior came from each group's understanding of what their work offered. By the early twentieth century waitressing was a permanent occupation for some women, and that realization encouraged them to organize. Spence looks at how women moved into the public arena of wage work and helps us understand how working women adapted a domestic ideology to support their new identities as wage earners.

> And fair woman—bless her picture!—we would save a little room
> To relate about the woman who is perched behind the broom;
> There are others whom I'd mention, but the praises now I chant
> Of the girl behind the counter in the smoky restaurant.[1]

Only recently have historians begun to take a hard look at the lives and labors of average, working-class women who, as the nineteenth century moved along, made up more and more of the fabric of an increasingly complex economic and social apparatus. At mid-century, domestic servants constituted the majority of women workers; by century's end, 64 percent of employed females continued to fall under domestic or other service categories,[2] but a subtle transition was under way. Many young women were moving out of service in private homes into service occupations in the public arena. Waitressing, one of their few escape hatches, was especially valuable to the young woman in the trans-Mississippi West where

Waitresses at Going-to-the-Sun Chalet, Glacier National Park. Courtesy National Park Service.

work in offices, factories, and department stores was either nonexistent or extremely limited. Furthermore, the high ratio of men to women during the frontier period fostered the lodging house, which in turn furnished patrons to a bewildering assortment of chophouses, coffeehouses, lunchrooms, restaurants, and taverns. In addition to the gender imbalance, the affluence of new urban areas, often the result of proximity to the mines, helped to create an "eating out" mentality in the West. With reference to San Francisco, Charles Loring Brace observed that "large numbers of people, who ought to be keeping house, live, whether from laziness or supposed economy, alone, or with their families, in hotels or boarding-houses." [3] One result was more employment opportunities in the restaurant industry for both men and women.

Waitressing was strenuous work, notorious for long hours, low pay, and backbreaking and bone-tiring labor. But to the young woman, it brought a sense of freedom and camaraderie not experienced in the dreary isolation of service in the private home. A quick mind was an asset, but a brief apprenticeship was sufficient for an average girl to learn the duties. Table waiting, too, was a step up the social ladder from domestic service, although rungs below dressmaking and millinery, two of the other major occupations open to women in the nineteenth century. Even so, in terms of interest, independence of action, and human relationship, it was a far cry from the life of the seamstress who often became bored with "stitch, stitch, stitch from morning until night, and nothing beyond"; more than one young woman forgot social status and exchanged her needle and thimble for a restaurant apron, even if the change did put her into close contact with men when they were likely to be in "their most animal moods." The prevalent Victorian concept of respectable womanhood excluded wage-earning women, especially those whose work left them open to improper advances and put them in the position of serving the personal needs of men outside a family relationship.

If waiting tables was an avenue open to the untrained girl, it also was a profession shared with men. In the nineteenth-century West, waiters outnumbered waitresses about two-to-one; not until 1920 did census figures show more women than men in the profession. Certain areas of the field were difficult to penetrate. Males never lost their dominance in service on ocean-going vessels or river steamers. Railroad dining cars were the special province of white-jacketed black waiters. At first, at least up to the 1890s, waitresses found formidable competition when they tried to gain entry to the dining rooms of the swank western hotels—the Palace in San Francisco, the Windsor in Denver, the Hotel del Monte on Monterey Bay, or the Coronado at San Diego. But soon they were making inroads, albeit slow and spotty: by the end of the century Pasadena's elegant Green Hotel was staffed by nearly ninety waitresses, some of whom may have shifted with their headwaiter during the summer off season to the famous Colorado Hotel at Glenwood Springs.[4]

Waitresses might be found presiding over the tables at nationally famous scenic attractions: at the Sentinel Hotel at Yosemite; at the Old Canyon Lodge in Yellowstone, singing "When the Dudes Come Marching In" as hungry guests collected outside the door; or at the international-minded Glacier National Park Hotel in Montana, clad in Swiss costumes in the dining room and Japanese in the grillroom. The bulk, of course, were employed in the hotels, commercial restaurants, and boardinghouses so common in every western locale with an urban pretense; but waitresses were to be found in many other settings. In the dusty, foresaken stagecoach stations and in the near-lethal eating houses along the Union Pacific Railroad, "neat-handed abigails," as one traveler called them, handed round dishes "fearfully and wonderfully made out of old satchels and seasoned with varnish." Others were employed in private mansions and clubs; some in corporate boardinghouses run by mining and smelting companies. After World War I, logging firms began substituting women for men at general table chores and in the process altered the life style of lonely timbermen. A few waitresses worked at isolated sheep camps, on dude ranches, at hospitals, sanatoriums, or mental institutions; and a handful traveled with circuses or carnival groups. The whole of the waitressing story or any of its parts deserves to be told.[5] In this article, however, the focus will be on three different, but fascinating, groups: the so-called "pretty waiters," the Harvey Girls, and the "union maids" in organized labor.

The first group reflects the limited range of occupations open to poverty-stricken and poorly educated women in the early West; it also confirms the Victorian social ideology that the very nature of restaurant work, with the attendant freedom of talking with strangers and the acceptance of tips, presented a peculiar moral danger to the young and inexperienced. Not all young women, of course, succumbed to temptation, but there was a sufficient number of "pretty waiters" who were "bad" to give waitresses a very negative image. As the nineteenth century wore on and more women entered the labor force, either by choice or necessity, the definition of respectable work broadened somewhat. Society also conceded the working women could act like ladies, although the standards of female behavior and respectability remained stringent and were often at odds with the reality faced by the majority of working women. The enterprising restaurateur Fred Harvey attempted to attract wholesome young women to his western eating establishments by providing sheltered working situations. These employees would not only serve his special business needs, but also reinforce Victorian images of niceness. The third small group of waitresses, the "union maids," while accepting some of the conservative ideology, attempted to arouse the consciousness of their fellow workers and to create new structures to achieve greater control over their lives and working conditions. Their public protests, including the walking of picket lines, placed them outside the bounds of "respectable" behavior, but at the same time fostered friendships and a sense of identity. No longer were these women willing to accept placidly what was offered by employers and society. An examination of these three groups of waitresses, then, can tell us something about all women who worked for wages in the West and how traditional ideology was accommodated to reality.

"PRETTY WAITERS"

Entrepreneurs of both sexes have long recognized the relationship between feminine pulchritude and the sale of "wet goods," especially in the nineteenth-century West, where women were in low supply and high demand. In the isolated mining camps, prospectors or miners would flock into any restaurant or saloon where a winsome woman worked, be she "a stout robust splendid looking German girl" at Humbug City in 1852 or "Sis," the first young lady at Georgia Gulch, out of Breckinridge, Colorado, a few years later.[6] Hinton R. Helper estimated that about one-quarter of the bars in San Francisco were attended by young women "of the most dissolute and abandoned character," with many men "being induced to patronize them merely for the sake of looking at them." Often dead tired or dazed with liquor, the so-called "pretty waiter girls" solicited orders and served drinks in uninhibited dress—hip-high skirts, unbuttoned blouses, in one dive no blouses at all. One operator of a place on Pacific Street decorated his girls in ostrich-feather hats and fancy jackets, with nothing below the navel. Slightly more respectable places, like the Bella Union Melodeon, with a free musical performance every night, depended upon the "pretty waiters" to swell the sale of "one-bit" drinks, as did the name-sake Bella Union in San Jose, with its billiard tables and small card tables, piano and violin in the background, and "2 young girls waiting on the motley crowd."[7]

In Deadwood late in 1876, Nuttal and Brown's Temple of Music adver-tised the "Best Entertainment in the City," only part of which was musi-cal, and promised to see its patrons "served by pretty waiter girls with the best Wines, Liquors and Cigars." Leadville's combined variety theater-saloon, the Carbonate Concert Hall, from 1879 used waiter girls to supply drinks, as did the Comique and its replacement, the Grand Central Variety Theater. In the 1870s, Denver's overlord of gambling, "Big Ed" Chase, erected at Fifteenth and Blake the impressive Palace Theater, capable of seating 750 burlesque fans and an additional 200 in the gambling room. Ostensibly a theater, it showed primarily leg art, with waitresses alter-nately serving drinks and performing in the chorus line, which ran contin-uously from 9:00 A.M. to 4:00 A.M.[8]

The Barbary Coast places were often dens of vice and crime, in which a girl's life was worth little; even in more elevated Virginia City, waiter girls might become the cause for violence from competing customers or even barkeepers. In order to keep their jobs, they had to be somewhat compliant in relationships with both employers and patrons. Typical were the cases cited by the Portland Vice Commission in 1913, which reported that of 1,504 arrests over an eighteen-month period for "crimes against decency and morality," almost 6 percent had been waitresses by occupation. The commission cited one instance of a Portland cook who boasted that he se-duced all the "fresh chickens" who came in from the country to work as waitresses, and another of a waitress in an amusement center restaurant who was constantly approached by unsavory types of men and testified, "A girl has to be some sport to work in this joint.[9]

With the coming of "civilization," leaders of urban reform movements, and Prohibition, especially, began to single out the iniquitous exploitation of women in the saloons, hurdy-gurdy houses, and dance halls. Generals in the cold-water army lamented the forty drinking places in Spokane with "wine rooms" attached, wherein transpired "immorality in its most de-praved form." Clearly, to reformers like the Reverend Mark Matthews, wine and women did not mix: "Combine the two and we get the lowest admixture of human vileness."[10] Thus, it is not surprising that one stan-dard solution for curbing excesses of dubious drinking establishments was to limit both alcohol and the role of women.

On the Comstock Lode, in western Nevada, in the late 1860s, aldermen began licensing dance halls and melodeons, and in 1867 required all own-ers of saloons with waiter girls to pay a quarterly license fee for each fe-male employed. An 1878 ordinance prohibited waiter girls from working between the hours of 6:00 A.M and 6:00 P.M., the intent being to reduce daytime rowdiness in saloons and allow respectable men and women to pass them without harassment.[11]

In 1868, Sacramento prohibited the playing of musical instruments and the presence of women—whether owners, patrons, or waitresses—in public drinking saloons after midnight, and sent at least two women to prison for violating the ordinance. In a habeas corpus proceeding, the women argued that the ordinance was repugnant to the state constitution, as well as to the Fourteenth Amendment of the United States Constitution, but the California Supreme Court disagreed. A dozen years later, the course reversed itself when it struck down a San Francisco ban on women as waitresses between 6:00 P.M. and 6:00 A.M. in places where liquor was sold, arguing conflict with the constitutional stipulation that "no person shall, on account of sex, be disqualified from entering upon or pursuing any lawful business, vocation, or profession." But in 1893, the state court accepted part of the San Francisco code which licensed the selling of liquor and barred licenses for dance cellars or dance halls that employed female waiters and where there was "any musical, theatrical or other public exhibition."[12]

When in 1895 Washington state law denying women employment in places selling alcohol was challenged, the Federal District Court upheld the statute. Nor was Montana out of step with its law banning liquor in any place frequented by women, either as actresses or as waitresses. It was in Colorado in 1901 that Judge Ben Lindsey began his reform career and "had the satisfaction of getting one heavy whack in on the snout of the Beast"—Denver's corrupt, graft-ridden city machine—when he held as valid a city ordinance excluding all women from drinking houses, arguing that under its police powers a community was entitled to take action to uphold public health, morals, and welfare, a decision ultimately sustained by the United States' highest tribunal.[13]

Women could find this burden of upholding morality costly. Early in the twentieth century, when the city of Los Angeles denied them work in businesses selling liquor, many suspected that southern California waiters were behind the ban. And when the legislature proposed a similar law for the entire state, the waitresses of Local No. 48 in San Francisco organized and helped defeat the measure. In both instances, it had not been the waiters, but a large Protestant migration at the turn of the century, that had made Los Angeles the center of Prohibition activity and spawned a vigorous Anti-Saloon League that was set on drying up California, bit by bit if necessary. Even as late as 1918, when Prohibition went into effect, it was clear the "pretty waiter" syndrome still lived. As a union spokesman in Los Angeles noted: "Practically all eating houses established in locations where bars were formerly located are employing girls, and the demand is for good-looking young girls, regardless of past experience."[14]

As Brick Pomeroy's 1871 article on the "pretty waiter girls" of New York indicated, this was not exclusively a western phenomenon, although the high man-woman ratio of the West no doubt helped perpetuate it. The term was not necessarily synonymous with prostitute, though often the line was thin between legitimate waitresses and whores. But here again the Victorian stereotype of the "bad" woman long persisted in connection with all waitresses. Given the limitations of realistic options for making a decent living in the male-dominated West, many women found the "naughty" route more rewarding; even those who did not, lived with the image.

HARVEY GIRLS

In marked contrast to the "pretty waiter girls" in life style and legacy were the Harvey Girls who staffed the numerous first-class lunch counters and dining rooms which Fred Harvey began establishing along the Santa Fe Railroad in 1876. Looking back in 1930 Whitfield Avery wrote:

This 2,000-mile dining room is a combination of more than 41 dining rooms, 25 hotels, 54 lunch rooms and 50 dining and cafe cars. . . . It stretches from the Great Lakes to the Pacific, from the Kansas Prairies to the Gulf of Mexico. It extends from Dearborn Station, Chicago, along the Santa Fe Railway, to California.[15]

A news story of 1929 reported that in "normal times" the Harvey Company employed 1,400 waitresses; and in 1961 a spokesman for the company's personnel department estimated that there had been around 100,000 Harvey Girls to that date.[16] Only in the Mojave Desert, where the heat was so intense, were waiters used for a time, but by 1910 the new El Garces Hotel, built especially to fit desert conditions at Needles, California, was staffed wholly by waitresses.[17]

Besides revolutionizing the railroad eating houses of the West and raising the standard of living for half a continent, Fred Harvey is credited with furnishing "pretty and useful wives for no man knows how many sighing swains." In the early days, according to tradition, it was all he could do to keep his stations staffed with waitresses because "they were carried off so rapidly by ranchmen and miners and trainmen who had formed some sort of combination with Cupid." Charles A. Brant, manager of El Tovar Hotel, Grand Canyon, Arizona, noted in 1908 that twenty-six female employees of that Harvey House had married since it opened in 1903, and of the sixteen he had brought out after he took charge in 1905, nine had opted for matrimony, "four to rich cattlemen." No doubt a few did marry ranchers, cowboys, or town promoters, but mostly they married the men with whom they worked, employees of the Santa Fe line or the Harvey chain.[18] And some seemed in no hurry to marry at all.[19] But they left behind a romantic image, which poets have been quick to capture:

> O the pretty Harvey Girl beside my chair,
>   A fairer maiden I shall never see,
> She was winsome, she was neat, she was gloriously sweet,
>   And she was certainly good to me.[20]

Usually with too little evidence, some writers have emphasized the virtue and good moral character of the Harvey Girls, who undoubtedly did raise the general stature of the waitress in the eyes of the public.[21] The fact that they lived in dormitories adjacent to the restaurants or in the upper rooms of the hotels where they worked, and were supposedly watched over by severe matrons who enforced curfew and other rules, only re-

inforced, at least for later generations, the image of niceness. But whether
naughty or nice, as Sharon Montalto has pointed out, the Harvey Girls
have the distinction of being the first group of oganizational women working in the West.[22]

Employees who lived at or near their place of employment were essential for a successful and efficient Harvey operation. Cooks and waitresses
must be prepared for the arrival of trains and their passengers, however
frequent or however late they might be. Joan Thompson remembered getting up at 5:00 A.M. on her wedding day to help serve a World War I troop
train; and Laura White noted that during three months in 1918 the Harvey
House at Gallup, New Mexico, fed three troop specials a day, in addition
to regular trains and local trade.

By ten o'clock at night all of us were walking in a daze. We would climb the stairs
and throw ourselves across the bed, clothes and all. Oblivion—never longer than a
minute, it seemed—then we heard the dreaded callboy marching down the hall.
    "Four o'clock!" he'd cry. "Five hundred Marines for breakfast this morning!"
    Wearily we'd pull ourselves off the beds, put on clean aprons, brush our hair
and start all over again.[23]

Fred Harvey demanded a high standard of performance and sought
young women who were strong, healthy, independent, and unafraid of
hard work. A few may have been college students and schoolteachers who
had wearied of the classroom, although managers thought teachers not
well suited to restaurant routine. Probably most waitresses were obtained
through employment agencies in such major cities as Chicago, Kansas
City, and Los Angeles.[24] According to Laura White, Harvey recruitment
signs were seen everywhere in Los Angeles in the autumn of 1917. By
1920, Harvey was advertising for waitresses in the classified, help-wanted
columns of city newspapers, but the practice proved too expensive and
was discontinued in 1922 in favor of building an applicant list on the basis
of information from former employees and reliable persons in the towns
where help was needed—in short, a combination of "old boy" and "old
girl" networking. Since candidates were not being screened by an employment agent and since the restaurant chain found it impossible to interview
all of them, Harvey began to require completion of a formal application, a
photograph, and names of references. By 1929 more than half of the new
Harvey Girls were being hired by correspondence alone. Managers of
Harvey hotels and eating houses could, and often did, hire waitresses
locally, and they could request the transfer or dismissal of a girl sent out by
headquarters.[25]

Harvey preferred inexperienced girls and started them out with a week
of training in the smaller units, then transferred them step by step to more
important dining rooms and restaurants. A waitress was hired for a minimum of six months and was furnished transportation and food from the
Santa Fe station nearest her home to her first assignment. After six months
she was entitled to a month's vacation without pay, and a railroad pass back
to her original Santa Fe point of departure. If she was dismissed during the

first term of her service, transport was provided to her starting point, but not if she left voluntarily.

The quality of the accommodations Harvey provided for its employees varied. Some were stark and perhaps cramped, but those at the new, luxurious El Garces Hotel in Needles were reported to be identical in most respects to those of the guest rooms except that they lacked private baths and telephones. Waitresses had access to the $75,000 library-reading-room-gymnasium the Santa Fe Railroad had built for its employees a half minute's walk from the hotel. Probably the most expensively constructed and appointed log house in America, El Tovar Hotel on the south rim of the Grand Canyon housed its employees in two separate buildings, one for males and one for females. Waitresses lodged two to a room and enjoyed steam heat and baths with water brought 127 miles by railroad, but many were happy to transfer because of the highhandedness of henna-haired Olga Brant, the assistant manager. At Gallup in 1910, Harvey Girls lived in three separate establishments: four were lodged with the manager and his wife; two lived together elsewhere; and one, listed as "head of household," had a farmer with two children in her dwelling. As automobile travel became more popular, Harvey located its houses with little reference to rail lines, and more of its waitresses came to be drawn from local areas and lived with their families.[26]

While the Harvey Girls' uniforms changed somewhat over the years, they were basically black dresses with white aprons (with or without bibs) and black shoes and stockings. The head waitress was recognized by her all-white uniform, and managerial status was indicated by a white blouse and black skirt. In the Southwest the prescribed attire seems to have been black for breakfast and white for luncheon and dinner. After Harvey modernized the old-fashioned, high-ceilinged dining facility in the Kansas City Union Station in 1937 and dubbed it the "Westport Room," cameo pins were added to the girls' uniforms of chintz and organdy; the skirts were cut in the fullness that marked the styles of the late nineteenth century when Kansas City was Westport Landing and the banjos played "Jubilo."[27]

Compensation varied over the years; in the early days it included board, room, and tips, plus $17.50 a month. The job paid $35.00 a month in 1929 with a $5-a-month increment after the first six months' service and annual increases thereafter until the maximum of $50.00 a month was reached. During the hiring process Harvey managers would not discuss the question of tips, nor would they hire a woman who was obviously concerned with the subject for fear she would not give the kind of consummate service for which the system was noted. Up to 1920 the standard tip was a dime, given as frequently by the poor as by the rich; despite modest salaries and gratuities, the manager of El Tovar boasted that all of his waitresses were saving money and that many had bank accounts of $1,000 to $4,000.[28]

Of the 197 Harvey waitresses identified in the 1900 and 1910 census records for selected towns, 183 were single, 7 were widows, 4 were married, and 3 were divorced. In age they ranged from fifteen to forty, but most were in their twenties. The few teenagers often had one or several relatives employed in the same restuarant, as in Dodge City, Kansas, where two sets of sisters worked: the Connelly sisters (Sadie, age fifteen, and Ollie, twenty-six) and the Moore sisters (Maggie, sixteen; Fannie, twenty-three; and Anna, twenty-six). Laura White became a Harvey Girl at fourteen when her mother was also hired. Married waitresses often had spouses employed in the system. For example, at Needles, Lula Wimsley served customers at the lunch counter while her husband managed the soda fountain of the same hotel.

Most of the waitresses had been born in the East or Midwest; very few came from the deep South. Canada and almost every country in Europe save Italy and Spain were designated as birthplaces by Harvey Girls, of whom 14 percent of those studied were foreign-born. There was a heavy Polish contingent at the Grand Canyon in 1910, some of them so recently arrived (1909) that they spoke only Polish. Most often, however, whatever their origins, those who had not yet mastered English were employed as pantry girls or chambermaids.[29]

Most western waitresses were mobile, especially the Harvey Girls, whose access to free railroad passes permitted easy movement within the system. The experiences of Laura White were not atypical. Within four years of her first job at Ash Fork, Arizona, she had waited tables at Gallup and Albuquerque in New Mexico, at La Junta in Colorado, and at Newton in Kansas. Of the twenty-one waitresses employed at the Harvey Alvarado in Albuquerque in 1909, only three were still there when the census was taken the next year; and none of the 1910 group appeared in the city directory for 1919.[30]

The Harvey Girls and the "pretty waiter girls," then, presented opposing images, but they are too easily reduced to the Victorian stereotypes of "good" and "bad" women. If Fred Harvey's sheltered working and living conditions represented a reinforcement of images of Victorian womanhood, they were at least partially motivated by his desire to control his work force and have employees available whenever trains arrived. Harvey waitresses were hardly delicate; they performed truly strenuous and demanding work under rush conditions.

"UNION MAIDS"

It would be fair to say that neither the Harvey Girls nor the "pretty waiter girls" could be classified as "union maids." Neither group was in the forefront of the twentieth-century trend of waiters and waitresses to unionize, though no doubt a few of the barroom waitresses in some of the major western cities were members of locals. On the surface there is no indication that the Harvey Girls were dissatisfied or sought to organize themselves, but it is strange that, living and working so close to railroad workers, where strong union ties were a tradition, they did not move in that direction. One factor may have been their unusual loyalty to their paternalistic employer[31] and another that they generally worked in smaller towns. Unions knew from experience how uncooperative waitresses could be even in places the size of Billings, Montana, and Cheyenne, Wyoming, where organizers despaired of organizing female table servers. "Too many of the 'Fluffy Ruffles' type, who can't be educated," one complained.[32]

Unionization would make its first inroads in the cities, beginning in Butte, Montana, where soon after the turn of the century a local of the Women's Protective Union was formed. It drew no color line and included women janitors, dishwashers, and cooks, as well as waitresses. Under the watchful eye of the powerful miners' union it was active in a number of restaurants and boardinghouses. The union was especially proud that it had reduced its members' daily working hours from fourteen or sixteen to eight.[33]

Elsewhere the movement was most vigorous on the Pacific Coast, where the active groups were affiliates of the American Federation of Labor, the Hotel and Restaurant Employees International Alliance, and the Bartenders International League of America, which by the end of 1920 had 156 locals in western states, perhaps one-third of them devoted to the table-waiting profession.[34] When their numbers were small, women were included in the waiters' locals, but in larger cities like Los Angeles, San Francisco, and Seattle, waitresses soon broke off into their own locals.[35]

In San Francisco in the summer of 1901 female members of Local No. 30 fought side by side with their male counterparts in a bitter strike that closed 184 restaurants, but in the end picketing, court orders, violence, and the calling out of the National Guard caused their defeat. Some waitresses were blacklisted, some left town, and others returned to work under the old conditions using assumed names.[36] But the setback was only temporary. Gradually, by perseverance, a steady but quiet campaign of education, and concentration of effort on one or two restaurants at a time, San Francisco waitresses made progress. When they were reorganized into their own Local No. 48, their hiring and bargaining rights were recognized by most of the city restaurants employing women. The union not only succeeded in raising wages (though invariably waitresses' pay fell considerably below that of waiters) but also achieved better hours and working conditions, especially in eliminating many of the additional chores that made serving tables so onerous. One waitress told a newcomer: "Women don't wash floors in San Francisco. . . . Women don't do any heavy work since the Union."[37] No longer were they required to shell peas, string rhubarb, peel apples, or clean coffee urns, windows, iceboxes, or chairs. No longer were lunch girls expected to sweep, polish silver, or wash mustard pots.

Probably Seattle's Local No. 240, organized in 1900, was the most tight-knit and best-disciplined group of waitresses in the West. For years its kingpin was Alice Lord, a conservative, aggressive New Yorker who had migrated to southern California and then to Puget Sound shortly before the turn of the century. The tough-minded Lord was remarkably successful in persuading new waitresses of the necessity of union membership, and with amazingly few strikes she led the "girls" to achieve many concessions from employers. When Local No. 240 was first organized, wages for Seattle waitresses ranged from $5.00 to $7.00 a week for a fourteen-hour day. By the end of 1904 the minimum scale was $8.50 for a ten-hour day, achieved even before the state mandated that schedule. In 1908, when restaurant owners fought to keep the seven-day week, Local No. 240 and its male counterpart, Local No. 239—600 strong—went off the job at eleven of the largest eating houses in town, and all but one owner quickly caved in. Among the waitresses there was but one black sheep—a woman who had been promoted to head waitress only a week before.[38]

Lord lobbied persistently in Olympia for the eight-hour day for women workers. Three times she saw her bills defeated in the legislature but succeeded on the fourth try in 1911. In the same year she expressed the unanimous sentiments of her "girls" when a Japanese man sought union recognition for his eating house. "No Japanese restaurant in Seattle will ever receive a union card if the Waitress Union can prevent it. . . . No waitress will ever work for a Japanese." At the time members of organized labor, male and female, were more violently opposed to Japanese and Chinese workers than they were to the new cafeterias and dairy lunch chains, which they detested. Asiatics were perceived as undercutting the scale of wages and hours; cafeterias eliminated jobs, while employees at the dairy lunch chains proved difficult to organize.

The waitresses of Local No. 240 demonstrated their esprit de corps by turning out en masse for annual Labor Day parades and the grand balls in the evening. When a member died, the local sometimes took charge of the funeral, as at a funeral in 1905, when every union waitress not on duty attended in a group: "It was a beautiful, although sad sight to see a procession of fully 170 working girls follow the remains of one of their number to the last resting place. . . . The Floral tributes were many, which goes to show the loyal generous hearts that beat in the bosom of the working girls," reported Alice Lord.

The union's vision of a place where waitresses might relax and even recuperate from illnesses became a reality in 1913, when Mr. and Mrs. Fred Keen presented the local with a new fourteen-room house, with grounds, to be used as a clubhouse and recreational facility. The place gave a magnificent view of lake and mountains, and in outfitting it, the waitresses included a library and facilities for modest lunches and parties.[39]

With the hope that it might be used as a weapon to improve working conditions, Lord favored the ballot for women, but unlike the suffragists, she and the union waitresses had no illusions about its being the working women's only shield and protection. Lord was not a "suffragette," and she had no desire to be classed as a "short-haired woman"; in fact, she gave thanks that her hair was long. The waitress union was her life, her first concern. She looked after her "girls" with the kind of concern, dedication, and tenacity that "Bridgie" Smith, veteran head waitress of the Castenada in Las Vegas, must have had toward her Harvey House crew down through the years.

As contrasted with the Harvey Girls and the "pretty waiter girls," Lord's "union maids," while certainly not free of the racist attitudes or the images of women common to their culture, sought to adapt by creating a new structure that would give them greater control over their working lives. For them, improvement in wages and working conditions became paramount, and public awareness of the reality of restaurant employment began to replace the stereotypes, both good and bad.

In 1930 there had been a definite improvement in the position of waitresses, not only in the West, but throughout the country. The unions and protective legislation had done much to rectify the barbarous conditions under which early waitresses were forced to work. Those conditions in the nineteenth century had been so bad that they attracted only dubious women whose physical charms were exploited by their employers for the purpose of selling drinks or who themselves made their work a blind for prostitution because waitressing gave them an opportunity to meet men. These practices created a basis for the lascivious image of the "bad" woman so common to the Victorian era.

In addition to improving actual working conditions, the unions were interested in gaining respect for the job and the wage earner; consequently, some contracts prohibited both employer and employee from using offensive language. But combating the negative image was uphill work, and Laura White, a member of Fred Harvey's cadre of specially trained waitresses—almost a new kind of woman with a positive image—recounts hearing a minister in one church declare, "I'd rather see the girls in this congregation in hell than working at that Harvey House." At another service a "pretty woman" closed her hymnal and moved to the far end of the pew when Laura sat down beside her to worship.

Although the number of union waitresses remained small, some locals were strong enough to set the standards of employment in nonunion houses. As elements of the work situation improved and the older stereotypes began to disintegrate, a higher class of women began to work in all kinds of restaurants, and they were able generally to raise the standard of the occupation. This advance took place simultaneously with changes in family and social life. The growth of hotels and apartment houses, the development of tourism in the West, and the escalating employment of women outside the home greatly increased the number of eating establishments.

Demand for waitresses, plus a growing emphasis on training, added respectability to the job. Large hotels established weekly classes with the object of instilling salesmanship and pride of work into each waiting person. Members of a high school vocational-guidance committee, Helen C. Hoerle and Florence B. Saltzberg, noted that "the job of a waitress is not one to be scorned if a girl can grow accustomed to the constant standing, and the carrying of heavy weights." [40] Classes in home economics began to include a unit in table service, and by 1930 trade schools were offering courses in waitress work. [41]

Waiting on tables might never be recognized as a "high calling," but it had been transformed from a dubious form of employment into a respectable trade that remained arduous and exacting. If the "pretty waiter girls" had projected the Victorian stereotype of "bad" women, it was the Harvey Girls—generally seen as the "good,"—and the "union maids"—who focused on working women's realities—who could claim some credit in this transformation.

Notes

1. E. A. Brininstool, "The Restaurant Girl," *Mixer and Server* 12 (15 Mar. 1903): 27.
2. Susan Estabrook Kennedy, *If All We Did Was to Weep at Home: A History of White Working Class Women in America* (Bloomington: Indiana University Press, 1979), p. 93.
3. Charles Loring Brace, *The New West; or, California in 1867–1868* (New York: G. P. Putnam & Sons, 1869), p. 42. The Reverend W. W. Ross thought that "the demoralizing custom of breaking up home and living in hotels, which obtains so largely in the eastern States," was carried much further in San Francisco *(10,000 Miles by Land and Sea* [Toronto: James Campbell & Son, 1876], p. 121).
4. "Trained Waitresses," *Hotel Monthly* (November, 1899): 16–18.
5. Earl Pomeroy, *In Search of the Golden West* (New York: Knopf, 1957), p. 161; *Yellowstone Cub,* 26 Aug. 1965; Philip Robinson, *Sinners and Saints* (London: Sampson, Low, Marston, Searle & Rivington, 1883), p. 53. For the general range of waitressing work in the West, see Mary Lee Spence, "They Also Serve Who Wait," *Western Historical Quarterly* 14 (January, 1983): 6–13.
6. Herman Francis Reinhart, *The Golden Frontier,* ed. Doyce Nunis (Austin: University of Texas Press, 1962), p. 29; Daniel Ellis Conner, *A Confederate in the Colorado Gold Fields,* ed. Donald J. Berthrong and Odessa Davenport (Norman: University of Oklahoma Press, 1970), p. 117.
7. Hinton R. Helper, *The Land of Gold: Reality Versus Fiction* (Baltimore, Md.: Henry Taylor for the author, 1855), p. 64; Richard Erdoes, *Saloons of the Old West* (New York: Alfred A. Knopf, 1979), p. 192; Evelyn Wells, *Champagne Days of San Francisco* (Garden City, N.Y.: Doubleday, 1947), p. 123; Walter Van Tilburg Clark, ed., *The Journals of Alfred Doten, 1849–1903* (3 vols., Reno: University of Nevada Press, 1973), 1:416, 680.
8. Watson Parker, *Deadwood: The Golden Years* (Lincoln: University of Nebraska Press, 1981), p. 191; Don L. and Jean Griswold, *The Carbonate Camp Called Leadville* (Denver: University of Denver Press, 1951), pp. 207, 223, 224; Thomas J. Noel, *The City and the Saloon: Denver, 1858–1916* (Lincoln: University of Nebraska Press, 1982), p. 38.
9. *Report of the Portland Vice Commission to the Mayor and City Council of the City of Portland, Oregon, January, 1913* (Portland, Oreg.: N.p., 1913), pp. 95–96, 186–87.
10. Quoted in Norman H. Clark, *The Dry Years: Prohibition and Social Change in Washington* (Seattle: University of Washington Press, 1965), pp. 60, 66.
11. Marion S. Goldman *Gold Diggers and Silver Miners: Prostitution and Social Life on the Comstock Lode* (Ann Arbor: University of Michigan Press, 1981), p. 146.
12. *Ex parte* Smith and Keating, 38 *California Reports* (October, 1869): 702–12; In the Matter of Mary Maguire, 57 *California Reports* (January, 1881): 604–12; *Ex parte* Joseph Hayes upon Habeas Corpus, 98 *California Reports* (June, 1893): 555–57.
13. In re Considine, 83 *Federal Reporter* (October, 1897): 157–58; Rex. C. Myers, "An Inning for Sin: Chicago Joe and Her Hurdy-Gurdy Girls," *Montana: The Magazine of Western History* 27 (April, 1977): 33; Ben B. Lindsey and Harvey J. O'Higgins, *The Beast* (New York: Doubleday, Page & Co., 1910), pp. 88–90, 91–92. See *Cronin* v. *Adams,* 192 *United States Reports* (October, 1903): 108–16.
14. *Mixer and Server* 18 (15 Nov. 1909: 12; ibid., 19 (15 July 1910): 48–49; ibid., 20 (15 Apr. 1911): 11; ibid., 22 (15 May 1913): 49; ibid., 27 (15 July 1918): 39.

15. Whitfield Avery, "The Dining Room That Is Two Thousand Miles Long," *Capper's Magazine* 12 (September, 1930): 23.

16. Doris I. Mirrielees to Alice Steele (Chicago, 30 Sept. 1928), Special Collection, Arizona State University, box 4, file 8; Byron Harvey, "The Story of the Harvey Girls," *Chicago Westerners Brand Book* 18 (October, 1961): 58.

17. The manuscript Twelfth Census, 1900, San Bernardino County, Calif., lists a total of nine waiters for the hotel on First Avenue in Needles, four for the lunch counter and five for the hotel, of which four were black. The manuscript Thirteenth Census, 1910, shows no waiters but lists one head waitress, fifteen waitresses, one serving girl, and one pantry girl. For a description of El Garces Hotel, see *Hotel Monthly* 16 (August, 1908): 39–42.

18. "The Harvey System," *Santa Fe Employees' Magazine* 1 (July, 1907): 271, 276; *Hotel Monthly* 16 (June, 1908): 19; Minnie Dubbs Millbrooke, "Fred Harvey and the Santa Fe," *Shawnee County Historical Society Bulletin*, no. 56 (December, 1979): 174; Laura White, "Harvey Girl," *Railroad Magazine* 37 (February, 1945): 78–100.

19. According to the manuscript censuses, the Harvey House at La Junta, Colorado, employed five single girls and one widow in 1900 and eight single girls in 1910, all between the ages of seventeen and thirty-seven. Yet not one is listed as having sought a marriage license in Otero County between 1900 and 1923.

20. S. E. Kiser, "The Harvey Girl," *Santa Fe Magazine* 1 (January, 1907): 43.

21. Clifford Funkhouser and Lyman Anson, "Cupid Rides the Rails," *American Mercury* (September, 1940): 42–46; James Marshall, *Santa Fe: The Railroad That Built an Empire* (New York: Random House, 1945), pp. 100–101; James D. Henderson, "Meals by Fred Harvey," *Arizona and the West* 8 (Winter, 1966): 305–22. Edna Ferber fictionalized the Harvey Girl in a short story entitled "Our Very Best People," Edna Ferber, *Mother Knows Best* (Garden City, N.Y.: Doubleday, Doran & Company, Inc., 1936). Three years after its publication in 1942, Samuel Hopkins Adams's novel *The Harvey Girls* became the basis for Metro-Goldwyn-Mayer's film starring Judy Garland.

22. Sharon Montalto, "The Harvey Girls: Naughty or Nice?" Paper delivered at the meeting of the Western History Association, Phoenix, Ariz., October, 1982. Montalto, who is making a thorough study of the Harvey Girls, traces the origins of the moral-character myth and contends that the true significance of this group of working women has been overlooked "in favor of a romantic view which sees their importance in terms of 'useful wives,' or as pretty 'skirts that hustle up the feeds.'"

23. Millbrooke, "Fred Harvey and the Santa Fe," p. 174; White, "Harvey Girl," p. 88.

24. Eugene Whitmore, "Fred Harvey's Employee Training Methods," *American Business* 8 (August, 1938): 42; Marshall, *Santa Fe*, p. 100. The Atchison, Topeka and Santa Fe Railroad recruited workers through the Kansas City Employment Agency at 605 Main Street; Montalto believes that the Harvey System did also, rather than by specific advertising in the 1880s. The agency wanted "girls for house and hotel work," "girls to go west, dining room girls for country town," "girls for New Mexico." *Kansas City Journal*, 10 Oct. 1882; *Kansas City Times*, 30 Jan., 1 March, 10 July 1883.

25. Mirrielees to Steele, 30 Sept. 1929.

26. *Hotel Monthly* 16 (August, 1908): 39–42; (June, 1908): 18–19; White, "Harvey Girl," pp. 89–90; manuscript, Thirteenth Census, 1910, McKinley County, Territory of New Mexico.

27. *Hotel Monthly* 16 (May, 1908): 20; Eugene Whitmore, "How Fred Harvey Finds New Ways to Increase Sales," *American Business* 8 (June, 1938): 18.

28. Dickson Hartwell, "Let's Eat with the Harvey Boys," *Collier's* (9 Apr. 1949); Mirrielees to Steele, 30 Sept. 1929; *Hotel Monthly* 16 (June, 1908): 19. Francis Donovan noted in 1917 that the standard tip in Chicago was a dime, whether at a hash house or at Usher Lane's exclusive tearoom for men *(The Woman Who Waits*, reprint, New York: Arno Press, 1974). Harvey had begun service at the Dearborn Union Station in Chicago in 1899.

29. Information on the 197 individuals in this and the previous paragraph has been drawn from the manuscript censuses of 1900 and 1910 for Trinidad and La Junta, Colorado; Dodge City, Kansas; Las Vegas and Gallup, Territory of New Mexico; Needles, California;

Williams and the Grand Canyon District, Territory of Arizona. All were from Harvey Houses or hotels along the Santa Fe railroad.

30. White, "Harvey Girl," *Worley's Directory of Albuquerque, New Mexico, 1909–1910* (Dallas, Tex.: John F. Worley Directory Co., 1909) and *Hudspeth's Albuquerque City Directory for 1919* (El Paso, Tex.: Hudspeth Directory Co., 1919). These results, of course, would be skewed if some of the women married and changed their last names so that they could not be traced.

31. By 1916, Elizabeth Cooper had been head waitress for seven years at Newton, Kansas, and Marie Abels had been in Houston since 1900. In October, 1917, Bridget Smith had been head waitress at the splendid Castenada dining room in Las Vegas for twenty years, and Jennie Flannigan had had many years at the Alvarado in Albuquerque. *Santa Fe Magazine* 11 (November, 1916): 65–66; ibid., 11 (October, 1917): 62.

32. *Mixer and Server* 11 (15 Apr. 1908): 49; ibid., 18 (15 June 1909): 43.

33. *Mixer and Server* 16 (15 Oct. 1907): 35.

34. Organized originally as the Hotel and Restaurant Employees' National Alliance in 1891, the union was broadened in 1898, and in 1981, with 400,000 members in 241 locals, the organization became the Hotel Employees and Restaurant Employees International Union.

35. On 22 May 1901, Local No. 30 of San Francisco had a membership of 2,462, including cooks and 263 waitresses. The cooks formed a separate union in 1902, and the waitresses were chartered into Local No. 48 in 1906. By January of the next year they had 225 members. *Mixer and Server* 10 (15 July 1901): 13; Edward Paul Eaves, "History of the Cooks' and Waiters' Unions of San Francisco" (master's thesis, University of California at Berkeley, 1930), p. 30; *Thirteenth Biennial Report of the Bureau of Labor Statistics of the State of California, 1907–1908* (Sacramento, Calif., 1908), p. 168.

36. *Twelfth Biennial Report of the Bureau of Labor Statistics of the State of California 1905–1906* (Sacramento, Calif., 1906), pp. 184–85; Lillian Ruth Matthews, *Women in Trade Unions in San Francisco* (Berkeley: University of California Press, 1913), pp. 76–78.

37. Maud Younger, "Taking Orders: A Day as a Waitress in a San Francisco Restaurant," *Sunset: The Pacific Monthly* 21 (October, 1908).

38. Mabel Abbott, "The Waitresses of Seattle," *Life and Labor* 4 (February, 1914): 48–49; *Mixer and Server* 13 (15 Nov. 1904): 30; ibid., 17 (15 Jan. 1908): 43–44.

39. *Mixer and Server* 14 (15 Feb. 1905): 39; ibid., 16 (15 April 1907): 34; ibid., 18 (15 April 1909): 51; ibid., 20 (15 July 1911): 37; ibid., 20 (15 March 1911): 41; ibid., 14 (15 Aug. 1905): 32; ibid., 16 (15 July 1907): 32; ibid., 16 (15 Aug. 1907): 34; ibid., 22 (15 Sept. 1913): 33–34; ibid., 17 (15 July 1908): 52.

40. Helen C. Hoerle and Florence B. Saltzberg, *The Girl and the Job* (New York: Henry Holt and Co., 1919), p. 43.

41. Lydia A. Salisch and Emily Palmer, *An Analysis of the Waitress Trade*, State of California, Department of Education Bulletin no. 21 (November, 1932). Congressional enactment of the Smith-Highes Act had stimulated the establishment of classes at the high school level in vocational education of all kinds. The Central Trade School of Oakland and the Frank Wiggins Trade School in Los Angeles also offered courses in waitress work, the latter in connection with the Pig 'n Whistle Confectionary Cafés.

PART FIVE   Expanding Our Focus

In our introduction, we said that western history must include women of all races and nationalities and that it must expand its time frame beyond the brief period of the Euro-American frontier. In this section we suggest what a wider framework can provide. These articles extend our time frame into the twentieth century, as women entered public life in the West through politics and wage work.

Traditional western history has told us that because American women first voted in the West, it was a land of opportunity for women. In the late nineteenth century western women entered public life, not (as has been assumed) as the passive beneficiaries of male generosity but through their own efforts. They not only voted but ran for public office and were elected. Winning the vote increased women's political power and was symbolically important. A more dramatic change in daily reality occurred in the twentieth century when many married Euro-American women entered the public world of wage work, as married women of different racial and ethnic heritages had earlier. The articles in this section explore the cultural values and the economic and social conditions that shaped women's options in these new arenas. The authors raise important questions about which cultural traditions influenced which groups of women and about whether and how those traditions "determined" women's choices.

It is dangerous to assume that participation in the public arena meant that western women were "liberated." Economic necessity has been the major influence over whether women worked for money, as it has shaped men's choices. The arena of women's work in the West simply shifted, with industrialization, from the family farm to the urban wage economy, as married women had to work ouside their homes to contribute to the family economy. From another perspective, as several authors in this section point out, the West was not liberating for women who lost their land and

235

were colonized by Spain or the United States. The lives of many western women remain difficult, bounded by poverty and racial prejudice. These women are as much a part of western history as their more privileged sisters.

So expanding our focus on women in the West means many things. It means bringing western history into the present and connecting the lives of our foremothers to women's lives in the contemporary West. It means expanding our sense of the centuries of western history and our awareness of the many people who have been westerners. And it means considering larger economic, social, and cultural changes that helped shape the lives of western women. As we see the women's West more broadly, our questions will go beyond the stereotypes with which we started and beyond simple questions of frontier liberation or oppression to a more complex understanding of how women helped build western society and culture and what their participation meant for them and for us.

16.

Distinctions in Western Women's Experience: Ethnicity, Class, and Social Change

ROSALINDA MÉNDEZ GONZÁLEZ

In this article, Rosalinda Méndez González greatly expands our focus to include the very different histories of women who were mistresses or servants, conquerers or conquered. Rather than filling in the details of those differences, she offers a historical framework through which to understand them. González writes from a Marxist perspective, which encompasses sex, class, ethnicity, and capitalist and colonial development. Her emphasis on groups is an important corrective or balance to the individualism we have traditionally associated with the West. It remains to be seen whether we can take this awareness of the larger economic and political forces that differentiated women's lives and weave it into what González calls "a single and common historical reality." She provides one historical model through which we can see how the West looked to different women. Many of the terms she uses are often found in European history, such as her discussion of primitive accumulation and early capitalism. If these concepts seem out of place in the American West, they would have seemed foreign to feudal peasants and lords too. As analytical tools they may help us connect the West of individualistic mythology to a larger understanding of economic and social development.

The issues of ethnicity, class, and social change as they relate to women in western history and to historical reevaluation derive in part from the social-change movements of the 1950s and 1960s. Until then academic research had tended to neglect the experiences of minorities, women, and the laboring classes or to justify their subordinate social condition. Then the civil rights, feminist, and nationalist movements raised challenges to these approaches.

The new research born of the rebellions of those exciting years sought to uncover and document the historical facts of the neglected groups; to critique the existing myths, stereotypes, and paradigms that veiled or rationalized the inequalities and the historical contributions of the affected social groups; and to examine and expose the structures of domination and subordination in our society.

At first, these investigations took a rigidly protective stance toward their subjects. Black or Chicano nationalist analyses tended to question all tra-

Hispanic women and children outside adobe near Trinidad, Colorado. Note the outdoor oven and the railroad tracks in the background. Courtesy Colorado Historical Society.

ditional assumptions and to defend all that was black or brown; women's analyses attacked institutions and ideologies as patriarchal without distinction as to class or ethnic inequalities; radicals imbued with class analysis criticized imperialism abroad and class structures at home without considering the ramifications of sex or ethnic discrimination. Those who sought to integrate the analyses of the various forms of social inequality were at first in the minority.

By the 1970s the diverse groups had successfully documented the importance of their subjects' contributions to historical development and demonstrated the existence of social structures of domination over each group. An effort began then to integrate this analysis and to arrive at a more complex, fundamental explanation of the interconnections among these distinct social-historical experiences.

The process of including women's history, black history, Indian, Chicano, Asian, immigrant, and labor histories in the chronicles of United States history has been a first step toward an integrated history. Now we are confronted with the next step of jointly interpreting our interrelated histories. This requires going beyond the empirical combination of facts, names, and dates to the conceptual problem of seeking an explanation of how the diverse experiences were daily woven by individual human beings into a single and common historical reality.

In outlining the factors involved in these interconnected experiences, we must be careful to search for both the subjective, cultural conditions that motivated the individual woman's experiences and perceptions, and the objective, political-economic conditions that shaped the experiences of each social group.

The use of diaries, personal testimonies, oral histories, and literature have proved to be effective for uncovering the first set of conditions: women's personal or subjective experiences. But there are shortcomings to this approach. Women of the poor, slave, or laboring classes do not tend to leave diaries. Different methods and different questions have to be posed if one is to recapture the personal experiences of Indian, Hispanic, black, Asian, and poor white women of the laboring classes.

To find a conceptual interpretation of these diverse personal experiences, we must address the objective conditions of western life. This involves first challenging the traditional Turnerian interpretation of western history as the "frontier" period. The evolution of the West spans hundreds of years of Indian society before the American frontier. It is important to understand Indian social relations and the role of women before the Europeans imposed a class society.

Four centuries of Spanish conquest and settlement left a legacy of cultural development and social relations which is still in force today as, for example, in the legislation of western states.[1] Then, overlapping the three decades of Mexican rule over large parts of the West, comes the relatively brief period of United States conquest, the "frontier" period which has so absorbed myopic western historians. Finally, it is important to keep in mind that western history also comprises the twentieth century development of women in the West.[2]

THE QUESTION OF CLASS

In studying western history since European penetration, one of the most obvious but often ignored conditions is the existence of social classes.[3] A class system was first introduced in the sixteenth century by the conquering Spaniards into the area that is now the southwestern United States.

Acknowledging the class character of Spanish and Mexican society in the Southwest penetrates the mist of generalizations which inaccurately assume classless homogeneity. Albert Camarillo's study of the Chicano communities in Santa Barbara and Los Angeles, California, delineates the four classes that comprised Mexican society: the elite rich "Californios," wealthy land-owning ranchers whose holdings averaged 25,000 acres; the middle class of small property owners and ranchers; the majority class of artisans and laborers living in humble dwellings; and the Indian population which was converted into laborers for the missions and menial servants for the wealthy Californios.[4]

In this society, what would it mean to talk about the life cycles of women? Certainly women's lives would appear different within the same household, where the wealthy Californios lived with their slave-like Indian female servants. Historian Elinor Burkett encountered this problem when she set out to study the relations of class, race, and sex in Spanish colonial South America. In feminist studies, Burkett notes, we often assume that:

sex is as important a force in the historical process as class. Thus, we deal with the domestic squabbles of the aristocracy and the survival trials of the black female in the same conference without feeling uncomfortable; frequently forget that the position of the one is maintained only through the exploitation of the other and that such a relationship leaves little concrete room for sisterhood.[5]

If western historians raised these questions they might uncover in verbal records the gulf between the experiences of women of different classes. For example, the following black lullaby from the southern United States laments a black mother's inability to be with her newborn child through early motherhood and nursing because she had to tend to the baby of her mistress.[6]

All the Pretty Little Horses

Hushaby, don't you cry.
Go to sleepy, little baby.
When you wake, you shall have cake,
And all the pretty little horses.
Blacks and bays, dapples and grays,
Coach and six-a little horses.
Way down yonder in the meadow,
There's a poor little lambie;
The bees and the butterflies pickin' out his eyes,
The poor little thing cries, "Mammy."
Hushaby, don't you cry,
Go to sleepy, little baby.

The evidence of working class women's experience is there, but the prevailing orientations of studying history, even women's history, steer us toward elite or educated women and their written records; then from this limited and class-biased evidence generalizations are drawn and applied to all women.[7]

In fact, if one looks at history through the eyes of the majority of women, the poor and the laboring classes, a very different picture of society emerges; the picture is far more complete, for elite eyes take *their* world as the standard and assume that all society exists, or should exist, in their image.

But to see through the eyes of the women on the bottom, is to see not only the lives of the vast majority, but also to look upward through all levels of society; the flaws and contradictions of the upper classes and of the social structure they maintain become exposed from this perspective. The elite class perspective tends to be biased, myopic, and class-centered; the majority laboring class perspective tends to be more critical and encompassing.

WESTWARD EXPANSION

A second major historical consideration in studying the objective conditions that shaped women's experiences is the process of United States "westward expansion" which ultimately resulted in the appropriation of Indian, French, Spanish, and Mexican territories by the United States and the subordination of local ethnic groups as dispossessed cultural or national "minorities."

The process of westward expansion brings into play a host of major economic, political, and social developments. In a historical and economic sense the conquest of the West can be interpreted as corresponding to the similar process undergone by the western European countries in the sixteenth, seventeenth, and eighteenth centuries; known as the original or "primitive" accumulation of land and resources, this process consititued the preliminary stage for the development of industrial capitalist society.[8] In what sense is the conquest of the West a primitive accumulation?[9] And what is the significance of this process for women's experiences in the West?

Frederick Jackson Turner wrote that "the existence of an area of free land, its continuous recession, and the advance of American settlement westward, explain American development." Yet in the process of westward expansion the leading political actors clearly recognized the true character of that expansion: not an acquisition of an unclaimed territory free for the taking, not the expansion of "free land," but a military and political conquest of an already inhabited territory.[10]

Without the United States Army, in fact, the West could never have been "taken" by the settlers and pioneers. What effect did the army, both in the conquest and in its subsequent preservation, have on women in the West? What effect did it have on creating, altering, or maintaining class, ethnic, or racial divisions? Indian reservations in California were inevitably placed next to army posts and outposts.[11] What impact did the army have on Indian women who survived the devastating wars of extermination against their people?

The railroads were also instrumental in the penetration of the West. The building of the railroads was a key to expansion, not just as a means of military transportation but more fundamentally because of what lay behind the conquest: the penetration of the West by eastern capital. Linking the West Coast to the East Coast not only opened up the ports and raw materials of the West for exploitation by eastern bankers, industrialists, and land speculators but, far beyond that, opened up the Asian subcontinent for exploitation in such a way that it placed the United States at the crossroads of international commerce between the Far East and western Europe. Thus, the military conquest of the Indian and Mexican West and the construction of the transcontinental railroads opened up both a national market and an international empire for giant eastern capitalists.[12]

The building of the transcontinental railroads affected women of diverse ethnic and class backgrounds in a variety of ways; the full effects remain to be studied. We know, for example, that the railroads, after the military, provided one of the most effective ways of destroying American Indian people's subsistence on the Plains, by establishing the policy of paying sharpshooters to kill the buffalo.

The railroads stimulated mass immigration from Europe into the United States and mass migration into the West and Southwest. The construction of the railroads was accomplished by exploiting immigrant laborers: the Chinese, Japanese, and Mexicans on the West Coast, the Irish and European immigrants on the East Coast.[13]

Yet the treatment of European immigrant laborers was qualitatively different, in a political sense, from that of the Asian and Mexican immigrants.[14] Chinese laborers, for example, were brought in as bound labor, as "coolies," a politically unfree form of contract labor. They were forbidden to bring their wives or families. This restriction had a negative and long-lasting impact on the development of Chinese communities in the West, and it led to the importation of Chinese women in the most brutal form of "white slave traffic," an experience quite distinct from that of European immigrant women in the East.[15]

The importation of Mexican labor by the railroads has also left a deep legacy. As with the placement of Indian reservations next to Army forts, maps show that the *colonias* or Mexican settlements in the first half of the twentieth century were invariably located along the railroad routes, since whole Mexican families were imported by the companies to clear, lay, and maintain the tracks. The railroad companies would segregate their work force along ethnic lines and establish Mexican colonies of boxcar residences in certain places along the track; thus, the phrase "the wrong side of the tracks" came to be applied to Mexican barrios.[16] In the growing search for roots among Chicanas and Chicanos, the oral histories and family records that are surfacing reveal, in instance after instance, the ties to the railroads among our parents, grandparents, and great-grandparents.[17]

Today many Chicano barrios are still alongside the "wrong side of the tracks." They developed on the original sites of the old railroad-track Mexican colonies; in cities throughout the Southwest from California to Texas, these barrios are still distinguished by adobe houses, unpaved dirt streets, lack of sidewalks, often in direct proximity to walled, modern, Anglo middle-class housing tracts with multitiered, air-conditioned, carpeted homes.

PROPERTY, PATRIARCHY, AND THE NUCLEAR FAMILY

What did the settlement of the land itself mean for women of different classes and ethnicity? Much of the preliminary analysis on women in the West focuses on pioneer women, and their lives are studied through the diaries or literature they left behind. But the majority of women in the nineteenth-century West neither read nor wrote English. Barbara Mayer Wertheimer points out that the ordinary American could not pack up and head West. "It took capital, about $1,500, to outfit a wagon, buy supplies, and tide the family over until the land began to produce. This was an impossible sum for most working-class families to come by." [18]

Without detracting from the courage and endurance of these pioneer women, we have to ask what the takeover and settlement of western lands really represents for the majority of Indian, Mexican, and immigrant women in the West. A more comprehensive answer has to be found by studying first what western conquest and settlement represented in American economic and historical development. The West was not really developed by individual pioneering men and women seeking land. Rather, the West was made economically exploitable by federal intervention in the form of massive land grants to railroads, mining companies, timber companies, and land speculators, and by virtue of federal legislation and funding that subsidized these private profit-making ventures and speculators at public expense. [19]

Industrial and financial magnates did not operate simply out of greed for lucrative profits; they were driven by the economic necessity for expansion, which is at the heart of this system of competition and property. When the United States broke away from England in 1783, capitalist expansion was faced with three obstacles: the plantation slave economy of the South which held onto a bound labor force, raw materials, and productive lands; the Indian tribes and nations which had been pushed together into the West; and the Mexican Northwest.

These barriers could only be overcome by the usurpation and appropriation that have characterized the birth of capitalism wherever it has appeared. This process essentially involves breaking up the existing economic system (e.g., feudalism, tribal societies, peasant communities), concentrating land and wealth in the hands of a few entrepreneurs, and uprooting the native peoples from their land and mode of living to provide a source of wage labor.

A bloody Civil War was launched to remove the first obstacle. Wars against the Indians removed the second, and an unprovoked war against Mexico eliminated the third obstacle. After the defeat of the slave plantation economy, Indian tribal societies, and Mexican feudalism in the Southwest, the United States engaged in accelerated expansion and conquest of western territories. This process involved plunder, massacres, swindling, and bribery. It succeeded in imposing capitalist private property and, equally important, individualism and the patriarchal nuclear family which is so necessary to sustain this form of property.

Various methods were used to impose this system of property and family in the West. In the accumulation of Indian lands, force was not the only technique applied. Andrew Jackson and subsequent presidents attempted to deprive the Indians of their lands by refusing to deal with them as tribes or to negotiate treaties with them as nations. Instead the government forced the Indians, through bribery, treachery, and legislation, to deal with the government as individuals; this policy set them up against each other with the incentive of immediate cash payment to individuals selling plots of land. By forcing the foreign system of private property onto them, the government was attempting to destroy the fundamental communal basis of Indian tribes.

The General Allotment Act, or Dawes Act, of 1883 sought to push the Indians out of the way of western penetration and open up their lands to exploitation, by alloting parcels of tribal land to individuals. The bill was condemned by Senator Henry Teller of Colorado as "a bill to despoil the Indians of their lands and to make them vagabonds on the face of the earth," yet Congress passed it with the justification that "Indians needed to become competitive." Senator Henry Dawes, principal proponent of the measure, argued that Indians "needed to become selfish." [20]

Two centuries earlier the French colonizers in Canada had been amazed at the egalitarianism and freedom among the women and men of the Montagnais tribe, at their disdain for formal authority and domination, and at the respect and independence between husbands and wives. Yet the Jesuit policy of colonization sought to "give authority to one of them to rule the others," and to teach them "to elect and obey 'Captains,' inducing them to give up their children for schooling, and above all, attempting to introduce the principle of binding monogamy and wifely fidelity and obedience to male authority." [21]

In a similar manner the United States recognized that to break down Indian resistance it was necessary to undermine the tribal and clan social organization of the Indians and to enforce upon them the individual nuclear family, with the husband the authority figure over the women and children. This attempt had the multiple purposes of forcing the Indians to alienate their communal tribal lands, breaking their economic and social clan organization, transforming them into individualist and competitive capitalist farmers, and providing the nuclear family institution through which the ideology of private property, individualism, and dominant-subordinate relations could be passed on.

Other American people—the small farmers, European immigrants, and settlers—also were subject to official policies promoting individualism in the process of westward expansion. The Homestead Act of 1862, which preceded the Dawes Act by almost three decades, forced individuals and individual families to settle independently; no land was made available for whole communities. On the other hand, huge tracts of land were made available only to the big companies penetrating the West: the railroads, banks, land speculators, and mining companies. While the individual homesteaders were told, "The government bets 160 acres against the entry fee of $14 that the settler can't live on the land for five years without starving to death," [22] the financial and industrial giants were granted all the land they wanted; the government even provided capital for the infrastructural construction they needed to operate and extract their private profits.

The fostering of private property, individualism, and the nuclear family in the West thus resulted on the one hand in the breakup of the population into individual, isolated, competitive miniscule units:—nuclear families; and the concentration of wealth and power in the hands of an increasingly smaller elite on the other—monopolies. For monopolization to take place, it was necessary to fragment the population through the imposition of private property.

The United States government promoted this process in the West. Neither the government's nor the monopolies' intention, however, was to perpetuate small-scale production and independence. Rather, they brought people in to clear the land, develop the resources, and make the area productive and, when this was done, usurped this settled population from their small plots and transformed them into the wage-labor force needed in the West. Both stages were accomplished by fostering private property, individual ownership of land, and the privatization of the nuclear family.

EXPLOITATION OF WOMEN'S DOMESTIC LABOR

The patriarchal nuclear family was important, not just as a means of preserving and transferring private property and the values associated with it, but also, for the families of the laboring classes, as a means of privately producing through the domestic labor of women the goods and services necessary to sustain the agricultural or industrial labor force needed by capitalist enterprises.[23]

Among Mexican immigrant families in the early twentieth-century Southwest, women's domestic labor was exploited indirectly by large employers as a means of subsidizing the payment of discriminatory and substandard wages to their Mexican workers.[24] This policy was refined by the monopolies engaged in developing the Southwest; these companies in the extractive, infrastructural, and agricultural industries first imported Mexican immigrants in large numbers at the turn of the century.[25]

The monopolistic pattern of southwestern land ownership and industry in many places retained vestiges of the feudal system, such as tenant or sharecropping systems in agriculture or debt peonage in company mining towns. These practices retarded the assimilation of Mexican immigrants into the working class, and had the effect of perpetuating the bondage of the wife and children under the patriarchal family. Patriarchal family relations were particularly strong in rural areas. Women who were hired as agricultural laborers to pick cotton were never paid their own wages; rather, these were paid to the father, husband, or brother. Because of this system of "family wages," feudal relations in the countryside were not easily broken down, and wage labor did not offer women the economic independence that weakened patriarchal relations as did urban or industrial employment.[26]

Even in urban areas, Mexican families found themselves segregated and living in boxcars or makeshift housing. Mario Garcia, in a study of Mexican families in El Paso, Texas, at the turn of the century, documented how their reduced standard of living provided a justification for the payment of wages far below the "American standard." Mexican families were forced to live "75 percent cheaper than Americans" by a series of economic and political mechanisms. Racial discrimination and starvation wages confined Mexicans to the worst slums, with overcrowded, inferior housing in adobes or shacks. These settlements were denied public services (water, paved streets, electricity, sewers) because the Anglo property owners refused to pay taxes to provide them and because the city, in turn, argued that Mexican residents were not property owners and taxpayers, and therefore not entitled to services.[27]

Given this living situation, the domestic labor of women and children was particularly arduous. They hauled water long distances from the river in buckets, hand-ground corn for hours, gathered and chopped wood for fuel, to make up for the lack of adequate wages and public services.

This extreme exploitation of family labor and the intense immiseration of the laboring communities caused high infant-mortality rates, infectious diseases, and malnourishment, while providing the justification for lower wages. It also provided a pool of severely underpaid Mexican female servants whose dusk-to-dawn exploitation in the homes of Anglo-American families freed the women of these families to seek outside employment and enter the industrial world. The economic advancement of many Anglo-American women in the Southwest was carried out on the backs of Mexican-American women, as it was in the South on the backs of black women, and the immediate beneficiaries were the banks and monopolies dominating the South and West.

THE QUESTION OF RESEARCH AND SOCIAL CHANGE

My discussion has not centered on individual heroines of different ethnic or class backgrounds nor on the important subject of women's struggles to change the conditions of ethnic, class, racial, or sex discrimination. I have sought to demonstrate the necessity of taking into consideration the larger, more fundamental political-economic forces in the development of the West, which must be studied if one is to understand the experiences of *all* women.

The forces that had come to dominate the West at the end of the nineteenth century have continued to shape the experiences of women in the twentieth century, the more so as economic concentration and its influence through the growth of government power has expanded. In 1962, the wealthiest 10 percent of the United States population controlled close to 70 percent of all personal wealth, while the other 90 percent of the population shared a little over 30 percent.[28] Even this small share of the pie was unevenly divided. Poverty in the United States was concentrated in the South and West, and among blacks and Mexican-Americans. In 1960, for example, official figures showed that in the Southwest 35 percent of the Spanish-surnamed families and 42 percent of nonwhite families were living in poverty. Among Anglo families, only 16 percent were listed in poverty, and yet this represented a very large number, since Anglos comprised 66 percent of all poor in the Southwest.[29]

Today we know that poverty and unemployment have worsened, that two out of every three persons in poverty are women, and that black women and Chicanas are among those most affected. This situation continues as the "minority" peoples of the Southwest are rapidly becoming the majority.

The trend toward greater inequality is growing. Richard M. Cyert, president of Pittsburgh's Carnegie-Mellon University, which houses the most advanced research and experimentation center in the robotics fields, recently stated, "I don't think there's any question that we're moving toward a society where income distribution will be even more unequal than it is at present and where unemployment is going to be even greater than it is now." [30]

The issue of inequality confronts anyone seeking to develop a historically accurate, comprehensive analysis that integrates the experiences of the majority of poor and working-class women, the experiences of black, Chicana, Indian, Asian, and immigrant women. We have been dealing with the divisions among us: while these divisions of race and class have existed, we also have to deal with the fundamental unity among us.

Our task is to discover both the causes of the artificial, socially created divisions that have kept us apart and ways to make our fundamental unity a reality. If we are concerned with social change, if our research is to involve a commitment to shedding light on the historical roots of contemporary problems and inequalities so that these inequalities can be abolished, then our research will have to address the issues of inequality, exploitation, and the related political question of democracy. For the history of the West, as the history of the United States, is a history of exploitation of the labor, land, and resources of diverse groups of peoples: Indians, indentured servants, black slaves, farmers, the working class, immigrants, and, not least, the exploitation of women in the home.

For this reason it is also a history of the unfolding struggle over democratic rights and against the powerful minority of anti-democratic forces who have sought to monopolize political power to ensure their economic concentration. This struggle for democracy has involved the Indians' struggle for their land and sovereignty; the struggle of immigrants, of blacks, of Chicanos; working-class and socialist struggles; and, integral to all of these, women's struggle for equality and political emancipation.

Notes

Special thanks to Nancy Paige Fernandez, of the Program in Comparative Culture at the University of California at Irvine, for her thoughtful critique of my first draft, and to Lisa Rubens, Lyn Reese, Deanne Thompson, and all the other women at the Women's West Conference whose warm encouragement and extensive discussions and comments enlightened my analysis and understanding.

1. E.g., community-property laws for married couples in many southern and western states (especially in former Spanish and French territories); and the Texas "cuckoo law," which allowed a husband to kill his wife's lover if he caught them "in the act." On community property consult Barbara Allen Babcock et al., *Sex Discrimination and the Law* (Boston: Little, Brown, 1975), pp. 604–13. On the Texas "cuckoo law" see "The 'Equal Shooting Rights,'" *Texas Observer,* 16 Mar. 1965; and "Origins of the Cuckoo Law," 2 Apr. 1965. The latter article observes, "Like so many of our especially Texan legal in-

stitutions (our homestead law, our venue statute, the independent executor, our adoption law, and our community property system), our legal attitude toward the cuckold's right to take vengeance for an affront to his conjugal honor is Spanish in origin." More accurately, they are feudal in origin.

2. If we include the twentieth century, certain "academic" problems are resolved, such as that there were few black women in "the West" narrowly defined as the frontier period. If we define the West more fully, the presence of black women emerges as a real issue. How, for example, did the development of Jim Crow in the South in the early twentieth century under the sponsorship of the large propertied and monied interests affect women when Jim Crow was imposed on black, Mexican, and Asian communities in the West?

3. Louis M. Hacker, in "Sections—or Classes?" *The Nation* 137, no. 355 (26 July 1933): 108–10 leveled a sharp critique at the Turnerian thesis of a unique and democratic frontier environment in the West. See also Barry D. Karl, "Frederick Jackson Turner: The Moral Dilemma of Professionalization," *Reviews in American History* 3, (March 1975): 1–7.

4. Albert Camarillo, *Chicanos in a Changing Society: From Mexican Pueblos to American Barrios in Santa Barbara and Southern California, 1848–1930* (Cambridge, Mass.: Harvard University Press, 1979). Other studies of sixteenth-to nineteenth-century Mexican families or women include Leonard Pitt, *The Decline of the Californios: A Social History of the Spanish-Speaking Californians, 1846–1890* (Berkeley: University of California Press, 1971); Richard Griswold del Castillo, *The Los Angeles Barrio, 1850–1890: A Social History* (Berkeley: University of California Press, 1979); Richard Griswold del Castillo, *La Familia: Chicano Families in the Urban Southwest, 1848 to the Present* (Notre Dame, Ind.: University of Notre Dame Press, 1984); Frances Leon Swadesh, *Los Primeros Pobladores, Hispanic Americans of the Ute Frontier* (Notre Dame, Ind.: University of Notre Dame Press, 1974); Ramon A. Gutierrez, *Marriage, Sex, and the Family: Social Change in Colonial New Mexico, 1690–1846* (Ph.D. diss., University of Wisconsin, Madison, 1980); Ramon A. Gutierrez, "From Honor to Love: Transformation of the Meaning of Sexuality in Colonial New Mexico," in Raymond T. Smith, ed., *Love, Honor, and Economic Fate: Interpreting Kinship Ideology and Practice in Latin America* (Chapel Hill: University of North Carolina Press, 1983); Ramon A. Gutierrez, "Marriage and Seduction in Colonial New Mexico," in Adelaida del Castillo, ed., *Mexicana/Chicana Women's History*, Chicana Studies Research Center (forthcoming); Gloria E. Miranda, *"Gente De Razon* Marriage Patterns in Spanish and Mexican California: A Case Study of Santa Barbara and Los Angeles," *Southern California Quarterly* 39 no. 1 (March 1957): 149–66; Jane Dysart, "Mexican Women in San Antonio, 1830–1860: The Assimilation Process," *Western Historical Quarterly* 7 no. 4 (October 1976): 365–75; Fray Angelico Chavez, "Dona Tules, Her Fame and Her Funeral," *Palacio* 57 (August 1950): 227–34; Marcela Lucero Trujillo, "The Spanish Surnamed Woman of Yester Year," in José Otero and Evelio Echevarria, eds., *Hispanic Colorado* (Fort Collins, Colo.: Centennial Publications, 1977); Daniel J. Garr, "A Rare and Desolate Lane: Population and Race in Hispanic California," *Western Historical Quarterly* 6, no. 2 (April, 1975): 133–48. A masterful bibliography on the "Borderlands," containing hundreds of references for further research, is Charles C. Cumberland, *The United States–Mexican Border: A Selective Guide to the Literature of the Region*, published by *Rural Sociology* as vol. 25, no. 2 (June 1970): 230 pp. The work includes references to Spanish-Indian relations in the region.

5. Elinor C. Burkett, "In Dubious Sisterhood: Race and Class in Spanish Colonial South America," *Latin American Perspectives* 4 nos. 1–2 (Winter–Spring, 1977): 18–26.

6. "All The Pretty Little Horses," in Middleton Harris et al., *The Black Book* (New York: Random House, 1974), p. 65. The book is a photographic documentary history of the black experience in the United States, including documents and graphics of blacks in the West.

7. For example, Barbara Welter's "The Cult of True Womanhood: 1820–1860," *American Quarterly* 18, no. 2 (1966): 151–74, reprinted in Michael Gordon, ed., *The American Family in Socio-Historical Perspective* (New York: St. Martin's Press, 1973). Welter assumes an upper-class, native WASP homogeneity of all women in America: "It was a fearful obli-

gation, a solemn responsibility, which the nineteenth century *American woman* had—to uphold the pillars of the temple with her frail *white hand"* (p. 225, emphasis added). Her article provides no discussion of property or of women and the family's relation to property. In her only (indirect) reference to the economic character of American society and its class divisions, she blithely passes by without acknowledging these contradictions: "America was a land of precarious fortunes. . . . the woman who had servants today, might tomorrow, because of a depression or panic, be forced to do her own work. . . . she was to be the same cheerful consoler of her husband in their cottage as in their mansion" (p. 238).

In fact, this section contains the only references to the existence of other classes of women: ". . . the value of a wife in case of business reverses . . . of course she had a little help from 'faithful Dinah' who absolutely refused to leave her beloved mistress" (pp. 238–239). Welter cites quotations linking the Cult of True Womanhood to a certain order of society ("that a stable order of society depended upon her maintaining her traditional place in it" [p. 242]), yet she never questions that order, never examines that society and why its maintenance depended on women's domestic subordination.

8. Cf. Leo Huberman, *Man's Worldly Goods: The Story of the Wealth of Nations* (New York: Monthly Review Press, 1936); Maurice Dobb, *Studies in the Development of Capitalism* (New York: International Publishers, 1947). An incisive presentation of primitive accumulation and its devastating impact on peasant families in Europe is found in Karl Marx, *Capital*, vol. 1, part 8 "The So-Called Primitive Accumulation."

9. Raul A. Fernandez, in *The United States–New Mexico Border: A Politico-Economic Profile* (Notre Dame, Ind.: University of Notre Dame Press, 1977), presents an analysis of the complex character of this process in the Southwest. Ray Allen Billington's classic *Westward Expansion* traces the historical facts of the process of westward expansion, though from the perspective of Frederick Jackson Turner's "frontier thesis."

10. Both Jefferson Davis and Captain Randolph B. Marcy compared the conquest of the West with the French imperialist conquest of Algeria, and both argued that the United States Army should apply the French tactics in that conquest to the conquest of the Indians in the West. Walter Prescott Webb, *The Great Plains* (Lincoln: University of Nebraska Press, ca. 1931), pp. 194, 195, 196.

11. Lynwood Carranco, *Genocide and Vendetta: The Round Valley Wars in Northern California* (Norman: University of Oklahoma Press, 1981). An excellent survey of government-Indian relations is found in D'Arcy McNichols, *Native American Tribalism: Indian Survivals and Renewals* (published for the Institute of Race Relations, London, by Oxford University Press, 1973). Indian women's resistance in the face of both the Spanish and United States conquests is presented in Victoria Brady, Sarah Crome, and Lyn Reese's "Resist and Survive, Aspects of Native Women of California," (MS Sarah Crome, Institute for the Study of Social Change, University of California, Berkeley, Calif.)

12. For a very explicit account of the connections between this internal conquest and the creation of a foreign empire by the United States, see Scott Nearing, *The American Empire* (New York: Rand School of Social Science, 1921). See also Leo Huberman, *We, the People* (New York, London: Harper Brothers, 1947).

13. A good overview of immigration in the United States is found in Barbara Kaye Greenleaf, *America Fever: The Story of American Immigration* (New York: New American Library, 1974).

14. Rosalinda M. González, "Capital Accumulation and Mexican Immigration to the United States" (Ph.D. diss., University of California at Irvine, 1981) offers a political-economic analysis of the discriminatory treatment of Asian and Mexican immigrants that differs from the traditional explanations in terms of racism.

15. Dorothy Gray, "Minority Women in the West, Juanita, Biddy Mason, Donaldina Cameron," in *Women of the West* (Millbrae, Calif.: Les Femmes Publishing, 1976), pp. 62–75; *Asian Women* (Berkeley: University of California, Dwinelle Hall, 1971); Ruthanne Lum McCunn, *An Illustrated History of the Chinese in America* (San Francisco: Design Enterprises, 1979).

16. Case studies of these barrios and their twentieth-century development appear in Arthur J. Rubel, *Across the Tracks: Mexican-Americans in a Texas City* (Austin: University

of Texas Press, 1966); and Ricardo Romo, *East Los Angeles, History of a Barrio* (Austin: University of Texas Press, 1983). The historical development of the Chicano people is examined in Carey McWilliams's classic *North from Mexico: The Spanish Speaking People of the United States* (New York: Greenwood Press, 1968); Rodolfo Acuna, *Occupied America: A History of Chicanos* (New York: Harper & Row, 1981); and the excellent bilingual pictorial history by Chicano Communications Center, *450 Years of Chicano History in Pictures* (South Pasadena, Calif.: Bilingual Educations Services, n.d.). A case study of how monopoly-motivated reforms of the Progressive Era were applied to Mexican immigrant communities at the turn of the century is found in Gilbert G. Gonzalez, *Progressive Education: A Marxist Interpretation* (Minneapolis: Marxist Educational Press, 1982). A historical analysis of Chicanas is presented in Martha P. Cotera, *Diosa y Hembra: The History and Heritage of Chicanas in the U.S.* (Austin, Tex.: Information Systems Development, 1976).

17. See, e.g., the beautiful and poignant description in Jose Lona's "Biographical Sketch of the Life of an Immigrant Woman," in Maria Linda Apodaca, "The Chicana Woman: An Historical Materialist Analysis," *Latin American Perspectives* 4, nos. 1–2: p. 70–89. The Institute of Oral History at the University of Texas at El Paso has a growing collection of over 500 taped interviews, many of which relate to the railroads.

18. Barbara Mayer Wertheimer, *We Were There: The Story of Working Women in America* (New York: Pantheon Books, 1977), pp. 249. Lillian Schlissel, in *Women's Diaries of the Westward Journey* (New York: Schocken Books, 1982), pointed out that most of the western pioneers were landowners and that their parents had also been landowners, "a class of 'peasant proprietors'" (pp. 10–11).

19. See, e.g., Gabriel Kolko, *Railroads and Regulation* (Westport, Conn.: Greenwood Press, 1976); Robert Wiebe, *The Search for Order, 1877–1920* (New York: Hill and Wang, 1968); James Weinstein, *The Corporate Idea in the Liberal State, 1900–1918* (Boston: Beacon Press, 1968); Matthew Josephson, *The Robber Barons* (New York: Harcourt Brace, 1934); and Matthew Josephson, *The Money Lords* (New York: Weybright and Talley, 1972).

20. McNichols, *Native American Tribalism*. For a brief description of the negative effects on tribal solidarity from the imposition of individualism and the nuclear family on Indian society, see the first two chapters of Keith Basso's *The Cibecue Apache* (New York: Holt, Rinehart and Winston, 1970).

21. Eleanor Leacock, "Women in Development: Anthropological Facts and Fictions," *Latin American Perspectives* 4, nos. 1–2.

22. Sheryll and Gene Pattersen-Black, *Western Women in History and Literature* (Crawford, Neb.: Cottonwood Press, 1978), p. 5.

23. An important article by Joan Jensen, "Cloth, Bread, and Boarders: Women's Household Production for the Market," *The Review of Radical Political Economics* 12, no. 2 (Summer 1980): 14–24, examines women's household production from the late-eighteenth to early-twentieth centuries. Jensen concludes that it increased the economic productivity of the family through women's provision of services and the home production of produce for domestic consumption and for local and regional markets. In rural areas the domestic labor of women allowed men to increase production of cash crops for urban markets without increasing food costs. "Low food costs combined with taking in boarders allowed the males of American urban families to work for lower wages than they might have required had women not contributed to the family income."

24. Rosalinda M. González, "Mexican Immigrants in the United States: Cultural Conflict and Class Transformation," *Labor History,* forthcoming; and Rosalinda M. González, "Chicanas and Mexican Immigrant Families, 1920–1940" in Joan Jensen and Lois Scharf, eds., *Decades of Discontent: The Women's Movement, 1920–1940* (Westport, Conn.: Greenwood Press, 1983).

25. Many of the leading entrepreneurs in western expansion also had their stakes in foreign conquest. In the Southwest, for example, Adolph Spreckles, who built his fortune in California and Hawaii sugar plantations, merged with Henry C. Havemeyer, the eastern sugar king, to form the sugar trust, which was obtaining concessions in Mexico to grant it complete monopolization. Spreckles was a close friend of the Southern Pacific Railroad, which under the leadership of Henry Huntington and subsequently under William Harriman

was gobbling up railroads in the United States and Mexico and absorbing steamship lines and ports. John Kenneth Turner, *Barbarous Mexico* (Austin: University of Texas Press, 1969); Carey McWilliams, *Factories in the Field* (Santa Barbara, Calif.: Peregrine Publishers, 1971).

26. Ruth Allen, *The Labor of Women in the Production of Cotton* (Austin, Tex.: University of Texas Press, 1931).

27. Mario T. Garcia, *Desert Immigrants: The Mexicans of El Paso, 1880–1920* (New Haven, Conn.: Yale University Press, 1981).

28. Institute for Labor Education and Research, *What's Wrong with the U.S. Economy?* (Boston: South End Press, 1982), pp. xi, 32.

29. Leo Grebler et al., in "A Preview of Socioeconomic Conditions," *The Mexican American People* (New York: The Free Press, 1970), pp. 13–34..

30. Donald Dewey, "Robots Reach Out," *United* (August 1983): 92–99.

17

The "Girls" from Syracuse: Sex Role Negotiations Of Kansas Women in Politics, 1887–1890

ROSALIND URBACH MOSS

What difference did the right to vote make in individual women's lives and in the ways the larger society viewed women? Rosalind Urbach Moss looks at the meaning of woman suffrage in Hamilton County, Kansas, where newly enfranchised women almost immediately were elected to public office. That women formed suffrage societies and moved quickly into politics tells us that they worked actively to enter public life. But, as Moss notes, all the records of these political pioneers are public records written by men, and they reflect the extent to which men continued to see women through the filter of domestic ideology. We do not know whether the women were as concerned with moral and domestic matters as the men suggest, and the records do not tell what their political success and their subsequent withdrawal from politics meant to them or to other women in the 1890s. That Moss could find no records to answer these important questions tells us a great deal about why we are so ignorant of our pioneer foremothers.

On April 4, 1887, the town of Syracuse, Kansas, became one of two communities in that state and in the nation to elect women to their municipal governments. Syracuse elected an all-female town council; Argonia in south-central Kansas elected a male council and the first female mayor in the country. (A year later, Oskaloosa near Lawrence elected women to both the mayor's office and the council.) Then in November 1887, Hamilton County (of which Syracuse became the seat) elected its first female county school superintendent, an office for which women had been permitted to run since 1872 but for which they still could not vote. Another woman succeeded her in 1890. Because of this burst of female political activity, Kansas provided the nation a testing ground for women's entry into politics; feminists, suffragists, and antisuffragists watched the Kansas towns eagerly for signs of support for their causes.[1]

As women entered politics in Hamilton County in the late 1880s, something else was occurring—the county's women and men were negotiating the place and proper activities of women in the West. The long-standing myth of the westerner's being freer than other Americans was put to a severe test when women entered local politics: Was the myth for men

City Council, Oskaloosa, Kansas, 1888. Courtesy The Kansas State Historical Society, Topeka.

only? In her book *Frontier Women,* Julie Roy Jeffrey demonstrates the pull of nineteenth-century domestic ideology on most female immigrants to the West; however, Sheryll Patterson-Black shows that some women *did* go west seeking different lives than they knew in the East. These two impulses met in Syracuse, Kansas, in the 1880s and sought mutual accommodation.[2]

Hamilton County lies in the far southwestern corner of Kansas, bordering Colorado. In the late 1880s this area consisted of rangelands, boomtowns, and dusty frontier homesteads. The county's major settlements, Coolidge, Syracuse, and Kendall, stretched between the Arkansas River and the Atchison, Topeka & Santa Fe Railroad tracks, along the old Santa Fe Trail. Although Syracuse and Coolidge had been settled since about 1873, the boom period began around 1885. By 1887 the towns were busily distancing themselves from the "wild West." Schools and churches were organized as more people, particularly more women, moved into the country. In 1885 there had been "not half a dozen women" in Syracuse; two years later there were enough "good" women to have organized Baptist, Methodist, and Presbyterian ladies' aid societies, even though separate churches had not yet been built. By the end of 1887 their influence was being felt: at least one "bad" woman ("Kate Evans, a courtesan") had been brought before the town judge.[3]

The years 1887 and 1888 are best remembered locally, however, for the drought and for the "county seat war." These disasters brought the county and its three warring towns close to financial collapse: At the same time the tax base was diminishing because of the drought, all three towns erected massive limestone schoolhouses to bolster their claims for becoming county seat. Worse, though, was the period of bitter and corrupt politics that competition for county seat initiated. At least once, this little "war" nearly became a shooting match.[4]

In the midst of this local uproar the Kansas Supreme Court ruled that the female municipal suffrage law passed by the legislature in January 1887, was valid. Notice of this ruling appeared in county newspapers in mid-March, giving barely three weeks' warning before the next town elections. Suddenly women as voters became participants in an ongoing political struggle within the Syracuse town council, the exact nature of which is unclear at this distance of time. Whatever the circumstances, on March 25, H. N. Lester, editor of the *Syracuse Journal,* published an announcement of a political meeting "for the purpose of nominating a law-abiding ticket for the city election. All voters, male and female, are expected to be present." Lester, one of the few remaining members of the original 1873 Syracuse colony, had plans to head up that "law-abiding" ticket, but he miscalculated his support. The *Sentinnel,* a rival paper, soon published a veiled accusation against Lester, calling for the election of officials "who will live up to the laws they make and enforce; . . . who will use their office for the public benefit and not to further their own personal designs." The *Sentinnel's* editor expressed confidence that "now that women can vote, there is no reason why men of known morality and upright character cannot be elected." He urged all women to vote, "but don't vote the way your husband, your best fellow, or any one else tells you without it suits."[5]

A week before the election, opposing political factions saw the women as votes to be won, but the women soon discovered their voting rights could produce something tangible. The *Sentinnel's* Will C. Higgins had joined forces with others to oppose Lester's candidacy and to elect as mayor N. E. Wheeler, a current council member. Wheeler's allies were the women of the church ladies' aid societies and their husbands, people interested in protecting their homes through municipal reforms. At some point (probably during a women's political meeting not quite a week before the election), this group decided to nominate an all-woman council slate. One of the candidates was Caroline E. Barber, like Lester an original settler, and the wife of the town's leading merchant, who was then a council member. The other council candidates were Sarah M. Coe and Mary E. Riggles (I have no information about them or their husbands); Hannah D. Nott, president of the Baptist Ladies' Aid, later elected president of the town council; and Lizzie M. Swartwood, active in the Methodist Ladies' Aid.[6] (Note that, as in much other women's history, none of these women left primary records of their actions and thoughts, and we must rely on secondary accounts of their public activities.)

Lester lost the mayoral race decisively (114 to 46) to the women's "City Ticket," largely because he failed to corral enough of the sixty-two women's votes, a fact he acknowledged, however condescendingly, in the *Journal's* headlines: "Syracuse Leads! The Ladies (God Bless Them) Rally to the

Polls and Rustle the Voters." Lester's official reaction in his article about the election was restrained, but he was careful to print the names of all those who had "planned the campaign" against him. He acknowledged, however, that the "ladies voted without hesitation and as if they had done so for the last twenty-one years." He even conceded that the election was "a great victory for the advocates of female suffrage." Lester reassured Syracuse citizens, and himself as well, that the "ladies elected are intelligent and worthy. Many of them have had extensive experience in business, are quick of perception, and more than ordinarily self-reliant. . . . At all events we are in favor of giving them a chance." [7]

Despite his official magnanimity, Lester could not resist getting in an oblique, ambiguous editorial comment elsewhere in the issue:

The ancient and eminent order of the Knights of the Garter has been reinstated in Syracuse, and at the next meeting of our city council the degrees will be conferred and a number of our prominent citizens decorated with the distinctive feature of the order for valiant service rendered in the "battle of the ballot."

Sentinnel editor Higgins published his own dig from another, more relevant perspective: "Don't you wish you had been a little mouse in the corner at the ladies' political meeting last week Wednesday?" [8]

Lester's world had changed even more dramatically than he thought. The election of an all-female town council had focused national attention on his frontier community. Not only did Laura Johns, president of the Kansas Equal Suffrage Association, decide to come to see for herself what was going on, but Syracuse faced less friendly and more facile scrutiny. On May 6, 1887, before he had had time to "give the ladies a chance," Lester was forced by his earlier magnanimity into defending the councilwomen from attack by (among others) his old hometown paper in Syracuse, New York. He reprinted the offending editorial and then accused its author of being "one of the original 'mossbacks' who cannot imagine a woman to be anything but a Victoria Woodhull or a Dr. Mary Walker, whenever she endeavors to take a position higher than a cook, washerwoman or handmaid." But Lester was not at home in his support of the women, and he allayed fears of "masculine women" and "petticoat rule" with the rather astounding assurance that

these women are ladies of refinement, culture and ability. None of them so far as we are informed, with one exception, is a woman suffragist in the common acceptation of the term . . . , but rather believe that by their example, moving in their own sphere, working by their own methods, they can transact public business and accomplish desired results without steeping themselves in corruption.

Lester's paradigm of "the way things are" was under severe stress, particularly if he could see five women sitting on the town council as "moving in their own sphere." He defended the councilwomen as best he could, however, leaving it to the more sympathetic Higgins of the *Sentinel* to report that the "ladies" of Syracuse had indeed organized their own equal suffrage society. Two of its officers, Nott and Barber, were council members;

the third officer was Mrs. Wheeler, wife of the new mayor.[9] There was more suffrage activity and support in town than Lester, and no doubt others, wanted to acknowledge, and they were going to have to live with it for the coming year.

After the women had completed their year in office, however, even Lester acknowledged that Syracuse had become "renowned as a city of good government, good morals, fine streets." Nothing catastrophic had occurred. The women had begun their administration by having the streets graded and ordering property owners to build sidewalks; later they voted on municipal bonds and split on an issue of business licensing. The women appear to have established a pattern of good government operated for the benefit of the community as a whole. But none of Syracuse's "city mothers" ran for reelection in 1888. The councilwomen evidently felt they had done their part to make the town better. They modestly retired in favor of male successors who would continue their course of municipal improvements geared toward making the place a "home" town.[10]

With no women at work in City Hall, it would have been easy for citizens to forget the questions about women's proper role raised by the presence of women in public office. By this time, however, another woman was keeping the issues alive by venturing into more turbulent county politics in the midst of the county-seat war. Elizabeth (Lizzie) Culver ran for the office of Superintendent of Public Instruction in the fall of 1887. Even though *Journal* editor Lester believed that the school superintendency was more "appropriate" for a woman than was serving on the city council, and although Culver's father was one of the county treasurers, her election was not an easy one. Owing to issues related to the county-seat war, as well as those raised by her gender, she had to fight to get and then to keep her post.[11]

Her father, Martin S. Culver, was a Texas cattleman who lobbied for the National Cattle Trail after the Kansas legislature quarantined Texas cattle in 1885. He was a founder of Trail City, two miles west of Coolidge, which was known as "the wickedest city in Colorado" during its brief life in the late 1880s. Culver had moved his family from Corpus Christi, Texas, to Coolidge and had become involved in county politics during the county-seat fight as the treasurer for the Kendall-Coolidge faction. In the fall of 1887, though ill, Martin Culver stood for reelection, while daughter Lizzie ran for the superintendency. She did not run on her father's Coolidge ticket, however: her "Independent County" ticket was nominated by Syracuse delegates disgruntled by two previous county conventions. Apparently her father's cronies did not agree with Lester that the superintendency was "a public position which . . . women are adapted to fill with credit to themselves and benefit to education."[12]

It is likely that, despite the politicization of the office of school superintendent by its being elective rather than appointive, many people in the county saw no problem with voting for a woman because they had come, like Lester, to see education as "woman's work." The factionalization of county politics at that time no doubt played a role in Culver's election, too.

The county newspapers characteristically provided few details of this campaign at the height of Kansas's longest county-seat war. Lizzie Culver won, however, against two opponents and by a nine-vote margin.[13]

Journal editor Lester again provides us with our only insight into this woman's experience in politics. Although Lester won the post of state legislator on the same ticket, he—and probably much of the rest of the county—knew little about Culver until after the election, when he announced in the *Journal* that she was "a Catholic and [had] received a convent education." Another of Lester's revelations provides an indication of what Culver's first campaign must have been like: Immediately afterward she hired a lawyer to sue the "colorful" Syracuse Methodist minister Sprague Davis for $5,000 in damages, charging him with slander. The basis of her slander charge was not reported in any county newspaper, but we can surmise what might have upset a Protestant preacher, whether or not he was aware of her Catholicism. Although she had left her father's political faction, Culver probably could not leave her association with Trail City wickedness. Her youth and her gender no doubt made her more vulnerable to attack when she entered public life. She was, after all, no matron as were the Syracuse councilwomen, whose status was at least a partial defense. During the campaign even one of her supporters, the *Syracuse Democratic Principle,* had made a thinly veiled reference to the beauty of one of the candidates. Not only had she entered the public arena very quickly after her father's death, but she probably had campaigned alone, both serious mistakes in the nineteenth century.[14] If these surmises are correct, the reactions they evoked undoubtedly led many county residents to question further the propriety of permitting women to become involved in politics.

After her election Culver moved to Syracuse and, staying with the Barbers, tried to carry out her official duties under difficult circumstances. The county records were being held at Kendall, whose citizens were contesting her election and where J. R. Campbell was acting as superintendent, though he had not run for the office. Culver kept a makeshift office in Syracuse when she could not get offices in Kendall, legally the temporary county seat. In the summer she organized and conducted the third normal institute held in the county. That fall she ran for reelection in a court-ordered contest after Syracuse had been declared the permanent seat. Culver was renominated, though not without challenges, and ran against Campbell, this time the official nominee of the Kendall-Coolidge faction.[15]

From all indications this election was also a nasty one, and Culver's earlier defection to Syracuse may have been a central issue. Lester encouraged his town to "be as true to [Culver] as she has been to us" because "petty jealousies in some localities may help Mr. Campbell." The other Syracuse papers, while more enthusiastic in her support, did not add other points in her favor; they repeated only that the election was "owed" her by Syracuse. This time Culver won by more than 100 votes, a good margin, though smaller than the margins of her male colleagues. When the Kansas dust settled, Culver married H. Clay Price, a rancher who had worked on her campaign committee. Their marriage, however, was not announced by the Syracuse papers, but rather by the *Kendall Boomer,* recently a bitter rival.[16]

Clearly she had made another mistake, though there is no way to know what people actually thought of Culver's marriage. The lack of any comment by her friends in Syracuse indicates ambivalence if not disapproval. The female city council members were already married when they won office, so being married in itself probably was not seen as a disqualification for office. But Lizzie Culver Price was a newlywed, a delicate condition for a nineteenth-century woman. She did not let this condition or people's opinions interfere with her duties as superintendent, however, as she energetically went about building and rebuilding the county school system. And she was not even slowed down at first by her pregnancy in 1890.[17]

Unlike the Syracuse councilwomen, Culver apparently did not realize that she should "retire" after she had made her point. Despite her convent education, she was after all, a cattleman's daughter and perhaps not as observant of social niceties as she might have been. She had already crossed two boundaries—the geopolitical and the moral ones between the cattle interests associated with Coolidge and Trail City and the settlement interests of many in Syracuse. Perhaps she was not aware that in failing to retire from public life and public view when her newlywed condition became even more "delicate" she was crossing another, more sensitive social border. Lizzie Culver Price had been a good superintendent, but the newspaper editors, and no doubt many others, did not—perhaps could not—acknowledge that fact until after she had left office. Even the formerly enthusiastic *Democratic Principle* in the summer of 1890 referred to her snidely as "the present incumbant who will not be a candidate again, she having tired of office life." [18] Lizzie Price's fine record as an officeholder had been obscured by her far from exemplary behavior as a conventional woman. Consequently, the question of women's suitability for public office became foremost in people's minds.

Even the woman who next ran for the superintendency felt her election had been jeopardized precisely because Price had not quit and had continued to "drive over the country in a very pregnant state, turning public opinion against her sex." It is unclear what bothered people most about Price's behavior: their assumption that pregnancy was incapacitating and therefore interfered with her public duties, or their objection to someone in such a "private" condition continuing to perform public duties. Whatever the reason, the next female candidate, Kate Warthen, found herself waging two campaigns—one for office and the other for the right of women to run for and serve in public office. She was eminently well equipped to do both and mounted a hard-nosed and quite modern "media" campaign for county superintendent in 1890.[19]

Sarah Catharine Warthen was born in 1866 and spent her early life in Indiana, the only daughter (with four brothers) of a Union Army veteran.

From the time she was fifteen, her family had homesteaded, first in Texas, then in southeastern Kansas. She had taught in country schools since she was seventeen, but in April 1887, she quit teaching and following her family to southwestern Kansas, determined to homestead land of her own. Her claim lay in the southeastern part of Hamilton County, while her parents' lay near Lakin, farther northeast in adjacent Kearny County. The Warthens moved to the area at what proved to be a very bad time. Owing to a drought and a hard winter, in 1887, Kate Warthen earned only $37.08 from her farm. She returned to teaching in a country school in Kearny County in March 1888.[20]

Warthen was ambitious, however, and by September 1889 she had been elected principal teacher of the big new limestone schoolhouse in Kendall. In April 1890 she decided to run for the superintendency. Warthen successfully negotiated political boundaries in the county, but it was harder to deal successfully with the problem of her gender, which had become more directly an issue because of Lizzie Culver's legacy. Indeed, Warthen had to worry a good deal more about being defeated by her sex than by her Democratic opponent, who clearly had neither the administrative nor the political qualifications she possessed.[21]

Typically, the issue of her being a woman was never raised directly in any of the county papers, but the *Syracuse Journal* approached the problem of "allowing women to hold office" obliquely when it published without comment an essay, "Women as Public Officers," signed only "Observer." Kate Warthen was the author. Although she offered primarily egalitarian feminist arguments, she buttressed these with assertions of women's special suitability for public office similar to those used by the Home Protectionists associated with the Women's Christian Temperance Union and other "social purity" groups. Significantly though, Lester and the other county newspaper editors stressed Warthen's competency in their endorsements, something they had not done—perhaps could not have conceived of doing—for Culver. Warthen managed to gain the support of all the county papers, even the *Democratic Principle,* which had to support her opponent perfunctorily because of its party affiliation.[22]

Once she had won the Republican nomination, Warthen campaigned actively over the entire county—careful always to be accompanied by one of her brothers. She won the election, 236 votes to 179. It was a smaller margin than Culver's in 1888, but considerably larger than those of the men elected with her to other county offices—a significant indication that her political acumen and competence won out over considerations of both partisan politics and women's proper place.[23]

Warthen's self-made feminism and open ambition pushed her to try herself further. Even while she served two terms as county superintendent from 1891 to 1894 and fulfilled her campaign promise to be a full-time professional administrator, she wrote as a small-time journalist, was commissioned a notary public (also an unusual job for a woman), and, after reading law with the county judge, became the first woman admitted to the county bar in March 1894. Indeed, Warthen's pursuit of traditionally male positions, from homesteader to politician and lawyer, was so determined that the community was quite surprised when, in late November 1894, she married. Warthen had learned from Culver's unfortunate experience to keep her private life to herself, and the people of the county had apparently written her off as a spinster, under the assumption that education and ambition were a double handicap in a woman's search for a man.[24]

The article in the *Syracuse Journal* about Warthen's wedding reads strangely like an obituary and indicates how much she had resolved for the people of the county by providing an acceptable model for a woman in public life. The editor drew a lesson for the community from her exemplary life: as she left public office, and the county, Warthen stood as a "shining example of the bright, versatile western girl who, while possessing all the fine womanly instincts of her eastern and southern sister[s], has besides the pluck and indominable [sic] energy peculiar to western progress and independence."[25] The western woman, it seems, did not rise fully formed from the prairie. She had to be cultivated arduously through the trial and error of collective experience. Local boundaries for western womanhood had been negotiated by the "girls" from Syracuse, Hamilton County, Kansas, in the 1880s and 1890s. The ideal respectable western woman was not, as it turns out, a larger-than-life "Marlboro woman" but a hybrid like Kate Warthen, who was able to combine competence with awareness and observance of the social limits of her conduct of public life. The limits Warthen observed remained unwritten barriers to middle-class women's participation in politics and, to a large extent, work until quite recently (i.e., if women must participate in either area, they should be unmarried professionals or experienced matrons).

Today the Syracuse councilwomen are remembered in Hamilton County as a list of names constituting a noteworthy but anomalous "first." Lizzie Culver is described only as a daughter of M. S. Culver, founder of Trail City, Colorado, and wife of H. C. Price, Hamilton County rancher. Kate Warthen, who left the state after her marriage in 1894, is recorded not at all in the county history. The negotiations of the 1880s about women's role in public life have likewise been forgotten. Lessons must become traditions to be truly learned; traditions depend on stable populations for transmission. Unfortunately, by the early 1890s, Hamilton County had reached the bottom of its population curve: many of those who had witnessed the negotiations left, to be replaced years later by others who were ignorant of that experience. More important, the newcomers were not presented with a living tradition. No women held public office in Hamilton County after 1894 until well into this century; the pioneers retired and were not replaced.[26] The new tradition of women in public life faded uncontested into rumor and then into dusty, documentary (as opposed to living, oral) history.

Notes

1. "Women in Office," *Kansas State Historical Society Collections* (Topeka) 12 (1911–1912): 400–401; the date of women's eligibility for the county superintendency comes from William Leach, *True Love and Perfect Union* (New York: Basic Books, 1980), p. 174; the Hamilton County newspapers found themselves responding to all sorts of reactions to the election from outside the town and the state; see also Monroe Billington, "Suzanna Madora Salter—First Woman Mayor," *Kansas Historical Quarterly* 21, no. 3 (Autumn 1954): 173–83, for reactions to the Argonia election. See Wilda M. Smith, "A Half Century of Struggle: Gaining Woman Suffrage in Kansas," *Kansas History* 4 (Summer 1981): 74–95, for a general history of suffrage in Kansas.

2. Julie Roy Jeffrey, *Frontier Women: The Trans-Mississippi West, 1840–1890* (New York: Hill & Wang, 1979), and Sheryll Patterson-Black, "Women Homesteaders on the Great Plains Frontier," *Frontiers* 1, no. 2 (Spring 1976): 67–88. See also Carl Degler, "What the Women's Movement Has Done to American History," in Elizabeth Langland and Walter Grove, eds., *A Feminist Perspective in the Academy* (Chicago: University of Chicago Press, 1981), for a discussion of the impact of the recovery of women's history on Turner's "frontier thesis."

3. *Syracuse Journal*, 11–18 Mar., 1887; *Syracuse Sentinel*, 9 Dec. 1887 (Evans was charged with "Lewdness and adultry"; she was acquitted). Early settler George F. Rinehart wrote in his memoir "An Early Day History of Hamilton County" (*Syracuse Journal*, 4 Oct., 1935) that many "bad men" came to Syracuse during that period and that "it took them a long time to get rid of the bad gang that hung around the boom town."

4. William F. Chollar, "A Pioneer History of Hamilton County, Kansas," (Master's thesis, University of Wichita, 1941); Floyd Edwards, ed., *Hamilton County, Kansas, History* (Syracuse, Kans.: Hamilton County Historical Society, 1979). George F. Rinehart, who served as the county's first school superintendent, described his observations of the conflict in the *Syracuse Journal*, 11 Oct. 1935: "The hue and cry that went up [over blatant ballot-stuffing] shocked the nation. Every leading newspaper in the United States featured the election on its front page. Syracuse got some bad advertising." Rinehart also reported that there was a rumor in Syracuse during the 1886 county-seat referendum that "Bat Masterson, the great gun man, was in the city to preserve order."

5. *Syracuse Journal*, 25 Mar. 1887; *Syracuse Sentinel*, 1 Apr. 1887.

6. Details about the councilwomen were compiled from items in the *Journal*, 11–18 Mar. 1887, and the "Pioneer Honor Roll" in the *Hamilton County History*, pp. 46–50. Of the two women, besides those elected to the council, who helped organize the campaign, Mrs. N. E. Wheeler, wife of the mayoral victor, was active in the Methodist Ladies' Aid; the husband of the other woman also worked on the campaign. Higgins's statements and the council's later actions provide evidence that the members of the "City Ticket" may have seen themselves as Home Protectionists, though they never used the term. "Home Protectionist" refers to those groups in the 1880s and 1890s that promoted women's participation in the public sphere as an extension of their moral role in the home. Women were going to "sweep out" corruption from politics and make the home safe from assaults from outside. The major elements of this movement were the Women's Christian Temperance Union and other temperance and "social purity" groups. One of WCTU leader Frances Willard's favorite mottoes was: "Woman will bless and brighten every place she enters, and she will enter every place"; Carolyn DeSwarte Gifford, "Home Protection: the W.C.T.U.'s Conversion to Woman Suffrage," Janet Sharistranian, ed., *Gender, Ideology, and Action: Historical Perspectives on Women's Public Lives* (New York: Greenwood Press, 1986), pp. 95–120. Also, George Rinehart recalled that Higgins and his brother Ed were "identified with all civic movements" in Syracuse (*Journal*, 11 Oct. 1935).

7. Lester reported the names of the men and women (including Will Higgins) who organized the victorious "City Ticket" in the 8 Apr. 1887, *Journal*. Higgins reported the returns and the number of female voters (62) in the 8 Apr. 1887, *Sentinel*. *Syracuse Democratic Principle*, 8 Apr. 1887. As for the women's business experience, contemporary newspaper sources indicate that Hannah Nott ran a millinery establishment; Caroline Barber undoubtedly helped her husband in his dry-goods store and land office.

8. *Syracuse Journal,* 8 Apr. 1887; *Syracuse Democratic Principle,* 8 Apr. 1887. It is safe to assume that Lester intended his joke to be directed at the men involved with the "City Ticket," not the female victors, who already had their garters. Unfortunately, I have been unable to uncover any record of the "ladies political meeting," so it is impossible to determine whether the nomination of the female council slate was a power play by an independent women's political caucus or an attempt by members of the incumbent male council to incorporate the new female vote to defeat other members. I suspect a coalition between the women and Wheeler's reform-minded faction.

9. *Syracuse Journal,* 29 Apr. 1887; *Syracuse Sentinel,* 13 May 1887.

10. *Journal,* 5 Apr. 1888. Lester refers to the council as "city mothers" (*Journal,* 8 Apr. 1887) and Higgins more familiarly as "city mammas" (*Sentinel,* 8 Apr. 1887). The councilwomen's achievements are collected from *Syracuse Journal,* 27 Apr. 1887, *Democratic Principle,* 14 Mar. 1888, and *Journal,* 6 May 1887, respectively. See June Underwood, "Civilizing Kansas: Women's Organization, 1880–1921" *Kansas History* 7 (Winter–Spring 1985): 291–306, for an excellent discussion of municipal reform issues women concerned themselves with during this period. The Syracuse councilwomen appear to have had similar concerns, although they disagreed about licensing a pool hall.

11. In the 22 Apr. 1887, *Journal,* Lester expressed his opinion about the school superintendency being a more appropriate office for women in the context of commenting on the worth of an unidentified woman (perhaps Culver) who he reported had sought the nomination. See Joanna Stratton, *Pioneer Women: Voices from the Kansas Frontier* (New York: Simon & Schuster, 1981), pp. 161–68, for an account of teaching and superintending in adjacent Kearny County in the late 1880s. Note also that, as with the councilwomen, no primary evidence of Lizzie Culver's private feelings about her public career survives.

12. Edwards, ed., *Hamilton County History,* pp. 59–60; Jimmy M. Skaggs, in *The Cattle Trailing Industry: Between Supply and Demand, 1866–1890* (Lawrence: University Press of Kansas, 1973), p. 92, states that many Dodge City saloonkeepers left that city after the Texas herds were quarantined and moved to Trail City. The *Hamilton County History* attributes to Culver the founding of Trail City and a major role in lobbying for the National Cattle Trail. Skaggs's only reference to Culver is as an "employee" of the Texas Cattle Raisers Association. Since he owned a ranch in south Texas, Culver could have been a working member of the association. Details of his participation in Hamilton County politics, as well as of his illness and death, come from "Some Lost Towns of Kansas," *Kansas Historical Collections* 12 (1911–1912): 457–63, and contemporary mentions in the *Coolidge Citizen* and the *Syracuse Journal;* at his death, the *Citizen* (7 Oct. 1887) described him as "perhaps our most prominent citizen." Lizzie Culver's candidacy was announced in the 28 Oct. *Syracuse Journal;* her hometown paper, the *Coolidge Citizen,* published her name in the listing of the "Independent County" ticket without comment.

13. The three candidates were Will Smoke, C. A. Warner, and Lizzie Culver; on 27 Apr. 1888, the *Syracuse Sentinnel* printed the election results because Kendallites were questioning the superintendent's portion of the 1887 election.

14. "Some Lost Towns of Kansas," p. 463; *Syracuse Journal,* 18 Nov. 1887; *Syracuse Sentinnel,* 21–28 Oct. 1887; *Journal,* 2 Dec., 11 Nov. 1887, respectively. In Culver's second campaign her party appointed a campaign committee (an unusual action for that time and place), which included her fiancé. Also, Kate Warthen, who ran for superintendent in 1890, was advised "by no means to campaign alone" (Warthen-Searcy Papers, Kansas Collection, Spencer Research Library, University of Kansas, Lawrence). Besides these gaffes there is evidence that Lizzie Culver had broken with her father before his death: the spring before she may have been the woman Lester referred to who had wanted to become superintendent, and she decided to seek public office with the Syracuse political faction just weeks after her father's death. Chollar describes Rev. Sprague Davis as "colorful" and says that he "attracted attention everywhere he went by his enormous and powerful physique . . . , [which] stood him in good stead in the many tight places a frontier preacher found himself" (pp. 68–69). He does not, however, mention Culver's suit, and I have not been able to discover its disposition.

15. *Syracuse Democratic Principle,* 29 Mar. 1888. George Rinehart relates in his memoir that Campbell had acted as Kendall's de facto school superintendent until the state su-

preme court recognized Rinehart as the legitimate superintendent (*Journal*, 4 Oct. 1935). The 19 Apr. 1888 *Democratic Principle* asked why Campbell was acting as superintendent, since he had not even run for the office in the 1888 election. "Some Lost Towns of Kansas," p. 462; though Syracuse had been legally declared the county seat in July, 1888, the "war" was not completely over until J. H. Borders, a crony of Martin Culver and his successor as Coolidge's treasurer, obeyed a court order and turned over the county's accounts in December 1888.

16. *Syracuse Democratic Principle*, 8 Nov. 1888; *Syracuse Journal*, 9 Nov. 1888; *Democratic Principle*, 4 Oct. 1888; Edwards, ed., *Hamilton County History*, p. 61; *Kendall Boomer*, 19 Jan. 1889.

17. Cf. Billington, "Suzanna Madora Salter," p. 178; Salter, Argonia's "lady mayor," gave birth to a child while in office, which produced primarily positive notoriety, at least locally.

18. *Syracuse Journal*, 16 Jan. 1891; *Syracuse Democratic Principle*, 26 June 1890.

19. Letter to researcher from Lucile Searcy, Kate Warthen's daughter, 2 July 1980, Warthen-Searcy Papers, Spencer Research Library, University of Kansas, Lawrence. For a complete discussion of Warthen's life and political career, see my "'Educated and Ambitious Women': Kate Warthen on the Kansas Frontier," in Sharistanian, ed., *Gender, Ideology, and Action*, pp. 121–55.

20. Details of Warthen's life are taken from documents in the Warthen-Searcy Collection and from correspondence and interviews with Lucile Searcy. More information exists about Warthen than about the other women, but far from enough to provide a well-rounded view of her life in county politics. Because no private documents survive for Warthen, newspaper accounts remain important in telling her story.

21. Warthen begins an unpublished essay describing her adventures being lost on the prairie with the statement, "I was ambitious," as an explanation of why she was the county superintendent (Warthen-Searcy Papers).

22. *Syracuse Journal*, 10 Oct. 1890; *Hamilton County Bulletin* (Coolidge), 31 Oct. 1890; *Syracuse Democratic Principle*, 16 Oct. 1890. On Sept. 25, 1890, the *Democratic Principle* stated that it would support Warthen if the Democratic county convention nominated no one for the office of school superintendent; its later comments about the man the Democrats nominated were lukewarm: "If [he is] elected, the county will be well looked after" (16 Oct. 1890).

23. *Journal*, 7 Nov. 1890; the next largest margin was 37 votes for county clerk.

24. *Journal*, 30 Nov. 1894, states that many of her friends considered "her's . . . a spinster's lot" (the editor of the *Journal* by this time was Henry Block, who had edited the Kendall *Boomer* during the county-seat war, and while Warthen was principal teacher and a contributor to the newspapers in Kendall and Coolidge). On her wedding trip to her new home in Tennessee, Kate Warthen Searcy insisted on stopping in Topeka to take—and pass—the state supreme court bar examination, probably the first woman to do so (4 Dec. 1894, according to the "Comprehensive Roster to July 1, 1935," *Reports of Cases Determined in the Supreme Court of the State of Kansas* 140 [Topeka, 1935]). She did not stay in the state to practice, however, as did Lilla Day Monroe after passing her examination the following year (Stratton, *Pioneer Women*, p. 19).

25. *Syracuse Journal*, 30 Nov. 1894.

26. Edwards, ed., *Hamilton County History;* actually, only Mrs. C. E. Barber, wife of a town father, is mentioned by name as a council member. Lizzie Culver's sister Ella is remembered as an "early schoolteacher" in Hamilton County; however, I found no mention of Ella as a county notable in any of the newspapers of the time (1886–94), although another sister, Nettie, attended the Normal Institute Lizzie organized in 1888 (*Journal*, 8 Aug. 1888). George Rinehart describes the county's natural disasters and "partial depopulation" in a memoir published in the 27 Sept. 1935, *Syracuse Journal*. A telephone conversation with Thelma P. McNeill, a current resident of Syracuse who is interested in local history, reveals that "an awful refuse problem started" the townspeople "electing women to office" again in the twentieth century (telephone conversation with researcher, 8 Jan. 1984).

18

Networking on the Frontier: The Colorado Women's Suffrage Movement, 1876–1893

CAROLYN STEFANCO

In this article about Colorado suffrage organizing, Carolyn Stefanco looks at efforts to win the vote from the women's perspective. This approach is a contrast to most studies of suffrage, which concentrate on the attitudes of male lawmakers and voters who finally granted the franchise. Stefanco shows us that suffrage campaigns were long and difficult, that they involved many different groups of women, and that suffrage advocates used arguments based in concepts of social justice, economic need, and genteel morality to justify women's right to vote. We need more work like this in other western states to understand why western women voted before women in the East. Stefanco shows women as activists for their own issues and takes us past simple answers to look at complex political coalitions.

Historians have frequently noted that western states more quickly approved woman suffrage than eastern states. Yet aside from speculation that such regional distinctions might reflect "frontier democracy" or more liberal male attitudes, little research has been done on the actual groundwork that led up to the enactment of woman suffrage. By examining the interlocking efforts of various women's groups for whom suffrage became a significant issue, one can begin to address this deficiency. Woman suffrage emerged as a plausible reform in Colorado largely as a result of the work of several women's associations, which eventually joined efforts to extend the franchise to women.[1]

The Colorado suffrage movement took place within a rapidly changing frontier environment. Denver attracted first miners and then settlers looking for economic opportunity. As in many other frontier cities that prospered, it became a regional transportation and commercial center, and witnessed a tremendous population growth between its founding in 1858 and the close of the century. Male immigrants outnumbered females throughout the nineteenth century in typical frontier fashion, but of the 133,000 Denver residents in 1900, there were more female than male inhabitants.[2]

As the largest urban center within the state, Denver acted as the focal point for suffrage activity in Colorado. Woman suffrage and related organizations counted their largest memberships in Denver and established

Women at Denver polling place. Courtesy Colorado Historical Society.

their state headquarters there. Members found it impossible to separate work carried out by state associations from that of local Denver organizations, and most viewed such efforts as one and the same.[3]

Suffrage sentiment emerged between the years 1868 and 1870 when former Colorado Territorial Governor John Evans and Territorial Governor Edward McCook asked the legislature to consider women's suffrage. However, women first organized and lobbied on their own behalf in 1876.[4] In that year Mrs. McCook, along with her sister-in-law Eliza Thompson, founded the first territorial suffrage society in Denver.[5] They invited interested women to join the society and to meet with them in early January 1877.

At that meeting they planned ways to convince the territorial constitutional convention to provide for equal suffrage in the new state of Colorado, and appointed a committee to address the constitutional convention. Although the convention delegates listened to the women "with respectful attention," a contemporary account of the suffrage campaign reveals the women had hoped that "the gentlemen . . . would have found it in their hearts to make some reply, even while disclaiming the official character of their act; but they preserved a decorous and non-committal, if not incurious silence, and the ladies withdrew."[6] Following the failure of this personal appeal, suffragists concentrated on circulating petitions and sent thousands of signatures to the convention. Despite all their efforts, in February the convention defeated the amendment to enfranchise women by a vote of 24 to 8.[7]

Morale remained high, however, since the women had gained concessions in the new state constitution. For the first time in Colorado women possessed the right to vote in school elections and to hold school district office. The Colorado constitution also mandated a referendum election on the suffrage question the following year, setting in place the mechanism by which women would eventually win the right to vote in all elections.[8] Article 7, section 2 stated that the people (or the male electorate, to be more specific) must in the future approve by a majority vote any law to extend voting rights.[9]

Colorado suffragists celebrated other achievements along with these legislative measures. They received financial support from Amelie Brocker, a long-term contributor who preferred to remain out of the limelight.[10] The women also found friends in the press. Suffragists persuaded William Byers, for example, to devote a weekly column to the cause in his newspaper, the *Rocky Mountain News*.[11]

A larger and stronger Colorado Suffrage Association met for its second annual convention in Denver on January 15, 1877, and ten days later applauded the legislature's passage of a bill providing for the referendum election on the suffrage issue in October. Denver women mounted a massive campaign during the intervening months. They held rallies and meetings, mostly within the city, and engaged speakers like Mary Shields from Colorado and Susan B. Anthony from the National Woman's Suffrage Association to tour the state. On election day, October 2, 1877, three or four women monitored every polling place in the city of Denver. Sitting demurely at tables decorated with flowers, they distributed handbills proclaiming "Woman Suffrage Approved" and tried to persuade the most recalcitrant male voters.[12] In spite of their efforts throughout the year, the measure lost, 14,053 to 6,612.

Denver newspapers explained the defeat by pointing to inappropriate female behavior. Local papers reported that the suffragists met on Sundays, when all decent women should be in church or at home with their families, according to nineteenth-century prescription; worse yet, the women intruded on the public sphere by working the polls on election day.[13] In response to such criticism, the suffragists replied that "whatever mistakes may have been made as to methods, we firmly believe that in the main tendency and total results of the campaign, immense gains in favor of equal suffrage will be found on the balance sheet." Along with emphatic statements regarding the progress of the movement, equal suffrage proponents offered their own explanation for the defeat of the amendment: the small number of active suffrage campaigners led men to believe that most women cared little about the right to vote.[14]

Suffragists assessed the 1877 defeat accurately. Most women in Denver, where suffrage activity was at its strongest, and certainly the great majority of women in other areas of the state, showed apathy at best and disdain at worst for the reform. In the next few years, although suffragists failed to engage these women in their struggle, they reached them through other, less threatening organizations.

Histories of the Colorado suffrage movement skim over the years between the 1877 and 1893 campaigns, judging them to be ones in which little activity occurred. But it was during these years that the movement developed an organizational base and built the momentum critical for success in the 1890s. Two factors emerged during these years which bridged the two seemingly unconnected suffrage campaigns. The first was individual initiative by "strong-minded women," and the second was the formation and growth of women's organizations.

Caroline Nichols Churchill, a maverick among women of her time, forced Coloradans to consider women's issues throughout the leanest years of the suffrage movement. To accomplish this, in 1879 she began publishing a monthly newspaper from her home in Denver. Called the *Colorado Antelope,* since, according to Churchill, a "little deer . . . is so difficult to overtake," the paper dedicated itself to the "interests of humanity, woman's political equality and individuality." [15] The paper covered a wide range of topics from class oppression to local history. Every issue, however, retained a primary focus on women's status.

Denver bookshops carried the *Antelope,* and Churchill personally delivered copies to stores in remote Colorado communities. Circulation increased substantially, and she sold more than 2,500 papers in the first three months of publication. Since Churchill believed that conversion took precedence over financial gain, she also gave issues away. She appealed specifically to her female audience and encouraged them to organize by offering free copies of the *Antelope* to women's clubs with five or more members. [16]

In spite of Churchill's pleas, few women's groups, with the possible exception of ladies' aid societies, existed in Denver during 1879. Churchill proselytized, nonetheless, and stated her explanations for women's inactivity in March 1880:

We are aware of the jealousies of many husbands in regard to any public work which the wife may become interested in, but women should remember that all the evils of society are caused by the bad management of men, and women are greatly to blame for folding their hands and permitting this state of things. [17]

Spurred by women like Churchill and by deplorable conditions in Denver, women took action, not directly on suffrage but on what they perceived to be the greatest evil confronting late nineteenth-century society: the liquor problem. In April 1880, Denver women joined the national movement for temperance by forming a state Women's Christian Temperance Union and a local union. In contrast to the conservative impulses that fed many unions across the country in the mid-1870s, Denver WCTU members exhibited some surprising attitudes.

To begin with, the Denver temperance union chose Mary Shields, the Colorado suffragist, to address the first state convention in Denver. One member who recalled their reasoning, explained that:

The year the question of Woman's Suffrage was submitted to Colorado [1877], Mrs. M. S. Shields lectured in its interests in Longmont, and had made a number of converts. Her pleasing manner, forcible logic, and the fact that she could speak in public, decided us in inviting her to be our speaker at the Convention.[18]

Shields, who also served on the executive committee of the territorial suffrage society in 1876, and who acted as an honorary vice president of the National Woman's Suffrage Association in 1880, was elected president of the state WCTU at the founding convention. She held the position for the next seven years.[19]

The WCTU attracted women like Shields who had participated in the suffrage campaigns of 1876–1877; but for the uninitiated, membership brought unexpected lessons in equal rights. A woman reported that Shields "directed franchise work so effectively [within the WCTU] that a separate suffrage organization was not deemed necessary."[20]

Some WCTU members thought otherwise, and they joined with women from across the state in issuing a call for a suffrage meeting on January 15, 1881. The notice, published by the *Rocky Mountain News,* read:

The women of Denver and the state at large are earnestly urged to attend to discuss the social and political status of women with a view to organizing a society through which they may help themselves and each other to self culture and self government.[21]

At the meeting five days later in Denver, the Colorado Equal Suffrage Association was formed. The members planned to hold meetings, circulate petitions, issue publications, and hire lecturers, but carried out few of these activities. As a result, a separate suffrage movement did not develop during the 1880s.[22]

Although individual WCTU members belonged to the suffrage association, the WCTU as a whole offered less than full support. This reluctance stemmed in part from the fact that Colorado suffrage societies used natural rights ideology to justify their claims, while the WCTU saw suffrage mainly as a tool for temperance. A WCTU member warned, for instance, that "if woman had the ballot in her hands it would not be many years before the mighty power of the liquor interest would tremble."[23] Temperance, not suffrage, motivated WCTU members and remained their top priority.

The society also met resistance from Caroline Churchill. Although she participated in planning the meeting, Churchill criticized the outcome. She resented the fact that women found it necessary, "for the sake of *respectability,*" to elect a man president of the suffrage society.[24] So instead of working with the group, Churchill concentrated on her own crusade in the *Antelope*.

These personal differences, along with halfhearted support from the WCTU, forced suffragists to work as individuals, as Churchill did, or through other women's organizations. Some continued to work within Denver temperance unions during these years, but many more also joined in a new movement of women—the formation of clubs.

Denver women's clubs, like their affiliates in other parts of the country, drew their inspiration from a combination of antebellum religious traditions and women's increased interest in education. Churches provided women with a socially acceptable meeting place and a Christian rationale for social action. Members of the Unity (Presbyterian) Church in Denver founded a Ladies' Aid Society in 1860, and women in other churches followed their example.[25] But while religious sentiment continued to motivate community activity, by the late 1870s and early 1880s, women had begun to form associations independent of the churches. The Central Presbyterian Ladies' Aid Society, for example, disbanded and regrouped in 1881 as the Monday Literary Club.[26]

Literary clubs provided intellectual stimulation for house-bound women, as well as a forum for suffrage proponents. Ione Hanna, for example, served along with her husband as an officer of the territorial woman suffrage society.[27] After the 1877 electoral defeat, Hanna (with eleven other women) formed the Denver Fortnightly Club. She hoped to encourage study, discussion, philanthropy, and "sisterly love and sympathy." The club retained a literary focus throughout most of the 1880s, while individual members like Hanna joined the WCTU, served in state temperance offices, and continued their interest in woman suffrage.[28] Club membership thus served to train women for leadership, and the outside interests represented within them by women such as Hanna provided political education.[29]

Hanna's participation in suffrage societies, women's clubs, and the WCTU exemplified the emergence of a women's network in Denver and revealed the interwoven history of female organizations. But while the memberships of many groups overlapped, some Denverites championed causes like suffrage in relative isolation, in part because political ideology and class status barred many women from middle-class associations such as the WCTU and women's clubs.

Working-class women in Denver agitated for suffrage during the late 1880s through the auspices of labor politics. The Union Labor party accepted women's inherent equality and proclaimed in its national platform that "all men and women are born free and with equal rights."[30] Female members of the Colorado Union Labor party addressed this topic frequently in speeches to the Rocky Mountain Social League, a Denver Socialist group that studied social issues. Rosa Cohen read an essay to a League meeting on "The Woman Question," and argued that "since time began woman has been thrust into an inferior position, [and] . . . her only hope . . . lay in Socialism which proposed to elevate woman into her true sphere of equality with man."[31] Leagues offered union women, as well as men, the chance to study pressing social concerns such as women's suffrage.

Some women utilized the support of radical politics and the skills acquired in social league meetings to forge a political role in late nineteenth-century Denver. They participated in party conventions and, according to the labor press, freed meetings "from the disgusting scenes always wit-

nessed in the . . . [other] party conventions." The Labor party also nominated women to political office. Socialists recommended that at least "one
firm independent woman [sit] on every school board," and in October 1887,
they proposed Miss L. E. McCarthy, who was described as a thinker,
speaker, and owner of a business in the dry-goods line, for the position of
superintendent of schools.[32]

McCarthy's defeat fueled the devotion of radical women to the suffrage
cause. Albina Washburn, who had sided with Caroline Churchill in the
1881 dispute over male officers of the suffrage society, began editing a
"Woman's Column" for the *Labor Enquirer* in December, 1887. Devoted to
obtaining the franchise for women, Washburn and other female columnists
made passionate arguments for equal suffrage, published national news on
the movement, and described working-class women's efforts in Denver. Socialist women circulated suffrage petitions, for example, in March 1888.[33]

As working-class women turned their attention to suffrage during the
late 1880s, middle-class WCTU members renewed their interest in the
cause. The state union finally agreed to create a department of franchise in
1888 and chose Julia Sabine to head it. Sabine organized petition drives
and distributed thousands of suffrage newspapers, magazines, and leaflets
to unions throughout the state. Under her leadership, the WCTU demonstrated a new level of commitment to the suffrage movement.[34]

Like their sisters in the WCTU, clubwomen acted on their own concerns
throughout the 1880s. Toward the end of the decade, however, they too
focused increasingly on women's rights issues and asserted a belief in the
power of the ballot. A Denver Fortnightly Club member reactivated the
campaign in 1890 by calling for the first suffrage meeting in the state since
1881.[35] Clubwomen spearheaded the effort to revive the Colorado Equal
Suffrage Association but recruited members primarily through Denver
temperance unions.[36]

The Colorado WCTU approved a resolution at its 1891 convention,
which stated in part: ". . . we pledge ourselves to work with the equal
suffrage societies to arouse every woman in our state to a sense of her
responsibility for the power she could have by claiming the franchise."[37]
Personal conviction and the exhortations of their state union persuaded
WCTU members to pledge themselves to the suffrage cause.

By the early 1890s, then, WCTU's, women's clubs, and Social Leagues
formed the backbone of a new women's suffrage movement. In spite of
their differences in motivation and long-term goals, the women represent-
ing these organizations found common cause in the struggle to win the
right to vote. They united first in school election campaigns in which
women already could vote. Denver women had expressed varying levels of
interest in these elections over the years, though suffragists had spent considerable energy urging them to vote. Churchill had run editorials in the
early 1880s which described candidates and announced polling places and
hours in the *Antelope* and in her new paper, the *Queen Bee*.[38] The WCTU
had passed resolutions encouraging members to exercise the school franchise and in 1884 had sent 11,000 letters to Denver women regarding a

municipal election.[39] The Union Labor party had nominated a woman for school superintendent in 1887.

It was not until the early 1890s, however, that Denver women showed enthusiasm for school elections. Drawing on renewed concern with the franchise, veterans of the Colorado suffrage movement sparked women's interest in the 1891 Denver city election by nominating a woman to political office. A Mrs. Saxton lost her bid for a position on the school board, in part because she had entered the race only weeks before the election, but Denver women learned a great deal from this experience. Success in the political arena required more than enthusiasm.[40]

The rapidly shifting political climate in Colorado during the early 1890s, and especially the rise of populism, gave women new hope in the political process. Endorsement of equal suffrage by the Populist state government brought statewide attention to the issue and, for many Coloradans, granted legitimacy to suffragists' claims.[41] Denver women recognized this opportunity and urged their sisters to join the movement. Churchill wrote, for example, that "the women . . . of Colorado, should be up and dressed with their lamps trimmed and burning for the present legislature. This question of woman suffrage ought to carry in Colorado with the Populists in state controle [sic]." [42]

The Populist party proved to be women's greatest ally, and it unwittingly served their cause in another way as well. In an attempt to create coalitions and, in effect, to blur distinctions between populism and other party platforms, Republican and Prohibition county conventions and the Democratic State General Committee also endorsed equal suffrage.[43] Despite last-minute support by these parties, it was the Populists who ensured passage of the woman suffrage bill.

The Ninth General Assembly of the state of Colorado took up the question of woman suffrage in January 1893. House Bill 118, entitled "A bill for an act to extend suffrage to women of lawful age, and otherwise qualified, according to the provisions of article 7, section 2 of the Constitution of Colorado," was introduced to the House on January 16. The House carried it on March 8 and the Senate passed it, in slightly modified form, on April 3. Passage of this bill by the assembly paved the way for the ensuing referendum election.[44]

The state suffrage organization, which had changed its name to the Non-Partisan Equal Suffrage Association of Colorado to avoid antagonizing political parties, officially entered the campaign in April, 1893 with only twenty-eight members, and twenty-five dollars in its treasury.[45] With scarce resources to carry out campaign work, the association appealed to women by publishing letters suggesting that "from this time onward, the women's organizations throughout Colorado, with their hundreds of active devoted members, should consecrate time, energy and means to the attainment of . . . [woman suffrage]." [46]

In the first test of their strength Denver suffragists nominated Ione Hanna for a position on the school board. Hanna's earlier work in suffrage societies, WCTUs, and women's clubs enhanced her popularity with the female electorate. With the force of organized womanhood behind them and in response to the anti-suffragists' refrain that all Colorado women opposed the vote, Denver women elected Hanna to office in May 1893 following a bitter campaign.[47]

Denver clubwomen like Hanna assumed leadership positions in politics and in the suffrage association, while WCTU members organized much of the work. At the 1893 convention the state Union adopted a resolution demanding "full political equality . . . because it is a right" and heard their president recommend that "from now until election day our forces be turned toward Equal Suffrage." Denver WCTUs had already held eleven meetings, sponsored ten suffrage addresses, and passed out thousands of leaflets.[48]

Most of the "house to house canvassers, distributors of literature and others who rendered most valuable assistance," however, belonged to the "wage-earning class." Some of these women received small salaries from the suffrage association so that they could participate without undue economic hardship. The national labor movement also sent Leonora Barry (Lake), the Knights of Labor general investigator for women's work, to aid the Colorado campaign in 1893.[49]

With the help of Barry and Carrie Chapman Catt, who represented the National American Woman's Suffrage Association, Colorado women from many organizations labored tirelessly throughout the campaign. On election day, November 7, they worked the polls as they had done sixteen years earlier. By the afternoon of November 8 partial returns heralded the good news: Colorado women had won the right to vote.

Enthusiasm overflowed as women celebrated their victory; Churchill described women's reactions to the news in an article entitled "Western Women Wild with Joy Over Colorado's Election."[50] The WCTU offered tributes to the 36,698 men who "placed the ballot in the hands of the women of our glorious state!"[51] And women's clubs, like the Monday Literary Club of Denver, "voted to go to the polls for the first time as a group."[52]

The successful referendum campaign in Colorado proved virtually impossible to repeat in other states until much later. Colorado women had created a social reform movement with characteristics unique for the period. The growth of equal suffrage sentiment depended on the work of individual women but also on the mobilization of women's organizations without obvious connections to suffrage societies. WCTU's, women's clubs, and social leagues differed in their motivations and priorities. Over time their members transformed these organizations into potent vehicles for women's political power. Joint affiliations and shared interests enabled women's groups to draw on a vast array of ideas, experiences, and skills. Networking focused energies and built momentum. The victory in Colorado demonstrated the powerful potential of women when they crossed and recrossed organizational boundaries.

274

The Women's West

Notes

I would like to thank William H. Chafe and the Women's West editorial board for their supportive comments and suggestions. Special thanks also go to my friends Kathi George and Barbara Parker for editorial advice and to Jane Slaughter for typing several drafts of this manuscript.

1. Representative interpretations of Colorado and western women's suffrage movements can be found in Carrie Chapman Catt and Nettie Rogers Shuler, *Women Suffrage and Politics: The Inner Story of the Suffrage Movement* (New York: Charles Scribner's Sons, 1926); Alan P. Grimes, *The Puritan Ethic and Women Suffrage* (New York: Oxford University Press, 1967); T. A. Larson, "Dolls, Vassals, and Drudges—Pioneer Women in the West," *Western Historical Quarterly* 3, no. 1 (1972): 5–16; Billie Barnes Jensen, "Colorado Woman Suffrage Campaigns of the 1870s," *Journal of the West* 12, no. 2 (1973): 254–71.

2. Aggregate statistics of Denver from the compendium of the eighth and twelfth censuses of the United States show a population increase from 4,749 in 1860 to 133,859 in 1900; in 1900 there were 67,267 women and 66,592 men. Racial breakdowns for 1900 indicate 129,609 whites, 3,923 blacks, 325 Chinese and Japanese, and two Indians.

3. A WCTU member wrote, for example, "It is very difficult, in fact well-nigh impossible to separate work done in the name of the state organization and work done by the Unions of Denver." See "Pages from Our History Book," TS (n.d.) Colorado Women's Christian Temperance Union Papers, box 5, ff.3, hereafter cited as WCTU Papers. This and all other WCTU Papers cited are in the Western Historical Collections, University of Colorado at Boulder.

4. Joseph G. Brown, *The History of Equal Suffrage in Colorado* (Denver: News Job Printing Co., 1898), p. 5; Billie Barnes Jensen, "The Woman Suffrage Movement in Colorado" (Master's thesis, University of Colorado, 1959), pp. 14–21.

5. "Mrs. Eliza Thompson Dies and City Loses a Notable Woman Leader of Old Days" (n.p., 10 Aug. 1916) Florence Burton Scrapbooks, 1877–1939, Western History, Denver Public Library.

6. Elizabeth Cady Stanton, Susan B. Anthony, Matilda Joslyn Gage, et al., *History of Woman Suffrage*, 7 vols. (Rochester: vols. 1–4, Susan B. Anthony, 1881–1902; vols. 5–7, New York: National American Woman Suffrage Association, 1922, vols. 5–7), 3:717. Mary G. Campbell and Katherine Patterson wrote this portion of the *History*.

7. Brown, *The History of Equal Suffrage in Colorado*, pp. 7–10.

8. This two-step process of amendment, first by legislative approval of a referendum election and then by popular vote, proved difficult across the country. Suffragists held 480 such campaigns in thirty-three states from 1870 to 1910. Of these, seventeen resulted in referenda, but only in Colorado (1893) and Idaho (1896) did women win the right to vote. See Eleanor Flexner, *Century of Struggle, The Woman's Rights Movement in the United States*, 2d ed. (1959; reprint, Cambridge, Mass.: Harvard University Press, 1975), p. 238.

9. Territory of Colorado, *Proceedings of the Constitutional Convention Held in Denver, December 20, 1875 to Frame a Constitution for the State of Colorado Together with . . . the Constitution as Adopted . . .* (Denver: Smith-Brooks Press, 1907), Article 7, sects. 1, 2, p. 683. Section 1 states, in part, that "no person shall be denied the right to vote at any school district election, nor to hold any school district office, on account of sex." Section 2 reads as follows: "The General Assembly shall at the first session thereof, and may at any subsequent session enact laws to extend the right of suffrage to women of lawful age and otherwise qualified according to the provisions of this Article. No such enactment shall be of effect until submitted to the vote of the qualified electors at a general election; nor unless the same be approved by a majority of those voting thereon."

10. "Pioneer Woman is Dead After a Romantic Life," (n.p., n.d.), Florence Burton Scrapbooks, 1877–1939, Western History, Denver Public Library.

11. Jensen, "The Woman Suffrage Movement in Colorado," p. 41.

12. *Denver Daily Times*, 2 Oct. 1877, p. 4.

13. "The Lost Cause," *Rocky Mountain News*, 4 Oct. 1877, p. 2; hereafter cited as *RMN*.

14. "The Woman's Column," *RMN,* 7 Oct. 1877, p. 1.

15. *Colorado Antelope,* November 1879, pp. 1–2; hereafter cited as *Antelope.*

16. *Antelope,* December 1879, pp. 4–5.

17. *Antelope,* March 1880, p. 6.

18. *Minutes of the Women's Christian Temperance Union of Colorado, Tenth Annual Session* (Denver: Dove, Printer, 1889), p. 26, WCTU Papers, box 6, bndl. 1; hereafter cited as *Minutes WCTU.*

19. Brown, *History of Equal Suffrage,* p. 10, lists Shields as a member of the executive committee. See "Officers of the National Woman's Suffrage Association for 1880–1881," *Antelope,* August 1880, p. 6, for mention of Shields as an honorary vice president. See *Minutes WCTU,* various places and publishers, 1882–1888, WCTU Papers, box 6, bndl. 1, on the Shields presidency.

20. Untitled TS (n.d.), WCTU Papers, box 5, ff 3.

21. "A Call For a Women's Meeting," *RMN* 15 Jan. 1881, p. 8.

22. "The Woman Suffrage Convention," *Antelope,* February 1881, p. 22.

23. *Minutes WCTU* (Colorado Springs: Gazette Publishing Co., 1882), p. 9. WCTU Papers, box 6, bndl. 1.

24. "Jokes and Gossip About the Late Woman's Rights Convention," *Antelope,* February 1881, p. 23.

25. Lyle W. Dorsett, *The Queen City: A History of Denver* (Boulder, Colo.: Pruett Publishing Co., 1977), p. 46.

26. For more information on Denver women's clubs, see the Denver Fortnightly Club Papers, hereafter cited as DFC Papers; and the Monday Literary Club Papers, Western History, Denver Public Library.

27. Brown, *History of Equal Suffrage,* p. 8.

28. See DFC Papers and "Minutes of the National Women's Christian Temperance Union," TS (1880) WCTU Papers, box 5, ff. 3, for Hanna's Colorado WCTU treasurer's report for 1880.

29. See Karen J. Blair, *The Clubwoman as Feminist: True Womanhood Redefined, 1868–1914* (New York: Holmes and Meir Publishers, 1980) for an excellent analysis of feminism within the women's club movement. Although the General Federation of Women's Clubs endorsed suffrage relatively late (1914), Blair demonstrates that clubwomen were "feminists under the skin."

30. "Platform of the Union Labor Party," *Labor Enquirer,* 16 July 1877, p. 3. The *Labor Enquirer* was the official newspaper of the Union Labor party of Colorado and served labor interests in Colorado, Wyoming, and Nebraska.

31. "Social League," *Labor Enquirer,* 15 Oct. 1887, p. 5.

32. Both quotations are from the "Union Labor Party," *Labor Enquirer,* 15 Oct. 1887, p. 5.

33. See "Jokes and Gossip About the Late Woman's Rights Convention," *Antelope,* February 1881, p. 23 for Washburn's position and "Woman's Column," *Labor Enquirer,* 24 Dec. 1887, 18 Feb. 1888, and 31 March 1888.

34. *Minutes WCTU* (1889), p. 60.

35. See DFC Papers; Brown, *History of Equal Suffrage,* p. 16; "Mrs. Katherine Patterson Dead," *Denver Times,* 17 July 1902, p. 6.

36. Jensen, "The Woman Suffrage Movement," p. 63.

37. *Minutes WCTU* (Colorado Springs: Republic Publishing Co., 1891), p. 60, WCTU Papers, box 6, bndl. 1.

38. See, for examples, *Antelope* (March 1881), p. 28; *Queen Bee,* 8 Nov. 1882, p. 1. The *Queen Bee,* a weekly, superseded the monthly *Colorado Antelope* on 5 July 1882. Both were published by Churchill in Denver. Although Colorado newspapers report that Churchill continued publication of the *Queen Bee* until shortly before her death in 1926, surviving issues exist only through 4 Sept. 1895.

39. *Minutes WCTU* (Colorado Springs, Colo.: Daily State Republic Printing House, 1884), Resolution 3, p. 28, WCTU Papers, box 6, bndl. 1.

40. Jensen, p. 63. Women also petitioned the Colorado legislature for a constitutional amendment on women's suffrage during 1891.

41. See James E. Wright, *The Politics of Populism, Dissent in Colorado* (New Haven, Conn.: Yale University Press, 1974). Wright's analysis of electoral returns by county shows a positive correlation between the Greenback and later Populist vote and the pro-suffrage vote.

42. *Queen Bee,* 11 Jan. 1893, p. 1.

43. Stanton, et al., *History of Woman Suffrage,* 4:516.

44. See Jensen, "The Woman Suffrage Movement," pp. 66–71, for a detailed discussion of the women's suffrage bill.

45. Brown, *History of Equal Suffrage,* p. 18.

46. This general letter was published, for example, in the *Colorado Temperance Bulletin,* 1 June 1893, p. 3, WCTU Papers, ff. 10 (oversized).

47. Jensen, "The Woman Suffrage Movement," p. 64; DFC Papers.

48. *Minutes WCTU* (Denver, Colo.: John Dove, Printer, 1893), pp. 35, 48, 78–79, WCTU Papers, box 6, bndl. 2.

49. Stanton, et al., *History of Woman Suffrage,* 4:516.

50. *Queen Bee,* 29 Nov. 1893, p. 1.

51. *Minutes WCTU* (Denver: John Dove, Printer, 1894), p. 53, WCTU Papers, box 6, bndl. 2.

52. Mabel Mann Runette, "In a Changing World, A History of the Monday Literary Club, 1881–1939," TS (n.d.), p. 39, Monday Literary Club Papers, Western History, Denver Public Library.

19.

The Myth of the Urban Village: Women, Work, and Family Among Italian-Americans in Twentieth-Century California

MICAELA DI LEONARDO

In the same way that historians assumed that the Cult of True Womanhood "determined" how Euro-American women behaved, many social scientists assumed that the actions of immigrant women were "determined" by the traditional cultural values of their old homeland. Yet histories of eastern immigrant women reveal a previously unrecognized variety of work and family roles. In this article anthropologist Micaela di Leonardo uses the case-study method to explore the choices of four California Italian-American women. Her approach reveals considerable variety in the women's options and choices and suggests that we need to look at how older cultural values changed and how individual women's possibilities were shaped by family needs, kin support, and the work available to women in their new communities. This approach is one way to look at how older traditions changed in the West. After all, if women's actions were entirely shaped by older values, we could not explain cultural transformation; if ideas entirely shaped behavior, the West would still be a cluster of traditional "urban villages."

This article and di Leonardo's The Varieties of Ethnic Experience *strongly suggest that our models of ethnic adaptation have been based too much on the experiences of eastern immigrants. The regional economies of the West and the varying times of ethnic migrations to the region created for the same group different options than those available in the East. The western experience, shaped in this instance by the California economy and ethnic-racial hierarchy, was different.*

> The assumption that women are in some sense by-products of their culture, that they are not actors, but victims of a set of institutions and of values that support them is one which distorts our understanding of the historical process.
>
> —ALICE KESSLER-HARRIS[1]

The 1970s witnessed a great outpouring of scholarly and popular interest in American white ethnics, the result in part of a response to the civil-rights movements of black and other minority Americans. The descendants of the "second wave" (1880s–1920s) of European migrants were inspired both by white racism and by a defensive response to racist stereotypes of themselves by other white Americans, organized academic and action groups, and published confessional accounts, local histories, and newsletters. Nonethnic scholars, particularly social and labor historians, joined in this effort to make visible a hidden ethnic past. Feminist scholars focused on the hardships of immigrant women's lives and on women's own accounts of migration and settlement.[2]

Most of this scholarly and political activity, however, took place in the metropolitan regions of the industrial Midwest and the eastern seaboard and carried forward an earlier model of white ethnic life. In this model, second-wave European migrants (with the partial exception of Jews) were seen as stolid, traditional peasants who flocked mindlessly to American cities. There they created "urban villages," ethnically segregated neighborhoods that were exact replicas of their European village communities. Each migrating group, however, had a distinct "ethnic culture," which determined its social and economic fate in the New World and which was transmitted to children by ethnic mothers in the home. According to this view, the structure and functioning of ethnic families were determined by their cultures. Ethnic women lived out their primordial roles as mothers, wives, and the conservative bearers of tradition.[3] Historian Virginia Yans-McLaughlin, for example, claims that "Italian cultural traditions" determined a rigid role for the Italian and Italian-American woman:

A wife's clearly defined family and household responsibilities included obedience to her husband, family loyalty, thrift, and, most important, childbearing. . . . Peasants looked disdainfully at wives who left the home to work, and few did so unless poverty required it.[4]

This model is simply empirically wrong. European migrants had a wide variety of economic experiences and skills, they left their countries for many strategic reasons, and they settled in various areas of the United States in response to specific demands for their labor. The United States was experiencing rapid industrialization during the peak years of migration. Companies' needs for inexpensive labor were so great that many advertised in Europe and even hired recruiters to increase the flow of migrants. Native-born Americans were migrating from rural to urban areas at high rates, and there was little opportunity to enter agricultural production niches in the Midwest and East.

In urban areas, ethnically segregated neighborhoods were created as much by the racism of the majority society as by migrant cohesiveness. In any event, neighborhoods fluctuated constantly as different groups moved in and out, businesses opened and closed, and immigrants themselves changed houses, streets, neighborhoods, and cities. Stephan Thernstrom points out that most identified residents in nineteenth-century city censuses were destined to vanish in the decade between enumerations.[5]

These varying individuals had "culture" in the sense that we all have culture: they had an array of changing cognitive resources with which they understood and acted upon the world. In the course of interacting with others from their own regions, from other regions, and from the majority society, they (and the others) coded their perceived differences in terms of ethnicity. But these notions of ethnic sameness and difference changed constantly and were profoundly connected to economic contexts.

Similarly, the households that immigrants formed, while labeled by themselves and others as "ethnic," varied greatly depending on region, era, and economic circumstance. Households might be nuclear, three-generation, "doubled up" (two nuclear families), or consist of kin and boarders. Some households were work sites; others were not. And the roles that household members took on varied with all these factors as well.[6]

These criticisms of the urban ethnic model apply particularly to its vision of ethnic women. Historical evidence indicates that, for example, Italian women as well as men had extensive and varied work experiences before migration. And it has been estimated that Italian women's labor-force participation varied greatly in different United States cities. This variation is directly linked to the local availability of employment for women and gives the lie to notions that "Italian culture" commanded women to stay at home. Ethnic women played complex roles in their nego-tiation of work, household, and public life in the New World, roles that cannot be understood from within the straightjacket of the urban eth-nic model.[7]

Just as the new historical and contemporary research on white ethnicity has neglected the West generally, so Italian settlement in California and the lives of successive generations of California Italian-Americans have been little studied. The few studies available reflect the false ethnic, urban-village model—as do, of course, many Italian-Americans them-selves. The model remains culturally pervasive; it is reflected particularly in the current advertising images of warm, cozy, patriarchal, working-class ethnic families.[8]

The experience of Italians in California and in the West generally is quite distinct from that of their compatriots farther east. They began to arrive much earlier than the second wave, during the gold-rush years of the 1850s, and encountered an expanding regional economy entirely distinct from the industrializing East and Midwest. Mining, logging, fishing, and agriculture were paramount in the economy. There was little manufactur-ing, and as that developed in California, it was largely in the realm of food processing, rather than textiles or heavy manufacturing. The population mix, too, was unique. California had significant Mexican, Chinese, and later Japanese and Filipino populations, while the Midwest and East had no large racial minority populations in metropolitan areas until the twen-tieth century was well under way.

These economic and demographic factors meant that Italians settling in California, even though they were clearly as capital-poor as those who settled further east, encountered a greater variety of economic opportuni-ties and a very different social climate. Farming, fishing, skilled work, and small business were open to them in the rapidly expanding economy. And Italians were seen as "white" in the popular mind, and thus distin-guished from Mexicans and Asians, who filled the most despised and poorly-paying occupations. In contrast, in Boston from the mid-nineteenth to mid-twentieth century, first Irish, then Italians and French-Canadians filled these economic and social slots.[9]

California's distinct climate of economic and social opportunities had particular consequences for Italian-American women. First, there were greater and more varied employment opportunities. Agricultural ventures involved women as much as men (although mining, lumbering, and fishing did not). Wider small-business opportunities allowed for women's equal entrepreneurship, as in "mom and pop" stores. The relatively higher level of social tolerance of white ethnics in the West allowed Italian-American women to achieve social status and gentility decades earlier than could their *sorelle* further east.

The households in which these women lived varied by members' involvement with the economy and over time. In fact, because of the unique agricultural tilt of California's Italian-Americans and the late industrial development of the state's economy, we can discern among Italian-American households structures similar to the evolution of what Louise Tilly and Joan Scott call the "family economy" through the "family wage economy" to the "family consumer economy."[10]

Tilly and Scott coined these terms to describe the changes in the relations among women's roles, domestic life, and work life for the broad mass of families over the course of the industrialization of the economies of western Europe. The "family economy" refers to the preindustrial, rural agricultural or urban artisanal family in which the family itself was a productive unit. Economic production and human reproduction were intertwined, and children were put to work at home very young, or apprenticed out. "Family wage economy" refers to the industrialized working-class family: production and reproduction were split with the rise of the factory system; women's lives were newly punctuated by movements into and out of the industrial labor market. Until the advent of child-labor legislation, all family members worked for, and pooled, wages. The "family consumer economy" refers to family patterns in the modern era as standards of living rose and mothers became family-consumption administrators, child-rearing experts, and managers of family's social presentations to the outside world.

In the course of my anthropological research among fifteen core cross-class Italian-American families in northern California (and many others related to the core families), I collected family histories which illustrate the three different household forms and illuminate women's lives within and outside them. In this article I present the household and family lives of four middle-aged women informants from the 1920s to 1979. The women are of the same generation, are Italian-American, and are married or formerly married. They differ greatly in economic status and in many other ways, and these differences help us discern the importance of historical and economic factors to what we have narrowly construed as the operation of "cultural tradition."[11]

DOROTHY DIVINCENZO

Dorothy DiVincenzo's northern Italian grandparents were immigrants. When Dorothy was a child in the 1920s and 1930s, her immediate family lived in two fluctuating, interconnected households. The first consisted of Dorothy's mother's parents, a changing array of other relatives, and, periodically, Dorothy and her siblings. The second household of Dorothy's father's father and his second wife was economically, but not socially, interconnected with the nuclear-family household.

Dorothy and her siblings lived periodically in the farm household of her mother's parents because their own house was small, and Dorothy's mother worked outside the home and needed child-care assistance, and because the children's labor was crucial to the successful operation of the farm. Other relatives in the farm household, mostly single men, received domestic services and contributed to the operation of the farm. The family as a whole straddled the family economy and family wage economy: Dorothy's grandmother's household was largely economically self-sufficient; her parents' household relied on the mother's wages and the father's small-business profits.

These household and kin patterns are clearly related to the material circumstances of immigration and economic adaptation: Dorothy's grandparents emigrated early, with capital, intending to settle in California. They prospered in farming because San Francisco's population grew enormously in the latter half of the nineteenth century, resulting in an increased consumer demand; they prospered in a small business that catered to the increased needs of farming families. These well-established farms and businesses survived the 1930s Depression intact. Women worked both at farm and household tasks, and in small businesses outside the home. The malleable household moved children where their labor could be used, and where their care was less of a burden. Because several generations now lived in the area and because of rural isolation, co-ethnic kin and friends formed a large, intermarrying, regionally homogeneous network.

Dorothy DiVincenzo's nuclear family moved into the city in the late 1930s. Her father, wishing to educate his children so they could work off the farm, had liquidated his business interests and invested in a business partnership in the South San Francisco Bay. The family moved in shifts, Dorothy and a brother boarding first with other Italian families until their parents and younger siblings joined them. Dorothy's mother worked at the store, but after her husband sold it and went into a different business, she became involved in the parochial school Mother's Club and hired a cleaning woman. The family had moved into the family consumer economy pattern.

Dorothy and her siblings went to the local college and lived at home until they married. Dorothy met Jarus DiVincenzo, also a third-generation, generation, college-educated Italian-American (but of Sicilian origin) whose family was in business, and married him in the mid-1940s. She became a housewife, having four children in the following decade and a half. She and her husband purchased a home, and then a more expensive home. Their children went to parochial schools and then to college.

ANGELA CAPUTO

In contrast to Dorothy DiVincenzo, Angela Caputo and her siblings lived in a strictly nuclear household throughout the 1920s and 1930s. Her mother had emigrated to San Francisco without capital around 1910; learning English rapidly, she worked at a variety of nonfactory jobs: as a cook, a housekeeper, and a seamstress. Working first for wealthy Italian-Americans from her region, she soon switched to Anglo employers to gain higher wages and less exploitative working conditions. Angela's father had emigrated earlier from the same region of northern Italy, and had gravitated to skilled work in San Francisco after working in the mines.

After the couple married, Angela's father strained the ties with Angela's mother's kin and friends. Family social life then revolved around the father's local farming and peddling kin across the Bay. In order to support her family, however, Angela's mother returned to domestic work whenever she could secure adequate child care, and she established patron-client ties with a succession of Anglo employers.

Angela's father invested his small savings in Transamerica stock (the holding company of the Bank of America) and became comparatively wealthy as the stock price rose in the 1920s. The entire family then returned to Italy and lived on this capital. When the stock price dropped after the crash of 1929, the suddenly impoverished family returned to San Francisco and both parents went back to work. Angela's father died, Angela's eldest sister went to work, and Angela's mother's kin provided their lodging.

This household existed apart from its North Beach environment throughout the 1930s. Late, solitary emigration, urban settlement, and lack of capital had determined some aspects of the family's household and economic arrangements such as the presence of only two resident generations, the small number of kin in the area, low-paying jobs necessitating two household incomes, and the lack of kin-centered child care arrangements. Other reasons for their isolation were the dislike husband and wife felt for each other's relatives and the social dislocation resulting from sudden wealth followed by equally sudden poverty.

Angela Caputo's elder sister, Caterina, took on the major burden of supporting the family at the start of the 1940s. Angela's mother retired and kept house while each daughter went to work full-time after she graduated from high school. When Angela was well-established at a clerical job (handing her mother her paycheck), and the younger sister Lina had married and moved out, Caterina enlisted in the Women's Army Corps and spent the rest of the World War II years abroad. She sent money home to support her mother. After the war, when Lina and her husband had settled in San Francisco and he had taken over his father's small business, Angela went to work for the federal government abroad. After some years she returned home, but soon married a non-Italian and moved out of state. Caterina moved up the job ladder in her company, taking a management position; she bought a home in a suburb. Their mother remarried, to an Italian man her age, and the couple bought a home in the suburbs as well. Lina by now had several children and she remained out of the paid labor force.

Angela and her husband settled in San Francisco. Caterina and Lina's husband tried to assist Angela's husband, but his business ventures failed and the couple again moved out of state. They separated; Angela returned to San Francisco and moved in with Caterina until she could support herself at a clerical job.

LUCIA MORNESE

Lucia Mornese's family, like Angela Caputo's, was also composed of solitary, late-arriving emigrants who settled in San Francisco and lived in a nuclear household; but it had otherwise a very different history. Lucia's mother arrived in San Francisco from a midwestern city in the 1910s, a widow with a small child, to live with her dead husband's kin. She went to work in a factory, and her sister-in-law cared for her child during the day. She met and married Lucia's father, who was boarding with an Italian-American family, and they set up a household and had Lucia and another child in the next five years. Wishing to escape the pollution of the factory, Lucia's mother persuaded her husband to lease a small store from a friend, and they worked in it together. The oldest child was boarded periodically with a farm family, at one point for two years, and Lucia and her younger sister were cared for by a non-Italian woman in her home for some years until Lucia herself was old enough to do most of the child care. From the late 1920s until the late 1930s Lucia and her parents ran the store together, working in shifts. Lucia's brother found employment and left home early; her younger sister was seriously ill in the early 1930s and convalescent for several years.

Because they began a small business with little capital, and because they had been running it only a few years when the depression struck, Lucia Mornese's family could not bridge the gap to the family consumer economy. All able family members worked thoughout the 1930s, and Lucia's mother had little time to spare for managing the family's self-presentation.

The 1940s greatly altered the structure and economy of the Mornese household. Lucia took an office job, then qualified for a better-paying government clerical job. She persuaded her parents to sell their business; her mother bought an apartment building with the proceeds and retired from market labor. Her father tried another business venture; when that failed, he took a job in the same sort of business he had operated. Lucia's older brother enlisted in the military and married; the family disapproved, and further relations were strained. Lucia's sister took a technical training course, found a job, and remained at home, turning over her paycheck.

Late in the war, Lucia was transferred to Italy; there she met and married an Italian national of bourgeois background. Salvatore Mornese was anxious to live in the United States; although he knew that his economic fortunes would decline, he wished to leave an overbearing father and the disorganization of postwar Italy.

The couple returned to San Francisco and moved into one of the apartments owned by Lucia's mother. Lucia had Linda, and then went back to work, with her parents providing child care. Salvatore at first could only find work as a ditchdigger, but he soon learned English, and began to work in a series of clerical jobs. He took technical courses and was offered a better-paying position with a branch of a large firm on the periphery of the Bay Area. The couple bought a house in a new subdivision filled with ex-servicemen who had been situated in California during the war, and had returned with their families to settle there. Lucia had a second child. Her parents and her sister's family visited often, staying for weekends in the cramped quarters of the tiny house.

After four years, Salvatore was transferred by his firm to southern California. The family of four moved again and spent several years isolated from kin and making few new friends. Lucia, bothered by the weather, persuaded Salvatore to quit his job and return to San Francisco. They bought a house in a section of the city with a concentration of Italian-Americans and enrolled their children in parochial schools. Salvatore found a job with a different firm and Lucia went back to work as well.

As the 1960s progressed there were further changes in household structure and economy. Lucia's father died, and her mother moved in with the family; the house was so small that the living room became the mother's bedroom. Linda went to junior college but soon quit and went to work, paying room and board to her parents; her brother did the same a few years later. Lucia became very ill and was forced to retire and to apply for disability payments. Finally, Salvatore was fired by his firm a few months before he would have qualified for his pension program. He took another job and a substantial cut in salary.

The Morneses' move into the family consumer economy was qualified by Salvatore's language handicap and later by Lucia's illness and by corporate venality. The children's wages and mother's board payments, added to Lucia's disability check and Salvatore's salary, allowed the family to retain its home, but the couple had experienced considerable lowering of their standard of living by the late 1970s.

CETTA LONGHINOTTI

Cetta Longhinotti's father, a nothern Italian, began working seasonally in the countries of western Europe as a young adolescent in the early years of this century. His father had died and the burden of support for his mother and younger siblings had fallen upon him. After some years, he began migrating periodically to the United States. He married Cetta's mother during an interim in Italy, and she lived with his family until she migrated permanently in the early 1920s with her first child to join him in an agricultural company town near San Francisco. Cetta's father taught his wife to cook, as she had only done farm labor in her own family in Italy, and she then kept a boardinghouse for single Italian men who worked in the town's processing plant. Cetta's father, still sending money home to his Italian family, managed to accumulate sufficient capital through factory work to open a small business with a partner. When the partnership dissolved the family, now with two children, bought an orchard in the central valley with another Italian family. Cetta's mother worked in the orchard and smokehouse; the farm prospered, and the family, now with three children, began buying their own farm. The older children went to school and worked on the farm after school and during the summers.

When the depression struck, demand for the farm produce dropped so sharply that Cetta's father could not make his payments. The bank foreclosed, and the family, now with four children, was forced to move into housing provided by charity. The family grew their own food; Cetta's father worked at temporary jobs; and the two older children found after-school occupations. After some years, Cetta's father was injured on a construction job; the family then had to survive on the older children's wages and on the seasonal field labor in which the mother and all the children, even the smallest, participated.

The family's fortunes improved during the war years. Cetta's father found a steady custodial job; the family grew most of its own food, and the father peddled the surplus, increasing the family's income. Cetta graduated from high school and could not find a job in the farming town, so she moved to San Francisco to live with her godmother and found a clerical job there. Her younger sister Anna lived with her during the summers, earning enough money in low-level clerical jobs to pay for her own clothing, school books, and medical bills. Other siblings had married, enlisted in the Army, or were still living at home and working after school.

Cetta entered a network of young San Francisco Italian-Americans through her godmother's daughter, and later through her brother, who came to live with her after he was demobilized. North Beach provided a lively setting for evenings spent dining at Italian restaurants, going to films, and attending Italian-American-sponsored dances in rented halls. In this way Cetta met Joe Longhinotti, who was stationed nearby. They married, Joe was demobilized, and they settled in San Francisco, Cetta continuing her clerical job and Joe entering GI Bill-sponsored training. Cetta became pregnant and quit her job; and Joe went into partnership with the husband of Cetta's godmother's daughter, who was starting a bakery in a small town outside of San Francisco. Cetta and Joe, buying a small home on the GI Bill, moved just before their first child was born. They lived almost a decade in this small town. Cetta had two more children; she placed them in the local parochial school and made friends with several other Italian-American mothers.

As the town increased in population, supermarket chains began moving in and small food stores lost business. Joe and his partner decided to cut their losses and move to a more remote small town northeast of San Francisco: "We left that town with Safeway on our tail," Joe recalled. Cetta and Joe bought a much smaller house, and the three boys slept in one bedroom. Joe and his partner opened a new store; but his partner, having more capital, also invested in real estate.

The next five years were lonely, since they could not afford to telephone or visit with kin, and the family was not in the habit of writing letters. Over this period the partners once again experienced supermarket competition and decided to sell out. Joe and Cetta moved to the East Bay, where Joe had grown up, and Joe tried to go into business on his own. When that venture failed, fearing loss of the larger home they had begun to buy, Joe went to work for a larger bakery as a union baker. Cetta had taken a job as a clerical in a large department store to buy furniture for the new home; after a few years Joe decided to sell their house and buy a smaller one, and Cetta remained at work of necessity since Joe's income had been cut significantly.

These women's life histories underline and flesh out the critique of the urban village model. In the first place, these Italian-Americans arrived in California with a range of skills and past occupations—farming, artisanal work, mining, transportation. The women were not "traditional" peasant women, and their backgrounds varied: Angela Caputo's mother had an extensive food-preparation background, while Cetta Longhinotti's mother had never cooked at all.

Second, the life histories demonstrate the variety of original urban, small-town, and rural settlements for Italians and the likelihood of geographic mobility; all four women had lived in at least three different homes before they married. Third, these histories illuminate the connection between regional economy and ethnic occupational pattern. Responding to regional economic opportunities, these women's parents and grandparents farmed, ran small businesses, worked as artisans, and engaged in service work. In just these four families in the 1920s through 1940s the female members did clerical work, various kinds of farming and ranching, cooking and cleaning for hire, and ran a store and a boardinghouse.

Fourth, the households in which these women lived reflected variety in economic strategies. Farming and small business allowed the family economy pattern. Wage labor, depending on its remuneration and the number of household workers, correlated with the family wage or family consumer economy. And professional occupations ensured the latter pattern. These different household types offered different opportunities and restrictions for women. Lucia Mornese's mother was an equal partner in her husband's shop; Dorothy DiVincenzo's mother took advantage of her husband's business success to "retire" to middle-class housewife status; Cetta Longhinotti's mother's farm work with her husband isolated her, and she was ill-prepared to cope with his incapacitation during the depression; Angela Caputo's mother, on the other hand, nearly divorced her husband during the early 1920s, a decision which only her urban location and ability to secure employment allowed her to contemplate. And, while most women have had difficulties rising in the business world, Angela Caputo's sister Caterina was encouraged in her efforts by her status as family provider and by her lifelong spinsterhood. It was not "Italian culture," then, that determined these foremothers' attitudes towards work, home, and husband, but their own particular life experiences.

My middle-aged women informants had lives that varied greatly from one another. Yet they also had many experiences in common not only with one another but with most American women of their generation. All of these women worked in clerical jobs before they were married and were part of the mass involvement of white American women in the burgeoning clerical sector in the first half of this century. Many quit work after they married or when they became pregnant, in fulfillment of the homemaker ideal that came into prominence in the 1950s. All, however, returned to the labor force eventually; for three of the four women, their supplemental wages became a crucial component of the family budget.

Finally, these Italian-American women reflect the range of perspectives expressed by the women in the larger sample. While they all identified strongly as Italian-American, and three of the four were practicing Catholics, they interpreted the meaning of that identity differently. Cetta Longhinotti, who lived most of her life in rural areas and small towns, expressed attitudes closest to the model of the urban ethnic woman. She felt that motherhood was sacred, that children should obey their parents, that members of other racial groups were to be feared and distrusted. In contrast, Angela Caputo, the product of a purely urban North Beach upbringing, was a progressive, a feminist, and a very articulate anti-racist.

Dorothy DiVincenzo and Lucia Mornese, with small-business backgrounds but very different life experiences and economic statuses, expressed mixed attitudes. Dorothy DiVincenzo was training to re-enter the labor force during my fieldwork; she eagerly articulated her resentment of her husband's lack of involvement in childrearing and her explicit desire to gain parity with him through leaving the home for paid work. Although she had been a very involved full-time mother, she wanted to relinquish control over and responsibility for her children. Lucia Mornese, on the other hand, had retired from her clerical position as a result of illness and saw her new leisure activities, many of which involved her kin, as part of a new liberated life. She had no need to control her children, as they actively involved themselves in her plans. She was successful in negotiating new housework responsibilities with Salvatore, and even in supporting her daughter-in-law's struggle to force Lucia's son to do housework. Lucia, however, consistently expressed racist attitudes, particularly toward recent Chinese migrants to San Francisco. Dorothy DiVincenzo did not, but

Dorothy was isolated from much contact with other races in an entirely white suburb.

These women's past lives and present experiences, when considered in the context of California social and economic history, help to give the lie to the urban villager model of white ethnic life. They show us the importance of regional economy, of historical era, and of women's autonomous experiences in the shaping of ethnic women's lives. Most importantly, they demonstrate the fact that "ethnic culture" is not an unchanging construct passed down by ethnic mothers, but the living result of the intersection of all members of a particular group with the economy and population of a particular region in a particular era. Ethnic women in the United States have not been simply the conservative bearers of tradition, and these California Italian-American women's life histories help us to construct a fresh vision of their varying experiences.

Notes

1. Alice Kessler-Harris, "Comments on the Davidoff and Yans-McLaughlin Papers," *Journal of Social History* 7, no. 4 (1970–71): 446–59, esp. p. 446.

2. For the white ethnic renaissance see Andrew M. Greeley, *Why Can't They Be Like Us? America's White Ethnic Groups* (New York: Macmillan, 1971); Michael Novak, *The Rise of the Unmeltable Ethnics* (New York: Macmillan, 1971). An example of American historians' interest in the hidden ethnic past is "Labor and Community Militance in Rhode Island," special issue of *Radical History Review* 17 (1978). Scholary interest in immigrant women's lives is exemplified by Miriam Cohen, "Italian-American Women in New York City, 1900–1950: Work and School," in Milton Cantor and Bruce Laurie, eds., *Class, Sex and the Woman Worker* (Westport, Conn.: Greenwood Press, 1977), pp. 120–43; Judith Smith, *Remaking Their Lives: Italian and Jewish Immigrant Family, Work and Community in Providence, Rhode Island, 1900–1940* (Ph.D. diss., Brown University, 1981).

3. This model is articulated in Herbert Gans, *Urban Villagers: Group and Class in the Life of Italian-Americans* (New York: Free Press, 1962); Nathan Glazer and Daniel P. Moynihan, *Beyond the Melting Pot*, 2d ed. (Cambridge, Mass.: MIT and Harvard University Presses, 1970).

4. Virginia Yans-McLaughlin, "A Flexible Tradition: South Italian Immigrants Confront a New York Experience," *Journal of Social History* 7, no. 4 (1974): 429–45, esp. p. 431.

5. This alternative model is documented in Micaela di Leonardo, *The Varieties of Ethnic Experience: Kinship, Class, and Gender Among Italian-Americans in Northern California* (Ithaca, N.Y.: Cornell University Press, 1984), chap. 2. See Stephan Thernstrom, *The Other Bostonians: Poverty and Progress in an American Metropolis, 1880–1970* (Cambridge, Mass.: Harvard University Press, 1973), p. 232.

6. See John Modell and Tamara Harevan, "Urbanization and the Malleable Household: An Examination of Boarding and Lodging in American Families," in Tamara Harevan, ed., *Family and Kin in Urban Communities, 1700–1930* (New York: New Viewpoints, 1977), pp. 164–86; Donna Gabaccia, "Houses and People: Sicilians in Sicily and New York City, 1890–1930" (Ph.D. diss., University of Michigan, 1979).

7. Miriam Cohen, "From Workshop to Office: Italian Women and Family Strategies in New York City, 1900–1950" (Ph.D. diss., University of Michigan, 1978).

8. See di Leonardo, *Varieties of Ethnic Experience*, chap. 5 for an analysis of this phenomenon.

9. See ibid., chap. 2.

10. Louise A. Tilly and Joan Scott, *Women, Work and Family* (New York: Holt, Rinehart and Winston, 1978).

11. Parts of the following analysis appear in di Leonardo, *Varieties of Ethnic Experience,* chap. 2. All names and some other details have been changed to protect informants' anonymity.

20.

The Impact of "Sun Belt Industrialization" on Chicanas

PATRICIA ZAVELLA

This article, like the previous one, challenges the belief that choices about women's work are determined by traditional ethnic values. While di Leonardo uses a case-study approach to demonstrate variety in the choices made by women of one ethnic group, Patricia Zavella uses the sociological survey to explore the work choices of Chicanas. Zavella surveyed Chicanas who had young children and who worked in the Albuquerque electronics and apparel industries in the 1970s and 1980s to discover why they worked, how they balanced work and family, and how they felt about their choices. This look at the twentieth-century "urban frontier" of women's wage work takes into account changes in the occupational structure as well as the personal meaning of the decision to work outside the home. Zavella reveals a variety of feelings, not the uniform response that would result if a single and unified set of cultural values were the sole determinant of Chicana behavior. This way of looking at the impacts of ideology and economics on cultural change in the modern West reveals women as important actors who help shape their culture.

Historically, Mexican-American women have had lower labor-force participation rates than Anglo or black women. In 1960 only 24.4 percent of Chicanas were employed, as compared to 34.5 percent of Anglo women.[1] Explanations of these disparities have relied on a model of cultural determinism that identified traditional cultural values and norms as the causal factors. Many authors assume that traditional family values alone determine whether Chicanas will enter the labor market, and that Chicanas violate those values when they work outside the home. According to the "traditionalist" model, Chicano "machos" prefer that their wives not work; since Chicanas value their homemaker roles over taking jobs, they submit to their husbands' wishes. A corollary notion is that acculturation occurs when Chicanas are employed and, consequently, they lose traditional family values.[2]

Over the last two decades, however, Chicanas have rapidly moved into the paid work force. Between 1960 and 1970, for example, married Chicanas entered the labor force at a national rate of 15 percent higher than their white and black counterparts.[3] In 1970, the gap in labor-force partici-

San Antonio cigar factory workers on strike, 1933. Courtesy *San Antonio Light* Collection, Institute of Texan Cultures.

pation rates had narrowed; 43 percent of all women worked as compared to 36 percent of Chicanas. By 1980, the gap between Chicanas and other women workers nearly disappeared: 52 percent of all women worked while 49 percent of Spanish-origin women were employed.[4]

At the same time, Chicanas consistently have had higher unemployment rates than Anglo women. In 1970, 14 percent of women of Mexican origin in the United States were unemployed, compared to 9 percent for all women. By 1980 Chicana unemployment decreased to 10 percent while that for Anglo women was 8 percent.[5] Technically, the unemployed are persons who are actively seeking jobs and are available for work. The official unemployment rate, of course, does not include the many "discouraged workers"—those who have completely given up the search for work. Groups with high unemployment rates usually also have higher numbers of discouraged workers.[6] The historically high Chicana unemployment rates, whether official or not, indicate that more Chicanas would work if they could find jobs. In addition, since Chicanas tend to have larger families than Anglo women, the availability of child-care facilities may have a greater influence on their ability to remain in the work force.

The traditionalist approach neither predicted nor explained these trends. Instead of using the data to challenge the traditionalist perspective, adherents of the model merely modified it and claimed that declining family values explained Chicanas' recent entrance into the labor force. Most au-

thors who support cultural determinism do not actually examine Chicanas' values and beliefs. A recent empirical study, however, investigated
how traditional values affect Chicana and Anglo women's labor-force participation. Vilma Ortiz and her colleagues found that "the cultural argument was not supported; traditional attitudes did not have a stronger impact for Hispanic females."[7] In addition, these researchers found that the
significant factor influencing Chicanas' commitment to the labor force was
prior work experience. Women with unskilled, low-paying jobs tend to
prefer homemaking, while those who have more stable jobs want to continue working. Ortiz argues that the availability of jobs, not traditional
culture, determines whether Chicanas are committed to the labor force
or not.[8]

   The traditionalist approach is ahistorical and does not consider variations or changes in regional economies. Yet regional economies are the
products of distinct patterns of accumulation and industrial development.
Storber and Walter show how the "spatial division of labor," or the regional variation in industrial location, is the product of managerial strategies for minimizing production costs. Managers choose locations for their
industries with lower labor costs to allow for new, less costly ways of
organizing production and workers.[9] Uneven regional development provides varied work opportunities for women workers. For example, two
studies show that even though Chicanas are generally segregated into the
lowest-paying jobs in most communities, there is regional variation in the
types of jobs they hold, in their employment rates, and in discrimination.[10]
The traditionalist argument also assumes that values determine behavior
by viewing the lack of employment as voluntary. Analyses of Chicana unemployment rates help to further illuminate the model's deficiencies.

   Rather than assuming that culture determines whether Chicanas enter
the labor force, a more fruitful approach is to examine changes in local
labor markets, structural defects in the regional economies, and the impact of women's work on their families. Such an approach provides a corrective to the traditionalist perspective which perpetuates the stereotype of
the reclusive, passive Mexican woman who devotes herself to motherhood, housework, and her man. Instead, I argue that Chicanas have always
placed a high value on work outside the home.

   This article analyzes data from a research project on women's work and
family strategies in the context of "Sun Belt industrialization" in Albuquerque, New Mexico.[11] In-depth interviews with twenty-two married
Chicana workers were conducted;[12] informants were employed in either
electronics or apparel factories, and had at least one child under the age of
six. These women had a mean age of twenty-nine and an average of two
children. Most of the women were entry-level electronics assemblers or
sewing-machine operators who had worked at their jobs for about three
years.

   Two related processes affected the relationship between work and family life for these women. Recent industrialization in Albuquerque created
jobs primarily for women. The state of the local labor market, including

the availability of jobs women consider to be good ones and the instability of men's jobs, was the primary reason Chicanas chose to enter and to remain in the labor force. Concurrently, women's work dramatically altered Chicano families. The evidence does not indicate a decline in family values, but a more complicated adaptation to new circumstances. The impact of women's work on Chicano families depended on factors such as the ages of children, the availability of child care, and the relative need for the women's wages. Furthermore, traditional values and norms should be viewed as family ideology, a set of values and beliefs which prescribe proper behavior for women and men and which are symbolically opposed to the world of work.[13] Women's views about being working mothers respond to the prevalent family ideology. All these related individual and familial processes must be viewed in the larger context of regional industrialization.

SUN BELT INDUSTRIALIZATION

The state of New Mexico has been slow to industrialize. As late as 1970, manufacturing jobs accounted for only about 6 percent of total employment. The service sector (including trade, finance, and public administration) provided over 60 percent of New Mexico's jobs.[14] Between 1960 and 1970, however, important changes began turning New Mexico into a southwestern industrial center. Significant growth of industrial jobs in the state has occurred because of the expansion of two industries: apparel and electrical machinery. Growth in both industries was dramatic; employment in electrical machinery manufacturing grew by 353 percent[15] and it quadrupled in the apparel industry.

Most of the recent industrial growth took place in Albuquerque, the state's largest city. Prior to industrialization, Albuquerque's economy was based on "guns and butter"—the military and related enterprises—and the public sector.[16] Besides the state of New Mexico, other large employers included Sandia Laboratories, Kirtland Air Force Base, the Veterans Hospital, and Air Force Special Weapons Center. Albuquerque, as the commercial center of the state, also provided a large number of sales and service jobs.

Albuquerque attracted manufacturers for several reasons.[17] A low wage scale existed, especially for women's jobs. The median pay for female manufacturing jobs during the 1970s was 44 percent of the wages for jobs held by males. In electrical machinery, for example, women earned about 44 percent of the wages of men, while in apparels women earned almost 70 percent of men's wages.[18] Taking inflation into consideration, average earnings in Albuquerque were almost 10 percent lower than national levels.[19] Few manufacturing plants are unionized, which partially accounts for lower wage rates. Another reason manufacturers chose Albuquerque was the available labor force, especially women.[20] In Bernalillo County, the unemployment rate of Anglo women was only 5 percent in 1960, but the figure grew to 6 percent in 1970 and to over 7 percent in 1979. During the same years, Spanish-surnamed women had unemployment rates of 5 percent, 8 percent, and 9 percent, respectively.[21]

The recent national recessions notwithstanding, Albuquerque has become a center of "Sun Belt industrialization.[22] Beginning in the late 1960s several companies—GTE Lenkurt, Singer Fridan, Levi Strauss, and Ampex—opened plants in or near the city. Subsequently, other firms such as Motorola, Digital, Honeywell, General Electric, Signetics, Sperry Flight Systems, and Ethicon built plants in Bernalillo County. Between 1969 and 1979 employment in manufacturing in Albuquerque grew more than 100 percent, while total employment increased only 60 percent.[23] By 1980 manufacturing was the third largest sector of Bernalillo County's economy, employing over 218,000 workers.[24]

Changes in industrial employment affected men and women differently. The bulk of new jobs were "women's jobs." In electronics the female labor force grew 680 percent; by 1970, women constituted 46 percent of the total electronics labor force. In the traditionally female apparel industry, the number of women employed increased fourfold, while male employment increased only 300 percent. By 1970, women formed 82 percent of the apparel labor force. These increases in women's employment occurred during a period when total manufacturing in the state dropped by 4 percent between 1960 and 1970. Male jobs, however, accounted for 16 percent of the decrease, while female employment increased by 58 percent. Women grew from 16 percent of the total manufacturing labor force in 1960 to almost 27 percent in 1970.[25] In sum, while manufacturing declined in the state as a whole, the electronics and apparel industries, which employed increasingly greater proportions of women, grew tremendously.[26]

While the growth of industrial jobs in Albuquerque primarily benefited women, Chicanas were affected the most. In the period of pronounced industrial growth, a large number of Chicanas entered the labor force. Between 1960 and 1970, the labor-force participation rate of Anglo women increased 18 percent while that of Chicanas rose by 66 percent.[27] The employment rate of Anglo women was 43 percent in 1970 and 40 percent for Spanish-surnamed women. By 1980, 52 percent of white women and 50 percent of Hispanic women were in the Albuquerque labor force.[28] Clearly, a significant proportion of Chicanas entered Albuquerque's labor market once industrial expansion began.

The women interviewed for this study entered the labor force during this time of rapid growth in the labor market. However, they were interviewed in 1982–1983 during a period of economic recession. Questions focused on two points: How has industrial employment affected these women? Have their family values changed?

WOMEN'S DECISIONS TO SEEK WORK

Our informants entered the labor force, as women increasingly are doing, when their children were under the age of six. The women had to secure satisfactory child-care arrangements; in addition, they struggled with the demands of caring for young children after work and the ideology that mothers—especially those with young children—should not work. According to the traditionalist viewpoint, we would expect these women to leave the labor force as soon as they could; but we instead found a more complicated situation.

When the women originally decided to seek wage work, most of them were in difficult financial situations and their primary motivation for seeking work was economic. While a few were working when they married, most started work after marriage. Many of the women entered the labor force when their husbands were either unemployed or earning low wages. The common refrain was: "The way it is now, everything's too high and we can't make it on one check." In the majority of couples, both husband and wife agreed that the woman should work. Eight of these husbands preferred that their wives not work, but agreed with the decision. In these cases, women's wage work was an economic strategy for families which had little choice.

Five of the twenty-two women wanted a job primarily to get out of the house; generally their spouses supported their decision. These women were critical of the boredom of housewifery. "I decided it (homemaking) wasn't for me," one woman noted. Sometimes they wanted personal satisfaction. One very independent woman said simply, "I'm a self-supporter."

WOMEN'S WORK HISTORIES

An examination of the women's work histories and family circumstances sheds light on the question of declining familism. Most of the women moved through a succession of low-paying, dead-end jobs as waitresses, fast-food workers, or cashiers before they acquired their current jobs. The apparel workers usually knew someone, often a relative, who already worked in the plant and notified them when the company was hiring; some of these women had not worked at a factory before. Electronics workers, however, had longer work histories and a wider base of comparison. These women tended to have had prior work experience in electronics production (as well as in apparel factories) and often had some technical training. Electronics workers usually applied for their present jobs without prior knowledge that the company was hiring and without the help of someone who was already employed there. These women heard through their training or through social networks that electronics factories pay better and provide good benefits. Electronics employees had worked less time on the job than apparel workers.

Compared to previous jobs, these women achieved job mobility in terms of pay, benefits, and job security. The benefits of factory work in particular, especially medical insurance and paid maternity leaves, were great improvements over their previous fringe-benefit packages. Women often received better job benefits than their husbands, so couples relied on the woman's medical insurance, for example.

Many women believed that their factories were relatively good places to work. Several women compared their present jobs to previous ones or to the general Albuquerque labor market. They were aware that in general, as one informant appropriately stated, "Albuquerque's (jobs are) always underpaid." However, women characterized the wages in electronics as "the best you can find in Albuquerque." Women recounted news stories regarding new firms offering employment, in which job seekers numbering in the hundreds waited for hours for the privilege of submitting job-application forms. Referring to these stories, or to the experiences of relatives who were chronically unemployed, one woman summed up the general view: "There's no place else. It's hard to get a job and I feel lucky to have this one."

THE ECONOMIC CONTRIBUTION OF WOMEN'S WAGES

It is important to emphasize the financial contribution that these women made to their families; their wages cannot be seen as supplemental. Electronics workers earned an average $5.25 an hour, and generally were the best paid blue-collar women in Albuquerque. There was considerable variation in wage rates for apparel workers, however, since they were paid on the piece-rate system. Depending on how fast they sewed, apparel workers earned between $4.00 and $7.00 an hour. On the average, electronics workers earned about $12,000 a year, while apparel workers earned about $9,500 annually.

One-third of our informants earned more than their husbands earned. These women were the economic mainstays of their households, since they earned over 60 percent of the total family income. The other women earned between 30 and 59 percent of the family income. Clearly, all these women made significant contributions to the support of their families.

But more than the amount of money that they contributed, women's wages were pivotal in terms of the families' economic stability. When both husband and wife were working, the family was relatively secure. Unfortunately, many of the women's husbands, particularly those who worked in construction, were periodically unemployed. These families were continually moving between the stability of two incomes and the hardship of having one wage. Therefore, the woman's income saved the family from financial disaster when husbands were laid off, and assured relative stability when he was employed.

The family incomes of the informants were slightly lower than those of other dual-worker families in Albuquerque, averaging $24,425 and ranging from $13,500 to $40,000 a year. The mean income of all families with two or more workers in Albuquerque was $26,846 in 1979.[29] However, compared to the rest of the state, where the median family income was $16,930 in 1979, our informants were relatively well-off. New Mexico Hispanics had a median family income of only $13,800 at this time, a significant disparity from other ethnic groups.[30]

The lives of the Chicanas surveyed in Albuquerque contrasted sharply

with those of their mothers. The majority were born and raised in Albuquerque, while their parents were born in rural areas and later migrated to
the city. Further, most of the women's mothers were housewives. When
they compared their standards of living with those of their kin from rural
areas, our informants' higher incomes were probably quite noticeable.

It is important to recall, however, that these were relatively young families with great economic needs. The men had not yet reached their peak
earnings, and many of them received low wages which were eroded by
inflation. Several of the women had recently taken maternity leaves which
considerably lowered the families' incomes. Since most of these couples
were buying or constructing homes, they had large payments to make.
When husbands went to work after periods of unemployment, there was
usually a time when the couples had to catch up on previously unmet
needs. Given the fluctuations and loss of real wages by husbands, the
women's wages were essential for family survival. These couples were
caught up in a national trend, in which the proportion of families with two
or more wage earners is increasing.[31] Most of our informants resigned
themselves to the fact that, as one woman said, "Nowadays, both people
have to work." Rather than diminished devotion to the family, changes in
the economy pushed these women into the labor force.

Taking jobs to provide financial support for the family could be seen as
an expression of traditional family values. But the women's economic contribution to their families was but one aspect of their commitment to the
labor force. Another important factor was the satisfaction they received
from their jobs.

JOB SATISFACTION

To gauge job satisfaction, informants were asked a number of questions:
what they liked and disliked about their jobs and their advantages and disadvantages; they were also asked to rank ten qualities of the job. Generally, the women believed that job security was the most important aspect
of a job, and most of them believed they had secure jobs. The women
chose pay as the second most important feature, and all of the women believed they had good pay. Most also believed they had good benefits, as
illustrated by one woman who observed, "That's the main reason I went
back to electronics." The women were generally satisfied with the economic features of their jobs. Beyond issues of remuneration, though, there
were important differences between electronics and apparel workers'
views regarding their jobs. These differences, of course, stem from the
distinct production processes.[32] Electronic workers, particularly those
who did not work as assemblers, had higher job satisfaction than apparel
workers.

In terms of the work process, two-thirds of the women believed they
could work at their own pace. Unfortunately, because of production quotas
in both industries, which women generally considered a disadvantage of
their jobs, self-pacing meant that women pressured themselves to work

fast. Assemblers lamented the physical discomforts (such as eyestrain, backaches, and headaches) resulting from the fast pace and the monotony. Apparel workers who sewed fast and who produced more than the production quota had more job satisfaction. These women believed that the piece-rate system allowed them to make good money. Women who missed or barely made their quotas disliked the pressure of the piece-rate system. Those women not meeting production quotas were either pressured to quit or, after a series of warnings, were fired. It is not surprising that the women found their work challenging.

Virtually all of the women in both industries believed their work place was safe. Furthermore, all of them said that their supervisors were good, and that there were ample opportunities to converse with co-workers.

The jobs had several disadvantages. Apparel workers had shortened work weeks during the 1982 recession, which most disliked. They preferred a forty-hour week so they could make steady wages. In addition, most of the women believed they were not paid well enough for the work performed, and some of them would have liked more appreciation for a job well done. Only half of the women believed they had opportunities for promotions.

Despite these reservations, however, the majority of the women liked their jobs, but for varied reasons. An assembler said: "I enjoy it. It's easy." A machine operator reported, "I like the work; I think it's interesting." A materials handler liked the autonomy of her job because "No one bothers me." An inspector cherished the opportunity to interact with friends and co-workers; "I like going to work," she said, "I get to talk to different people. It makes me forget half of my problems." Another assembler made an analogy between her department and home, saying, "It's like a family." A quality control worker could find nothing wrong with her job, claiming, "I like everything about that job." These comments were not unusual; on the whole, the women valued their jobs.

WOMEN'S VIEWS ON BEING WORKING MOTHERS

Women's views on their status as working mothers reflected the contradictions between economic circumstances, on the one hand, and family obligations and ideology on the other. Traditional family ideology asserts that women should stay home and care for their families, especially young children. Finding the balance between these "competing urgencies" is difficult and filled with frustrations.[33] In an attempt to understand their values and attitudes, women were asked to indicate whether they agreed or disagreed with several statements regarding gender roles and women's work. The women's responses to these statements illustrated both how they construct the meaning of family and how their circumstances tempered their beliefs and values. Probably the most striking aspect of the women's views was their variation; they ranged from traditional to egalitarian viewpoints; some were ambivalent and even inconsistent.

Given the state of Albuquerque's economy, with inflation and relatively high male unemployment, it was not surprising that virtually all the women agreed with the following statement: "Women need to work to help their families with the high cost of living." Their responses to other economic issues, however, were less clear. Most of the women disagreed with the notion that it is better for a marriage if a husband earns more money than his wife; of the six who agreed, only two earned more than their husbands. Apparently, even if a woman earned higher wages than her husband, she did not necessarily believe that he should earn more. In addition, the majority of the women disagreed with the more general view that men should get most of the higher-paying jobs because they have families to support. These women's experience with relatively high-paying jobs led them to reject the view that men should be primary breadwinners. According to several women, "Women have to support families too."

Child-care arrangements profoundly affected the women's views on being working mothers. Two-thirds of the women had their husbands or female kin to care for their children. Others took their children to a private baby sitter or a day-care center. Many of these women had frequently changed child-care providers and had bad experiences with former baby sitters. When we interviewed them, though, most were generally satisfied with their child-care arrangements.

Despite this satisfaction, some women felt sorrow and guilt about leaving their young children in child care. The statement that elicited the most responses was: "Working mothers miss the best years of their children's lives." Most of the women agreed with this statement, and believed that by going to work while their children were young, they missed those important "first steps" in the children's development. Several of the women delayed entering the labor force, not only because they did not want to leave infants with a sitter, but because they wanted to enjoy their children's developmental progress. For example, Mrs. Armijo[34] wanted to wait until her daughter was one year old before going back to work, but circumstances forced her into the labor force for three months when her daughter was six months old. Mrs. Montoya was defensive on this issue. When her baby-sitter informed her that her son said the word "cookie," she replied: "Yeah, I know, I taught him how." She went on, "I felt like I heard it first."

Working while having young children placed certain demands on women's time. Women had to miss work to take their children for medical care. Many women indicated that the hardest aspects of a working mother's life were the lack of time to accomplish everything that needs to be done at home and their fatigue from working and parenting very active youngsters. It is understandable, then, that the majority of women agreed with the statement: "It would be much better all around if a woman can stay home and take care of her family instead of having to work."

Regarding the household division of labor, we found variation. Five of the women had relatively egalitarian divisions of housework with their husbands. Couples in these households either divided the work (she washed clothes while he took out the garbage, for example), or both performed the same chores. Several of these couples negotiated a more equitable division of labor after the women complained they were doing too much. A second group of nine women performed most of the housework. The remaining couples fell between these extremes, with women taking on a greater share of housework. However, three-quarters of the couples divided the child-care chores equitably. These differences between the sharing of housework and of child care was reflected in the women's responses to several statements. Every woman agreed that "taking care of the children should be shared equally between husband and wife." Furthermore, most of the women agreed that "sometimes I think that I cannot do enough for my family when I work," and "that sometimes I feel it is unfair that I have to work and also spend so much time taking care of my home and my children." [35]

Finally, women were asked if they ever thought of quitting their present jobs. Most of them had considered leaving, but for varied reasons, usually the frustrations or boredom of the work itself, the pressures of the piece rate or of managing home duties and a job, and the desire for higher wages (especially by apparel workers). Only a few of the women wanted to stay home and rear their children. The others wanted better opportunities, specifically a job that paid more and allowed some advancement. Most of the electronics workers who wanted better jobs preferred to remain in the electronics industry.

One woman's statements illustrated how most women vacillated between their desires to support their families and to care for their young children at home. When asked whether she ever thought of quitting, she stated: "I always wanted to work, it's a habit I have. I can't be without work. I can't stay home; it's so boring. I have to work or else I won't be happy." Later, however, when asked whether she would quit if she did not have to work, she contradicted herself: "It's kind of hard. I do like to work, but I think my family is more important." She realized she was contradicting herself, so she joked: "Maybe I like to work because I need the money."

Whether or not these employed Chicanas held traditional views regarding family, the economic needs of their families often took precedence. Each family must find the balance in meeting these competing needs, and women constructed meanings for their decisions that took each need into consideration. Thus, despite the women's misgivings about not being able to spend time with their children, most agreed that: "Working is an important part of my life that would be hard for me to give up," and "Even if I didn't need the money, I would continue to work." Finally, virtually all of the women believed that their work did not conflict with family responsibilities.

An analysis of the changing local economy—including job opportunities for women—and its multiple effects on women and, in turn, on the family economy, must be examined before traditional norms can be interpreted as labor-force determinants. Contrary to the traditionalist viewpoint, those Chicanas interviewed for this study indicated a strong commitment to their jobs. Women's employment had a significant positive effect on the family economy. The impact on family ideology, however, was more complex. Once Chicanas entered the labor market, some of their views regarding family changed, while others remained the same. The extent to which women accepted the prevalent ideology or constructed a new meaning depended on their particular work histories and job satisfaction, their economic contribution to family economic status, and the demands at home. In other words, rather than continuing an ideological separation between work and family, based on the assumption that family values determine women's labor-force participation, one must investigate the reciprocal effects of work and the family on women employees. Clearly, a combination of factors determines whether Chicanas prefer to continue wage work or not, factors similar to those that influence other American working-class women.

Notes

I want to thank Micaela di Leonardo, Denise Segura, Elizabeth Jameson, and Albert Camarillo for their helpful comments on an earlier draft of this paper.

1. Rosemary Santana Cooney, "Changing Labor Force Participation of Mexican American Wives: A Comparison with Anglos and Blacks," *Social Science Quarterly* 56, no. 2 (1975).

2. See Elizabeth M. Almquist and Juanita L. Wehrle-Einhorn, "The Doubly Disadvantaged: Minority Women in the Labor Force," in Ann H. Stromberg and Shirley Harkess, eds., *Women Working, Theories and Facts in Perspective* (Palo Alto: Mayfield Publishing Co., 1978); Walter Fogel, *Mexican Americans in Southwest Labor Markets*, UCLA, Mexican American Study Project, Advance Report 10, 1967; Roberta V. McKay, "Employment and Unemployment among Americans of Spanish Origin," *Monthly Labor Review*, April 1974; Cooney, "Changing Labor Force Participation"; Vernon M. Briggs, Jr., Walter Fogel, and Fred H. Schmidt, *The Chicano Worker* (Austin: University of Texas Press, 1977). For a full critique see Patricia Zavella, "Women, Work and Family in the Chicano Community: Cannery Workers of the Santa Clara Valley" (Ph.D. diss., University of California, Berkeley, 1982).

3. Cooney, "Changing Labor Force Participation," p. 253.

4. U.S. Department of Labor, *Employment and Training Report of the President* (Washington, D.C.: U.S. Government Printing Office, 1982); *1970 Census of Population, Persons of Spanish Origin*, PC(2)-1C (Washington, D.C.: U.S. Government Printing Office, 1973); *1980 Census of Population, Provisional Estimates of Social, Economic and Housing Characteristics*, PHC80-S1-1 (Washington, D.C.: U.S. Government Printing Office, 1982). Statistics on women of Mexican origin only were not available at the time of this writing.

5. U.S. Bureau of Census, "Persons of Spanish Origin in the United States: March 1976," *Current Population Reports*, Series P-20, no. 310 (Washington, D.C.: U.S. Government Printing Office, 1982); *1980 Census of Population, Provisional Estimates of Social, Economic, and Housing Characteristics*, PHC80-S1-1 (Washington, D.C.: U.S. Government Printing Office, 1982).

6. U.S. Department of Labor, *Employment and Training Report of the President* (Washington, D.C.: U.S. Government Printing Office, 1982). Discouraged workers have neither worked nor looked for work during the four-week period before an unemployment survey. Nearly 75 percent of the recently discouraged workers cite labor-market factors as the reason for not looking for work.

7. Vilma Ortiz, Rosemary Santana Cooney, and Ronald Ortiz, "Sex-Role Attitudes and Labor Force Participation: A Comparative Study of Hispanic Females and Non-Hispanic

White Females," paper presented at the American Sociological Association meetings, 7 Sept. 1982, p. 13.

8. A 1979 study by the Census Bureau found that Hispanic women left their careers for family reasons at about the same rate as white women. *San Francisco Chronicle*, 18 July, 1984.

9. Michael Storber and Richard Walter, "The Spatial Division of Labor: Labor and Location of Industries," in Larry Sawers and William K. Tabb, eds., *Sunbelt/Snowbelt* (New York: Oxford University Press, 1984).

10. Laura Arroyo, "Industrial and Occupational Distribution of Chicana Workers," *Aztlan* 4, no. 2 (1973); Tacho Mindiola, "The Cost of Being a Mexican Female Worker in the 1970 Houston Labor Market," *Aztlan* 11, no. 2 (1980).

11. Special thanks go to Louise Lamphere and Peter B. Evans, the principal investigators. This project is sponsored by National Science Foundation grant no. BNS-8112726.

12. Both the women and their husbands were interviewed twice. The total sample includes Chicano and Anglo dual-worker couples, as well as Chicana single parents, who are not discussed here. Informants were not randomly selected, but were referred to us from a variety of sources. Since we interviewed women in a particular stage of the life cycle, it is unclear how representative they are of the total female work force in Albuquerque. Other research shows variation in family strategies depends on women's age, marital status, skills, and the nature of the labor market. See Louise Lamphere, Filomena M. Solva, and John P. Sousa, "Kin Networks and Family Strategies: Working Class Portuguese Families in New England," in Linda S. Cordell and Stephen Beckerman, eds., *The Versatility of Kinship* (New York: Academic Press, 1980); Zavella, *Women, Work and Family*, 1982.

13. Rayna Rapp, "Family and Class in Contemporary America: Notes Toward an Understanding of Ideology," *Science and Society* 42, no. 3 (1978); Jane Collier, Michelle Z. Rosaldo, and Sylvia Yanagisako, "Is There a Family? New Anthropological Views," in Barrie Thorne and Marilyn Yalom, eds., *Rethinking the Family, Some Feminist Questions* (New York: Longman, 1982).

14. *1970 Census of Population, General Social and Economic Characteristics*, PC (1)-C33, cited in Peter B. Evans, "Comparisons of Labor Force Structures of New Mexico and Rhode Island" (manuscript, n.d.).

15. Evans, "Comparisons of Labor Force Structure."

16. Joseph V. Metzgar, "Guns and Butter: Albuquerque Hispanics, 1940–1975," *New Mexico Historical Review* 56, no. 2 (1981).

17. Recent studies indicate that a good business climate and right-to-work laws are the most important motivations for new plant location. See Roger Schmenner, *The Manufacturing Location Decision* (Englewood Cliffs, N.J.: Prentice-Hall, 1982), cited in Bennett Harrison, "Regional Restructuring and 'Good Business Climates': The Economic Transformation of New England Since World War II," in Sawers and Tabb, eds., *Sunbelt/Snowbelt*.

18. Evans, "Comparisons of Labor Force Structure."

19. City of Albuquerque, "Social Profile of Albuquerque" (Manuscript, Department of Human Services, n.d.).

20. The city of Albuquerque provided tax incentives to attract new manufacturing plants to the area and is considered to have a good business climate. Albuquerque is only a four-hour flight from California's "Silicon Valley," which makes it relatively inexpensive to transport materials. Other features include a relatively good housing market, especially an interesting cultural environment—with a history of Indian, Spanish, and Anglo settlement—and proximity to the art center of Santa Fe. These features make Albuquerque a good place either to start new plants or, like GTE Lenkurt, relocate the firm's headquarters.

21. Figures for 1960 and 1970 are from Patrick H. McNamara, "A Social Report for Metropolitan Albuquerque," Albuquerque Urban Observatory, *Studies in Urban Affairs*, no. 16 (1973). Figures for 1979 are from New Mexico Employment Security Department, "Affirmative Action Information," Research Statistics Section (1979), p. 2.

22. Other new industrial centers include Austin, San Antonio, Dallas, Tucson, Phoenix, Colorado Springs, El Paso, and Raleigh-Durham, North Carolina. Increasingly, high-tech

firms are relocating from Silicon Valley. See Anna Lee Saxenian, "The Urban Contradictions of Silicon Valley: Regional Growth and the Restructuring of the Semiconductor Industry," in Sawers and Tabb, eds., *Sunbelt/Snowbelt;* "High Technology Companies are Making Moves," *Washington Post,* 26 Dec. 1982.

23. Evans, "Comparisons of Labor Force Structure."

24. U.S. Bureau of Census, *County Business Patterns, New Mexico, 1980* (Washington, D.C.: U.S. Government Printing Office, 1981).

25. Evans, "Comparisons of Labor Force Structure."

26. The feminization of the working class in Albuquerque can be seen in the following table:

Year	Anglo men		Chicanos		Anglo women		Chicanas	
	LFPR*	%U+	LFPR	%U	LFPR	%U	LFPR	%U
1970	77.6	4.5	76.8	5.7	42.9	6.5	40.2	8.3
1980	64.0	6.3	62.1	8.7	51.8	6.3	49.8	7.8

Source: *1980 Census of Population: General Social and Economic Characteristics, New Mexico* (Washington, D.C.: U.S. Government Printing Office, 1983), pp. 105, 129; *1970 Census of Population: Characteristics of the Population, New Mexico* (Washington, D.C.: U.S. Government Printing Office, 1973), p. 151.
* LFPR = labor force participation rate.
+ %U = unemployment rate

Between 1970 and 1980, Anglo and Chicano men declined in their labor-force participation rates while Chicanas and Anglo women increased their labor-force participation rates. Chicanas had a higher unemployment rate than Anglo women in both years, but a lower rate than Chicano men by 1980. Chicano men had the highest unemployment rate of all in 1980.

27. U.S. Bureau of Census, 1972, cited in Patrick H. McNamara, "A Social Report for Metropolitan Albuquerque." In 1960, "Spanish-surnamed" means white persons with a Spanish surname; in 1970 "Spanish-surnamed" includes those women who speak Spanish as a native language as well as those with a Spanish surname. "Anglo" means the total population of women excluding black and Spanish-surnamed women.

28. These figures are rounded off. *1970 Census of Population, Characteristics of the Population, New Mexico; 1980 Census of Population, General Social and Economic Characteristics, New Mexico.* The term "Hispanic women" refers to all women of Spanish origin, rather than only women of Mexican origin. These were the only statistics available.

29. U.S. Bureau of Census, *Advance Estimates of Social, Economic and Housing Characteristics for New Mexico,* PHC80-S2-33 (Washington, D.C.: U.S. Government Printing Office, 1980).

30. U.S. Bureau of Census, *Provisional Estimates of Social, Economic and Housing Characteristics,* 1980 Census of Population and Housing Supplementary Report, PHC80-S1-1, cited in "La Red/The Net," newsletter of the National Chicano Research Network (Austin, Tex.), June 1982, p. 1.

31. Of all husband-wife families in 1980, 42 percent were dual-worker families, while in 38 percent only the husband was employed. See. U.S. Department of Labor, *Employment and Training Report of the President.* This report did not specify, but apparently the other 20 percent of husband-wife families had only the wife employed.

32. For a discussion of the differences between women's work in the apparel and electronics industries in northern Mexico, see Maria Patricia Fernandez-Kelly, *For We Are Sold, I and My People: Women and Industry in Mexico's Frontier* (Albany: State University of New York Press, 1983).

33. The phrase was coined by Arlie Hochschild and quoted in Lillian B. Rubin *Intimate Strangers, Men and Women Together* (New York: Harper & Row, 1983).

34. Women's names are ficticious.

35. For a full analysis of these patterns, see Patricia Zavella, "The Effects of Women's Work: Chicano and Anglo Working Class Families" (unpublished paper).

Western Women's History: A Challenge
for the Future

SUZAN SHOWN HARJO

In her moving article, which was the concluding speech at the 1983 Women's West Conference, activist and poet Suzan Shown Harjo presents an important challenge for western women's history. She tells us that we cannot separate ourselves from our past and that who we are affects how we see history. Our determination to include women of all heritages in western history cannot succeed until women of all cultures help write, as well as make, history.

Harjo tells us with her poet's voice why this involvement is crucial, why it is more than an interesting academic exercise. An inclusive history is important, she says, because people are important. A history that excludes us trivializes our lives and our needs; it tells us that we were, and are, marginal. Harjo reminds us that we need to write all women into western history, not just to understand our past but to change the ways we see ourselves and envision our future. We need to reclaim our own voices not only for ourselves, but also for our children, whose identities require access to their foremothers' histories.

Because I feel it is important to know the background and biases of persons who present perspectives for my consideration, I will tell you what I feel is important for you to know about me. I am culturally Cheyenne and Creek, and politically a citizen of the Cheyenne and Arapaho tribes of Oklahoma. My mother is Cheyenne and Pawnee, a descendant of those who entered into the treaty providing that Pawnees would stop stealing the Cheyenne horses if the Cheyenne stopped eating the Pawnees' yellow dogs. My mother is Tsistsistas, a Human Being, our name for ourselves. Lakota people had a hard time saying Tsistsistas so they used two words: Sheyela, meaning people who talk funny (or people who lead and speak beautifully with their words, if they were speaking to a Cheyenne), and Sheyena, which means Red People. The French fur trappers heard these words and, not being able to pronounce Tsistsistas for some reason, called us Cheyenne, and it stuck. My mother is from the line of Bull Bear, Buffalo Walla, and others who won the battle of Little Big Horn, she is a daughter of the prophecy to flee the coming of the white destruction. My father is half Scots by blood, from a father he never knew, and half Creek. The Muscogee language was his first language. He is Hodulgee Muscogee, which means the First People or Wind Clan of the Creek Nation, from the Nyaka tribal town. I am the mother of an eighteen-year-old daughter and a ten-year-old son and widow of a Muscogee man of the Watko or Raccoon Clan, who passed into the spirit world at age thirty-five.

I was born in western Oklahoma in El Reno, twenty-eight miles from Oklahoma City, and grew up in part in eastern Oklahoma on a farm of my grandfolks near Beggs, near Tulsa. We ate lots of squirrel and deer and corn cooked about ninety-nine ways, and we had no electricity, newspaper for wallpaper, and a three-seater with the most advanced of catalogues. It was neither good nor bad. It simply was. Because my father was a cryptographer with Allied Forces Southern Europe at one period of his life, I went to school in my early teen-age years in Naples, Italy. I was thereby spared the experience of spending the delicate adolescent years in racially biased Oklahoma; that atmosphere exists today as strongly as it did in the late 1950s and early 1960s when I was away. Because of some early, psychologically damaging experiences, such as being thrown out of a second-story window in the El Reno grade school by a teacher who just didn't like Indians, I avoided school as much as I could and have, therefore, little formal education.

I am a poet and have also worked in theater, radio, and print. For nearly a decade I've worked in Washington, D.C., as a lobbyist for the National Congress of American Indians, the Department of the Interior, and the Native American Rights Fund, as legislative liaison for the Fried, Frank, Harris, Shriver, Kampelman law firm, which serves as D.C. counsel for a number of Indian tribes. I have worked on over 200 legislative and appropriations matters, including those dealing with land claims, particularly in Maine and Rhode Island; fishing rights in the Pacific Northwest; and health, education, child welfare, and religious freedom issues.

The emphasis lately has been on appropriations, since the Reagan administration has targeted the federal Indian budget for severe cuts—anywhere from 30 to 100 percent—in all areas of Indian life. One small example is its effort to decrease the funds for the prevention of diabetes, which occurs at a higher rate amongst Indians than in any other population in the United States, and to increase by a roughly equal amount the program for surgical amputation of limbs, most of which results from untreated diabetes. These programs and services result from the treaties and other legal, contractual arrangements that provided that Indians would receive in perpetuity sustaining goods and services in exchange for land cessions. Among the myths of the West—which West, by the way, also brought us this western-movie cowboy hero in his current role as president—are that Indians were greedy, wanting all the land for ourselves; we were unwilling to share and therefore had to be eliminated or defeated, or assimilated; and that today's Indians are on the welfare dole and need to be taken off it, by hook or crook, in order to assume our place as near-white people. These notions are as foolish and inaccurate as many of the other myths about the West that oppress us as people.

Women of the West are still possessed of inaccurate information about who we are collectively, who we are individually, and who we have been. We view each other through layers of racial, ethnic, and class biases, perpetuated by the white, male ruling institutions, such as the educational system that teaches in the early years and controls later research in the history of women in the West. This institution teaches that white people have history, while Asian-Americans, blacks, Hispanics, and Native Americans have legends, tales, stories, and oral (translated: suspect) history. It is an institution that teaches that white people have true religions—as Mark Twain said, "several hundred of them"—while non-whites have rites, rituals, ceremonies, cults, myths, and primitive belief systems. Each person who has a Ph.D. or who is working on one understands the institutional pressures to conform to these views and some have done so willingly, while others have resisted and suffered no small consequence for so doing. During my address at the Women's West Conference, a goodly number of white women were present in the roomful of historians. No Asian-American or black women were counted; four Hispanic and two Indian women were there. I leave it to the academics to interpret the sample.

The challenge for the women of the West is to avoid the mistakes and biases of the men of the West and to recognize the origin of stereotypes and biases in our forefathers and our foremothers. We need to create new definitions: that of the frontier period, for example, and who is included in it. We need to remember that what some called hard times settling in a foreign land was home, life, and daily living for others. And that black buffalo soldiers—who were underclass white property pitted against Indians, the enemies of their masters—did not live in the West without black women. And that the frontier mentality extends to the Japanese internment camps. And that the frontier period extends through today in white America's fight against Indian America for precious resources and against Hispanic Americans for immigration and voting rights.

We need to appreciate silence, to understand it and hold it dear, and to share some of the secrets of our silences with each other—if not in as great detail as each would like, at least so that we understand what it is we hold in our hearts. The challenge for the future of western women's history is that, in attempting to uncover the truth of the past, we do not miss the essence of what is happening today and how it is happening. In order to have a future with women living and describing it, we must find ways to apply common sense and modern sensibilities to lessons learned from pure research and documentation. And we need to accept that the clouded personal memory is as valid or invalid as the dusty distorted page.

How are we to meet these challenges? The answers lie within ourselves. In order to find them, we must ask ourselves the right questions and be clear about our responses. I have a few questions to submit for women's historians: What are my personal and altruistic reasons for pursuing this research—that is, education, job, money, security, prestige, perhaps to change existing inequities, perhaps to preserve the present system? Do my motivations influence my methodology? Is my research related to living and evolving history? If not, why not? If so, why? How integrated is my perspective? How much do I compartmentalize the subjects of my research? What are my own biases and how do they manifest themselves in my work? What is my ethical standard? Are my eyes open to the exciting changes that are taking place around me?

We must add dimension to history, and to policy, if we are to survive it. We must mold future policy and law to make them consistent with natural law because common sense tells us that natural law will not change. There is no changing mother earth.

We need to move beyond negative actions, guilt, self-oppression, and viewing ourselves as survivors, or the chosen, or the mistresses of anything but our own fates. We need to advance beyond sharing our commonality to respecting our differences, without attempting to convert each other to anything. We can no longer use the old oppressive models, either in research methods or in something as simple as conference style. If we wish to follow democratic models we should look to my people, to our own bodies—to circles for meetings where we can look across at each other and no one person is above another.

We can no longer be polite about laws and institutions that discriminate in favor of anyone to the advantage of any other. We can no longer be polite about the fascism in our own communities and about those who would inhibit, restrict, or control us by reason of any part of our identity. We can no longer be polite about the agents or instrumentalities that would sacrifice our mother, the earth, on the altar of materialism. We have an obligation as people to protect our future generations, not just our personal blood line or our relations, and not just humankind, but all the beings of the universe. We have tremendous power to destroy and to perpetuate destruction by denying our responsibility in our own small spheres, or by our silence. We have the power, but we do not have the right.

I would like to conclude with a very personal challenge that is contained in a poem I wrote some time ago. This particular one is about kinship and about my son. (I have poems about my daughter, as well, so don't get upset.)

WAKING UP THOUGHTS

a small, gentle kicking awakens me at dawn
my little one beside me, tired from the evening's work
chasing fireflies and snakedoctors in his sleep
now breathing in my time, as before birth
now a once, twice smile, shuddering as young ones do
warming my blanket, changing my dreams with his crawling
taking me from cold death-caves to yellow medicine-flower fields

my little son, destiny boy-child
"give me a boy," said my man, "on my father's day"
and it happened that way without effort
but, before his black eyes lost their newborn glaze

his belly felt the white man's doctor knife
carving an early sterile scarring mark to last a lifetime
soon, after learning to stand on two feet, then to balance on one,
his legs began to quiver as the foul air invaded his chest
fumes from the below garage rising in search of young bodies,
leaving one nightworker dead, another mechanic purple-faced and foaming
then, later, the corner city crashing of cars
before he had anything to say for himself

last night we grown-ups told old stories and new tales of near misses
we drank day-old coffee and watched smoke and sadness fill the air
i saw her dry eyes form the words her mouth could not release
her knowing and forgetting eyes saw a certain kinship
in our shaking, working, living and dying-hard hands

Lakota woman, sister-friend, once-wife of my brother,
i mourn your little one, burning in a closet in Kyle,
putting her clothes out with her hands, too stunned to cry out
i mourn your little one, living for so long after, her tiny body blackened
then dying, just when there was hope, they said

Lakota woman, mother-daughter, once and now family of mine,
i mourn your memories of fire, of charred hands
i mourn your todays of gunfire, of fear and threats
i know you show these midnight tears because they were absent at her feast
your broken nose making tears the more painful, an accident, they said

Lakota woman, sister in sorrow, now and then friend of mine,
it is fortunate for the fine and upstanding,
those masters of cheap shots and shell games,
that flaming bodies and bloody faces leave no traces of fingerprints

Lakota woman, my little ones are yours this hour until you are stronger
or until they no longer need us in that sweet, holding-on way
let's rest today, tomorrow you must find your own way home
to the other small ones, eating beans for breakfast, over half a world away
right under the noses of good fathers and mothers who look out for their own
tomorrow we will have bigger concerns, tonight we will think of ourselves
tomorrow we will worry about a way to find water that is free of tetanus
on the next tomorrow we will worry about how the air will be rationed
then, on the day after that tomorrow, who will have compassion
for my sleeping one, this gift of the sun?

The Contributors

KATHRYN ADAM is Director of Continuing Education and Summer Sessions, College of St. Catherine, St. Paul, Minnesota. She holds B.A., B.S., and M.A. degrees in English and education and is an independent scholar in midwestern women's history and literature. She has lectured extensively on Laura Ingalls Wilder with Minnesota Chautauqua, a community-education program funded by the Minnesota Humanities Commission.

PATRICIA ALBERS and WILLIAM JAMES received Ph.D.s in anthropology from the University of Wisconsin, Madison. Albers teaches anthropology at the University of Utah and has several publications on women and American Indians, among them *The Hidden Half: Studies of Plains Indian Women,* coedited with Beatrice Medicine (University Press of America, 1983). James teaches economics at the University of Utah and has published on American Indians and Latin America. Recently, both have published extensively on photographic images of American Indians.

SUSAN ARMITAGE, Director of American Studies and Associate Professor of History at Washington State University, has been writing about western women since 1974. She is the author of a number of articles, among them "Women and Men in Western History: A Stereoptical Vision," *Western Historical Quarterly* (October 1985). She is studying the ways in which women participated in the founding and development of communities in the West.

CORLANN GEE BUSH, who prefers to be called "Corky," is Affirmative Action/Human Resources Director at Montana State University. Her undergraduate training in American Studies led her to an interest in art history; her interest in the American West led her to examine how separate messages about men and women are codified, conveyed, and reinforced in western art and other expressions of popular culture.

ROSALINDA MÉNDEZ GONZÁLEZ is Associate Professor of Mexican-American Studies at San Diego State University. Her research findings on immigration, southwestern labor, women, and United States-Latin American relations have appeared in many journals, among them *The Review of*

Radical Political Economics, Southwest Economy and Society, and *Latin American Perspectives.* Her article "Chicanas and Mexican Immigrant Families: Family Labor and Class Exploitation" appeared in Joan Jensen and Lois Scharf, eds., *Decades of Discontent: The Women's Movement 1920–1940* (Greenwood Press, 1983).

MELODY GRAULICH is Associate Professor of English at the University of New Hampshire where she teaches American literature and women's studies. She has published essays on several women writers and is currently at work on the book, *Liberating Traditions: Women Writers and the American West.*

ELIZABETH HAMPSTEN teaches in the English Department of the University of North Dakota. She is the author of *Read This Only To Yourself, The Private Writings of Midwestern Women 1880–1910* (Indiana University Press, 1982), and edits the journal *Plainswoman.*

KATHERINE HARRIS'S article is based on a chapter in her dissertation, "Women and Families on Northeastern Colorado Homesteads, 1873–1920" (University of Colorado, 1983). Harris has also written several articles on the Colorado Women's Christian Temperance Union, but her top priority is to continue research on homesteading women as she revises her dissertation for publication.

SUZAN SHOWN HARJO, a member of the Cheyenne and Arapaho tribes of Oklahoma, is a poet and an activist. She currently works with the National Congress of American Indians in Washington, D.C.

ELIZABETH JAMESON has taught women's history and United States social history at the Universities of Michigan, Colorado, and Virginia, and Loretto Heights College in Denver. She has written on women's history and working-class history. Her publications include "Imperfect Unions: Class and Gender in Cripple Creek, 1894–1904," in *Class, Sex and the Woman Worker,* Milton Cantor and Bruce Laurie, eds. (Greenwood Press, 1977) which is part of her forthcoming larger study of working-class culture in the Cripple Creek gold-mining district.

SUSAN L. JOHNSON received her M.A. from Arizona State University, and subsequently served as managing editor of *Signs: A Journal of Women in Culture and Society.* At present she is a graduate student in history at Yale University.

MICAELA DI LEONARDO is a native Californian and third-generation Italian-American. She holds a Ph.D. in anthropology from the University of California at Berkeley, and has done postdoctoral work in economics. She has taught at Berkeley, George Washington University, and Oberlin College, and currently holds a joint appointment in women's studies and anthropology at Yale University. Her research interests center on issues of women, work, family, and culture. Her article in this volume is part of a larger study, *The Varieties of Ethnic Experience: Kinship, Class and Gender Among California Italian-Americans* (Cornell University Press, 1984).

NORMA J. MILTON, an independent historian in Calgary, Alberta, will soon publish "The Scots of Alberta" in *The People of Alberta*, edited by Howard and Tamara Palmer.

ROSALIND URBACH MOSS earned her M.A. in English from the College of William and Mary. Now a Ph.D. candidate in American Studies at the University of Minnesota (Minneapolis), she is currently working on her dissertation, a study of the images of and ideas about never-married women (particularly spinster schoolteachers) in American culture between 1880 and 1960. "Educated and Ambitious Women: Kate Warthen on the Kansas Frontier," an essay related to her article in this book, was published during 1986 by Greenwood Press in a two-volume collection, *Women's Public Lives*.

MARY MURPHY is a Ph.D. candidate at the University of North Carolina, Chapel Hill. She is co-author of *"Like a Family": An Oral History of the Textile South, 1880–1940,* forthcoming from University of North Carolina Press, and is continuing research for her dissertation, a social history of Butte, Montana, in the 1920s and 1930s.

SHERRY SMITH received her Ph.D. in history from the University of Washington. She has taught western and Indian history at the University of Colorado, University of Wyoming, and (currently) at the University of Texas, El Paso.

MARY LEE SPENCE is a member of the history faculty at the University of Illinois, Urbana-Champaign, where she teaches courses on American women and American Indian-white relations. A past president of the Western History Association, she has edited (with Donald Jackson) *The Expeditions of John Charles Fremont* (3 vols).

CAROLYN STEFANCO is Assistant Professor of History at Wheaton College. She has been Visiting Assistant Professor of American women's and social history at Oklahoma State University and the former coordinator of the Women's Studies Program at Duke University. Her article is part of a larger study entitled "Pathways to Power: Voluntary Associations and the Politics of Women's Culture, Denver, Colorado, 1853–1893."

SYLVIA VAN KIRK, a westerner from Edmonton, Alberta, is Associate Professor of History and Women's Studies at the University of Toronto.

The author of *"Many Tender Ties": Women and Fur Trade Society in Western Canada, 1670–1870,* she has written numerous articles, including entries for the *Dictionary of Canadian Biography,* on the early history of Western Canada. Van Kirk was a founding member of the Canadian Women's Studies Association and served on the board of the Canadian Research Institute for the Advancement of Women from 1981 to 1984. She is currently working on a social history of the Cariboo gold rush in British Columbia, 1858–1870.

ELLIOTT WEST is Professor of History at the University of Arkansas and a specialist in the social history of the American West. He is author of numerous articles, co-editor of two volumes of essays, and author of *The Saloon on the Rocky Mountain Frontier.* He is currently researching the history of children on the American frontier.

PATRICIA ZAVELLA, an anthropologist, is an Assistant Professor on the Community Studies Board at the University of California, Santa Cruz. She is completing a book on *Women's Work and Chicano Families: Cannery Workers of the Santa Clara Valley,* to be published by Cornell University Press. She is also working on a book with Louise Lamphere, Felipe Gonzales, and Peter Evans entitled *Working Families and Sun Belt Industrialization: Changes in the Workplace and in the Home* to be published by Basic Books, Inc.

Index

Ables, Lottie: 201
Abortion: 117, 197–99
Abuse: *see* violence
Acuna, Pancha (Pancha Jackson): 79, 86
Africans: 4
Albuquerque, N.Mex.: 293–99
Alcohol: 58, 200
All Saints Home for Girls (Edmonton): 215
American Federation of Labor: 229
American Indians: and appropriations, 306; contemporary women, 305–309; exclusion of, from prescriptive literature, 147; and loss of lands, 243–45; and "maiden" image, 48; postcard portraits of, 35–49; and "princess" image, 14, 35, 46, 48, 65, 72–73; and railroads, 242; and "squaw" image, 14, 48, 65; stereotypes of, 14, 35, 41, 45, 48–49, 65, 72–73; and U.S. history, 51, 238–39, 247, 307; in western art, 19, 21, 26–28; women and fur trade, 53–61; women and intermarriage, 55–61; women and military men, 63–74; women in warfare, 68–69; women's lives, 15; at Women's West Conference, 307; *see also under names of tribes*
American Indian studies: 5–6
Anderson, Mary: 174
Anglo-Americans: economic advancement of, 246; and Mexican women, 78–82, 88; and American Indian women, 63–74; and poor-white experience, 239; women and miners, 78, 82–88; women in labor force, 291, 292, 294–95; *see also* Euro-Americans
Anthony, Susan B.: 267
Anthropology: 5, 15, 51
Anti-Saloon League (Los Angeles): 224
Apache Indians: 64–65, 68, 69, 71–72
Apache Princess, An (King): 71
Apparel industry: 293–99
Arapaho Indians: 70, 305
Archaeology: 5
Argonia, Kans.: 253
Arizona: 77–88
Army, U.S.: 241; officers, 63–74
Art, cowboy: 19–32

Arthur, Dolly: 196, 199, 201
Asian-American studies: 5
Asians and Asian-Americans: and American history, 238, 239, 307; in California, 279, 287; exclusion of, from prescriptive literature, 147; immigration of, to West Coast, 15; and Japanese internment camps, 307; and labor unions, 230; and railroad construction, 242; stereotypes of, 14; and women's inequality, 242–47; at Women's West Conference, 307
Austin, Mary: 111, 112
Averell, William Woods: 67, 72
Avery, Whitfield: 225

Bachichia, Juanita: 77–80, 86
Bama, Jim: 30–32
Banning Committee (1876): 69
Barber, Caroline E.: 255, 256, 258
Barden, Ollie: 173, 174
Barden, Willis: 173
Barnitz, Capt. Albert: 70
Barrangia: 81; *see also* unions, informal
Barrios: 242
Barry, Leonora (Leonora Barry Lake): 273
Bartenders' International League of America: 229
BAS (writer): 209–11
Beierman, William: 196
Bella Union (San Jose, Calif.): 223
Bella Union Melodeon (San Francisco): 222
Benteen, Capt. Frederick: 70, 71
Berger, John: 24, 39
Bernahillo County (N.Mex.): 294–95
Biederwolf, William: 203
Birth control: 117, 151–53, 197
Blacks: and American history, 238–39, 307; exclusion of, from prescriptive literature, 147; as waiters, 221; unions of, with Anglos, 82, 86; in the West, 15; women in labor force, 291; and women's inequality, 240, 246–47; at Women's West Conference, 307
Black studies: 5
Blair, Madeleine: 197, 202
Boast, Mrs. (friend of Ingalls family): 109
du Bois, Col. John Van Deusen: 69, 71